The Ships That Saved An Army

Patrick Stephens Limited, part of Thorsons, a division of the Collins Publishing Group, has published authoritative, quality books for enthusiasts for more than twenty years. During that time the company has established a reputation as one of the world's leading publishers of books on aviation, maritime, military, model-making, motor cycling, motoring, motor racing, railway and railway modelling subjects. Readers or authors with suggestions for books they would like to see published are invited to write to: The Editorial Director, Patrick Stephens Limited, Thorsons Publishing Group, Wellingborough, Northants, NN8 2RQ.

The Ships That Saved An Army

A comprehensive record of the 1,300 'Little Ships' of Dunkirk

Russell Plummer

Patrick Stephens Limited

First published in 1990

British Library Cataloguing in Publication Data

Plummer, Russell
The ships that saved an army: a comprehensive record of the 1,500 'Little Ships' of Dunkirk.
1. World War 2. Dunkirk Campaign. Evacuation of Great Britain. Army. British Expeditionary force.
I. Title
940.54'21

ISBN 1-85260-210-4

Patrick Stephens Limited is part of the Thorsons Publishing Group, Wellingborough, Northamptonshire NN8 2RQ, England

Printed and bound in Great Britain by Butler & Tanner Ltd, Frome and London

10 9 8 7 6 5 4 3 2 1

Front endpaper *Tin helmeted troops huddle together while a pitiful few strike out from the beach at La Panne in a dinghy. The abandoned* **Devonia** *is in the background with the Thames paddler* **Royal Eagle** *seen in the distance.* (Imperial War Museum)

Rear endpaper *Some of the 5,677 men returned by HMS* **Codrington** *wait their turn to disembark in Dover, while another equally heavily laden vessel is moored alongside. Note the pile of discarded rifles at the* **Codrington's** *stern.* (Times Newspapers)

Contents

Foreword by Leslie Aitken, MBE

National Chaplain of the 1940 Dunkirk Veterans' Association 1953–89

This book has been painstakingly compiled and fills a gap in the literature concerning Dunkirk. It outlines the story of the involvement of a maritime force of small vessels which was described by Winston Churchill as 'The Mosquito Armada', and goes on to supply details of the individual ships which must be the most comprehensive to appear in one volume. Its scope is wider, too, than its title suggests. It relates moving stories of the men of the sea, professional and amateur, whose heroism has become legendary.

It was to the men of the sea that the defeated Allied Armies looked at the end of May and the beginning of June, 1940. The speed of the success of the German invasion of France and the Low Countries soon made it apparent that nothing short of a miracle could prevent enormous numbers of men from annihilation. Indeed, on 23 May, General Alan Brooke confided in his diary that, 'Nothing but a miracle can save the BEF now'. Two days later, General Ironside wrote, 'We shall have lost practically all our trained soldiers by the next few days, unless a miracle appears to help us'. When the evacuation of the Allied forces was accomplished, with over one third of a million men recovered, General Pownall wrote, 'The evacuation from Dunkirk was surely a miracle'. Speaking in the House of Commons, Winston Churchill declared that it was 'A miracle of deliverance'.

The Miracle of Dunkirk consisted of several constituent parts. One, which has touched the hearts of many, was that wrought through the heroic actions of men, many of them civilians, who manned the Little Ships. Although this aspect of the story has become legendary, as the stories told here show why, there has been a lack of information published concerning the vessels themselves, and it is due to Russell Plummer's initiative that so much information is now available in one volume.

In *The Miracle of Dunkirk*, Walter Lord wrote that there have been so many books published on the subject of Dunkirk that they 'could fill a warehouse'. Of these, there are not many which one could recommend for serious study. On account of its scope, as this concerns small vessels of so many types, this book will be added to the few which one can recommend.

Introduction

'SO long as the English tongue survives, the word Dunkirk will be will be spoken with reverence. In that harbour, such a hell on earth as never blazed before, at the end of a lost battle, the rags and blemishes that had hidden the soul of democracy fell away. There, beaten but unconquered, in shining splendour, she faced the enemy, this shining thing in the souls of free men which Hitler cannot command. It is in the great tradition of democracy. It is a future. It is victory.'

New York Times, 1st June 1940.

HALF a century after those words were written by a columnist on the other side of the Atlantic, 'Dunkirk' can still tug at the emotions. Even as the number of survivors among rescuers and the rescued thins with the passage of the years, the name of the French sea port still symbolises one of the darkest and, in its way, most glorious phases in Britain's military and maritime history. So many families throughout the land had someone, or knew of someone, who was at Dunkirk, either as a member of the British Expeditionary Force that was plucked from under the enemy's nose, or aboard one of the huge fleet of ships, both naval and civilian, which crossed the English Channel in a desperate mission to save an entire army. Sadly, despite almost superhuman efforts, many both ashore and afloat did not return.

The sequence of events triggered by the start of Germany's advance on the Low Countries on 10th May 1940 and the resulting Dunkirk

Dunkirk! The destroyer **Javelin** *lies to the east of the Mole with a hospital carrier, possibly the* **Worthing**, *visible to the right. On the left, the half submerged wreck of a twin-funnel naval vessel is pinpointed by the Dunkirk lighthouse standing out white against the acrid smoke.* (The late L. A. Baker's collection)

evacuation, Operation Dynamo, has been the subject of hundreds of thousands of words. We begin with a brief outline simply to set the scene for the purpose of this work, a detailed analysis of the multitude of ships that answered a call of duty at Dunkirk. It is doubtful whether a full list of the participating naval and merchant vessels will ever now be compiled but I believe what follows is the most comprehensive record of individual ships and their contribution to Operation Dynamo so far attempted. It has been made possible thanks to the help of many people, both friends and others who were total strangers when we started, with just a shared interest in the ships and the crews who performed so heroically.

Just as organisations such as the Dunkirk Veterans' Association have kept alive the bond of comradeship that existed between the men, the ships themselves have not been forgotten and the Association of Dunkirk Little Ships is well established and works to foster the spirit of those who manned the vessels in the early summer of 1940. Well over a hundred 'little ships' still survive and many of them have been back to Dunkirk as part of an ADLS fleet that makes a commemorative crossing every fifth year. Apart from the motor cruisers and yachts, a number of small excursion craft can still be found in commercial operation such as the Thames vessel *Kingwood* which goes about its business from Westminster Pier with the St. George's Cross flag of the Association always fluttering proudly at the bow. Incredibly, two of the paddle steamers that earned a special place in the Dunkirk legend also survive. One, *Princess Elizabeth,* is on the River Seine in France while the other, *Medway Queen,* a particular Dunkirk heroine, is being restored in a backwater of the River Medway.

On the other side of the Channel, the character of the port of Dunkirk has changed considerably. The shattered locks and basins were soon restored after the war and train ferry connections with Dover, including the prestigious 'Night Ferry', resumed. But the old harbour is a lot quieter since the ferry traffic was moved to a new purpose-built tidal port known as Dunkirk West and close to Mardyck, from where in 1940, enemy shore batteries pounded the harbour and made life difficult for passing rescue craft. To the east, the Mole thrusting out, almost a mile to the harbour entrance, and which had an important but largely unexpected part to play in the evacuation, is no more. Only a short stretch of the seaward end of the structure remains, the rest having been demolished and replaced by a breakwater consisting of granite blocks. Close to its starting point on shore begin the beaches, running right across the Belgian border, that were black with men during those harrowing days at the end of May and in early June 1940. Now, as summer holidaymakers crowd the whiteish sand as far as the eye can see, only a simple stone memorial stands sentinel. It faces, not out to sea, or even towards the harbour, but along the beaches, and there is a particular local feel to the area, the monument's simple inscription commemorating the sacrifice of the airmen, sailors and soldiers of France and her allies. Nowhere is Britain mentioned specifically.

The simple memorial on the seafront at Dunkirk. The small plaque beneath the city's coat of arms was unveiled in 1980 to mark the 40th anniversary of the evacuation. (Author)

Operation Dynamo

THE signal officially starting Operation Dynamo, the evacuation of the British Expeditionary Force from Dunkirk, was made by the Admiralty at 6.57 a.m. on Sunday 26th May 1940. It ended when the old and battered destroyer *Shikari* left Dunkirk's East Mole at 3.40 a.m. on Monday 3rd June, and was responsible for the safe return to British shores of the staggering total of 338,226 men in an armada of ships of all shapes and sizes estimated to number between 800 and 1,200. Precise figures of vessels used will never now be known and it is in respect of what have since come to be called 'the little ships of Dunkirk' that the official records are most limited.

Disaster or deliverance? Triumph or humiliation? The Dunkirk evacuation, most widely acclaimed as a nine-day miracle, has remained a contentious issue ever since. An Admiralty communiqué issued within a few hours of the final vessels landing their troops on British soil on 3rd June 1940 stated:

> The most extensive and difficult combined operation in naval history has been carried out during the past week. British, French and Belgian troops have been brought safely to this country from Belgium and Northern France in numbers which, when the full story can be told, will surprise the world. The withdrawal has been carried out in face of intense and almost continuous air attack, artillery and machine-gun fire. The success of this operation was only made possible by the close co-operation of the Allies and of the Services, and by never flagging determination and courage of all concerned. It was undertaken on the British side by several flotillas of destroyers and a large number of small craft of every description. This force was rapidly increased and a total of 222 British naval vessels and 665 other British craft took part. Through the operation of the Small Craft Registration Order, the Admiralty already had full details of all available small vessels. The order for the assembly of these vessels met with

A Royal Air Force Hudson patrols overhead as more than 30 naval and merchant vessels lay off La Panne. From the right a paddle minesweeper, most probably the **Sandown,** *bustles through the screen of destroyers to join the rescue fleet of mainly Dutch skoots.* (Imperial War Museum)

instantaneous response. Fishermen, yachtsmen, yacht builders, yacht clubs, river boatmen, and boat-building and hireing firms manned their craft with volunteer crews and rushed them to the assembly point, although they did not then know for what purpose they were required. They operated successfully by day and by night under the most difficult and dangerous conditions. The Admiralty cannot speak too highly of the services of all concerned. They were essential to the success of the operation and the means of saving thousands of lives.

The whole operation was screened by naval forces against any attempt by the enemy at interference at sea. In addition to almost incessant bombing and machine-gun attacks on Dunkirk, the beaches and vessels operating off the port, and shipping plying to and fro, were under frequent shellfire. This was to some extent checked by bombardment of the enemy artillery positions by our naval forces. A withdrawal of this nature and magnitude, carried out in face of intense and almost continuous air attack, is the most hazardous of all operations. Its success is a triumph of Allied sea and air power in face of the most powerful air forces the enemy could bring to bear. Dunkirk has been blocked by the sinking of concrete filled block ships. The sea gates of the canal and the lock-working mechanism have been demolished. The lock gates have been blocked. The other ports now in enemy hands have been rendered virtually useless. Fuel stocks have been destroyed. Naval bombardment also protected the flanks of the withdrawal. The enemy was active with submarines and high-speed motor torpedo boats. Losses have been inflicted upon both these forces. The operation was rendered more difficult by shallow water, narrow channels and strong tides, the situation was such that one mistake in the handling of a ship might have blocked a vital channel of that part of the port of Dunkirk which could be used.

The losses sustained by our Naval forces have been comparatively light. The loss of His Majesty's destroyers, *Grafton, Grenade* and *Wakeful* was announced on May 30th. HM destroyers *Basilisk, Keith* and *Havant* have also been sunk by enemy action. Of more than 170 minor war vessels of the British fleet engaged in the operation, 24 have been lost. These comprise: 1 Fleet minesweeper – *Skipjack*; 1 gunboat – *Mosquito*; 1 Fleet Air Arm tender – *Grive*; 5 paddle minesweepers – *Brighton Belle, Gracie Fields, Waverley, Medway Queen, Brighton Queen*; 1 minesweeper – *Crested Eagle*; 8 trawlers – *Polly Johnston, Thomas Bartlett, Thuringia, Stella Dorado, Argyllshire, Blackburn Rovers, Calvi, Westelia*; 3 drifters – *Girl Pamela, Paxton, Boy Roy*; 2 armed boarding vessels – *King Orry, Mona's Isle*; 1 dan laying vessel – *Comfort*; 1 tug – *St. Fagan*. The next of kin of all casualties are being informed as details become available.

The following day, in an additional statement, the Admiralty reported:

The paddle minesweeper *Medway Queen*, believed lost, has now arrived safely in port.

Thus, in about 700 words, one of the most remarkable achievements in British maritime history, and certainly one of the least orthodox, was officially summed up. But perhaps the secret of Dunkirk's success – and it has to be judged that, if only on the basis of the sheer number of men brought home – was the way in which so many facets of the operation were conducted off the cuff. There was simply no time for elaborate advance planning and the strength of many of the key decisions lay in the fact they were taken not at the Admiralty in London, or even in the Dynamo control room at Dover, but by men in the thick of the turmoil and carnage in Dunkirk itself.

The credit for such people being in the right place at the right time – and for so many other pieces of the Dynamo jig-saw being made to fit precisely – belonged almost solely to Bertram Home Ramsay, Vice-Admiral, Dover. From his sparse accommodation in the bowels of the chalk below Dover Castle, the quiet-spoken, slightly-built Ramsay planned and executed the evacuation brilliantly. From scattered and limited resources Ramsay put together a rescue fleet and somehow managed to maintain the momentum of the evacuation in the face of tremendous odds, with perhaps the greatest strength of his leadership being a willingness to delegate coupled with a talent for choosing the right men to shoulder the responsibility.

Ramsay had finished the Great War commanding the destroyer HMS *Broke* of the Dover Patrol and his administrative efficiency then brought steady progress up the promotional ladder. Excelling as Captain of the battleship *Royal Sovereign*, he was appointed Home Fleet Chief of Staff in 1935 with a rank of Rear-Admiral, but resigned within a few months after a clash of temperaments with his Commander-in-Chief, Sir Roger Backhouse. He later turned down an appointment in the Far East to command the Yangtse gunboats and by 1938 had been placed on the retired list. Ramsay was not idle for long

Bertram Ramsay, Vice-Admiral, Dover, the man responsible for the creation from scattered and limited resources of the greatest evacuation fleet in maritime history and with the execution of Operation Dynamo. Ramsay's brilliance as an organiser was tested again in 1944 when he planned the Royal Navy's part in the Normandy Landings. Tragically, he was killed in an air crash near Paris in January 1945. (Imperial War Museum)

and, as the international climate worsened, he was appointed to report on the state of Dover Harbour and its facilities. The findings pinpointed years of neglect at a port familiar from his own early career and resulted in a £750,000 programme to revive Dover as a naval base. Much more important as events proved was an understanding that, in the event of war, Ramsay would take command at Dover. In September 1939 he moved in as Flag Officer and quickly the Dover area was made independent of the Nore Command with Ramsay appointed Vice-Admiral, Dover, and answerable direct to the Board of the Admiralty.

The opening months of the war proved fairly quiet for Ramsay and his staff. To lessen threats from enemy air power, the large-scale outward movement of troops and equipment of the British Expeditionary Force was from South Coast ports to western France and the army continued to be supplied mainly through Cherbourg or Le Havre and then overland to the front by way of Amiens and Arras. As late as 15th May 1940 the Ministry of Shipping was advised by the War Office that changes might have to be made to the lines of supply with a greater reliance on the ports in Ramsay's area of command. Within a fortnight it became clear that his role was not to supply the army, but to rescue it!

Much of the Allied defensive strategy had been based on the invincibility of the Maginot Line, the complex French system of fortifications stretching for hundreds of miles along its borders with Germany. But the Maginot Line did not extend across northern France (in part because of the cost, the low-lying terrain and the need to support Belgium, but also to prevent this important French industrial region from becoming a battlefield); thus it simply ended in the middle of nowhere at Longuyon and offered no protection on the northern flank across some 200 miles to Channel coast. The BEF, under the command of Lord Gort, was one of five armies strung out across this part of the front, on the frontier with Belgium and Luxembourg, the British being in position from Bailleul to Maulde, with the French Seventh Army between them and the sea. To the east came the French First Army in the valley of the Oise, the Ninth Army between the Oise and Sedan and the Second Army from the area of Sedan to the end of the Maginot Line.

It was not intended to fight on this frontier, the plan being for the Allied Armies to swing forward into Belgium and confront the advancing Germans, who, it was wrongly assumed, would mount their main attack from the north across the Flanders Plain. This plan was put into effect when the Germans invaded France and the Low Countries on 12th May, with the BEF crossing the Belgian border and taking up its assigned position on the River Dyle. To the left of the BEF, the French Seventh Army moved through

Belgium to the Scheldt and into Holland, but on the BEF's right flank things did not go as well. Although the First Army's cavalry reached high ground between the Dyle and the River Meuse, the main body of its troops were slower moving up and the Ninth Army, of second rank troops including two light cavalry divisions still on horse-back, failed to cover its allotted section of the front, which was precisely where the first German thrust came.

Originally, the Germans had planned on placing the main weight of their assault – some 37 divisions – in the north and on using a further 27 divisions to make a supplementary attack in the south. This is what would have happened had the advance started when first intended in November 1939, or in January 1940. Various postponements had followed one another, ostensibly because of the weather, and by the time the order to attack was finally given on 10th May the emphasis had been switched to the south, with 44 divisions, 7 armoured and 3 motorised, unleashed through the Ardennes while 28 divisions (3 with armour and 1 motorised) attacked further north across the Flanders Plain. The Allied supreme commander, General Gamelin, who had considered the hilly, wooded Ardennes country impossible for armour, was proved tragically wrong and on 13th May, just three days after the assault began, Major-General Erwin Rommel's 7th Panzer Division had obtained bridgeheads over the Meuse, while Colonel-General Heinz Guderian's XIX Panzer Corps burst across at Sedan.

In the north things were going equally badly for the Allies. The Germans overwhelmed Holland on 14th May and although the BEF held its own, a badly mauled French Seventh Army was falling back towards Antwerp and the First Army's front had been broken. On 16th May, Gort was ordered to pull the BEF back to the River Senne and in two more stages a withdrawal to the River Escaut was completed on the 19th. By this time, in the south, the Germans had crossed the Canal du Nord and were continuing

Prior to the start of Operation Dynamo on Sunday 26th May, passenger vessels had been arriving in Dover and Folkestone with surplus personnel brought home under the so-called 'useless mouths' scheme. After one such crossing the steamer **Manx Maid** *is being berthed at the South Pier, Dover, loaded with Royal Air Force men, and a similar complement, also newly arrived from France, can be seen bottom left at the stern of another Isle of Man ferry, the* **Mona's Queen.** (Imperial War Museum)

in full cry for the coast, cutting off the three armies from their main supply centre at Abbeville. Gort, in conference with corps commanders decided it would be difficult to hold their Escaut positions for more than a day and decided the best course would be to withdraw to their old frontier positions where use could be made of anti-tank works, pillboxes and trenches prepared during the previous winter. Gort also felt that the possibility of a withdrawal towards the Channel ports should be considered as a further alternative and late on the 19th his views were reported to a War Office meeting originally convened to consider organising alternative supply routes.

Admiral Ramsay's Dover administration was represented and a plan formulated for a start to be made from the 20th to bring out surplus BEF personnel at a rate of 2,000 a day. This was to be followed, if needed, with an evacuation of up to 15,000 base unit, hospital staff and other miscellaneous personnel from the night of 22nd May. A third element touched upon, but considered unlikely to be needed, was the evacuation of very large forces. By the time Admiral Ramsay presided at a meeting in Dover to discuss implementing these decisions just 24 hours later, the position on the other side of the Channel had changed so much that the question of how substantial numbers of troops could be brought back to England was on the agenda.

Ramsay and his staff decided that by using passenger ferries as many as 30,000 men a day could be evacuated in an operation spread evenly between the ports of Boulogne, Calais and Dunkirk. Sufficient ships were to hand at Dover to make a start and others were immediately available at Southampton, where more were put on stand-by to be called forward if needed. The meeting continued at the War Office next day and the Sea Transport officers at centres along the South Coast from Weymouth and Poole round to the Thames Estuary, and up the East Coast as far as Harwich, were ordered to prepare lists of all small craft including excursion vessels of up to 1,000 tons and arrange for the details to be sent to Dover. During the same meeting Captain J. Fisher, director Coastwise and Short Sea Shipping, brought to Admiral Ramsay's attention the large numbers of Dutch coastal motor vessels which had crossed to England following the fall of their country a few days earlier. It was decided that some forty of these schuits – or 'skoots' to which their name was soon anglicised – should be commissioned with Royal Navy crews.

To cope with the fast-growing work-load, a whole new organisation had to be set up and the focal point in Admiral Ramsay's headquarters, deep in the chalk cliffs below Dover Castle, became what was known as the Dynamo Room. The network of galleries had been hewn out of the chalk by French prisoners during the early nineteenth century and enlarged in the First World War; the Dynamo Room, normally used for conferences and from which the code-name for the whole operation was taken, being so-called because it had housed an electrical generator during that war. The adjoining network of rooms were fairly basic and one of the galleries, leading to an opening in the cliff face, was Ramsay's own office. From there he worked throughout 22nd May bringing together the multitude of elements of an evacuation plan, word coming from the War Office that no decision to begin an evacuation was expected prior to Friday 24th.

Well before then, Ramsay had been forced to drastically revise his preparations. During Thursday morning, shell flashes from the German attack on Boulogne could be clearly seen in Dover and with Calais seriously threatened reserves were sent to help the hard-pressed garrison. The beleagured British forces battled on all through Friday, into Saturday and not until the evening of Sunday did the final resistance cease. It was a heroic stand and bought precious time for the BEF which had already started falling back on Dunkirk. General Gamelin had been succeeded as Allied supreme commander on 21st May by veteran French General Maxime Weygand who planned an offensive with new French forces fighting their way north to meet up with its own First Army, the BEF and remnants of the Belgian Army who were to strike out south-west to cut directly across the German route to the coast. There had already been a counter-attack by the BEF to hold Arras but as the Germans simply swept past the town Gort ordered the troops to pull back on the 24th, by which time it was clear the Weygand plan existed only in the 73-year-old General's mind.

Gort was left with little alternative but to make a tactical withdrawal towards Dunkirk – the only port left open – and also to the long open beaches stretching from the town to the Belgian border and beyond. The simple strategy was to fight by day and retreat towards the coast during darkness over a period of three days and nights, the hope being that all troops would be inside the perimeter by the end of Wednesday 29th with bastions created covering each of ther embarkation points. Gort gave orders for the retreat to begin on Saturday 25th without entering into any consultation with the French and obviously abandoning any thought of participating in Weygand's combined offensive. By the time Gort telegrammed news of his course of action to Anthony Eden in London, the Secretary of State for War was aware that the French push from the south was just a figment of Weygand's imagination. Eden said in his reply to Gort: 'The French offensive from the Somme cannot be made in sufficient strength to hold any prospect of functioning with your Allies in the North. Should this prove to be the case you will be faced with a situation in which the safety of the BEF will predominate. In such conditions the only course open to you may be to fight your way back west where all beaches and ports east of Gravelines will be used for embarkation.' Gort was anything but optimistic and in a further message said: 'I must not conceal from you that a great part of the BEF and its equipment will inevitably be lost even in the best circumstances.'

That the BEF was able to disengage and begin to fall back was largely due to an unexpected halt in the German advance. General Guderian's XIX Panzer Corps had taken Boulogne and, with Calais encircled, one of its divisions was sent towards Gravelines with the intention of continuing up the coast towards Dunkirk, when he was ordered to stop and fall back on the Au Canal. The decision that the push should cease was taken by the German Army Group A commander, General Gerd von Rundstedt, and confirmed on a visit to the Charleville headquarters by Adolf Hitler, who had been unnerved by the degree of success and was wary of what might yet happen to the south. Concerned that the Panzers were in danger of out-running lines of supply and might become bogged down in the low-lying terrain around Dunkirk, some of it already flooded, Rundstedt had no difficulty convincing Hitler that by staying put his army could form a buffer against which the Allies could be crushed by General Fedor von Bock's Army Group B sweeping down from the north. Hitler also agreed that the Panzers would be best saved for the attack that would then be made southwards into France and he looked favourably on a plea from Field Marshal Hermann Göring that the task of wiping out Allied forces trapped in the Dunkirk pocket should go to the Luftwaffe. It was a full two days before Guderian's Panzers were ordered to move again, and by then it was too late. The greater part of the BEF, and substantial numbers of French troops, had slipped through and were inside the Dunkirk perimeter.

The Admiralty signal officially starting Operation Dynamo reached Dover at three minutes before seven on the evening of Sunday 26th May and, at that moment, Admiral Ramsay already had personnel carriers actually loading in Dunkirk. They had been sent in the afternoon and were the latest in a stream of ships sent back and forth in the previous few days as base personnel, communication troops, training units and other so-called 'useless mouths' were brought out. By midnight on Sunday almost 28,000 men had been landed in Dover, but they were not included in the Operation Dynamo totals which started from the following day.

Up to that time all vessels dispatched by Ramsay had taken the most direct route, a 39 nautical miles run across the English Channel to turn east at No. 6 Buoy off Calais for a final leg along the coast to Dunkirk. This was designated Route Z and before the end of the first full day of the evacuation shore batteries near Gravelines caused so much trouble to passing ships that it was only safe for the passage to be used in darkness. This left Ramsay with two possibilities. Next shortest was Route X of 55 miles passing through the Downs, the historic anchorage between the Goodwin Sands and the Kent coast, and then from the North Goodwin light vessel to cross the Ruytingen Bank and join Route Z between Gravelines and Dunkirk for the last few miles. Then there was Route Y of 87 miles which also went inside the Goodwins before striking-out for a long haul towards Ostend, and made a dog-leg turn at Kwinte Buoy to approach Dunkirk from the east through the Zuydecote Pass. There was a threat from mines on each of the longer passages and after German artillery reached the Belgian coast at Nieuport, Route Y ships came under fire as they closed on the coast. Minesweepers had been sent out to clear Route Y

Dunkirk from land and sea. The outskirts of the town on the road from St. Omer, with every building in sight damaged in this German photograph taken after Dynamo was over. The Bergues Canal formed part of the inland perimeter to the evacuation area (Imperial War Museum). *Below, the harbour entrance with its backcloth of the pall of black smoke from the oil storage tanks that blazed throughout the operation. A Royal Navy destroyer is standing off as the paddle minesweeper* **Queen of Thanet** *is about to round the lighthouse at the end of the West Mole. Either the Isle of Man Steam Packet Company vessel* **Tynwald** *or sister ship* **Fenella** *is seen on the left, moored on the outside of the East Mole.* (Imperial War Museum)

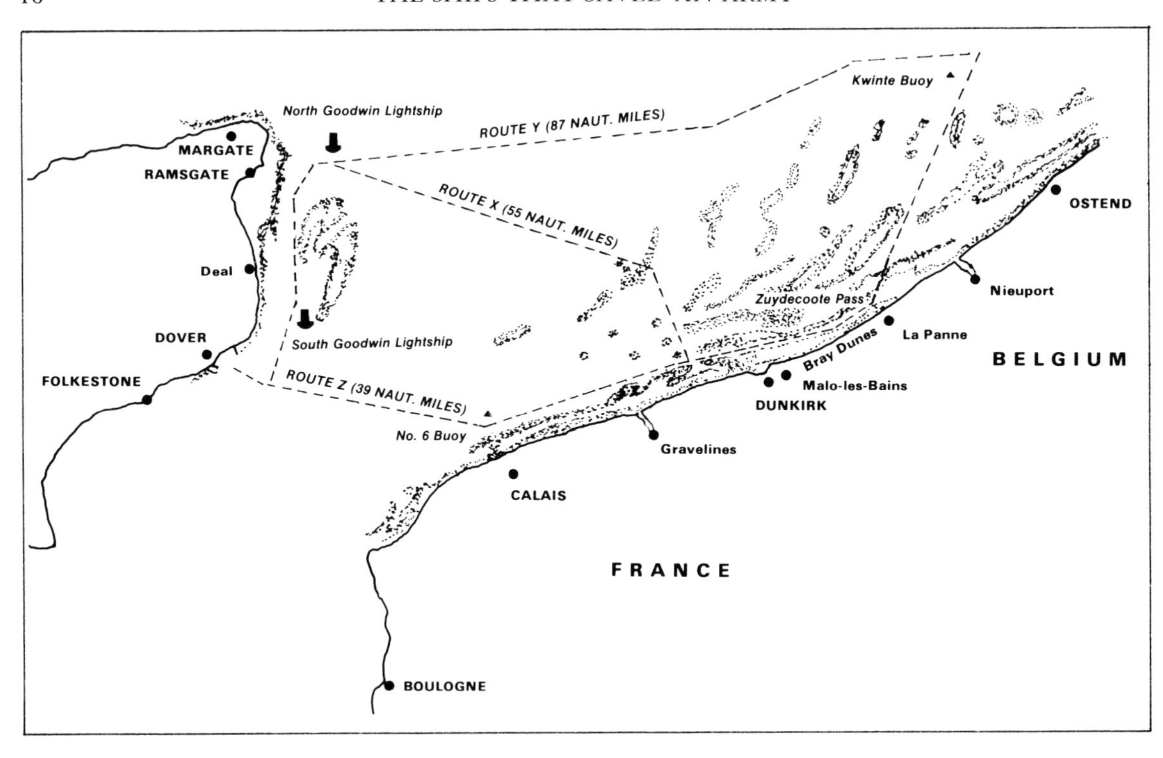
North Goodwin Lightship
ROUTE Y (87 NAUT. MILES)
Kwinte Buoy
MARGATE
RAMSGATE
ROUTE X (55 NAUT. MILES)
OSTEND
Deal
Nieuport
Zuydecoote Pass
DOVER
South Goodwin Lightship
La Panne
Bray Dunes
BELGIUM
FOLKESTONE
ROUTE Z (39 NAUT. MILES)
Malo-les-Bains
DUNKIRK
No. 6 Buoy
Gravelines
CALAIS
FRANCE
BOULOGNE

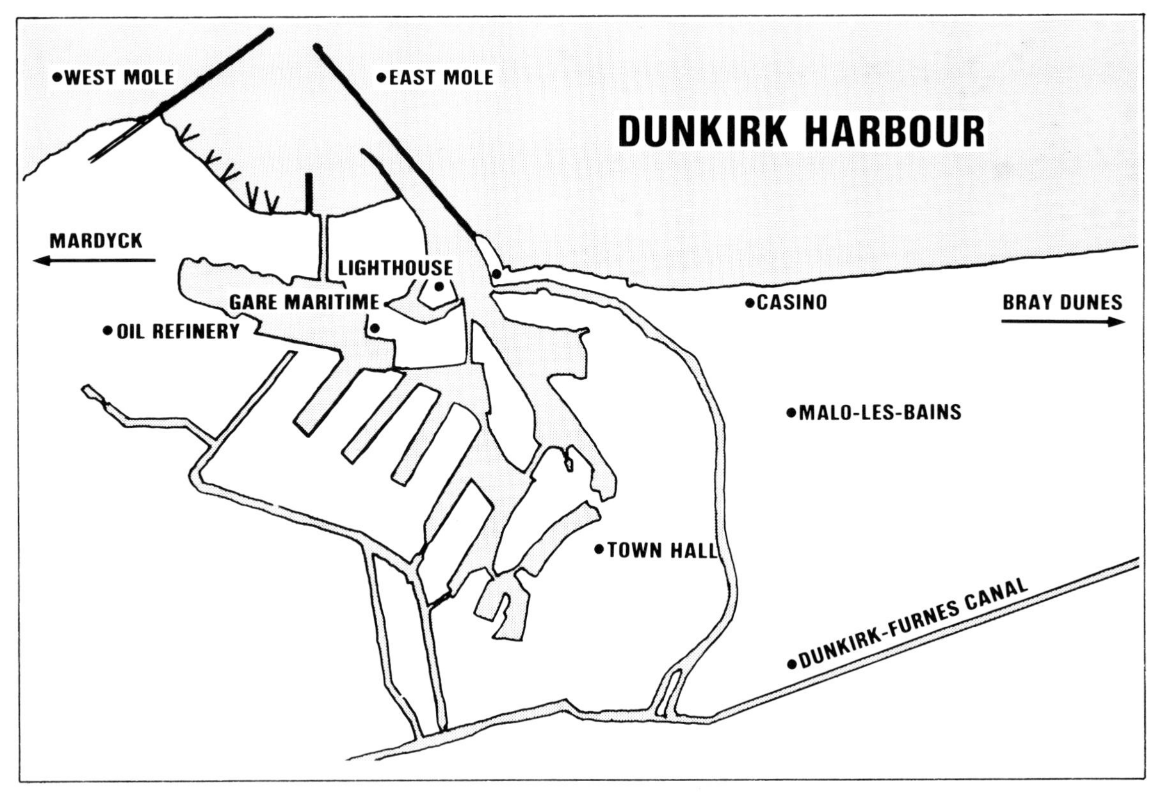
WEST MOLE
EAST MOLE
DUNKIRK HARBOUR
MARDYCK
LIGHTHOUSE
GARE MARITIME
OIL REFINERY
CASINO
BRAY DUNES
MALO-LES-BAINS
TOWN HALL
DUNKIRK-FURNES CANAL

but Ramsay had to take the risk of using it before they had time to complete their work and before lunch on Monday two personnel ships, two hospital ships and a pair of escorting destroyers set off.

One of the officers who volunteered to assist in the organisation of the evacuation, Captain William Tennant, chief staff officer to the First Sea Lord at the Admiralty, was sent over to Dunkirk during Monday afternoon to become senior naval officer on shore. He crossed in the destroyer *Wolfhound,* taking with him a dozen officers, communications staff and 160 ratings, arriving at around six in the evening. Tennant found much of the town ablaze and the facilities of what had been one of Europe's most modern ports in ruins. The lock system for the seven main dock basins, stretching well into the town was wrecked, leaving most of the five miles of quays useless, and only two long piers stretching out to the harbour mouth appeared undamaged. The West Mole came out at angle from the oil storage area where tanks blazed all through the evacuation and the resulting pall of black smoke became Dunkirk's major landmark. The longer East Mole began close to ancient fortifications on shore and ran 1,400 yards to the harbour entrance.

Although Tennant had been in Dunkirk barely two hours, the seriousness of the situation was immediately apparent and he quickly signalled a request to Dover for all available craft to be sent to the beaches to the east of the harbour, adding the comment: 'Evacuation tomorrow night is problematical.' Ships already there were distributed along the coast and used their lifeboats to

A turning point in the evacuation as far the numbers of troops handled was the discovery late on Monday 28th May that large personnel vessels could moor alongside the East Mole at Dunkirk. Tin helmeted soldiers are streaming along the Mole to board the destroyer seen in the foreground as the twin-funneled **Maid of Orleans** *departs for Dover. This Southern Railway steamer made several visits to the Mole and averaged more than 1,000 men a crossing after spending five or six hours alongside loading.* (Popperfoto)

ferry troops, but the gently shelving beach meant that vessels had to stand a long way off and with small boats in short supply the process of loading was agonisingly slow. Despite all the effort only a disappointing 7,669 men reached England during the 27th and, in the hope of speeding up the lifting of troops, Tennant decided to experiment during Monday evening to see whether vessels could berth alongside the East Mole. A structure consisting of concrete piles with a narrow railed planked walk-way on top, it was just about wide enough for three men to walk abreast and certainly not designed for ships to lie against. There were no bollards to which lines could be attached and the surge of the tides through the piles was a further headache. But Tennant had to gamble and one of the personnel ships, believed to have been the Thames excursion motor vessel *Queen of the Channel,* was called in and managed to get alongside safely.

Soldiers wait patiently in line up to their necks in the sea to be hauled aboard the minesweeper **Oriole,** *beached off the Belgian resort of La Panne on 29th May 1940. It is perhaps the most widely published picture of the evacuation but rarely, if ever, has the photographer, John Rutherford Crosby, a Sub-Lieutenant serving in the converted Clyde paddle steamer, been credited. (It has also on occasion been decried as a fake – a montage – on the assumption that no ship could get so far inshore without running aground!)*

The news was relayed to Dover and from this point the evacuation gathered momentum. As the larger vessels started to move to the harbour a second great priority was the provision of small craft to work off the beaches. Thus the collection of launches, motor cruisers and yachts by the Admiralty's Small Vessels Pool began in earnest. Quite fortuitously, an appeal for small pleasure craft to be registered by their owners had gone out earlier in the month as the Admiralty sought to meet a short-fall in vessels for harbour and other auxiliary duties. By the evening of Monday, owners were being contacted and some of Dunkirk's real 'little ships' were moving down the Thames to Sheerness.

Throughout Monday the BEF continued to fall back and, despite communications worries and a generally confused situation, the day ended with Gort satisfied there was cover on all flanks. Tuesday saw the evacuation continuing from the beaches with 5,930 troops transported to safety and, more significantly, almost 12,000 were taken from the harbour in the face of shelling and almost constant air attacks. The Navy's destroyers were pressed into transport roles and carried prodigious loads, their high speed enabling some of them to complete two or more round trips in a day. A total of 17,804 men were taken out during the 24 hours up to midnight on the 28th and Ramsay had reason to feel that the operation was proceeding satisfactorily.

Wednesday 29th brought severe losses among personnel ships, naval vessels and small craft alike and in the evening there was another shattering blow for Ramsay when the Admiralty ordered the withdrawal of all the operation's most modern destroyers. With three sunk and six more badly damaged during this day alone, Ramsay had to release all remaining units from the H, I and J Classes and was left with just 15 of the older craft. The destroyers took a large percentage of the 33,558 troops moved from the harbour during the 29th yet there was little Ramsay could do but get on with the job.

Loading from the beaches was becoming better organised however, and with 13,752 men safely transported from those areas the total for the day grew to 47,310. It had to. German pressure was on and during Wednesday evening nowhere was the front line more than five miles from the sea. The perimeter contracted still further to little more than 30 miles on Thursday, two thirds of it held by the BEF forces with the French hanging on roughly from the area of Bergues to the coast.

East of Dunkirk itself, three main loading beaches had been been identified at Malo-les-Bains, Bray Dunes and La Panne, with gaps of about a mile between them. Thursday brought the greatest concentration of effort there in response to a message in the early hours of the morning from the British headquarters at La Panne which warned in plain language that 'the perimeter cannot be held for long.' All manner of craft were by then in use ferrying troops from the beaches for an equal variety of vessels to make the passage to the ports and piers of Kent. Supplies of food, drinking water and ammunition were sent over in Thames sailing barges which were driven ashore and, in most cases, destroyed after being unloaded. Dutch skoots and some of the equally shallow draught paddle minesweepers steamers were deliberately run aground to allow troops to wade out as the tide receded and by midnight 29,512 men from the beaches were back on English soil, together with 24,311 from Dunkirk itself, this figure clearly reflecting the disappearance of the larger and faster destroyers, plus some losses among vessels using the Mole. But the day's total of 53,823 men was still the best so far.

By this time the Germans were withdrawing units to prepare for the attack southwards into France and late on Thursday it was decided that all operations in connection with Dunkirk should be left to Army Group B, with Rundstedt quickly initiating a regrouping of the Panzers of his Army Group A for that. There was certainly no lessening in the intensity of the attack on Dunkirk and the perimeter continued to shrink. An onshore breeze blew up on Friday morning which cleared much of the haze and smoke, allowing artillery as close as Mardyck to begin shelling the harbour with great accuracy. The beach at La Panne also suffered regular artillery barrages from guns moved up to the area of Nieuport. If this attention was not sufficiently unwelcome, the breeze caused surf off the beaches and for a time it became almost impossible to handle small boats.

The same morning brought communications problems with Dover and none of over a dozen personnel or hospital ships sent over the previous evening had returned. Gradually they began to come in and Ramsay pressed on with a plan to send over his final reserve of small craft for a major effort at the beaches in the early hours of Saturday. The task of getting the assortment of vessels across the Channel was mostly entrusted to tugs or skoots while a few of the larger motor cruisers and yachts themselves towed other craft. What became known as the 'special tows' began setting off from Ramsgate, where they had been collected, at 1pm and soon there was a continuous line of ships stretching over five miles. The Admiralty had already advised Admiral Ramsay that equal priority should be given to the evacuation of French troops in British vessels and Saturday produced the biggest evacuation total of them all, 68,014 men – 45,072, including 15,000 French, from Dunkirk and 22,942 off the beaches – taking the total for the operation as a whole close to 200,000 in five days.

Lord Gort reluctantly left French soil on Friday evening after handing over command of the remaining elements of the BEF to General Alexander, his request to be allowed to remain until the very end receiving an emphatic refusal from London. Gort went out from La Panne to the minesweeper *Hebe* as the headquarters was closed down and he later transferred to the fast anti-submarine boat *MASB 6* for the crossing to Dover. Alexander was to oversee a further withdrawal to a line from near Bergues through to the villages of Uxem and Ghyvelde, but feared it might not be possible to hold the perimeter for long after midnight Saturday.

At sea, things also went badly during the first day of June. The destroyer *Wakeful* was lost on Friday and three of Ramsay's remaining destroyers, *Basilisk, Havant* and *Keith* were sunk in the space of a few hours on Saturday when four more were damaged seriously. The personnel vessels large and small were also taking a battering as the Luftwaffe filled the skies and it became so hazardous that a decision was taken in Dunkirk to allow no ships to sail after 3am on Sunday morning. The Admiralty stepped in to suspend movements from the port after 7am with

Going home! The expressions on the faces of the troops say it all. Some stand and chat, others sleep in the early summer sunshine and the rest gaze over the rails as the paddler **Oriole** *churns her way back to the Kent coast and safety.* (John Rutherford Crosby)

Ramsay reluctantly agreeing that the risk to ships operating in daylight was out of all proportion to the number of troops evacuated. Some vessels still lingered until it was getting light and 1st June again saw over 60,000 men landed in England, 47,081 leaving the harbour, the largest concentration of the evacuation.

Although troops continued to be lifted from the beaches, the Germans had been moving down the coast from Nieuport and only the section between Malo-les-Bains and Dunkirk could be used. There were now only between three and four thousand members of the BEF left, together with French personnel originally estimated to total some 25,000. The French were holding the perimeter and during Sunday they even counter-attacked in one area until progress was halted by the Luftwaffe near the tiny village of Notre Dame

TROOPS LANDED IN ENGLAND

	From Dunkirk Harbour	From the Beaches	Day's Total	Grand Total
Monday 27th May	7,669	Nil	7,669	7,669
Tuesday 28th May	11,874	5,930	17,804	25,473
Wednesday 29th May	33,558	13,752	47,310	72,783
Thursday 30th May	24,311	29,512	53,823	126,606
Friday 31st May	45,072	22,942	68,014	194,620
Saturday 1st June	47,081	17,348	64,429	259,049
Sunday 2nd June	19,561	6,695	26,256	285,305
Monday 3rd June	24,876	1,870	26,746	312,051
Tuesday 4th June	25,553	622	26,175	338,226
Totals:	239,555	98,671	338,226	

HMS **Icarus** *storms past the* **Oriole** *and the camera of Rutherford Crosby, her after decks crowded by some of a total of 4,704 troops she carried to Dover during the evacuation. One curiosity not explained is the apparent absence of two of the vessel's main armament turrets, forward and aft.*

des Neiges. The personnel vessels returned late on Sunday and, at 11.30 p.m., after the last British elements were embarked, Captain Tennant was able to signal Admiral Ramsay with the news: 'BEF evacuated.' Of 26,256 men embarked in that period, well over 20,000 were French and during the 24 hours to midnight on Monday another 26,746, again mostly from Dunkirk Harbour, were transported to England, some of the vessels returning only sparsely loaded after encountering difficulties in finding troops.

As Monday progressed, it became clear to Ramsay that yet another lift would be necessary that night and the remaining destroyers, personnel vessels and some of the little ships crossed yet again, despite the fact that Dover had no really accurate figure of the number of French troops to be brought out. When the first vessels reached the Mole, machine-gun fire could be heard from Dunkirk's outskirts and although some of the exhausted French preferred to stay behind, again more than 26,000 had left by the time the destroyer *Shikari's* departure at 3.40 a.m. on Tuesday brought Operation Dynamo to an end. Later on Tuesday morning the last defenders surrendered.

Personnel Vessels

NEARLY one third of all the troops brought back from Dunkirk made the crossing on passenger ferries. Around 50 vessels were involved, operating almost exclusively in and out of Dunkirk Harbour and with most departures from the East Mole. A majority of the ships had been in use as transports on the English Channel since early in September 1939 when, within hours of war being declared, requisition orders were placed on not only the ferries of principal South Coast operators such as the Southern Railway and Great Western Railway, but also on ships from the London and North Eastern Railway's Harwich fleet and others then employed on the Irish Sea by the London and Midland and Scottish Railway and under the Great Western Railway's management between Fishguard and Rosslare.

An equally heavy call was made on the fleet of the Isle of Man Steam Packet Company, whose eight ships which took part in Operation Dynamo were credited with transporting one in every 14 of the troops landed in Britain. Large summer excursion ships from the Thames, and vessels more accustomed to cruising amid the splendour of the Western Isles of Scotland, were also called south, mostly sailing with their civilian crews and being used to transport the British Expeditionary Force and Royal Air Force support personnel to France before settling into a routine of crossings to maintain lines of supply, particularly to Le Havre and Cherbourg from Southampton.

During the opening months of the war, and into 1940, limited cross-Channel services continued but these were concentrated between Folkestone and Calais after first Dover, and later Boulogne, were closed to civilian traffic. BEF leave sailings were also provided between Folkestone and Calais but, by May 1940, with the situation on the other side of the Channel altering rapidly, the ferries had to be used for evacuation purposes for the first time with civilians and military personnel brought over from Belgian and Dutch ports.

Although the need for an evacuation of forces from France in substantial numbers began to look increasingly likely as the month of May wore on, as late as the 20th the enormity of the task had still not been realised. It was still being reasoned that if an evacuation became necessary, in the region of 30,000 troops a day could be brought out. This assumed that the ports of Dunkirk, Calais and Boulogne would all be available to handle around 10,000 men in each 24-hour cycle and allowing for what was described as 'moderate interference' from the enemy.

The bulk of the transportation was to be put in the hands of the ferries operating in pairs to all three ports and with the sailings timed in such a way that no more than two ships would be alongside a French quay at any one time. Admiral Ramsay already had some ten ferries lying in Dover or Folkestone, a further half dozen on stand-by at Southampton and yet more able to be brought forward at comparatively short notice. In addition there were eight hospital ships, all converted ferries, at Southampton or Newhaven to handle wounded on separate sailings and make it possible for able bodied personnel to be loaded more quickly on to the passenger ships.

It all looked very practical on paper. The ferries were still largely manned by peacetime crews who, on the short rail-connected services across the Dover Straits especially, were well versed in getting passengers on and off in quick time and using a number of gangways. In reality it was very different. There was one barely accessible embarkation port instead of three, an almost total lack of conventional berthing facilities and intense enemy artillery and air activity.

Later in the war, the Thames excursion ship *Royal Daffodil,* one of the stalwarts of the evacuation, caused quite a stir in Dover when putting down seven gangways to await the arrival of two troop trains which arrived simultaneously at the Marine Station by different routes. The 1,500 men they conveyed were run on to the quay at the double and the ship sailed fully loaded just seven minutes after the trains had stopped. During trips to Dunkirk there was little scope for such expertise and on numerous occasions officers from vessels like *Royal Daffodil* had to go ashore and actually search for troops to carry.

The ferries returned from Dunkirk to Dover and Folkestone where full advantage was taken of rail facilities in the ports, most of the loads of troops being transferred direct from ship to train and moved quickly away from the immediate vicinity. While the ships were fuelled and supplied for another crossing, many of the trains went only a short distance before halting at small stations in the Kent countryside where local voluntary services were waiting with food and drink.

A number of the vessels had been involved in difficult rescue sailings from the Low Countries in the fortnight before Dunkirk and, as Operation Dynamo continued, there were quite serious problems among the crews as sheer fatigue began to take its toll. The policy adopted by Admiral Ramsay was to put in a naval commander and a stiffening of RN personnel into such ships. But it all took time and crossings were lost, from Folkestone in particular and, as will be seen later, one vessel left the area altogether and proceeded without orders to Southampton.

Even when Dynamo ended there was no let-up for the undamaged personnel vessels, with further evacuations soon necessary from north-west France and the Channel Islands. And when in June 1944 the British Liberation Army returned to France with the Americans as allies, a contingent of the Dunkirk ferries were there again for the Normandy Landings, this time converted to Landing Ships Infantry and going to the beaches carrying half a dozen assault craft apiece.

Vessels which survived the war and were returned to civilian service tended to be overtaken quite quickly by the car ferry revolution and, by the end of the 1960s, most had been displaced by new multi-purpose tonnage and scrapped. Amongst larger ferries the Isle of Man Steam Packet Company's *Lady of Mann* lasted until the summer of 1971 and the Clyde veteran *King George V* ran until 1974 and was not finally scrapped until 1984 after a fire ruined plans for the vessel to be established as a floating restaurant in London.

ARCHANGEL

Built: 1910 by John Brown & Co, Clydebank, as *St. Petersburg* for the Great Eastern Railway. Renamed *Archangel* 1914, transferred to London & North Eastern Railway, 1923.
Gross Tonnage: 2,410.
Length: 331 ft.
Width: 43 ft. 2 in.
Machinery: Direct drive Parsons turbines, triple screw.
Speed: 20 knots.
1939 route: LNER Harwich–Zeebrugge service.

Archangel was renamed when requisitioned in 1914 for First World War service as a hospital ship. She was called-up a second time in December 1939 and sent to Southampton to assist with troop movements across the English Channel. Immediately before the start of Operation Dynamo *Archangel* sailed from Southampton under the command of Captain Arthur Greenham carrying troops from the Queen Victoria Rifles and Rifle Brigade to defend Calais, but was forced to turn back to Southampton after coming under heavy fire from shore batteries at Gravelines. Although listed among ferries on stand-by at Southampton as the evacuation began, it is unclear whether *Archangel* was called forward to Dunkirk and the vessel is not listed as transporting any troops. *Archangel* did take part in attempts to pick up troops cut off on the French coast at St. Valery a week later and at the end of the month assisted in the evacuation of the Channel Islands with crossings to Jersey. By the following year *Archangel* was operating in more northerly waters and on 16th May 1941,

An early post-war view of **Autocarrier** *showing the fairly primitive arrangements for transporting cars across the English Channel that were offered from 1931.* **Autocarrier** *was extensively used as a cargo ship in the opening months of the war and made three crossings to Dunkirk before a later involvement in the evacuation of the Channel Islands.* (Skyfotos)

during a passage from Kirkwall, was bombed and 17 crew members were killed. The vessel was beached and subsequently declared a total loss.

AUTOCARRIER

The Southern Railway responded in 1931 to competition from the car carrying service of Dover-based Townsend Bros by completing a cargo vessel then under construction on the Clyde to take about 30 crane-loaded cars and 120 passengers under the name *Autocarrier*. With SR master Captain C. H. Masters remaining in command, *Autocarrier* saw much use as a cargo vessel in the early months of the war and made a first appearance at Dunkirk on 2nd June but was unable to find any troops and returned to Dover. A second visit on 3rd June was more successful, 712 men being taken aboard after Captain Masters succeeded in berthing *Autocarrier* on the outside of the East Mole despite difficulties caused by the combination of a freshening easterly wind and a fast running tide. *Autocarrier* was back before the end of 3rd June and in the evening, together with *Newhaven*, evacuated final French troops and naval personnel. *Autocarrier* then moved west and on 14th June made the final civilian sailing from St. Malo to St. Helier before playing a part in the evacuation of Jersey. *Autocarrier* was next used as a Royal Navy recreation ship until starting sailings out of Southampton as a cargo vessel until the summer of 1946. In the final phase of her career, until broken up at Ghent, Belgium, in 1954, she mainly operated as a cargo vessel from Dover or Folkestone and only occasionally carried cars and passengers.

Built: 1931 by D. & W. Henderson, Glasgow, as *Autocarrier* for the Southern Railway.
Gross Tonnage: 822.
Length: 270 ft.
Width: 26 ft.
Machinery: 8-cylinder triple-expansion, twin screw, coal-fired.
Speed: 15 knots.
1939 route: Southern Railway Dover–Calais car ferry service (crane-loaded).

BEN-MY-CHREE

The first oil-burning vessel to be built for the Isle of Man Steam Packet Company, *Ben-my-Chree* earned a deserved reputation during the 1930s as a flier, regularly averaging over 20 knots on

Built: 1927 by Cammell Laird, Birkenhead, for the Isle of Man Steam Packet Company.
Gross tonnage: 2,586
Length: 355 ft.
Width: 46 ft.
Machinery: Two single-reduction Parson geared turbines
Speed: 22.5 knots.
1939 route: Isle of Man Steam Packet Liverpool–Douglas service.

Despite the abundance of smoke, **Ben-my-Chree** *was the Isle of Man Steam Packet Company's first oil burner and is clearly ready to start one of the fast passages for which she was noted. Painted white from 1932 onwards and quickly pressed into service as a transport when the war started, the* **Ben-my-Chree's** *Dunkirk contribution was cut short after a collision off Folkestone on 2nd June. Damage to the starboard side amidships was extensive as seen in the lower picture taken during repairs at Birkenhead. An area of the hull two decks in height had to be replaced and some of the buckled plates can be seen on the quayside after being cut away. Note the 'Out of Bounds to Troops' sign at the top of the Boat Deck companionway.* (Richard Danielson collection)

crossings to and from the Mersey. She was requisitioned for duties as a transport within a few days of the outbreak of war and retained a Steam Packet crew under Captain G. Woods. *Ben-my-Chree* had completed three or four trips to Dunkirk by 1st June, landing a total of 4,095 men, but the officers and men were close to exhaustion and relief naval personnel had been introduced by the time the vessel left Folkestone on 2nd June. Soon after sailing *Ben-my-Chree* was in collision and sustained severe damage on the starboard side amidships and was unable to take any further part in the evacuation. Following repairs she was used on transport duties from northern ports to Iceland until converted on the Tyne early in 1944 to serve as a Landing Ship Infantry. With six landing craft she was headquarters unit of the 514th Assault Flotilla in the Normandy Landings, carrying US Rangers to Omaha Beach. The vessel later undertook cross-Channel sailings until released in May 1946 when a lengthy overhaul was necessary before Steam Packet service resumed. She was broken up in Belgium at the end of 1965.

Southern Railway steamer **Biarritz** *ran between Dover and Boulogne as a forces' leave ship until a little more than a month before Operation Dynamo. Then, after bringing out Dutch nationals from Rotterdam,* **Biarritz** *was severely damaged in the boiler room when shelled from the French coast during a first trip to Dunkirk on 27th May and had to retire to Southampton for repairs.* (A. M. S. Russell collection)

BIARRITZ

Requisitioned by the Admiralty immediately upon completion early in 1915, *Biarritz* was converted to operate as a minelayer and saw service in the North Sea and Dardanelles and did not finally begin Dover–Calais sailings until 1921 following overhaul by Vickers Armstrong at Barrow. After a further extensive refit by Dennys in the winter of 1925–26, *Biarritz* and sister ship *Maid of Orleans* switched to a year-round Folkestone–Boulogne service which continued until the war started in 1939. *Biarritz* operated between Dover and Boulogne as a leave ship for the BEF from December 1939 to April 1940 and then went to Rotterdam to bring out Dutch nationals. *Biarritz* and the Thames excursion vessel *Queen of the Channel* carried the 20th Guards Brigade to Boulogne on 22nd May and although at Dover and immediately available to Admiral Ramsay when the Dunkirk operation began, she was prevented from playing a major part after suffering serious damage in her boiler room from shellfire off the French coast on 27th May. After the shell hit, Fireman A. Phillips died attempting to turn off fuel and his efforts were mentioned in despatches together with the name of the master, Captain W. A. Baker. Engineer J. L. Crockett was awarded the DSC for his work in the crisis. *Biarritz* was sent to Southampton for repairs and later had spells on the Stranraer–Larne service and as a target ship for naval pilots before being converted to act as a landing ship in the Normandy invasion. *Biarritz* remained in grey livery until overhauled by Dennys in 1947 and continued on troop and displaced person sailings mainly from Harwich, until scrapped at Dover in the winter of 1948.

Built: 1915 by Wm Denny & Bros, Dumbarton, for the South Eastern and Chatham Railway; transferred to the Southern Railway, 1923.
Gross tonnage: 2,495.
Length: 341 ft. 3in.
Width: 45 ft.
Machinery: Parsons geared turbines, twin screw.
Speed: 23 knots.
1939 route: Southern Railway services, Folkestone–Boulogne.

CANTERBURY

Provided for the sea connection of the prestigious 'Golden Arrow' London–Paris rail service, *Canterbury* originally carried only 300 first class passengers, although second class facilities were added from 1932. Before Dunkirk, *Canterbury* operated on cross-Channel trooping runs and, on 25th May, showed the evacuation potential of the personnel ships, taking on 1,246 men at Dunkirk's Gare Maritime, a load mainly made up of base personnel who were no longer required.

Canterbury, *the ferry which sailed into the 1930s taking just 300 first class passengers on the 'Golden Arrow' service and provided for them facilities including a Palm Court and 20 private cabins, left Dunkirk on 29th May 1940 with almost 2,0000 battle weary troops crowded aboard. Credited with making four crossings in all,* **Canterbury** *sailed with loads in excess of 1,200 men on two other occasions. After a varied war career including a role in the Normandy Invasion as a Landing Ship (Infantry),* **Canterbury** *was back on the 'Golden Arrow' run in 1946 and although soon relegated to less prestigious duties, completed 35 years' service before being withdrawn in 1964.* (Skyfotos)

Next day *Canterbury* arrived at Dunkirk in the evening, berthing alongside *Maid of Orleans* to load 1,340 men and after returning on 29th May, she left with nearly 2,000 men aboard during a ferocious air attack. *Canterbury* suffered serious bomb damage, yet repairs were completed in time for the ferry to appear at Dunkirk again on 3rd June when 659 French troops were loaded and taken to Dover. Briefly used as a target ship for the Fleet Air Arm, she then had a year on the Irish Sea's Stranraer–Larne service before conversion to a Landing Ship at Ardrossan in 1943. After participating in the Normandy invasion carrying six small assault craft slung outboard from hand-operated davits, *Canterbury* ran from Dover and Folkestone as a military leave ship and was refitted on the Tyne prior to returning to the 'Golden Arrow' service in April 1946. Soon displaced by larger tonnage, the vessel sailed between Folkestone and Calais until 1948, switching to Folkestone–Boulogne summer sailings which kept her occupied until withdrawn in the autumn of 1964. She was broken up in Belgium during the following summer.

Built: 1929 by Wm Denny & Bros, Dumbarton, for the Southern Railway.
Gross tonnage: 3,071.
Length: 341 ft. 6 in.
Width: 47 ft.
Machinery: Parsons single-reduction geared turbines, twin screw.
Speed: 21 knots.
1939 route: Southern Railway 'Golden Arrow' service between Dover and Calais.

COTE D'ARGENT

The French-crewed *Cote d'Argent,* which came under the orders of Admiral Ramsay together with sister vessel *Cote d'Azur,* made five trips from Dunkirk, transporting 5,754 men. She was one of the vessels that got alongside the East Mole on 2nd June in conditions made extremely tricky by wind and tide, more than 1,000 troops boarding before the ferry sailed for Dover half an hour after midnight. A few weeks later, at the end of July 1940, the *Cote d'Argent* was caught

The French cross-Channel ferry **Cote d'Azur,** *reversing towards Admiralty Pier in Dover, was sunk near Dunkirk on 27th May but later raised by the Germans and used as a minelayer. Sister ship* **Cote d'Argent** *survived the evacuation only to fall into enemy hands in July 1940 and was also converted into a minelayer. Both vessels were later sunk,* **Cote d'Azur,** *then named* **Ostmark,** *in April 1945, and* **Cote d'Argent,** *which became* **Elsass,** *in June of the previous year.* (John de S. Winser collection)

Built: 1932 by F & C. de la Mediterranée for the Society Anonyme de Gerance et d'Armement (SAGA).
Gross tonnage: 3,049.
Length: 325 ft. 10 in.
Width: 45 ft.
Machinery: Two Parsons single-reduction geared turbines.
Speed: 23 knots.
1939 route: SAGA Calais–Dover service.

on the 26th at La Pallice by the rapid German advance and suffered extensive damage. The vessel was later towed to St. Nazaire for repairs and then commissioned by the Germans as the minelayer *Elsass,* in which guise she was mined and sunk near Namsos in June 1944.

COTE D'AZUR

Cote d'Azur was requisitioned early in May 1940 to assist in the evacuation of French troops from Flushing and later took Belgian troops and civilians from Ostend. She was then sent to Dunkirk but was bombed and sunk on 27th May. The wreck was raised by the Germans during the following year and after conversion for Baltic service as a minelayer under the name *Ostmark*

Built: 1932 by F & C. de la Mediterranée for the Society Anonyme de Gerance d'Armement (SAGA).
Gross tonnage: 3,047.
Length: 325 ft. 10 in.
Width: 45 ft.
Machinery: Two Parsons single reduction geared turbines.
Speed: 23 knots.
1939 route: SAGA Dover–Calais service.

was sunk on 21st April 1945 when caught near Anholt by RAF Mosquito aircraft.

FENELLA

The versatile *Fenella,* and sister vessel *Tynwald* which was also at Dunkirk, were built to provide winter sailings from Douglas to Liverpool as well as playing a full part in handling the Steam Packet

Built: 1937 by Vickers-Armstrongs, Barrow, for the Isle of Man Steam Packet Company
Gross tonnage: 2,376.
Length: 314 ft. 6 in.
Width: 46 ft.
Machinery: Two single-reduction geared turbines.
Speed: 21 knots.
1939 route: Various Isle of Man Steam Packet services, including winter sailings between Liverpool and Douglas.

Company's extensive seasonal traffic. The *Fenella* was requisitioned as a transport before the war was a week old, taking with her an almost exclusively Manx crew under Captain W. Cubbon. She set off to Dunkirk on 28th May and berthed on the outside of the East Mole and had loaded about 650 troops when coming under fire in the day's third massed air attack, receiving hits from three bombs in rapid succession. The first bomb penetrated the promenade deck, a second hit the Mole and blew pieces of concrete through the hull below the waterline before another bomb, exploding between the Mole and the vessel, wrecked the engine room. The troops were hurriedly disembarked on to the Mole before the vessel sank, some of them, and survivors from the *Fenella's* 48-strong crew, going to the paddle steamer *Crested Eagle,* which was also bombed and sunk almost soon as she had cleared the pier. Junior steward Tom Helsby, age 19, from Liverpool, suffered severe burns and became a prisoner of war, receiving expert treatment from German doctors. The only Steam Packet crew member to be taken prisoner, he returned to serve the company for many years and was chief steward of the car ferry *Ben-my-Chree.*

HYTHE

Built: 1925 by D. & W. Henderson, Glasgow, for the Southern Railway.
Gross tonnage: 829.
Length: 229 ft. 6 in.
Width: 35 ft. 9 in.
Machinery: Steam reciprocating, twin screw.
Speed: 15 knots.
1939 route: Cargo services Dover–Folkestone to Calais–Boulogne.

One of three similiar cargo steamers built for the Southern Railway, *Hythe* worked from Dover or Folkestone until the war and then, although not provided with accommodation for more than a handful of passengers, was used as a transport. Prior to Dunkirk *Hythe* had been running out of Southampton and was sent from there on 30th May to anchor in the Downs and await orders. These were not long in coming and *Hythe* crossed to the beaches in the early hours of Friday 31st, accompanied by sister vessel *Whitstable.* Hythe's master, Captain R. W. Morford, was not impressed when given an army map from which to navigate and after arriving off the beaches and seeing the difficulties being caused to small boats by the surf, decided to go in to Dunkirk Harbour. Shells fell ahead and astern of the ship as it entered but Captain Morford managed to swing and get alongside a stone pier at the shore end of the East Mole. Troops, some carrying wounded on stretchers, were taken on board and *Hythe* left with 674 men some two hours later. *Hythe* re-opened the Dover–Calais cargo service in August 1945 and also made the first cargo sailing to Boulogne in March of the following year. The steamer continued to serve Boulogne until withdrawn in 1956 and scrapped at Dover.

KILLARNEY

This veteran former Irish Sea ferry was the oldest of the larger personnel vessels at Dunkirk and a harrowing return crossing on 29th May was

Idyllic surroundings for the Coast Lines' Scottish summer cruise ship **Killarney,** *anchored off Arrochar at the head of Loch Long in June 1935. Five years later, as the veteran steamer headed home from Dunkirk, shore batteries fired an estimated 90 shells at her in the space of 30 minutes. Miraculously there was only one direct hit, at the stern, which killed eight men and wounded 30.* (Graham E. Langmuir)

certainly in marked contrast to her pre-war role making leisurely cruises from Liverpool to the Western Isles of Scotland. Whilst waiting off Dunkirk the *Killarney* was not far away when *Mona's Queen* was mined and sank, the vessel then going in to the East Mole to load almost 900 men, who were squeezed into every available foot of space below and on the open decks. The master, Captain R. Hughes, made smoke as the 6-inch guns of the shore batteries near Gravelines opened up and, despite the narrow channel,

Built: 1893 by Harland & Wolff, Belfast, as *Classic* for the Belfast Steamship Company; renamed *Magic* 1919; acquired by the City of Cork Steam Packet Company and renamed *Killarney* 1924; taken over by Coast Lines 1931.
Gross tonnage: 1,849.
Length: 311 ft. 3 in.
Width: 38 ft. 3 in.
Machinery: Triple-expansion, twin screw.
Speed: 18 knots.
1939 route: Summer cruises from Liverpool to the Western Isles of Scotland.

zig-zagged at full speed. There was also a threat from mines as *Killarney* was not degaussed. An estimated 90 shells were fired by the Germans in the space of a little over half an hour and one hit at the stern killed 8 men and wounded a further 30. Later, a German aircraft machine-gunned the vessel before being shot down by an RAF Spitfire and crashed into the sea half a mile away. The *Killarney* also took a French officer and two Belgian soldiers off a home-made raft consisting of pieces of wood and an old door. A little surprisingly perhaps, the Western Isles cruises resumed after the war and the old steamer, by then named *Lady Killarney,* was used until scrapped without replacement in 1956.

KING GEORGE V

The first passenger vessel to be built with high-pressure turbine machinery, *King George V* actually carried the monarch in whose honour she was named for the opening of the King George V Dock on the Clyde in 1931. In this period the steamer was used mainly on a summer run from Princes Pier to Loch Fyne until sold in 1935 to David MacBrayne Ltd and based at Oban for the next four summers, sailing to Staffa and Iona. While most excursion services ceased immediately the war started, *King George V* continued at Oban until 14th September 1939 and was then requisitioned as a transport and based at Southampton, sailing to the French ports. Although a good deal smaller than many of the cross-Channel ferries used in a similiar role, *King George V* was extremely valuable, being capable of not far short of 20 knots and able to take over 1,000 troops.

Built: 1926 by Wm Denny & Bros, Dumbarton, for Turbine Steamers Ltd; bought by David MacBrayne Ltd, 1935.
Gross tonnage: 815.
Length: 260 ft. 6 in.
Width: 32 ft. 1 in.
Machinery: Single-reduction Parsons turbines.
Speed: 20 knots.
1939 route: Summer excursions Oban to Staffa and Iona.

From the Spring of 1940, *King George V* took part in evacuations from Rotterdam (where she narrowly escaped serious bomb damage), Ostend, Boulogne and Calais, before becoming one of the earliest visitors to Dunkirk. *King George V* made six crossings to and from the harbour, loading around 700 troops each time and landing a total of 4,300 men in Dover. Both *King George V's* skipper, Captain R. McLean

One of the longest-surviving Dunkirk vessels, **King George V** *remained in service until 1974 and was not finally scrapped until ten years later after a serious fire halted preparations for a new static role as a pub and restaurant on the Thames in Central London. Most closely associated with the Oban–Staffa–Iona excursion,* **King George V** *is seen on the Clyde in 1946 passing* **Queen Elizabeth,** *then newly emerged in peacetime colours* (W. Ralston)

and Chief Engineer W. McGregor were awarded the DSO and the bosun, D. McKinnon, received the DSM. She went back to the Clyde to perform tender duties and in 1941 carried Winston Churchill to the battleship *Prince of Wales* prior to a visit to the USA to meet President Roosevelt. She was overhauled by Dennys and resumed MacBrayne cruises on the Clyde in 1946, going back to Oban in 1947 and continuing there each summer until withdrawn after the 1974 season. Quickly sold, the steamer languished in dry dock at Cardiff until conversion work began in 1981 for use a pub and restaurant on the Thames. Alas, it was not to be and, after a serious fire whilst fitting out, the gutted wreck was broken up in 1984.

Immaculately turned-out as part of the David MacBrayne fleet in 1971, the only major changes from **King George V's** *early years are the addition of a wheelhouse and radar.* (Author)

LADY OF MANN

Built: 1930 by Vickers-Armstrongs, Barrow, for the Isle of Man Steam Packet Company.
Gross tonnage: 3,104.
Length: 360 ft.
Width: 50 ft.
Machinery: Single-reduction geared turbines.
Speed: 23 knots.
1939 route: Fleetwood–Douglas service and other Isle of Man Steam Packet Company routes.

Completed in 1930, the centenary year of the Isle of Man Steam Packet Company, *Lady of Mann* was its largest ship and became well-known on the Fleetwood run during the 1930s, for most of which period the hull was painted white. Requisitioned before the end of September 1939, *Lady of Mann* carried troops across the Channel from Southampton before being moved to the Dover area as the situation in France worsened and played a big part in the Dunkirk evacuation bringing 4,262 men back to Folkestone and Dover. Although not equipped as a hospital ship, *Lady of Mann* was sent over on 31st May to load casualties and, after being attacked from the air and shelled by shore batteries on the way, spent six hours alongside taking on stretcher cases and walking wounded. When she got back to Folkestone there were several holes in the starboard bow near the waterline and three lifeboats were splinter damaged. With the damage patched up, *Lady of Mann* was back at Dunkirk next day to take on 1,500 men, including more wounded, and 2nd June brought a third appearance off the port but there were no troops to embark and the vessel turned back, Captain T. C. Woods stopping on the way to pick-up 18 Frenchmen from a small boat. *Lady of Mann* was one of a group of ferries sent over on the evening of 3rd June to bring out the final French troops and was the first to arrive but failed to get alongside because French fishing vessels, originally ordered to go further into the harbour, were moored on both sides of the Mole. After two hours of waiting *Lady of Mann* finally managed to get alongside and 1,244 men were embarked in little more than an hour.

Within a fortnight, *Lady of Mann* was being used as part of a fleet of personnel ships involved in the evacuations from Le Havre, Cherbourg and Brest. One of the last ships to leave Le Havre under sustained air attack, *Lady of Mann* was said in some estimates to be carrying nearly 5,000 troops. From August 1940 until April 1944 *Lady of Mann* ran between Scottish ports, the Shetlands and Faroes before being converted to serve

Marine artist John Nicholson's pen and ink drawing captures the imposing lines of **Lady of Mann,** *which served with distinction in peace and war for more than 40 years.*

as a Landing Ship Infantry in the style of other ferries with three hand-hoisted landing craft carried on either side. *Lady of Mann* was headquarters vessel of 521st Assault Flotilla in the Juno sector near Courselles during the Normandy Landings and later had a further spell as a transport running from Dover and Harwich to Ostend and the Hook of Holland until released early in 1946, when her return to Douglas was marked by a civic reception. She resumed Steam Packet service after refitting at Birkenhead and remained in the fleet until August 1971 when sold for scrap and broken up on the Clyde.

'Greetings from Fleetwood' . . . in 1940 the place-name of this 1930s postcard depicting what was described as the 'Big Five' of the Isle of Man fleet could easily have been changed to Dunkirk, for all these vessels were there, **Fenella** *and* **Mona's Queen** *being lost during the evacuation, while* **Tynwald** *became a casualty later in the war. The* **Lady of Mann,** *one of the front-line Steam Packet ships to wear a white livery during much of the 1930s, steamed on until after the summer season of 1971. Also featured is the* **Ben-my-Chree.** (Richard Danielson collection)

LOCHGARRY

A long-serving Irish Sea steamer bought in 1938 by David MacBrayne Ltd and thoroughly renovated internally to become the company's summer cruise vessel in the West Highlands. On a first crossing to Dunkirk, on the night of 28th May, *Lochgarry* came close to colliding with the unlit North Goodwin lightship after picking her way from Dover through the Downs, where many anchored vessels were also showing no lights. The next morning *Lochgarry* arrived off Dunkirk as *Killarney*, also a West Highland cruise ship a year earlier, left the harbour. Loading proceeded but was hardly uneventful with frequent air raids and shell fire. For a time *Lochgarry* had a destroyer alongside loading across her decks and, when the time came to sail, Captain Ewen MacKinnon found it difficult to get out as there were three destroyers immediately astern. A drifter that tried to assist only succeeded on cutting *Lochgarry's* degaussing wires which started a small fire, and then when joined by HMS *Greyhound* outside the harbour, both vessels suffered near misses after two successive salvos from the shore. A third salvo hit the destroyer, which was holed in the engine room, and *Greyhound* instructed *Lochgarry* to proceed independently. The *Lochgarry* finished the week with some superficial damage and had transported 1,001 troops. She later operated from Scotland to Iceland as a transport and was lost in this role off Rathlin Island in 1942.

Built: 1898 by A. & J.Inglis, Pointhouse, as *Vulture* for G. & J. Burns Ltd; transferred to Burns and Laird Line 1922; renamed *Lairdsrock* 1929; sold to David MacBrayne Ltd and renamed *Lochgarry* 1937.
Gross tonnage: 1,670.
Length: 265 ft.
Width: 33 ft. 6 in.
Machinery: Triple-expansion.
Speed: 15 knots.
1939 route: David MacBrayne West Highland summer cruises.

LORINA

Built: 1918 by Wm Denny & Bros., Dumbarton, for the London and South Western Railway; transferred to the Southern Railway in 1923.
Gross tonnage: 1,475.
Length: 299 ft.
Width: 36 ft.
Machinery: Parsons single-reduction turbines.
Speed: 19 knots.
1939 route: Southern Railway service Southampton–Channel Islands, and Channel Islands–St. Malo.

The first London and South Western Railway vessel to be ordered from the Denny yard, *Lorina* was taken over by the Admiralty while under construction at Dumbarton and completed as a troopship. Handed to her owners before the end

Pictured off Dunoon in August 1939 just a fortnight before the start of the Second World War, **Lochgarry** *was a former Irish Sea packet bought when 40 years old in 1938 and fitted with extensive cabin accomodation to cruise along the West Coast of Scotland. The* **Lochgarry** *transported over 1,000 men from Dunkirk and was lost in 1942 while operating as a transport between Scotland and Iceland.* (Graham E. Langmuir)

Sunk in shallow water in Dunkirk Roads after a direct hit on 29th May, and with flags still defiantly flying, the Southern Railway steamer **Lorina** *became a point of navigation for other vessels taking part in the evacuation. Later, the wreck was boarded by men from* **HMS Winchelsea** *and some of her lifeboats lowered and used to ferry troops from the beaches.* (Ambrose Greenway collection)

of 1919, *Lorina* had a fairly uneventful career apart from an incident in September 1935 when the hull was severely damaged after striking a rock near St. Helier. When the war started *Lorina* was quickly pressed into service as a transport and was called from Southampton to Dover after Operation Dynamo began. On 29th May *Lorina* was off the beaches when caught in a dive-bombing attack and suffered a direct hit amidships which broke her back, the vessel going down in shallow water despite the determined efforts of skipper Captan A. Light to beach her. Eight crewmen lost their lives. Two days later the wreck was boarded by men from the destroyer *Winchelsea* who lowered undamaged lifeboats from the *Lorina's* davits and used them to ferry troops from the beaches.

MAID OF ORLEANS

Built: 1918 by Wm Denny & Bros, Dumbarton, for the South Eastern and Chatham Railway; transferred to the Southern Railway in 1923.
Gross tonnage: 2,384.
Length: 341 ft. 3in.
Width: 45 ft.
Machinery: Parsons geared turbines, twin screw.
Speed: 23 knots.
1939 route: Southern Railway services Folkestone–Boulogne.

Ordered by the South Eastern and Chatham Railway as a sister vessel to the *Biarritz*, construction was held up by the start of the First World War and *Maid of Orleans* was taken over by the Admiralty and completed as a troop

A 1936 view of **Maid of Orleans,** *the Southern Railway ferry that was setting out from Dover for a sixth crossing to Dunkirk when put out of action after colliding with the destroyer* **Worcester.** *Used on the Folkestone–Boulogne service from 1926 until 1939,* **Maid of Orleans** *was mined and sunk in June 1944.* (Ambrose Greenway collection)

transport in the summer of 1918. It was 1920 before she started at Dover on her designed service to Calais, switching with *Biarritz* to run between Folkestone and Boulogne from 1926. Duties as a leave ship in the early months of 1940 were followed by a dash to Rotterdam to bring out Dutch nationals before the vessel made a major Dunkirk contribution, carrying well over 5,000 men in five crossings. *Maid of Orleans* first sailed on 26th May loaded with 1,200 gallons of water in cans and carrying 250 RASC and Signal Corps men whose task was to try and achieve some semblance of organisation ashore. Shelled passing Gravelines, the *Maid of Orleans* arrived off Dunkirk in a heavy air raid and after lying off for a time was recalled to Dover – but berthed safely after crossing a second time later in the day. *Maid of Orleans* sailed for Dover with 988 men and was back on the 29th, spending five hours alongside and taking on 1,372 troops. On 30th May another 1,253 were loaded from the Mole and on 1st June the vessel was alongside for six hours, two destroyers using her as a floating landing stage to take on over 1,000 men apiece, *Maid of Orleans* following herself with 1,400 British and 400 French troops crowding the decks. In the evening *Maid of Orleans* was starting out for Dunkirk again when she collided heavily with the destroyer *Worcester* which was limping into harbour after being damaged by bombs earlier in the day. *Maid of Orleans* was able to take no further part in the evacuation but was again in the thick of things during the Normandy Landings in 1944, being mined and sunk on 28th June with the loss of six crewmembers.

The civilian-manned **Malines** *achieved some notoriety as the ship which pulled out of the evacuation fleet and sailed to Southampton without orders. However, the LNER vessel was by no means the only transport whose crew was close to breaking point—and she also operated in and out of Folkestone, where overall supervision was not quite as close or immediate as that for the larger ships using Dover and in sight of Admiral Ramsay's staff.* (Philip. J. Cone collection)

MALINES

Malines has gone down in history as the ship which pulled out of the Dunkirk evacuation and headed back to Southampton without authority from the Admiralty. She was not by any means the only civilian-manned ship whose crew came close to cracking under the enormous pressures of the period and, equally, through sheer exhaustion, and the decision of the *Malines*' master Captain G. Mallory – which he considered 'to be in the best interests of all concerned' – needs to be seen not only in the context of Dunkirk but, in the case of this vessel, also bearing in mind the crew's experiences earlier in May. *Malines* had remained at Harwich, from where all LNER passenger services ceased even before the declaration of war on 3rd September, and was used on various transport duties from Parkeston Quay which had been taken over by the Admiralty. As the German advance swept through Holland, *Malines* and

Built: 1921 by Armstrong Whitworth, Wallsend, for the Great Eastern Railway; transferred to London and North Eastern Railway in 1923.
Gross tonnage: 2,969.
Length: 310 ft. 7 in.
Width: 43 ft. 2 in.
Machinery: Four single-reduction geared turbines.
Speed: 18 knots.
1939 route: LNER Harwich–Antwerp service.

Harwich fleet-mate *St. Denis* were sent to Rotterdam on 10th May to evacuate the remaining British subjects. With the city suffering intense bombing, the two masters were ordered to destroy all confidential papers and sail, *Malines* getting clear under cover of darkness to land 178 people at Tilbury. *St. Denis* failed to get away and was scuttled on 12th May.

Malines made two trips from Folkestone to Dunkirk, bringing back 1,500 men, among them survivors taken from the torpedoed destroyer HMS *Grafton* which had been carrying 800 men loaded from small boats off Bray beach. As Operation Dynamo's first week drew to a close, crews of several of the larger transports were showing signs of strain and naval personnel were put in to stiffen their resolve. At Folkestone the problems were more acute and on 2nd June the men of *Malines* and the *Ben-my-Chree* and *Tynwald* were unwilling to sail. Relief personnel were eventually drafted on to the two Manx packets which had been moved alongside the quay from anchor, but whilst this was being sorted out, *Malines* left the anchorage and sailed to Southampton. The vessel was soon pressed into service again and in the two weeks to 17th June made two trooping trips to Cherbourg and one to Le Havre before running from Weymouth to Jersey later in the month when the Channel Islands were being evacuated. In 1941 *Malines* was converted to serve as an escort vessel and went to the Mediterranean, being sunk off Port Said in July 1942. Raised in January 1943, she was used as a depot ship in the Suez Canal until broken up on the Tyne in 1946 after an eventful and long-winded tow back to England the previous year.

MANXMAN

Built for the Midland Railway's Heysham–Belfast route, *Manxman* had visited the Isle of Man on seasonal services before the First World War and was sold to the Admiralty in 1915 and converted to operate as a seaplane carrier. Put up for sale at the end of 1919, she was bought by the Isle of Man Steam Packet Company in the

Built: 1904 by Vickers Sons and Maxim, Barrow in Furness, for the Midland Railway; sold to the Admiralty 1915; bought by Isle of Man Steam Packet Company in 1920.
Gross tonnage: 2,030.
Length: 330 ft.
Width: 43 ft.
Machinery: Three Parsons turbines, triple screw.
Speed: 22 knots.
1939 route: Liverpool–Douglas and other Steam Packet services.

'Liverpool Steamer' proclaims **Manxman's** *destination board as the one-time Midland Railway vessel backs away from Douglas at the start of a crossing to the mainland.* **Manxman** *was hard aground for several hours during a first crossing to Dunkirk on 28th May and later took part in the evacuations from Cherbourg and St. Malo.* (Richard Danielson collection)

following year and, in 1921, became the first Steam Packet vessel to be adapted to burn oil fuel. Quickly requisitioned in the autumn of 1939, *Manxman* was used for cross-Channel trooping duties before transporting 2,394 men on three trips from Dunkirk and made a fourth uncredited crossing but failed to find any troops. The first trip on 28th May could easily have ended in disaster, *Manxman* sailing with the hospital ship *Paris* and the Harwich ferry *Prague* by Route Y, the longest passage to Dunkirk. None of the trio had adequate charts and all of them grounded when attempting to go through the Zuydecoote Pass off the French coast. The *Paris* and *Prague* re-floated quickly but *Manxman* was stuck fast for several hours, although eventually getting off without suffering any damage. After Dunkirk, *Manxman* was heavily involved in evacuations from Cherbourg, the crew cutting mooring lines with axes prior to a final departure as German tanks advanced along the quayside. *Manxman* also lifted troops from St. Malo and was later fitted out as a Radio Direction Finding vessel and based in the Isle of Man and later on the Clyde. When repaired after being driven ashore near Greenock during a gale early in 1943, *Manxman* resumed duties as a personnel ship and latterly served Dutch and Belgian ports from Tilbury and Harwich. She did not return to the Steam Packet Company and was scrapped at Preston in 1949.

MANX MAID

Designed for the London and South Western Railway's Southampton–Channel Islands services, *Caesarea* spent the opening year of the First World War as an armed boarding vessel and then returned to the Channel Islands run. She was sold to the Isle of Man Steam Packet Company for a modest £5,000 in 1923 and while

Built: 1910 by Cammell Laird, Birkenhead, as *Caesarea* for the London and South Western Railway; sold to Isle of Man Steam Packet Company and renamed *Manx Maid* in 1923.
Gross tonnage: 1,504.
Length: 284 ft. 6 in.
Width: 39 ft. 1 in.
Machinery: Three Parsons turbines, triple screw.
Speed: 20 knots.
1939 route: Isle of Man SP Liverpool–Douglas route and other services.

undergoing repairs to hull damage sustained when striking rocks near St. Helier. A £22,500 refit followed and the steamer was converted to burn oil fuel at an additional cost of £7,000 before commencing Steam Packet operations as *Manx Maid*. Designated a 'special services' vessel in the Second World War, there are conflicting stories concerning her involvement in Operation Dynamo, although claims that *Manx Maid* took no part in the evacuation through being under repair at Southampton tend to be refuted by the

One of several second-hand ships bought by the Isle of Man Steam Packet Company between the wars, the **Manx Maid** *had a 40-year career which lasted until 1950. Her Dunkirk role has remained somewhat obscure although there is photographic evidence of an involvement in the early stages of the evacuation at least.* (Richard Danielson collection)

photograph on page 12 which shows her at Dover's South Pier in the early stages of the evacuation when the many of the men crowding the decks are in RAF uniforms. On the other hand, *Manx Maid's* name does not figure in the list of personnel vessels and numbers of troops they landed. *Manx Maid* did take part in later evacuations from Western France and, although unable to enter St. Malo, she more than made up with a lift of 3,000 men from Brest which represents more than double her peacetime passenger complement of 1,470. After further war service as a Fleet Air Arm target ship, *Manx Maid* paid off at Ardrossan in 1945 and returned to serve the Steam Packet Company until scrapped at Barrow in 1950.

MONA'S QUEEN

Designed to carry almost 2,500 passengers with a high standard of accommodation including 20 private cabins, the imposing *Mona's Queen* sported a white hull from new and made a big impression in her first five summers running from Liverpool. *Mona's Queen* was requisitioned immediately war broke out and was soon carrying troops across the English Channel,

Built: 1924 by Cammell Laird, Birkenhead, for the Isle of Man Steam Packet Company
Gross tonnage: 2,756.
Length: 337 ft.
Width: 48 ft.
Machinery: Two single-reduction geared turbines.
Speed: 22 knots.
1939 route: Liverpool–Douglas and other Steam Packet services.

moving east in May with trips to Dutch ports to bring out civilians and troops. Commanded by Captain R. Duggan, the vessel was at Boulogne on 23rd May and left for Dover with 2,000 troops as German Panzers entered the town; then, on 26th May, *Mona's Queen* was one of the first personnel ships to reach Dunkirk after coming under heavy fire from the shore and being dive bombed on the way across. A total of 1,200 men were loaded and *Mona's Queen* arrived in Dover on the night of the 27th. With Captain A. Holkham taking over from Captain Duggan, *Mona's Queen* sailed again in the early hours of 29th May carrying hundreds of cans of drinking water but at 5.30 a.m., and when only half a mile off Dunkirk harbour entrance, she struck a mine and went down inside two minutes. Twenty-four crewmembers lost their lives, more than half of them in the engine and boiler rooms, while 32 survivors were picked-up by the destroyer *Vanquisher*.

With a livery of white hull and a black-topped, scarlet funnel from completion in 1934, the **Mona's Queen** *brought an almost yacht-like appearance to the Mersey when arriving daily from the Isle of Man.* (Richard Danielson collection)

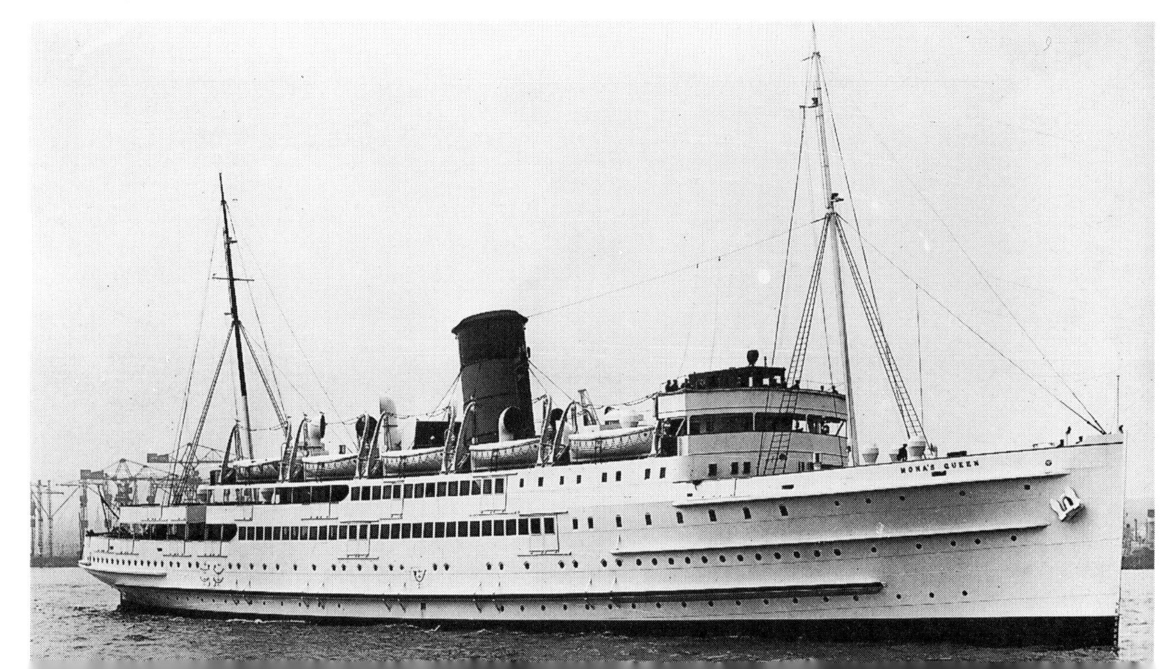

A dramatic shot of **Mona's Queen** *breaking in two after striking a mine early on the morning of 27th May and when only half a mile from the entrance to Dunkirk Harbour. The vessel went down in two minutes, taking 24 of the crew with her. Some of the 32 survivors are seen, below right, pulling alongside the destroyer* **Vanquisher.** (Imperial War Museum)

NEWHAVEN

Originally twin funnelled, both *Newhaven* and sister ship *Rouen,* also at Dunkirk, were extensively rebuilt in 1929–30 and received single funnels when converted to burn oil fuel a little later. They were built as part of the French Western Railway's contribution to the Dieppe–Newhaven service, a joint operation with the London, Brighton and South Coast Railway, and after French Navy service early in the First World War, *Newhaven* transferred to serve as a hospital ship for the British Admiralty. Requisitioned again in 1940, *Newhaven* was one of four French ferries which took part in Operation Dynamo and is recorded as landing 1,841 men in British ports, although this figure is probably inaccurate. Following the early loss of *Cote d'Azur,* the remaining three French vessels were credited by British sources with transporting 7,454 men while their own records claimed carryings closer to 12,000. *Newhaven* was among the last personnel ships to go to Dunkirk, leaving on 3rd June carrying French headquarters staff.

Built; 1911 by F. & C. de la Mediterrannée for the Societé de Chemin de Fer de l'Etat; transferred to SNCF 1936.
Gross tonnage: 1,546.
Length: 301 ft. 9 in.
Width: 34 ft. 7 in.
Machinery: Three direct-coupled Parsons turbines, triple screw.
Speed: 21 knots.
1939 route: SNCF/Southern Railway joint service, Newhaven–Dieppe.

Later she took part in evacuations further west but was seized by the Germans at Rochefort on 26th July and was used as an auxiliary patrol vessel, then as a depot ship and finally for accommodation purposes. She was returned from Kiel late in 1945 and then lay at Le Tréport until scrapped in Belgium during 1949.

NORMANNIA

Built: 1912 by Fairfield Shipbuilding Co, Govan, for the London and South Western Railway; transferred to the Southern Railway in 1923.
Gross tonnage: 1,567.
Length: 290 ft.
Width: 36 ft.
Machinery: Parsons single-reduction geared turbines, twin screw.
Speed: 19 knots.
1939 route: Southern Railway Southampton–Le Havre night service.

After years of reliable if unspectacular service to Le Havre, the *Normannia* continued to operate out of Southampton when the war began in September 1939 and towards the end of the following May was one of a group of ferries on stand-by there as Operation Dynamo got into its stride. Quickly called into the action, *Normannia* was off the coast near Mardyck following a first crossing on 29th May when caught and bombed by a flight of German Heinkel aircraft near No. 6 Buoy, and went down in shallow water with flags flying.

PRAGUE

Prague was one of a trio of ships which considerably raised standards on the Harwich–Hook night service from the beginning of the 1930s and after the war started she remained at the East Coast port until requisitioned and sent to Southampton in the middle of December 1939. Called forward to Dover, the *Prague* sailed on 28th May in company with *Manxman* and *Paris,* grounding briefly on the way in the Zuydecoote Pass. After successfully loading at Dunkirk she sailed for Folkestone to disembark troops. Fog forced Captain Cliff Baxter to anchor off Folkestone for several hours before she could set sail again and, by the time a fresh load of troops had been taken onboard in Dunkirk, the vessel was hard on the harbour bottom. It took a considerable effort from the tugs *Lady Brassey* and *Foremost 87,* and judicious use of *Prague's* own engines, to get underway. On 1st June the steamer returned to Dunkirk having already transported 3,039 men and this time Captain Baxter managed to berth her on the western side of the outer harbour close to the lock and an estimated 3,000 French troops were taken aboard. After departing, *Prague* quickly came under fire from the shore and was dive-bombed, twice suffering near misses, concussion from one of the explosions astern putting the starboard engine out of action. Although continuing at her best speed on the remaining engine, *Prague* began taking water and in a remarkable operation as she

Built: 1930 by John Brown & Co, Clydebank, for the London and North Eastern Railway.
Gross tonnage: 4,218.
Length: 350 ft. 8 in.
Width: 50 ft. 1 in.
Machinery: Four single-reduction Brown-Curtis geared turbines, twin screw.
Speed: 20 knots.
1939 route: Harwich–Hook of Holland night service.

Left *The London and North Eastern Railway's* **Prague** *arriving at Parkeston Quay, Harwich, in 1936 after an overnight crossing from the Hook of Holland.* (E. L. Cone)

Below *Down by the stern and with one engine out of action after being dive-bombed off Dunkirk on 1st June 1940, the* **Prague,** *her troops taken off by other vessels, is being towed by the* **Lady Brassey** *to be beached between Deal and Ramsgate.* (Newhaven Historical Society)

struggled towards the Kent coast all but a handful of the troops were transferred to other vessels. First alongside was the destroyer *Shikari* which took on 500, then the paddle minesweeper *Queen of Thanet* moved in and more than 1,500 men stepped from ship to ship before another 200 crossed on to the corvette *Shearwater*. While *Queen of Thanet* and *Shearwater* were taking their extra loads of troops to Margate and Sheerness respectively, *Prague* was beached near Deal and both Captain Baxter and Chief Engineer Bill Oxenham received the DSM in recognition of their efforts. After temporary attention the *Prague* was able to steam to the Thames and permanent repairs were carried out in the West India Dock.

Prague later served as a hospital ship with United States Forces and made more than 50 trips to and from the Normandy coast after the invasion of June 1944. The distinction of re-opening the Harwich–Hook of Holland service after the war fell to the *Prague* on 14th November 1945 and early in the following year the vessel was sent to the Clyde for a major refit. While at the John Brown yard on 14th March 1948 a fire in the engine room led to an explosion and firemen struggled in vain for twelve hours to save the ship, which heeled over to rest against the side of the dock. The *Prague* was only fit for scrap and was towed to Barrow later in the same year and broken up by T. W. Ward.

Princess Maud, *seen at Gourock in March 1939, was damaged before even reaching Dunkirk and it needed considerable skill from her master and frantic work by the crew to get her back to Dover for repairs. Five days later* **Princess Maud** *was able to re-join the evacuation fleet and was one of the last large ships to leave on 4th June.* (Graham E. Langmuir)

PRINCESS MAUD

Built: 1933 by Wm Denny & Bros, Dumbarton, for the London, Midland and Scottish Railway (Stranraer Section).
Gross tonnage: 2,886.
Length: 319 ft. 2 in.
Width: 49 ft. 1 in.
Machinery: Four single-reduction geared turbines.
Speed: 21 knots.
1939 route: Stranraer–Larne passenger service.

Although a coal-fired ship, *Princess Maud* had mechanical stokers and refinements throughout the passenger accommodation including an automatic fire sprinkler system. Within a couple of days of the war starting in 1939 *Princess Maud* was requisitioned for transport duties and sent to Southampton, from where she was moved to Dover as Operation Dynamo got into its stride the following May. Setting off on Thursday 30th, *Princess Maud* came under shore fire immediately after turning off Calais to proceed along the French coast past Gravelines and was holed aft on the starboard side and in the engine room where the shell made a hole three feet wide in the hull, wounding four crewmembers who later died of their injuries. A desperate effort was made to plug the hole and Captain H. Clarke managed to list the vessel to port by draining storage tanks and even swinging out port lifeboats as he carefully turned and nursed the ship back to Dover. The *Princess Maud* entered Wellington Dock for repairs which were completed in time to sail on the evening of 3rd June. She arrived in Dunkirk just after midnight. Despite being struck by the French ferry *Cote d'Argent* and a trawler, *Princess Maud* was slotted into a berth by Captain Clarke and took on 1,270 men before sailing at 1.50 a.m. when, with *Royal Sovereign*, she was the last of the large personnel vessels to leave. *Princess Maud* was one of the ferries converted to act as a Landing Ship Infantry for the Normandy invasion in 1944 and in the following year was a forces leave ship mainly between Folkestone and Calais. Before returning to the LMS in 1946 *Princess Maud* was converted to burn oil fuel and then became a relief vessel, operating on most of the Irish Sea routes at different times each year. Withdrawn in September 1965 and bought by Cypriot interests, *Princess Maud* had three years in the Mediterranean as *Venus* before ending her days as an accommodation vessel in Denmark.

QUEEN OF THE CHANNEL

Completion of *Queen of the Channel* in 1935 marked something of a revolution in the Thames day excursion trade, for the vessel which entered the hitherto undisputed domain of the paddle steamer was not only propelled by screws but also had diesel machinery. Builders Dennys, determined to demonstrate the progress made since the failure of the large-screw vessel *Kingfisher* on the Thames before the First World War, formed a company in conjunction with the New Medway Steam Packet Company specifically to introduce the *Queen of the Channel.* A handsome white-painted vessel with an enclosed promenade deck much in the style of the Clyde turbine steamers, she had twin yellow funnels, the forward of which was a dummy. *Queen of the Channel* ran cross-Channel excursions from Gravesend and Tilbury to Boulogne, Calais and Ostend and in 1936 there was a special two day excursion to the Solent to see the *Queen Mary's* maiden departure from Southampton to New York.

When the war started the *Queen of the Channel* was among Thames vessels were used to evacuate children from London to Yarmouth, after which transport duties followed. *Queen of the Channel* helped to convey the 20th Guards Division to Boulogne on 21st May and a week later was one of the first large vessels to work off the beaches to the east of Dunkirk. She arrived in the afternoon of 27th May, entering the harbour and took on about 50 men before being ordered to the beaches. After loading during the night *Queen of the Channel* sailed at dawn with 920 troops and was attacked, a single plane securing a direct hit which broke her back. As she went down by the stern the troops and crew were taken off by the store ship *Dorrien Rose* which was positioned bow to bow so that survivors were able to step from ship to ship.

Built: 1935 by Wm Denny & Bros, Dumbarton, for the London and Southend Continental Shipping Company, and managed by the New Medway Steam Packet Company, to whom ownership was later transferred.
Gross tonnage: 1,030.
Length: 255 ft.
Width: 34 ft.
Machinery: Two Sulzer 8-cylinder two-stroke diesels.
Speed: 21 knots.
1939 route: Cross-Channel sailings to Ostend, Calais and Boulogne and other excursions from Thames piers.

The motor vessel **Queen of the Channel** *was to bring a striking new look to the Thames when completed in 1935 and marked the start of a transition from steam and paddle propulsion for London's major excursion ships. Prior to Dunkirk,* **Queen of the Channel** *took reinforcements to Boulogne. She was lost on 28th May after an attack by a single German aircraft.* (Ambrose Greenway collection)

A Weymouth-based cargo vessel from the Great Western Railway's Channel Islands fleet, the **Roebuck** *was sent to Dunkirk purely as a personnel ship and succeeded in bringing back more than 600 men, over 100 of them wounded and including 47 stretcher cases.* (E. H. Cole)

ROEBUCK

The Great Western Railway's nineteenth-century practice of naming its Weymouth ships after animals was revived when *Roebuck* and sister *Sambur* were introduced on the Channel Islands cargo services in 1925. *Roebuck* was unloading produce from the Islands at Weymouth when a requisitioning order was received on 29th May 1940 and by late afternoon the vessel was heading for Dover, anchoring next day at 07:00. Not until after midnight did the master, Captain W. Larbalestier, receive orders to proceed to La Panne. The vessel arrived safely despite a total lack of appropriate charts and an encounter with a destroyer which collided with the stern near No. 6 Buoy. A freshening north easterly breeze made it almost impossible for small craft to work from the beach and following a frustrating spell in which she could render no real assistance *Roebuck* was ordered to Dunkirk Harbour, entering after the hospital ships *St. Julien* and *Paris* had left. In all 47 stretcher cases, 72 other wounded and 570 troops embarked over improvised gangways before *Roebuck* sailed at 3.35 p.m., arriving off Dover at 7.30 p.m. but being unable to berth until 5 a.m. next day. The trip was completed without the vessel having any degaussing equipment and as, by then, more ships with protection against magnetic mines were available, *Roebuck* was sent back to Weymouth. However, she was again requisitioned (together with *Sambur*) on 9th June and after being degaussed at Portland, took part in the unsuccessful attempt to evacuate British troops from St. Valery-en-Caux, west of Dieppe. Later *Roebuck* was converted to serve as a barrage balloon ship in the Thames Estuary, based at Sheerness. She returned to the Channel Islands run until withdrawn in 1965.

Built: 1925 by Swan Hunter & Wigham Richardson, Wallsend, for the Great Western Railway.
Gross tonnage: 866.
Length: 211 ft.
Width: 34 ft.
Machinery: Steam reciprocating, twin screw.
Speed: 12 knots.
1939 route: GWR Weymouth–Channel Islands cargo service.

ROUEN

Rouen joined elder sister *Newhaven* on the Dieppe–Newhaven run in 1912. Two years later, she was requisitioned by the French Navy and because of her speed – she achieved 24 knots on trials when new – was used as an auxiliary scout with the 2nd Light Channel Squadron. Torpe-

When the French ferry **Rouen,** *pictured at her home port of Dieppe in the mid-1930s, left Dunkirk carrying over 420 wounded on 26th May, the British troops in this complement were dismayed when taken, not to Dover or Folkestone, but down channel to Cherbourg, from where they were eventually transported to Southampton.* **Rouen** *later crossed from Dunkirk to the Kent ports and survived the war despite falling into German hands in August 1940. Returned to the SNCF in 1945,* **Rouen** *was never put back into service and was scrapped four years later.* (Newhaven Historical Society)

doed by a German submarine off St. Malo in 1916, the vessel was repaired and served as a seaplane carrier before going to the Mediterranean for use as a transport. Substantially rebuilt to become a single funnel steamer in the winter of 1929–30, *Rouen* was an early arrival at Dunkirk on 26th May and took on 420 wounded before heading for Cherbourg. She was back on 2nd June but grounded on mud inside the harbour and despite the attempts of two different tugs, *Foremost 22* and *Sun X*, had to wait for the rising tide before refloating and crossing to Dover the following morning. *Rouen* went over again in the company of sister ship *Newhaven* on the evening of Monday 3rd and a load from the harbour boosted her total number of men transported to 2,886. *Rouen* later took part in evacuations from more westerly French ports but was caught by

Built: 1912 by F. & C. de la Mediterranée for the Societé de Chemin de Fer de l'Etat; transferred to SNCF in 1936.
Gross tonnage: 1,546.
Length: 301 ft. 9 in.
Width: 34 ft. 7 in.
Machinery: Three direct-coupled Parsons turbines, triple screw.
Speed: 21 knots.
1939 route: SNCF/Southern Railway joint service Newhaven–Dieppe.

the Germans at Le Verdon in August and used by them in 1941 as an auxiliary cruiser and later as an experimental vessel, in which guise she was damaged by a mine in the Baltic during 1943. *Rouen* was returned to Dieppe in October 1945 but did not resume in service and was scrapped there in 1949.

ROYAL DAFFODIL

The scepticism which greeted *Queen of the Channel* in 1935 quickly disappeared and *Royal Daffodil* became the third large Thames motor excursion ship when commissioned in April 1939. Primarily built for long cross-Channel trips, *Royal Daffodil* had barely completed her inaugural season when the war started and during September 1939 she carried some 4,000 women and children evacuees from London to Lowestoft and was then sent to Southampton and assisted in taking the BEF to France.

Royal Daffodil had been at Calais a week before Operation Dynamo and then, as personnel vessels faced increasing shore fire between

Built: 1939 by Wm Denny & Bros, Dumbarton, for the General Steam Navigation Company.
Gross tonnage: 2,060.
Length: 299 ft. 7 in.
Width: 50 ft. 1 in.
Machinery: Two 12-cylinder Sulzer diesels, twin screw.
Speed: 21 knots.
1939 route: GSNC–New Medway excursions from Thames resorts, including cross-Channel sailings to Ostend, Calais and Boulogne.

Calais and Dunkirk, she was among the first group of larger vessels to be sent with a destroyer escort by the longer Route Y, sailing on 27th May with *St. Helier* and the hospital ships *St. Julien* and *St. David*. This was the first of six crossings and by the time *Royal Daffodil* put her final troops ashore at Ramsgate on 2nd June she

A contrast of colours and mood with the **Royal Daffodil** *in war and peace. The Thames excursion ship is seen in rust-streaked grey during war service when not far short of two and a half million personnel were transported – as many as 9,500 of them during six trips from Dunkirk.* **Royal Daffodil** *resumed summer cruises in 1947 and the lower view clearly shows the amount of open deck space available to London day trippers in addition to extensive restaurant and lounge accommodation below.* (Author's collection and Skyfotos)

was officially recorded as having transported some 7,552 men, although in all probability the true figure was nearer 9,500 as claimed by her crew, *Royal Daffodil's* biggest carryings including 2,000 French on 30th May and a further 1,600 on 1st June. By then personnel vessels were using Route Z and on 2nd June, while returning by this 55-mile passage and near the Ruytingen Buoy, *Royal Daffodil* came under sustained attack by six German aircraft; although five bombs missed, a sixth hit and passed through three decks and entered the engine room before exploding just after going out of the starboard side. With the engines stopped and water coming in through the hole in the hull and an increasing list developing to starboard, the enemy aircraft returned to rake the ship with machine-gun fire. *Royal Daffodil's* master, Captain G. Johnson, refused to be beaten and his crew set about moving gear and the human cargo over to the port side, where lifeboats were also lowered to deck level and filled with water to counter the list. In the engine room, chief engineer J. Coulthard and second engineer W. Evans, stuffed matresses into the hole and the latter then stood up to his neck in water to keep the bilge valve open. Even more amazingly, Coulthard managed to restart the main engines and the ship was able to crawl back to Ramsgate, despite a mixture put at three parts water to one of fuel reaching the engines.

After repairs, *Royal Daffodil* went to the Irish Sea in 1941 and ran between Stranraer and Larne until 1945 when switched to English Channel Dover–Calais and Newhaven–Dieppe crossings, plus British Army of the Rhine leave sailings before being released in January 1947. By then, in the course of her war service, *Royal Daffodil's* officers and crew had been awarded three DSCs, a DSM and three mentions in despatches. The vessel herself carried 2,443,979 service personnel and covered 170,000 miles. After a refit by Dennys, *Royal Daffodil* resumed Thames sailings in 1947 but no cross-Channel trips were possible and passengers had to be content with cruises to view the French coast and it was not until 1955 that 'no passport' landing trips were permitted. *Royal Daffodil* made a special 10th Anniversary trip to Dunkirk on 31st May 1950 and continued to appear each summer until a shock announcement after the 1966 season that her operators were withdrawing from the excursion business. *Royal Daffodil* was quickly bought by Belgian shipbreakers and made a sad last voyage to Ghent under her own power early in 1967.

ROYAL SOVEREIGN

Following the success of *Queen of the Channel*, the New Medway company and Dennys again joined forces to produce an enlarged and improved version of the design. New Medway was then bought by the General Steam Navigation Company who had the new motor vessel launched as *Royal Sovereign*. This single funnel ship was given extra beam by extending the three upper decks from the side of the hull on sponsons, almost in the style of paddle steamers, and it was a feature repeated in the larger *Royal Daffodil*. In common with the other Thames motor ships, *Royal Sovereign* was used for evacuation trips from London in the early weeks of the war, taking children and expectant mothers from the Dagenham area to Great Yarmouth. She then made trooping sailings from Southampton to Le Havre and Cherbourg.

Built: 1937 by Wm Denny & Bros, Dumbarton, for the New Medway Steam Packet Co but delivered to General Steam Navigation Company following its acquisition of the New Medway Steam Packet Company.
Gross tonnage: 1,527.
Length: 269 ft. 6 in.
Width: 47 ft.
Machinery: Two 12-cylinder Sulzer diesels, twin screw.
Speed: 21 knots.
1939 route: Excursions from Thames resorts, including cross-Channel sailings to Ostend, Calais and Boulogne.

Completed in 1937, **Royal Sovereign** *was licensed to take over 1,300 passengers, and this capacity was repeatedly put to the test during Operation Dynamo, when the vessel's officially recorded carryings of 6,772 troops could well have been a couple of thousand wide of the mark. One of the last large personnel ships to leave Dunkirk, together with the* **Princess Maud,** *the* **Royal Sovereign** *was mined and sunk in the Bristol Channel in December 1940.* (Ambrose Greenway collection)

With well-known Thames excursion skipper Tommy Aldis in command, *Royal Sovereign* was reckoned to have carried one tenth of all the troops transported by personnel vessels during the evacuation and her performance is remarkable not only for the regularity of appearances off the French coast but for the speed with which the men were loaded whilst she was there. *Royal Sovereign* arrived in Dunkirk for the first time and moored against the East Mole in the early hours of 29th May and took on a full load of troops in an hour. Sailing at 4.45 a.m., she reached Margate at 12.15 p.m., discharged by 1.30 p.m., was back off La Panne at 5.30 p.m. and had commenced loading off the beaches by 6.20 p.m. This took longer, but at 5.30 a.m. *Royal Sovereign* was heading for Margate, arriving at 11.35 a.m. By around 1 p.m. all the troops and their equipment were ashore and, taking full advantage of the vessel's 21 knots capability, Captain Aldis was again off the beaches by evening and ready to take on a third load. At daybreak on 31st May, *Royal Sovereign* was officially unaccounted for, then just after 7 a.m. she turned up at Margate, almost as if running to a schedule. She crossed to Dunkirk in the evening and anchored off the harbour until ordered to La Panne, from where she left at 2.30 a.m. on 1st June with crowded decks in spite of coming under heavy fire whilst loading. Before the end of the day yet another voyage was undertaken, but this time even the redoubtable Captain Aldis could not get through and, after two air attacks and shore fire from the Gravelines shore batteries, *Royal Sovereign* headed back to Margate to await instructions. They were not long in coming and after arriving late on 2nd June it was probably fitting that *Royal Sovereign*, together with *Princess Maud*, was the last personnel vessel to leave Dunkirk in the early hours of 3rd June. *Royal Sovereign* was lost on 9th December 1940 after striking a mine in the Bristol Channel.

ST. HELIER

St. Helier was sent from Southampton to Folkestone to await orders on 22nd May and air activity continuing on a bright moonlit night, *St. Helier* was eventually ordered to leave and

Originally a two-funnel ship, this was how the **St. Helier** *looked up to the start of the Second World War, the dummy after funnel having been removed in 1928 and the remaining stack shortened by five feet in 1937 when the naval type cowl was added.* **St. Helier** *was officially recorded as landing 6,584 men from Dunkirk and later took part in other evacuations from Western France and the Channel Islands.* (Ambrose Greenway collection)

crossed to Dover. Next day the steamer went to Dunkirk and brought back 1,500 English and French evacuees without incident. After spending the 24th refuelling and taking on stores at Dover, the *St. Helier* sailed for Dunkirk on the 25th but was ordered back because the newly-positioned shore batteries at Gravelines had started taking a toll among vessels using the direct route. By 27th May the longer Route Y was in use and *St. Helier* sailed among a group of vessels including her Channel Islands run sister *St. Julien* which was serving as a hospital ship. *St. Helier* was among the earliest large vessels to moor against the Mole and succeeded in carrying 2,000 men to Dover, returning to France later on 30th May and reaching Dover, again well laden, at 7 a.m. on Friday 31st. On 1st June *St. Helier* arrived back in Dunkirk amid a ferocious air attack and spent seven hours alongside during shelling by German artillery. On 2nd June, continued to Calais to embark troops, but found few of the projected 2,000 waiting. With enemy Captain R. Pitman refused an offer of relief but a naval commander and 10 ratings were put aboard to assist the crew before *St. Helier* sailed again as the last of the BEF were waiting in Dunkirk. The steamer made a final lifting and after her departure at 11.30 p.m., Captain William Tennant, senior naval officer in the port, made the signal: 'BEF evacuated.' *St. Helier* later took part in evacuations from other French ports and the Channel Islands and was then used by the Navy as a depot ship for coastal forces on the River Dart. In 1942 she was converted to operate as a Landing Ship (Infantry), taking part in the Normandy landings. *St. Helier* returned to the Channel Islands run in 1946 and was scrapped in Belgium some twenty years later.

Built: 1925 by John Brown & Co, Clydebank, for the Great Western Railway.
Gross tonnage: 1,855.
Length: 291 ft. 3 in.
Width: 42 ft. 6 in.
Machinery: Parsons single-geared turbines.
Speed: 18 knots.
1939 route: Weymouth–Channel Islands.

Despite working both off the beaches and from Dunkirk Harbour, **St. Seriol** *was listed as landing only 672 men at the Kent ports. This figure almost certainly relates to her visit on 27th May and loadings for a further crossing on the 28/29th appear to have been overlooked. Later used between Larne and Stranraer, the* **St. Seriol** *re-opened the excursion service from Liverpool to North Wales in 1946 and was scrapped in Belgium after lasting until the end of the 1961 season.* (Skyfotos)

ST. SERIOL

Built: 1931 by Fairfield Shipbuilding Co, Govan, for the Liverpool and North Wales Steamship Company.
Gross tonnage: 1,586.
Length: 269 ft. 7 in.
Width: 37 ft. 1 in.
Machinery: Four double-reduction geared turbines.
Speed: 18 knots.
1939 route: Seasonal services Liverpool–Llandudno, Llandudno–Anglesey, Llandudno–Douglas, Isle of Man.

Built to act in a supporting role to the Liverpool and North Wales Company's larger turbine steamer *St. Tudno*, the *St. Seriol* became equally well-known during the 1930s and was twenty miles out of Liverpool on a Sunday sailing to North Wales when news of the start of the war was received by radio. The vessel went on to land passengers at Llandudno before returning to Liverpool and was soon requisitioned and put to work as a troop transport out of Southampton. After taking a full load of men to Cherbourg on 20th May 1940, *St. Seriol* was ordered to Dover to embark units of the Canadian Provost Corps and sail to Calais, but the decision was later reversed and the troops put ashore again. On 27th May *St. Seriol* was among the first large vessels to work off the beaches, sending her own lifeboats inshore to bring off troops. She was then ordered to Dunkirk Harbour and took off over 600 men and survived four air raids while this was in progress. Naval personnel relieved some crew members prior to a crossing on 28th May and next day *St. Seriol* was sent from the harbour to the beaches and was nearby to rescue troops and crewmembers when the paddle steamer *Crested Eagle* was bombed and sunk. Later in the war *St. Seriol* operated between Scotland and Northern Ireland and, when released, was sent back to her builders for reconditioning prior to taking the first post war sailings from Liverpool at Easter 1946. Regular visits to the Isle of Man from Llandudno were added to the steamer's traditional programme and *St. Seriol* continued in service until the end of the 1961 season. After being put up for sale at the beginning of 1962, she was bought by Belgian breakers and demolished at Ghent.

SCOTIA

The last of a quartet of London and North Western Railway steamers for the Holyhead mail service to Kingstown, or Dun Laoghaire as the port is now known, *Scotia* had been used for cross-Channel troop runs before being called to Dover and sent on a first trip to Dunkirk on 29th May by Route Y. Accompanied by the LNER steamer *Malines*, she came under fire from shore batteries near Nieuport when closing the French coast and then, owing to the dense smoke and

The sinking of the **Scotia** *on 1st June was one of the most costly of Operation Dynamo, the former Holyhead mail steamer going down with 300 troops and 30 crewmembers after being attacked off Calais by a dozen enemy aircraft which came over in flights of four. In an earlier crossing on 29th/30th May* **Scotia** *had sailed with an estimated 3,000 troops, almost certainly the largest single load by any vessel during the evacuation.* (W. Robertson)

Built: 1921 by Wm Denny & Bros, Dumbarton, for the London and North Western Railway; transferred to the London, Midland and Scottish Railway in 1923.
Gross tonnage: 3,441.
Length: 380 ft. 5 in.
Width: 45 ft. 2 in.
Machinery: Four single-reduction geared turbines.
Speed: 25 knots.
1939 route: Holyhead–Dun Laoghaire mail service.

bombing, missed the entrance to Dunkirk Harbour. After sailing on to the west, *Scotia* was shelled by shore batteries near Mardyck while attempting to turn and received one hit aft of the engine room. *Scotia's* master, Captain W. Hughes, estimated that 3,000 troops were loaded at the East Pier before *Scotia* sailed to Margate. There the entire crew turned out to coal the ship before she crossed again on 1st June and took on 2,000 French troops at the West Mole. Returning by the most direct route, *Scotia* had reached No. 6 Buoy off Calais when attacked by a dozen German aircraft which came over in formations of four. Heavy damage was done aft and *Scotia* went down by the stern, an estimated 300 troops and 30 crewmen losing their lives despite gallant efforts by several drifters which were in the area.

TYNWALD

Built side-by-side with sister *Fenella* and launched on the same day in December 1936, *Tynwald* also failed to survive the war but the success of their design with its definite eye to year-round service can be judged by the Steam Packet Company's decision to use it as a basis for a six-ship post-war fleet replacement programme between 1946 and 1955. *Tynwald* was requisi-

Tynwald *was completing only a second summer of service to the Isle of Man when the war started and was quickly sent to the South Coast for troop carrying duties. Heavily involved all through the Dunkirk evacuation,* **Tynwald's** *total of almost 9,000 men transported was the highest recorded for any of the personnel vessels. Later commissioned by the Royal Navy as an anti-aircraft ship,* **Tynwald** *was lost off the Algerian coast during the North African landings of 1942.* (Richard Danielson collection)

It was claimed that one in every 14 of the troops landed in Britain travelled back on a vessel from the fleet of the Isle of Man Steam Packet Company. This complement from the **Tynwald** *are crossing the decks of another Steam Packet vessel, probably the* **Ben-my-Chree**, *to land at the Admiralty Pier, Dover.* (Times Newspapers).

Built: 1937 by Vickers-Armstrongs, Barrow, for the Isle of Man Steam Packet Company.
Gross tonnage: 2,376.
Length: 314 ft. 6 in.
Width: 46 ft.
Machinery: Single-reduction geared turbines.
Speed: 21 knots.
1939 route: Liverpool–Douglas winter sailings and other seasonal Isle of Man Steam Packet routes.

tioned in the first week of the war and was on the South Coast throughout the winter and became involved in the Dunkirk evacuation on 28th May. When it ended a week later *Tynwald* had transported 8,953 men, the largest total of any personnel vessel. Sent across for the first time on the evening of the 28th, *Tynwald* was one of ten personnel ships to bring almost 15,000 men away from the East Mole on 29th May and after a quick turn-round in Folkestone was back on Thursday 30th to take on 1,153 men. The Manx vessel made a third trip on 31st May but by then the strain was beginning to tell and Captain W. Qualtborough told the authorities that his officers and crew were totally exhausted. Relief personnel were provided by the navy and *Tynwald* sailed on 2nd June with chief officer J. Whiteway in command and brought back another 1,200 men. Her final crossing was on the evening of 3rd June and *Tynwald* left Dunkirk early on the 4th with a further load of well over 1,000 men. Towards the end of 1940 the vessel was fitted out as an auxiliary anti-aircraft ship and commissioned as HMS *Tynwald* and used mainly to escort coastal convoys. She went to the Mediterranean for the North African Landings of 1942 and was lost while taking part in an action off Bougie, east of Algiers, on 12th November.

WHITSTABLE

Designed for Southern Railway Dover–Folkestone cargo runs, the *Whitstable* had been used for war transport duties based at Southampton until sent to Dover on 30th May, and lay in the Downs before being ordered across on 31st with sister ship *Hythe*. The *Whitstable* went to Bray Beach, and although arriving at 08:20, had to wait for six hours before the first troops were brought out and it was a further hour before the steamer was able to sail. Later in the war, *Whitstable* was used on crossings between Stranraer and Larne, but returned to Boulogne services in the middle of 1946. Her last few months in operation were spent running from Weymouth to the Channel Islands until sold for breaking up in Belgium during 1958.

Built: 1925 by D. & W. Henderson, Glasgow, for the Southern Railway.
Gross tonnage: 865.
Length: 229 ft. 6 in.
Width: 35 ft. 9 in.
Machinery: Steam reciprocating, twin screw.
Speed: 15 knots.
1939 route: Cargo services Dover–Folkestone to Calais–Boulogne.

Armed Boarding Vessels

A NUMBER of merchant ships, including both passenger ferries and small cargo units, were requisitioned soon after the start of the war for use in coastal waters as Armed Boarding Vessels. Usually the armament consisted only of a single 4-inch or 4.7-inch gun mounted forward and as the operation of such vessels proved less than successful, most of those which survived were switched to other duties or returned to the merchant fleet.

Three ABVs from the Dover Patrol were responsible for transporting almost 5,000 troops from Dunkirk and it seems highly probable that a fourth vessel was also involved. All of them had been taken off patrol duties and placed at Admiral Ramsay's disposal prior to the start of Operation Dynamo.

Used solely as personnel ships for the duration of the evacuation, one of them, the *King Orry* from the Isle of Man Steam Packet Company's fleet, was among the first large ships to enter Dunkirk Harbour and had completed a round trip carrying more than a thousand men before being lost when making a second visit on the night of 29th–30th May.

KING ORRY

The Steam Packet's first unit powered by geared turbines soon found itself serving as an armed boarding vessel during the 1914–18 war and in November 1918 had a prominent place in the centre line as the German Grand Fleet steamed to Scapa Flow to surrender. *King Orry* received a major refit in 1934 and was converted to burn oil

A veteran of the 1914–18 war, **King Orry** *was used in a similar role as part of the Dover Patrol from the autumn of 1939 but was lost after making a second crossing to Dunkirk on 29th May. The vessel had been peppered by shore batteries en route and sank while efforts were being made to beach her.* (Richard Danielson collection)

fuel only a few months before the start of the Second World War. By the end of September 1939 *King Orry* had been commissioned as an armed boarding vessel and moved south as part of the Dover Patrol, but was taken off regular duties on 22nd May 1940 and put on stand-by for the evacuation of the BEF.

Built: 1913 by Cammell Laird, Birkenhead, for the Isle of Man Steam Packet Company.
Gross tonnage: 1,877.
Length: 313 ft.
Width: 43 ft.
Machinery: Single-reduction geared turbines.
Speed: 22 knots.
1939 route: Liverpool–Douglas and other Steam Packet routes.

The *King Orry* was one of the earliest ferries to arrive off Dunkirk and succeeded in entering the harbour and took on 1,131 men before departing at breakfast time on the 29th. She was damaged by shore fire near Calais and had suffered casualties as well as structural damage by the time she reached Dover at noon. *King Orry* returned to Dunkirk on 29th May and again came in for persistent attention from shore batteries, a direct hit at the stern wrecking the rudder and steering gear. She drifted against the East Mole and was secured to allow an examination of the damage, so many shrapnel holes being discovered that it simply became a race to move her before she sank and blocked the harbour entrance. After a wait of two hours until the tide rose it took almost another two hours of manoeuvring using the engines to get clear of the Mole. The original intention was to beach *King Orry* away from the main channel but while this was in progress the steamer suddenly began to list to starboard and sank.

LAIRDS ISLE

When new, *Riviera* (and sister *Engadine*) replaced the last paddle steamers on the Dover–Calais route to which she returned after First World War service as a seaplane carrier. Bought by Glasgow interests in 1932, *Riviera* was resold to Burns and Laird the following year and converted to burn oil before a debut on the Ardrossan–Belfast summer day service as *Lairds Isle*. She was back in familiar waters when called up to serve as part of the Dover Patrol in the first winter of the war and although not credited with any troop carrying from Dunkirk, it seems highly probable that *Lairds Isle* played some role.

Built: 1911 by Wm Denny & Bros, Dumbarton, as *Riviera* for the South Eastern and Chatham Railway; sold to Burns and Laird Lines and renamed *Lairds Isle* in 1933.
Gross tonnage: 1,675.
Length: 316 ft.
Width: 41 ft. 1 in.
Machinery: Three Parsons single-reduction geared turbines.
Speed: 23 knots.
1939 route: Ardrossan–Belfast summer day service.

The steamer later acted as a troop landing ship for the Normandy invasion but was back on her old Irish Sea route from the summer of 1946 and still had a fine turn of speed. *Lairds Isle* was unexpectedly withdrawn in August 1957 and within two months was being broken up at Troon.

Another vessel of the Dover Patrol, the involvement of the **Lairds Isle** *in the evacuation has never been clarified. She later underwent conversion to serve as a troop landing ship during the invasion of Normandy. Pictured towards the end of a career spanning 46 years,* **Lairds Isle** *retained a fair turn of speed to the very end.* (Colin Campbell collection)

LORMONT

A cargo vessel used by General Steam for services to the near Continental ports before going rather further afield after being sold to Moss Hutchinson. Requisitioned as an armed boarding vessel and commanded by Lieutenant Commander W. Smithies, *Lormont* transported 1,083 men from Dunkirk and was also involved in evacuations from St. Malo. The vessel was lost on 7th December 1940 following a collision in the Humber Estuary.

Built: 1927 by Greenock Dockyard Co. as *Woodcock* for the General Steam Navigation Company; sold to the Moss Hutchinson Line, and renamed *Lormont* in 1939.
Gross tonnage: 1,561.
Length: 241 ft. 4 in.
Width: 40 ft. 2 in.
Machinery: Triple expansion by Kincaid & Co, Greenock.
Speed: 12 knots.
1939 route: UK–Mediterranean ports cargo sailings.

MONA'S ISLE

One of five similiar Denny vessels which represented the pioneer English Channel turbine steamers, *Onward* was used as a transport from South Coast ports during the First World War. After catching fire at Folkestone in September 1918 she had to be scuttled to put out the blaze but was salvaged and refitted on the Thames. It was from there that the *Onward* was bought by the Steam Packet company and entered service to the Isle of Man as *Mona's Isle* in May 1920, becoming most closely associated with summer links from Douglas to both Belfast and Dublin. *Mona's Isle* followed Steam Packet fleet-mate *King Orry* to Dover as an armed boarding vessel soon after the start of the Second World War and spent the winter of 1939–40 patrolling in the North Sea.

Mona's Isle claimed to be the first personnel vessel to complete a round trip to Dunkirk and was already crossing when Operation Dynamo officially started just before seven in the evening on 26th May. A total of 1,420 troops were loaded from the harbour and when *Mona's Isle* was returning to Dover there were several near misses from shore batteries and 23 men died and 60 were wounded when the vessel was machine gunned by a German aircraft. *Mona's Isle* completed a second return trip carrying a further 1,234 troops. She was later based in the Tyne and then used as an accommodation ship before a new role as an English Channel transport following D-Day. Sent back to the Steam Packet Company in 1946, *Mona's Isle* served the Isle of Man briefly until broken up at Milford Haven in 1948.

Built: 1905 by Wm Denny & Bros, Dumbarton, as *Onward* for the South Eastern and Chatham Railway; bought by the Isle of Man Steam Packet Company, and renamed *Mona's Isle* in 1920.
Gross tonnage: 1,691.
Length: 311 ft. 2 in.
Width: 40 ft. 1 in.
Machinery: Parsons geared turbines, triple screw.
Speed: 21 knots.
1939 route: Douglas–Dublin; Douglas–Belfast summer services.

A poster promoting the Royal Mail Lines passenger service to South America looks curiously out of place as exhausted troops await onward transportation from Dover Marine station.

Hospital Carriers

IN ADDITION to the ferries pressed into service as military transports from the earliest days of the war in September 1939, further passenger steamers were selected for rapid conversion to serve as Hospital Carriers. They emerged with peacetime saloons converted into wards capable of carrying more than 200 patients and were also fully repainted, receiving white hulls carrying broad red stripes and red cross symbols.

Newhaven was designated as the main ambulance port for the British Expeditionary Force and the Hospital Carriers also served the Netley Hospital through Southampton, although there was so little military activity during the first winter of the war that none of the eight ferries thus converted made more than a handful of crossings out of Dieppe or Cherbourg.

As the following record of the individual ships shows, the picture altered considerably during May 1940 and they were in the thick of things at Dunkirk and consistently came under attack despite wearing obvious internationally recognised markings. One Hospital Carrier, the twin funnelled *Paris*, used before the war on Newhaven–Dieppe services, was lost on 2nd June and a further vessel, *Isle of Guernsey*, suffered so much superficial damage that further crossings were impossible.

The use of such vessels in and out of the wrecked port posed special problems and the wounded often had to be carried for long distances through all manner of debris to the waiting ships, this task frequently being performed by volunteer crewmembers in the absence of stretcher bearers.

Later in the war, some of the surviving Hospital Carriers were converted and used to take assault craft to the Normandy Beaches and one of them, the Southern Railway steamer *Dinard*, was among the last of the large Dunkirk ferries to remain in service, running between Sweden and Finland as *Viking* until 1970.

DINARD

An early priority after the Southern Railway came into being in 1923 was improvement of the Southampton-based services to France inherited from the London and South Western Railway and *Dinard* was one of a pair of vessels contracted with Dennys which really represented an improved version of the *Lorina* ordered from the same builders by the LSWR during the First World War. The *Dinard* made her debut on the St. Malo service in July 1924 and continued until the service was withdrawn on 6th September 1939. After a brief spell of relief work on the Le Havre service, the steamer was requisitioned early the following month and converted to serve as Hospital Carrier No. 28. *Dinard* spent much of the winter lying at Cherbourg but was not required and by the beginning of May 1940 had made only two trips with patients, one to Newhaven from Dieppe in February and another between Boulogne and Southampton towards the end of April.

Dinard left Cherbourg on 25th May with 118 stretcher cases and 135 walking wounded and was sent straight from Southampton to Dover for a first crossing to Dunkirk on 28th May. After loading 271 wounded she left on the 29th and was

Four different phases in the 50 year life of the Southern Railway steamer **Dinard,** *completed in 1924 and not finally broken-up until 1974 in Finland.* **Dinard** *is seen (left) as new when making a first visit to Jersey on 4th July 1925* (Ambrose Greenway collection); *and then in Red Cross markings (right) following conversion in 1939 to serve as Hospital Carrier No. 28* (John de S. Winser collection). *After finishing the war as a troop transport,* **Dinard,** *originally able to carry 1,340 passengers as a conventional ferry, was sent to the Tyne and rebuilt to run as a car ferry between Dover and Boulogne (centre right), accommodating up to 80 vehicles and just 360 passengers* (Skyfotos). *Although displaced following the arrival of purpose-built car ferries in the autumn of 1958,* **Dinard** *was bought by Finnish interests and used to start the first drive-on/drive-off service across the Baltic between Sweden and Finland. As* **Viking** *(bottom right) she gave her name to what has become the most influential ferry operation in Scandinavia, continuing to run until 1971 and being scrapped three years later. The vessel's Second World War battle honours plaque and other relics have been preserved in the maritime musuem at Mariehamn, the Aland Islands' capital* (Anders Ahlerup).

attacked from the air while near Kwinte Bank on the longer Route Y, but reached Newhaven safely. She came under heavy artillery attack when returning to Dunkirk on the night of the 30th and left on an ebbing tide when there was only a foot of water beneath her keel. Captain J. W. A. Jones used a torch to try to identify buoys as the vessel picked its way out of the harbour. One of the *Dinard's* peacetime stewardesses, Mrs Amy Goodrich, stayed with the ship for both crossings and was mentioned in despatches, the only woman whose name appeared in the list of Dunkirk honours. In the middle of June *Dinard* made a trip from Cherbourg and later went to the Irish Sea before being based at Aultbea from April 1941. She returned briefly to the South Coast towards the end of the year and received attention from Dennys early in 1942 prior to commencing an Aberdeen–Scapa Flow supply run. Early in the following year more work was done on the Clyde before *Dinard* went to the Mediterranean and made many sailings from Southern Italy, Sicily and North Africa until recalled to Britain to support the Normandy Landings in 1944. On a first crossing to the French coast *Dinard* struck a mine and suffered serious damage forward and had to spend a month in dry dock for repairs. Throughout the summer the vessel carried casualties and prisoners of war from France and her spell as a hospital ship ended with visits to Ostend and a stint between Dover and Boulogne.

Released after a further spell of work as an ordinary cross-Channel transport, *Dinard* returned to the Southern Railway but instead of resuming on her old service to St. Malo was extensively rebuilt on the Tyne and in June 1947 began operating from Dover to Boulogne as a car ferry taking 80 vehicles and 360 passengers. Initially, cars were craned on and off but from 1952 *Dinard* had stern doors and continued on the service until put on the market in the autumn of 1958. Bought by Finnish interests, she was renamed *Viking* and in June 1959 began the first drive-on/drive-off ferry service linking Sweden and Finland via Mariehamn in the Aland Islands. By the time *Viking* was withdrawn in August 1970 she had carried more than three quarters of a million passengers between Sweden and Finland and the consortium of companies which took its marketing name from the vessel was well on the way to becoming established as one of the world's most influential ferry concerns. *Viking* was finally broken up at Helsinki in 1974.

Built: 1924 by Wm Denny & Bros, Dumbarton, for the Southern Railway.
Gross tonnage: 2,294.
Length: 325 ft.
Width: 43 ft. 9 in.
Machinery: Four single-reduction geared turbines.
Speed: 19 knots.
1939 route: Southampton–St. Malo.

26
28

VIKING LINE

One of three similar ships completed between 1930 and 1932 for the Southern Railway's Channel Islands run from Southampton, the **Isle of Guernsey** *visited Dunkirk three times as a hospital ship before an accumulation of damage from air attacks made a further crossing impossible. A picture of* **Isle of Guernsey** *as a hospital ship appears later in 'The Seafarers' Stories', accompanying the Dunkirk account of one of the doctors serving aboard.* (Skyfotos)

ISLE OF GUERNSEY

The second of a trio of Denny-built steamers for the Southern Railway's Southampton–Guernsey–Jersey route, *Isle of Guernsey* was quickly taken out of civilian service in September 1939 and used to carry Royal Air Force personnel to France before being requisitioned on the 23rd of the month to be converted to serve as a hospital ship. Sent to Dieppe to await casualties, she made only a handful of crossings before returning to Southampton at the end of January 1940. A brief appearance at Newhaven was followed by an overhaul in April and *Isle of Guernsey* made one trip to Boulogne and two visits to Cherbourg in mid-May prior to leaving for the Dover area on the 25th. After awaiting orders in the Downs she sailed late on the morning of the 26th together with the hospital ship *Worthing* and took on 346 stretcher cases in Dunkirk Harbour and then went overnight to Newhaven. Back at Dunkirk on the 27th, *Isle of Guernsey* loaded 450 stretcher cases and sailed direct to Newhaven. After leaving again in the early hours of the 29th, *Isle of Guernsey,* although fully painted with Red Cross markings, was fired on by an enemy plane while stopped to pick up an airman from the sea. Despite being shaken every few minutes by bombs exploding on the quay and in the water, *Isle of Guernsey* was able to load 490 stretcher cases and many more less seriously wounded in Dunkirk Harbour and carry them safely to Dover. The vessel had so much superficial damage that a further crossing was ruled out and she was sent to Newhaven and then on to Southampton for repairs.

In October 1940 *Isle of Guernsey* became a training and target ship and was at centres on the west coast of Scotland until converted to serve as a Landing Ship Infantry late in 1943. After putting Canadian soldiers ashore near Berniers on D-Day she carried more troops across on sailings from Newhaven and became the second ship to enter the Mulberry Harbour at Arromanches. *Isle of Guernsey* had the distinction of re-opening civilian services between Britain and France on 15th January 1945, sailing from Newhaven to Dieppe, the only French port which was available. The following April she also restored services to the Channel Islands after a break of five years, although it was not until April 1947 that a fully refitted *Isle of Guernsey* returned to the route on a permanent basis. She continued until the service from Southampton

Built: 1930 by Wm Denny & Bros, Dumbarton, for the Southern Railway.
Gross tonnage: 2,198.
Length: 306 ft.
Width: 45 ft.
Machinery: Four single-reduction geared turbines.
Speed: 19 knots.
1939 route: Southampton–Channel Islands.

During the first winter of the war, long periods of inactivity were common for the **Isle of Thanet,** *seen above at Dieppe* (Imperial War Museum), *and most of the other ferries converted to serve as hospital ships. Everything changed from the middle of May 1940 and* **Isle of Thanet** *first visited Dunkirk on the 23rd, just a couple of days after sister vessel* **Maid of Kent,** *also serving as a hospital ship, was lost at Dieppe.* **Isle of Thanet** *made sailings with casualties to both Newhaven and Dover before suffering bow damage in a collision and is pictured below in dry dock at Southampton on 6th June undergoing repairs* (John de S. Winser collection).

was closed in May 1969 and then operated some relief sailings from Weymouth for a few weeks until sold and scrapped in Belgium.

ISLE OF THANET

Another product of the Southern Railway's Channel Fleet replacement programme in the 1920s, and, almost inevitably, a Denny-built turbine steamer, *Isle of Thanet* was capable of 22 knots and could take 1,400 passengers on the Dover–Calais run. After work as a transport in the early weeks of the war both *Isle of Thanet* and sister vessel *Maid of Kent* were converted at Southampton to serve as hospital ships, the latter being bombed and sunk at Dieppe on 21st May 1940. Two days later *Isle of Thanet* left Newhaven for Dunkirk and, despite an air raid, loaded 300 wounded at the Gare Maritime,

Built: 1925 by Wm Denny & Bros, Dumbarton, for the Southern Railway.
Gross tonnage: 2,664.
Length: 342 ft.
Width: 45 ft.
Machinery: Two single-reduction geared turbines.
Speed: 22 knots.
1939 route: Dover–Calais passenger service.

leaving at 11 in the evening. These men came mainly from base hospitals and on the 25th the vessel sailed again as a concerted effort was made to clear the last of these casualties. Sailing at 1.15 a.m. on the 26th, *Isle of Thanet* was in Newhaven by 08:00 and on the 27th she was again off Dunkirk but unable to enter the harbour. A second attempt in the evening succeeded and after taking on a full load of casualties *Isle of Thanet* left for Dover in the early hours of the next morning. During this crossing *Isle of Thanet* collided with the examination vessel *Ocean Reward* which sank immediately without survivors.

Isle of Thanet subsequently served as a target ship for the Fleet Air Arm and, following conversion to operate as a Landing Ship Infantry in 1943, was headquarters vessel of Force J in the Normandy Landings of June 1944. When returned to the Southern Railway in 1945, *Isle of Thanet* first served between Newhaven and Dieppe for a year before returning to her original route. However, from 1948 she was based at Folkestone, surviving until 1963 although used towards the end only for relief sailings and excursions. *Isle of Thanet* was scrapped at Blyth in 1964.

PARIS

A real flier in her day, the high speed of *Paris* was utilised during the First World War when she operated as a minelayer. After returning to the Dieppe service *Paris* underwent major modifications in 1929–30 when the superstructure was plated-in and she received new oil-fired boilers in 1932. From 1934 she became well known at Brighton when undertaking twice weekly summer day trips from the resort's Palace Pier to Dieppe. After the war started *Paris* was used as a transport until converted into a hospital ship in January 1940. Like her contemporaries the *Paris* saw little use until May but then things changed quite dramatically and she had been at Calais immediately prior to the start of Operation Dynamo. Her first arrival in Dunkirk was with *Isle of Thanet* on 25th May and three days later she was one of three ferries to ground in the Zuydecoote Pass when attempting to approach Dunkirk from the east. *Paris* was disabled by bombing when crossing again on 2nd June with the loss of some 20 crewmembers. Although the tug *Sun XV* attempted to tow the vessel to safety, the *Paris* sank some 10 miles from the shore following more air attacks.

Built: 1913 by Wm Denny & Bros, Dumbarton, for the London, Brighton and South Coast Railway; transferred to the Southern Railway in 1923.
Gross tonnage: 1,774.
Length: 301 ft.
Width: 35 ft. 6 in.
Machinery: Four Parsons compound-geared turbines.
Speed: 24 knots.
1939 route: Southern Railway/SNCF Newhaven–Dieppe joint service.

Capable of 24 knots, the **Paris,** *seen entering the harbour at Newhaven* (P. J. Cone collection), *was well-known to countless Brighton holidaymakers for cross-Channel day trips to Dieppe from 1934 to 1939. After working as a troop transport, the vessel was converted to serve as a hospital carrier, above right, in January 1940 and sank on 2nd June while under tow after being disabled by air attack.* (Newhaven Historical Society)

ST. ANDREW

Introduced on the Fishguard–Rosslare route with sister ship *St. David,* the *St. Andrew* was requisitioned on 11th September 1939 and fitted out as a hospital ship based at Southampton and serving Netley Hospital. The opening months of 1940 produced comparatively little activity until *St. Andrew* was ordered to Boulogne to evacuate wounded on 20th May, lying alongside overnight during bombing raids until casualties arrived from base hospitals next morning. After returning with them to Southampton, *St. Andrew* completed a trip to Cherbourg on 22nd–23rd and was refuelled and put on one hour stand-by to sail to Dover, the movement order coming through on the evening of the 23rd. Next day *St. Andrew* was sent to Calais, only to be recalled to Dover after the intensity of enemy fire twice thwarted efforts to enter the port. That evening (24th May), she crossed to Dunkirk and succeeded in getting into the port despite the air bombardment. But with no medical staff other than the ship's own, and no stretcher bearers, the master, Captain H. Bond, had to call for volunteers, and bombs fell all around as her officers and men spent over two hours going back and forth carrying casualties aboard. She sailed direct to Newhaven and came under fire from Gravelines as she had when sailing in the other direction. On 25th May *St. Andrew* returned to Dunkirk via Dover and twice tried to get into the harbour before being ordered to withdraw by naval authorities. On Monday 27th she was sent by Route Y with another hospital ship, *St. Julien,* and waited off the harbour whilst personnel vessels *St. Helier* and *Royal Daffodil* went in.

Built: 1932 by Cammell Laird, Birkenhead, for the Fishguard and Rosslare Railways and Harbours Company and managed by the Great Western Railway.
Gross tonnage: 2,702.
Length: 327 ft. 9 in.
Width: 49 ft. 1 in.
Machinery: Four Parsons single-reduction geared turbines.
Speed: 21 knots.
1939 route: Fishguard–Rosslare.

Both the waiting ships came under attack and *St. Andrew* was again ordered back to Dover, anchoring in the Downs where she was subjected to further low-level bombing attention. The vessel was then sent to Southampton where she was oiled and stored and workmen fitted concrete shields to the bridge and wheelhouse. Orders to return to Dover were received on 30th May and the following afternoon the *St. Andrew* sailed to Dunkirk, berthing at the East Mole and then moving further into the harbour. The

The hospital ship **St. Andrew** *amid the carnage of Dunkirk, most probably departing on 31st May. After initially getting alongside the East Mole, seen in the foreground, the steamer twice moved to other berths nearer the town but even then the volunteer stretcher bearers drawn from the crew had a long and dangerous carry.* (Imperial War Museum)

inevitable air raid was in progress and the vessel was shifted a third time before it was possible to load any wounded, the crew again acting as stretcher bearers for what was a long and difficult carry. *St. Andrew* then played a part in the evacuations from the north-west of France with sailings from Cherbourg and St. Malo before being directed to ports in the Bay of Biscay. She was released to reopen the Rosslare service in 1946 and remained there apart from odd relieving spells elsewhere until withdrawn at the end of December 1966. She was scrapped in Belgium, at Antwerp, during 1967.

ST. DAVID

St. David was requisitioned from the Fishguard–Rossslare service for use as a hospital ship on 23rd September 1939, just 12 days after sister ship *St. Andrew* departed for similar conversion. The *St. David* saw limited use to and from French ports until ordered to Dover on 24th May 1940 and from there was sent immediately to Dunkirk, arriving during the following morning and coming under shore fire from Gravelines when making a return dash to Newhaven. The steamer arrived back at Dunkirk late on 28th May and lay

St. Andrew's *sister ship* **St. David,** *seen in a Great Western Railway postcard view, was also at Dunkirk as a hospital ship but after two trips was bombed while lying off Dover and had to go on one engine for repairs at Southampton following damage to the port propeller shaft. Later converted to operate as a Landing Ship (Infantry),* **St. David** *was sunk in the Anzio landings at the beginning of 1944.* (Ambrose Greenway collection)

Built: 1932 by Cammell Laird, Birkenhead, for the Fishguard and Rosslare Railways and Harbours Company and managed by the Great Western Railway.
Gross tonnage: 2,702.
Length: 327 ft. 2 in.
Width: 49 ft. 1 in.
Machinery: Four Parsons steam reciprocating geared turbines.
Speed: 21 knots.
1939 route: Fishguard–Rosslare.

overnight while crew members acted as stretcher bearers to embark wounded in the absence of RAMC personnel. She set off on a third crossing during Friday 31st, arriving to find *St. Andrew* and another hospital ship *St. Julien* already alongside and no other berth available. In the absence of orders, Captain B. Mendus, who had relieved Captain C. Joy after the first two trips, tried to enter the harbour but was driven back and forced to return to Dover. While anchored off the coast a bombing near miss damaged the port shaft and *St. David* proceeded to Southampton on the starboard engine for repairs. During 1943 *St. David* was fitted out as a Landing Ship Infantry and was lost in this role on 24th January 1944 while taking part in landings on the Italian coast.

ST. JULIEN

The *St. Julien* was taken off Channel Islands sailings on 9th September 1939 and sent to Avonmouth three days later, making two trips carrying troops from the Bristol Channel port to St. Nazaire. In October, the vessel arrived at Southampton and was converted to serve as a hospital carrier, although until early April 1940 *St. Julien's* only work in this capacity was half a dozen trips between Dieppe and Newhaven. It was from Newhaven that *St. Julien* was sent to Dunkirk and her story is similiar to that of the other hospital ships, with wounded being carried aboard by the ship's own crew amidst a

Two views of **St. Julien** *as a hospital ship provide an interesting comparison with a pre-war appearance represented by sister ship* **St. Helier** *(page 47). In the stern view,* **St. Julien** *is at her home port of Newhaven with the hospital ship* **Dinard** *ahead* (Imperial War Museum). *The other shot overleaf was taken at Dieppe in 1940 prior to Operation Dynamo. Before* **St. Julien** *went to the Mediterranean in 1943, the lifeboats were replaced by powered hospital tenders and a fully-equipped operating theatre was fitted. The vessel was subsequently mined in the early stages of the Normandy invasion* (John de S. Winser collection).

continuous hail of bombs and shelling. Accurate information on *St. Julien's* crossings is sparse and, surprisingly, she is listed as transporting only 287 men. The vessel was at Dunkirk on 27th May having taken the long Route Y passage with a destroyer escort but, with *St. Andrew*, did not succeed in getting into the harbour and was ordered back. She certainly made it on 31st May after naval personnel were put aboard to assist the weary crew and loaded in Dunkirk, crew-members assisting the wounded.

St. Julien took part in evacuations from north-western France and was later fitted with an operating theatre and powered ambulance tenders before going to the Mediterranean in 1943, with service including a role in the landings at Anzio and Salerno. *St. Julien* came back to south coast ports in the build-up to the Normandy Landings but was damaged by a mine on 5th June. Although resuming sailings to the Channel Islands in 1945, the *St. Julien's* Great Western connections were severed in the following year when the Weymouth operation passed to the Southern Region of the British Transport Commission. Replaced by new tonnage in 1966 and sold to Belgian breakers, she was used for a time as a dockers' recreation centre before being finally cut up.

Built: 1925 by John Brown & Co, Clydebank, for the Great Western Railway.
Gross tonnage: 1,855.
Length: 291 ft. 3 in.
Width: 42 ft. 6 in.
Machinery: Parsons single-geared turbines.
Speed: 18 knots.
1939 route: Weymouth–Channel Islands.

WORTHING

Built: 1928 by Wm Denny & Bros, Dumbarton, for the Southern Railway.
Gross tonnage: 2,288.
Length: 306 ft.
Width: 38 ft. 6 in.
Machinery: Two single-reduction geared turbines.
Speed: 24 knots.
1939 route: Southern Railway/SNCF Newhaven–Dieppe joint service.

Launched by a French Vicomtesse, *Worthing* was always a noted flier and on a trial run in 1928 was timed pier head to pier head from Dieppe to

The Southern Railway steamer **Worthing** *had a varied war career, including service as Hospital Carrier No. 30 (above) at Dunkirk* (John de S. Winser collection) *before later spells as a target vessel and Landing Ship under the name* **Brigadier.** *Restored to the Newhaven–Dieppe service in 1945, a well-loaded* **Worthing** *(below) is seen near the end of a six-year spell of English Channel crossings before sale to Greek interests in 1951* (Skyfotos).

Another view of the **Isle of Thanet**, *still in hospital ship colours later in 1940 and lying at Newhaven. Later service as a target ship for the Fleet Air Arm was followed by conversion to operate as a Landing Ship Infantry.* (Newhaven Historical Society)

Newhaven in 2 hours 38 minutes, an average speed in excess of 24 knots. After the war began, *Worthing* was fitted out as Hospital Carrier No. 30 by Harland & Wolff at Southampton and based at Newhaven from where she was dispatched to Dunkirk with *Isle of Thanet* to bring out wounded on 23rd May. Then, on the morning of 26th May, some seven hours before Operation Dynamo began officially, the *Worthing* crossed again, accompanied by *Isle of Guernsey.* The vessel's speed came in useful on 2nd June when she was set upon by a dozen aircraft *en route* for Dunkirk. Captain C. Munton increased speed to 24 knots and took violent evasive action as a vessel clearly identified as a hospital ship was attacked in broad daylight. Two bombs exploded within a few feet of her and although taking water she returned safely.

On 11th June the *Worthing* loaded wounded from launches at Le Havre and had a spell at Weymouth as evacuations from western France continued. Next came conversion to operate as the target ship HMS *Brigadier* in the Firth of Forth until 1942 when there were further alterations at West Hartlepool with a change of role to Landing Ship Infantry. *Brigadier* carried commandos across to Arromanches on D-Day and then switched to transport duties from Southampton. In this role she suffered severe bow damage when colliding with the Combined Operations HQ ship *Hilary* in Spithead in November 1944. A month later the *Worthing* reverted to her old name when taken over by the Ministry of Transport and, following repairs, went on to the Newhaven–Dieppe run from March 1945. Surplus to requirements in 1951, *Worthing* was sold off. As the Greek *Phryne,* after a spell on a service between Piraeus and Crete, and limited work as a pilgrim carrier, she was scrapped in 1964.

Cargo Ships

CARGO vessels ranging in size from coastal tramps and colliers to the large, modern, deep-sea cargo liner *Clan MacAlister* had a part to play before, during and even after the very end of the evacuation. This heading embraces what were largely merchant ships sent initially to perform tasks at Dunkirk other than bringing out troops, although many slotted into this role as well and acquitted themselves with great distinction.

One of the most impressive records belongs to the steamer *Dorrien Rose*, a Liverpool-registered coastal tramp which went across carrying stores and returned to land 1,494 troops, some 900 of them taken off the sinking personnel vessel *Queen of the Channel* in an exercise demonstrating outstanding seamanship by the skipper Captain W. Thompson. Another tramp, the *Yewdale*, brought back 890 men, and motor coasters such as *Bullfinch, Ngaroma* and *Scottish Co-operator* transported more than 500 men to safety. Other cargo steamers from the railway fleets were called forward from Southampton and sent across specifically to lift troops and have already been listed among the personnel ships.

Losses were quite heavy among the cargo vessels themselves, with the most important casualty the valuable *Clan MacAlister*, commandeered at Southampton because of an ability to handle assault landing craft using her own cranes. Three of the smaller coastal vessels to be lost, *Bawtry, Spinel* and *Williamstown*, were all salvaged by the Germans and put back into service.

A final sacrifice was the decision to sink six elderly cargo vessels, three of them originally Danish, as blockships in the entrance to Dunkirk Harbour. Only four of them ended their days in this manner, the other two sinking en route.

ABUKIR

Built for the London–Guernsey–Jersey trade of the London and Channel Islands Steamship Company as *Island Queen*, she later became *Kyle Queen* for Monroe Brothers of Liverpool before being sold as *Abukir* for the Khedivial Mail Steamship Company. She passed through two other Mediterranean owners before sale on 15th May 1940 to the Ministry of Shipping and was placed under the General Steam Navigation Company's management. Although not strictly taking part in the evacuation, *Abukir* is generally listed in Operation Dynamo losses after being sunk by an E-Boat north of Dunkirk on 28th May while on passage from Ostend to the Downs with a cargo of army lorries and 210 troops and refugees, of whom only 21 survived together with 5 of the crew of 21.

Built: 1920 by Swan Hunter & Wigham Richardson, Sunderland.
Tonnage: 689.
Length: 173 ft. 5 in.
Width: 12 ft. 9 in.
Machinery: Triple expansion by Swan Hunter, Newcastle.

BAWTRY

Completed as *Tourmaline* for William Robertson, Glasgow, one of the biggest British oper-

Built: 1898 by J. Shearer & Sons, Glasgow.
Tonnage: 835.
Length: 200 ft.
Width: 30 ft. 1 in.
Machinery: Triple expansion by Muir & Hutson, Glasgow.

ators of steam coasters, becoming *Bawtry* in 1938 when bought by the London-based Bawtry Steamship Company. She arrived at Dunkirk in ballast from the Tees on 13th May and was bombed and sunk there on the 21st. After being declared a war prize the wreck was raised by the Germans and taken to Antwerp, later being put back into service as *Rival* by a Kiel company. The vessel was finally destroyed during a bombing raid on Hamburg by the American Eighth Army Air Force on the last day of 1944.

BEAL

Built for Tyne-Tees Steam Shipping and employed on regular routes to the near Continent. Made three crossings to the French coast near La Panne loading troops from small craft on 28th, 29th and 30th May 1940 and transported a total of 364 men to Ramsgate. After the war became *Sylvan Coast* when Tyne Tees was taken over by Coast Lines in 1949 and then *Lairdsburn* from 1959 for another member of the group, Burns and Laird. Sold in 1966, the vessel was used for tramping in the Mediterranean for a succession of Greek owners and was lost as *Ariadne* after hitting a breakwater at Augusta in March 1978.

Built: 1938 by Hawthorne, Leslie & Co, Newcastle.
Tonnage: 504.
Length: 165 ft. 3 in.
Width: 27 ft. 2 in.
Machinery: Humboldt-Deutz oil engine, speed 9.5 knots.

BULLFINCH

Although not fast, *Bullfinch* was used by General Steam Navigation Company on regular liner routes to ports in France, Holland and Belgium. She crossed to La Panne on 28th May but the skipper, Captain H. Buxton found that while the beaches were crowded with troops, evacuation was being held up by a shortage of small boats. He was ordered to beach *Bullfinch* at first light next day but the kedge anchor failed to hold and the coaster was left grounded broadside. Lines were run to the shore and boats pulled backwards and forwards until the tide dropped, enabling men to wade out. *Bullfinch* had to wait until refloating at 6.15 p.m. and came under air attack both when grounded and after getting underway. Near misses astern damaged the steering gear and she had to hove-too off Dunkirk for repairs, eventually reaching the Downs and unloading 600 men at Ramsgate. After serving GSNC until 1963, the *Bullfinch* had two years as Commodore Shipping's *Norman Commodore* and after going to the eastern Mediterranean in 1965 was only finally broken up at Piraeus in 1985.

Built: 1936 by Caledon Shipbuilding Co, Dundee.
Tonnage: 433.
Length: 174 ft. 1 in.
Width: 31 ft. 1 in.
Machinery: British Auxiliaries oil engine, speed 9.5 knots.

CLAN MACALISTER

Built: 1930 by Greenock Dockyard Co.
Tonnage: 6,787.
Length: 453 ft. 8 in.
Width: 62 ft. 3 in.
Machinery: Triple-expansion by Kincaid & Co, Greenock.

This modern cargo liner owned by Clan Line Steamers was lying in Southampton when commandeered to carry eight assault landing craft to Dunkirk as deck cargo. The vessel used her own derricks to hoist them onboard on 27th May prior to sailing later the same day, also carrying a naval party of 45 ratings and two reserve officers to man the craft. *Clan MacAlister* reached Dunkirk Roads on the morning of 29th May and began discharging the assault craft, two being severely damaged in the process. While the six remaining craft began ferrying troops, *Clan MacAlister,* despite presenting an irresistible target to the Luftwaffe, was told to await further orders. As air activity intensified the vessel was hit and set on fire, HMS *Malcolm* moving in to

The largest cargo vessel to be directly involved in the evacuation, **Clan MacAlister** *was used to carry eight assault landing craft from Southampton to Dunkirk Roads. After unloading the craft with her own derricks, the near 7,000-ton steamer became a target for the Luftwaffe after, surprisingly, being ordered to remain at anchor to await orders. Quickly set on fire, she was abandoned and the crew and some troops taken off by other ships.* (World Ship Photo Library)

take off troops who had been brought out from the shore. Efforts to control the blaze were to no avail and *Clan MacAlister* was abandoned, her crew being taken off by the minesweeper *Pangbourne*. The vessel went down on an even keel in shallow water and then performed perhaps her most useful role as German aircraft continued to shower the wreck with bombs.

CLEWBAY

Built: 1904 by Ailsa Shipbuilding Co, Troon.
Tonnage: 645.
Length: 183 ft.
Width: 28 ft. 6 in.
Machinery: Two-cylinder compound by Muir & Hutson, Glasgow.

A steam collier built as *G. Player* for Teignmouth owners and used on the East Coast until acquired by John Kelly Ltd of Belfast and renamed *Clewbay* in 1914. She carried coal from the Mersey or South Wales to Belfast until the war started and was ordered to Dunkirk on 24th May after moving up to Dover from Newhaven where a cargo of explosives had been loaded. *Clewbay* came under air attack whilst crossing and succeeded in entering the harbour but could find nowhere to unload and, in the absence of instructions, returned to Dover and finally discharged in Littlehampton on 31st May. *Clewbay* resumed trading on the Irish Sea until broken-up in Belgium during 1959, having been renamed *Ballygilbert* in 1952.

CORINIA

Corinia was built by the Williamsons for their own Northwest Shipping Company, the family, shipbuilders first and foremost, turning out vessels to their own account when orders were slack. A quite large coastal tramp steamer, *Corinia* was taken across to Dunkirk by her

Built: 1928 by R. Williamson & Son, Workington.
Tonnage: 870.
Length: 188 ft. 3 in.
Width: 30 ft. 2 in.
Machinery: Triple-expansion by Beardmore & Co, Coatbridge.

master J. R. Hughes and loaded troops from small craft off La Panne and carried them safely to a Kent port, believed to be Ramsgate. She was lost on 10th March 1941, mined south of Beachy Head whilst en route from Blyth to Cowes with a cargo of coal.

The master, mate and chief engineer of the Mersey-based steam coaster **Dorrien Rose** *each received the DSM and there were honours for four other crewmembers after a remarkable rescue of nearly 1,000 men from the sinking* **Queen of the Channel** *on 28th May.* **Dorrien Rose** *had carried stores to Dunkirk and came through the war to continue in service until 1959.* (World Ship Photo Library)

DORRIEN ROSE

Liverpool-based Richard Hughes, one of the biggest Mersey coaster operators, built the largish *Dorrien Rose* in 1922 as part of an ambitious expansion following the First World War. The depression brought financial ruin and the company was taken over by Cardiff shipping agent Thomas Tierney who continued to trade as Richard Hughes. *Dorrien Rose* went to Dunkirk as a store ship and early on 28th May was able to rescue over 900 troops when the Thames motor vessel *Queen of the Channel* was bombed shortly after leaving Dunkirk, being skilfully taken alongside the sinking vessel. In all *Dorrien Rose* carried almost 1,500 men back to England and her master W. Thompson, mate T. O'Hanlon and chief engineer B. Murphy were all awarded the DSC and four other crewmembers the DSM. After the war, *Dorrien Rose* steamed on until sold in 1951 and had spells as *Fairwood Elm* (Fairwood Shipping, Swansea), *Cupholder* (Glynwood Navigation Company, Hull) and *Holdernore* (Holderness Steamship Company, Hull) until scrapped at Dublin in 1959.

Built: 1922 by John Fullerton & Co, Paisley.
Tonnage: 1,034.
Length: 210 ft. 4 in.
Width: 33 ft. 2 in.
Machinery: Triple-expansion by Ross & Duncan, Glasgow.

EDVARD NISSEN

Built: 1921 by Sturhs M/S, Aalborg, Denmark.
Tonnage: 2,062.
Length: 282 ft. 5 in.
Width: 42 ft. 7 in.
Machinery: Triple-expansion by A/S Frichs, Aarhus, Denmark.

Built as *Thorsdal* for Norwegian owners and became *Edvard Nissen* when bought by the Danish Vendila Steamship Company in 1928. The vessel is thought to have escaped from Denmark and to have laid-up in Britain until taken over by the Ministry of Shipping earlier in 1940 with Newcastle collier operators Witherington and Everett appointed as managers. *Edvard Nissen* was one of six cargo vessels singled out for use as blockships and was sunk at Dunkirk for this purpose on 4th June.

ESKBURN

Originally commissioned as *Northwick* for Pike & Co. of London, and used in the East Coast coal trade, there was a change of name to *Eskburn* in 1919 following purchase by Middlesbrough owners. An interesting further sale took place in 1928 to William James, the last operator to be based in Cardigan, and this continued to be

The tramp steamer **Foam Queen** *was beached off La Panne and a line taken ashore and attached to an abandoned lorry. The ship's own lifeboat was hauled back and forth to help load more than a thousand troops, who were landed at Ramsgate.* **Foam Queen** *was torpedoed by an E-Boat off the Sussex coast in 1943 while carrying coal from Goole to Poole.* (Roy Fenton collection)

the headquarters after the company changed its name to British Isles Coasters in 1935 – although the *Eskburn* is thought rarely, if ever, to have negotiated the River Teifi to visit the port. The *Eskburn's* name appears in official lists of Dunkirk small craft but her exact part in the evacuation is not clear. After changing hands in 1941 and becoming *Springburn* she was eventually converted to a sand pump dredger in 1948 and put in a further thirteen years of service in this role until scrapped at Swansea in 1961.

Built: 1917 by Swan Hunter & Wigham Richardson, Sunderland.
Tonnage: 427.
Length: 158 ft. 2 in.
Width: 26 ft. 1 in.
Machinery: Triple-expansion by Beardmore & Co, Glasgow.

FIRTH FISHER

Built as *Freeland* for Freeland Shipping, managed by Joseph Fisher, and sold to the Barrow operation of distant relative James Fisher at the end of 1933, the small tramp steamer appeared as *Firth Fisher* the following year. She was mined and sunk just before Operation Dynamo striking a mine half a mile east of Boulogne on 21st May while sailing to the French port from Dover and Littlehampton with a cargo of army stores. Seven of a crew of ten were drowned.

Built: 1919 by John Lewis & Sons, Aberdeen.
Tonnage: 574.
Length: 164 ft. 8 in.
Width: 27 ft.
Machinery: Triple-expansion by builders.

FOAM QUEEN

A general cargo tramp put into service by Cardiff owners as *River Exe*, she passed to the London and Channel Islands Steamship Company as *Foam Queen* in 1928 and continued to trade on general tramping to Continental ports and London–Channel Islands services after the owners were taken over by Coast Lines and became British Channel Islands Shipping in 1937. Captain A. T. Mastin sailed his vessel to near La Panne on the evening of 31st May and beached her in an attempt to overcome the shortage of small boats for ferrying. Lines from the ship were

Built: 1922 by London and Montrose Shipbuilding & Repair Co.
Tonnage: 811.
Length: 189 ft. 2 in.
Width: 30 ft. 3 in.
Machinery: Triple-expansion by Beardmore & Co, Coatbridge.

tied to a lorry on the beach and *Foam Queen's* own lifeboat was hauled backwards and forwards. The vessel refloated at 03:00 on 1st June and returned with nearly 1,200 men to Ramsgate. *Foam Queen* was torpedoed by an E-Boat on 2nd November 1943 when between Dungeness and Beachy Head with a cargo of coal from Goole to Poole. The stern was blown off and 11 of a crew of 15 and three gunners were lost, but the wreck was towed into Dover where the coal was discharged. The hulk was taken to Muckling Flats and used for experimental purposes.

GATESHEAD

Gateshead was the third name carried in little more than a dozen years by this coastal tramp which was built for J. Leete and Sons of London as *Catherine Anne* and then became *The President* after sale to Glasgow company J. Hay and Sons in 1922. Bought by the Tyne Tees Steam Shipping Company in 1933, the *Gateshead* was sent to the Dunkirk area on 30th May, carrying supplies to Malo-les-Bains and returning with troops. The steamer was renamed *Persian Coast* in 1946, returned to the West Coast as *Celia Mary* for Liverpool owners in 1951 and was broken up in Holland during 1956 after a short spell with Hull's Glynwood Navigation Company as *Cupholder*.

Built: 1919 by Forth Shipbuilding & Engineering Co, Alloa.
Tonnage: 746.
Length: 190 ft. 9 in.
Width: 29 ft. 2 in.
Machinery: Triple-expansion by builders.

GLENARIFF

Built: 1936 by John Lewis & Sons, Aberdeen.
Tonnage: 868.
Length: 197 ft. 7 in.
Width: 30 ft. 7 in.
Machinery: Triple-expansion by builders.

Another of the John Kelly fleet of colliers based at Belfast, *Glenariff* was used mainly to carry coal from South Wales, the Mersey and Ayrshire to Belfast. *Glenariff* spent most of 31st May lying with the *Whitstable* off Bray Beach waiting for troops but eventually left with only 26 aboard. She came through the remainder of the war and operated until broken up at Faslane in 1963, being named *Ballyknock* for the last eleven years of service.

GOURKO

Built for the Humber–Scandinavia services of Ellerman's Wilson Line, *Gourko* originally had first class accommodation for 27 passengers and was also fitted with refrigerating machinery.

Built: 1911 by Earle's & Co, Hull.
Tonnage: 1,975.
Length: 318 ft.
Width: 42 ft. 2 in.
Machinery: Triple-expansion by builders.

Purchased by the Admiralty in August 1914, she was used during the First World War as a canteen and amenity ship at Scapa Flow before being sold back to Wilson's in 1919 and refitted for further service. *Gourko* was requisitioned on 21st May 1940 to be used as a blockship at Dunkirk but sank en route on 3rd June.

HOLLAND

Another Danish tramp steamer which came under the Ministry of Shipping's control during 1940. She had been built as *Dansted* for Rodby owners and was named *Holland* upon changing hands in 1923. After being taken over in 1940, *Holland* was placed under the management of R. Dalgleish Ltd., until selected for use as a blockship at Dunkirk but, like *Gourko,* the vessel was lost on its way on 3rd June.

Built: 1919 by Sturhs M/S, Aalborg, Denmark.
Tonnage: 1,251.
Length: 238 ft. 7 in.
Width: 36 ft. 2 in.
Machinery: Triple-expansion by A/S Frichs, Aarhus, Denmark.

KOHISTAN

A cargo vessel built for the Persian Gulf trade of Strick Line, *Kohistan* appears to have been involved in one of the pre-Dunkirk evacuations, arriving at Dover on 24th May carrying large

Built: 1930 by John Redhed & Sons, South Shields.
Tonnage: 5,884.
Length: 425 ft. 8 in.
Width: 55 ft.
Machinery: Triple-expansion with low-pressure turbine by builders.

numbers of troops and being berthed at Admiralty Pier by the tugs *Simla* and *Lady Brassey*. *Kohistan* survived the war and operated until arriving at Kure, Japan, for demolition in November 1959.

LEVENWOOD

Levenwood, built for prominent Middlesbrough owners the Joseph Constantine Steamship Line, was similar to *Corinia* from the same Workington yard. Used in the East Coast coal trade, *Levenwood* went to Dunkirk with military stores on 31st May. Captain W. Young beached his vessel in eight feet of water and used her lifeboats

Built: 1924 by R. Williamson & Son, Workington.
Tonnage: 803.
Length: 186 ft. 5 in.
Width: 29 ft. 4 in.
Machinery: Triple-expansion by Beardmore & Co, Glasgow.

to carry supplies to the beach 800 yards away, also bringing off 60 troops who were landed in Dover. Changing hands in 1944 and again in 1945, she became *Devonbrook* and was wrecked off Blyth on 28th August 1946 when sailing in ballast from London.

LOWICK

A modern Dutch-built motor coaster added to the fleet of Tyne-Tees Steam Shipping, *Lowick* was sent to Dunkirk with supplies and then loaded troops from small craft off Bray Dunes on 1st June. The *Lowick* was renamed *Frisian Coast* in 1946 and received new Mirlees engines nine

Levenwood *was another steamer beached off the coast after crossing to Dunkirk and used its own lifeboats to take military supplies almost half a mile to the shore, with some troops ferried out as the boats returned. After surviving the war,* **Levenwood** *was lost off the Northumberland coast in 1946, by which time she had changed hands and was operating as* **Devonbrook.** (World Ship Photo Library)

Built: 1937 by Scheepsbouw Gideon, Groningen, Holland.
Tonnage: 586.
Length: 195 ft. 9 in.
Width: 31 ft. 6 in.
Machinery: Humboldt-Deutz oil engines.

years later. She became *Agia Eleni* when sold for service in the Mediterranean during 1967 and, ten years and two further Greek owners later, was stranded at Rhodes after her moorings parted in bad weather on 26th November 1977.

MOYLE

This steam collier, built for the Shamrock Shipping Company of Larne, had five years in

Built: 1918 by Ailsa Shipbuilding Co, Troon.
Tonnage: 1,761.
Length: 275 ft. 2 in.
Width: 36 ft. 1 in.
Machinery: Triple-expansion by builders.

the colours of Normandy Shipping of London from 1918 before being re-sold to the Ulster concern. *Moyle* was bought by the Admiralty on 21st May 1940 and sunk as a blockship at Dunkirk on 4th June.

NEPHRITE

A steam coaster built as *Burstow* for Edward T. Lindley of London, she became *Nephrite* following purchase by William Robertson in 1930 and was mainly used to carry coal or limestone. *Nephrite* had been acquired by Stephenson, Clarke and Associated Companies earlier in 1940

Built: 1927 by John Lewis & Sons, Aberdeen.
Tonnage: 927.
Length: 199 ft. 7 in.
Width: 30 ft. 9 in.
Machinery: Triple-expansion by builders.

and was used as a store ship during Operation Dynamo and, with Captain C. G. West in command, transported 504 troops. She became *Portslade* in 1946 and *Rosefleet* after sale to the Ouse Steamship Company of Goole in 1956, but her career under this name was short. Later in the same year, on 29th October, after leaving Dunkirk for Goole in ballast, *Rosefleet* sank at Mardyck, some kilometres west of the port, and the wreck was demolished where it lay by a Belgian contractor.

NGAROMA

Built: 1931 by N.V. Industrieele Maatschappi De Noord, Alblasserdam, Holland.
Tonnage: 503.
Length: 159 ft.
Width: 25 ft. 7 in.
Machinery: Humboldt-Deutz oil engines.

Ngaroma was the first new building for William A. Wilson, a Southampton shipowner who ran coal from South Wales and the North East to London and the South Coast ports. The vessel was also among the first of its size to be motor powered and went to Dunkirk under the command of Captain J. W. Dickenson, probably making two crossings and carrying 100 troops. *Ngaroma* returned to coal carrying and was lost on 15th August 1942 after striking a rock near the Scillies when on passage from Barry to Plymouth.

PACIFICO

Built as *Princess Helena* for coastal cargo liner operators M. Langlands and Sons, she became *Moray Coast* after the Glasgow company was swallowed up by Coast Lines in 1919. There were a succession of owners from 1935 when the vessel operated as *Olga*, *Olga S.*, and *Caper*

Built: 1905 by the Caledon Shipbuilding Co, Dundee.
Tonnage: 677.
Length: 210 ft. 5 in.
Width: 31 ft. 5 in.
Machinery: Triple-expansion by builders.

before acquisition in 1938 by Alcyon Shipping of London as *Pacifico*. She came under Admiralty control in October 1939 and was sent to Dunkirk and sunk as a blockship on 4th June.

QUEENSLAND

Built for a Dutch coal importer as *Beijerland*, the vessel was renamed *Queensland* when transferred to an associated British company, Shipping and Coal of London, in 1936, but continued trading

> **Built:** 1928 by Jan Smit, Czn., Alblasserdam, Holland.
> **Tonnage:** 1,617.
> **Length:** 242 ft. 8 in.
> **Width:** 38 ft. 1 in.
> **Machinery:** Triple-expansion by Maatschappij de Schelde, Flushing.

from Goole and other British East Coast ports into Rotterdam. She presumably carried stores to Dunkirk but is not recorded as transporting troops. After a career spanning 40 years, the *Queensland* was scrapped in Belgium during 1958.

ROYAL SCOT

Ordered by the London and Edinburgh Shipping Co. of Leith and used to carry cargo in their

> **Built:** 1930 by Caledon Shipbuilding Co, Dundee.
> **Tonnage:** 595.
> **Length:** 271 ft. 3 in.
> **Width:** 31 ft. 6 in.
> **Machinery:** Triple-expansion by builders.

regular service between the Forth and Thames, the *Royal Scot* was recorded as a merchant vessel taking part in Operation Dynamo, having been sent forward from Southampton, but did not, apparently, transport troops. The steamer was mined and sunk in the entrance to the Humber on 10th June 1941.

SANDHILL

Sandhill, delivered to Tyne-Tees Steam Shipping, was a repeat of the *Lowick* completed by the same Dutch yard a year earlier and was one of four vessels from the Newcastle company's fleet to take part in Operation Dynamo as a store ship, crossing to Dunkirk on 24th May with a cargo of 940 tons of explosives which the crew unloaded, using the ship's own cranes, during bombing raids. The *Sandhill* made a second trip on 30th

A Dutch-built steamer, the **Queensland** *was employed in the East Coast coal trade for 40 years until scrapped in 1958.* (A. Duncan)

Royal Scot *was one of a number of vessels held at Southampton before the need for an evacuation and, although recorded as crossing to Dunkirk, did not carry troops. She was lost little more than a year later, striking a mine at the mouth of the Humber.* (A. Duncan)

The modern Dutch-built motor coaster **Sandhill,** *and her identical sister* **Lowick,** *were among four vessels of the fleet of Tyne-Tees Shipping to take part in Operation Dynamo.* **Sandhill** *unloaded a cargo of explosives at Dunkirk amid bombing raids and lifted troops from La Panne on a second crossing. Seen here in the late 1950s as* **Durham Coast,** *the vessel continued in service, latterly in the Mediterranean, until 1979.* (A. Duncan)

Built: 1938 by Scheepsbouw Gideon, Groningen, Holland.
Tonnage: 586.
Length: 195 ft. 6 in.
Width: 31 ft. 6 in.
Machinery: Humboldt-Deutz oil engines.

May, loading troops from small boats off La Panne. She went on to complete a career of over 40 years and was broken up in Italy during the winter of 1979–80 as *Margarita P*, her eighth name. In the post-war period there were spells as *Valerian Coast* and *Hebridean Coast* before a move to the Irish Sea as *Ulster Chieftain* in 1953. She returned to the East Coast in 1956 as *Durham Coast* prior to yet another spell on the Irish Sea from 1960 as *Wicklow*. Then it was off to the Mediterranean as *Sinergasia* with a last name change in 1974.

SCOTTISH CO-OPERATOR

Built: 1939 by Industrieele De Noord, Alblassardam, Holland.
Tonnage: 513.
Length: 216 ft.
Length: 31 ft. 3 in.
Machinery: Oil engines by Atlas Diesel A/B, Stockholm, Sweden.

Built to bring in foodstuffs and other materials for the Scottish Co-operative Society of Leith, *Scottish Co-operator* participated in Operation Dynamo as a merchant vessel and transported over 500 men. She was ordered across from anchorage in the Downs, and Captain T. Robertson, taking responsibility for his own actions, eased *Scottish Co-operator* into Dunkirk Harbour. There, some 50 stretcher cases, 150 walking wounded and a further 300 troops were taken aboard. The wounded were transferred to a hospital ship before the vessel returned, coming under air attack on a number of occasions. She was then sent immediately to Sheerness for repairs. After the war *Scottish Co-operator* returned to East Coast cargo services until sold in 1950 to another Leith concern, London and Scottish Lines as *Edinburgh Merchant,* continuing until passing to Greek owners as *Annika* in 1959.

SEQUACITY

Built: 1937 by Goole Shipbuilding & Repairing Co.
Tonnage: 570.
Length: 196 ft. 2 in.
Width: 30 ft. 2 in.
Machinery: Oil engine by British Auxiliaries, Glasgow.

A modern motor coaster from the extensive fleet of F. T. Everard, the Thames-based company who started building sailing barges and became noted for their ability to convey anything from anywhere around the British coast or to the near Continent. *Sequacity* was crossing to Dunkirk, having originally sailed from Greenhithe in ballast, when she and the Glasgow coaster *Yewdale* came under fire from shore batteries at Cap Gris Nez. *Sequacity* suffered three hits and went down two miles east of Calais, all her crew being picked up by the *Yewdale.*

SODALITY

Laid down by Williamsons for their own account in 1932 but left unfinished on the stocks, the hull was launched and towed to Goole six years later to be completed and delivered to F.T. Everard as *Sodality*. The vessel was at Dunkirk before the start of Operation Dynamo, loading supplies at Deptford Victualling Wharf on 20th May and arriving in Dunkirk on the 22nd, where crewmembers operated shore cranes to unload the cargo. After lying overnight, the *Sodality* sailed for Dover next morning and landed six army lorries at Dover. *Sodality* remained in the Everard fleet until sold for breaking up at Grays in 1958.

Built: 1932–1938, laid down by R. Williamson & Sons, Workington, completed by Goole Shipbuilding and Repairing.
Tonnage: 829.
Length: 188 ft. 4 in.
Width: 30 ft. 3 in.
Machinery: Oil engine by Newbury Diesel Co.

SPINEL

A motor general cargo coaster built for William Robertson, the *Spinel* sailed to Dunkirk from Poole with a cargo of cased petrol but was bombed after arriving on 25th May and had to be abandoned by her crew. At the beginning of July 1940 the wreck was salvaged by the Germans, repaired and put into service supplying the then occupied Channel Islands, arriving in St. Helier for the first time on 4th October 1940. She was recovered when the Islands were liberated in May

Built: 1937 by Henry Robb, Leith.
Tonnage: 650.
Length: 185 ft.
Width: 28 ft. 7 in.
Machinery: Oil engine by British Auxiliaries, Glasgow.

Although completed for F. T. Everard in 1938, the **Sodality's** *hull had remained on the stocks unfinished for six years, which partly accounts for the rather old fashioned lines. Even in the week before the start of the evacuation, and after arriving in Dunkirk with provisions and military supplies, the* **Sodality's** *crew had to operate shore cranes themselves to unload the cargo.* (Skyfotos)

Above *Abandoned at Dunkirk, salvaged by the Germans and used to supply the occupied Channel Islands, the* **Spinel's** *eventful war continued when she was recovered in 1945. Eventually re-acquired by her original owners during the following year,* **Spinel** *sailed on until 1970.* (Skyfotos)

Below *The steam coaster* **Westown,** *pictured after the war as* **Holdernook** *for Hull owners, went to Dunkirk as a store ship. In all she served under four names in a lengthy career and was broken up at Dover early in 1957.* (A. Duncan)

1945 and renamed *Empire Spinel* by the Ministry of War Shipping and put into the hands of William Robertson as managers. Robertsons re-acquired the vessel in 1946 and, after reverting to its original name, *Spinel* served them well until scrapped at Dalmuir on the Clyde in 1970.

WESTCOVE

A collier built for William Cory and Son as *Cove* which spent all its working life on the East Coast apart from a spell during the First World War carrying mines, stores and railway materials to

France for the British Expeditionary Force. There was a change of name to *Corcove* in 1920 and another to *Westcove* seven years later following a sale to Westwick Steamship Company, of London. The old steamer was sailed to Dunkirk on 3rd June and scuttled as a blockship in the harbour approaches.

Built: 1912 by S. P. Austin & Son, Sunderland.
Tonnage: 2,734.
Length: 312 ft. 5 in.
Width: 45 ft. 3 in.
Machinery: Triple-expansion by George Clark, Sunderland.

WESTOWN

Built: 1921 by C. Rennoldson & Co, South Shields.
Tonnage: 710.
Length: 180 ft. 4 in.
Width: 28 ft.
Machinery: Triple-expansion by Day, Summers & Co, Southampton.

Built as *Channel Queen* for the London–Guernsey–Jersey trade of the London and Channel Islands Steamship Company, she became *Westown* in 1937 when sold to the Brook Shipping Company and placed under the management of Comben Longstaff. *Westown* went to Dunkirk as a store ship under Captain R. W. Shanks and continued tramping after sale in 1941 to George W. Grace and Co, London, and then to Holderness Steamship Company, Hull, in 1946, by whom she was renamed *Holdernook* in the following year. The vessel switched to Glynwood Navigation Company, Hull, as *Logholder* in 1956 and arrived at Dover for breaking up on the 28th December of that year.

WILLIAMSTOWN

Built for Williamstown Shipping with Comben Longstaff management, *Williamstown* was listed as participating in Operation Dynamo as a merchant ship. Sold later in 1940 to Southampton owner William A. Wilson, the vessel joined Ellerman's Wilson Line in 1946 as *Electro* and received new British diesel engines, serving until sold to Greek owners in 1967 and renamed *Georgios*. She changed hands again at the beginning of 1972, becoming *Nicholas C* for a Cypriot company but was lost after catching fire on her first voyage to Portugal.

Built: 1937 by Scheepsbouw Gebruder van der Werf, Deest, Holland.
Tonnage: 793.
Length: 198 ft. 9 in.
Width: 29 ft. 1 in.
Machinery: Oil engines by Motorenwerke Mannheim AG, Germany.

WORTHTOWN

A rather unlucky ship, being lost twice by the same owners! After entering service for Williamstown Shipping Company, with Comben Longstaff as managers in 1939, *Worthtown* was bombed and sunk by aircraft off Dunkirk on 27th May. The wreck was salvaged as a war prize and put back into service by the Germans during 1942 as *Ilse Schulte*. After British Forces recovered the vessel at Schlei in April 1945 she was named *Empire Worthtown* by the Ministry of War Transport and ran under Comben Longstaff management until sold back to Williamstown Shipping in 1946. The ship, renamed *Glamorganbrook*, sank on 11th October, 1946 after springing a leak during a voyage from Blyth to Cowes with coal.

Built: 1939 by John Lewis & Sons, Aberdeen.
Tonnage: 868.
Length: 205 ft.
Length: 32 ft. 3 in.
Machinery: Triple-expansion by builders.

YEWDALE

Glasgow owner John Stewart used *Yewdale* mainly on Irish Sea services and the vessel proved its worth at Dunkirk, transporting 890 troops

Built: 1929 by Scott & Sons, Bowling.
Tonnage: 823.
Length: 195 ft.
Width: 31 ft. 2 in.
Machinery: Triple-expansion by J. Abernethy, Aberdeen.

Seen during her later years when running as **Ballygilbert**, *the 1904-built* **Clewbay** *was typical of British steam coasters represented at Dunkirk. After surviving a hazardous crossing to Dunkirk with a cargo of explosives, and the rest of the war,* **Clewbay** *sailed on until her 55-year career ended in 1959 at a Belgian breaker's yard.* (World Ship Photo Library)

back to English soil. The steamer sank on 30th September 1944 after striking a submerged object off the northern coast of France while carrying a cargo of coal from Grimsby. During the following month, the *Aaro*, a Danish steamer under Ministry of War Transport ownership, ran over the wreck of *Yewdale* after dragging her anchors in a gale and was also lost.

YEWGLEN

Completed as *Fairmuir* for James Inglis of Leith but went through two other Scottish owners before a sale to an Italian company in 1921 who registered her in Dubrovnik as *Lokrum*. The vessel was back in Scottish waters as *Yewglen* for John Stewart from 1924 and went to Dunkirk at the same time as *Yewdale* from the Stewart fleet. *Yewglen* was bought by Holderness Steamship Company of Hull in 1945 and served them as *Holderness* until scrapped at Dover in 1955.

Built: 1915 by Ardrossan Dry Dock & Shipbuilding Co.
Tonnage: 607.
Length: 175 ft. 8 in.
Width: 28 ft. 1 in.
Machinery: Triple-expansion by Lidgerwood, Coatbridge.

The Paddle Steamers

A TOTAL of 23 paddle steamers were officially recorded as taking part in Operation Dynamo. All but one of them appear to have crossed to the French coast at least once and there is a strong probability that a further four side-wheelers played at least some part in the evacuation. A majority of the steamers had been requisitioned in the early days of the war and commissioned by the Royal Navy as paddle minesweepers, several hoisting the white ensign before the end of September 1939. Others followed in the remaining months of the year and at the beginning of 1940, and more than a dozen of them had served in a similar capacity during the 1914–18 war.

The paddle minesweepers, representing all the major British peacetime excursion fleets, were initially formed into five flotillas. Four of them – the 7th based at Granton on the Forth, 8th at North Shields, 11th at Greenock and 12th at Harwich – each consisted of five steamers, and the 10th Flotilla, based at Dover, of eight. All but the Clyde-based 11th Flotilla were involved in Operation Dynamo – veterans completed before the turn of the century contrasting with large Thames and South Coast boats only a few years old.

Many were still coal-burners and even with the weight of equipment for Oropesa minesweeping and armament, generally consisting of an ancient single 12-pounder gun mounted forward and various lighter weapons, a lot of them still managed a fair turn of speed. In fact, prior to Dunkirk, the sprint back to base after a day's sweeping in the North Sea, was one of the few highlights for the Granton and North Shields boats which regularly worked in pairs and indulged in some spirited unofficial races. They came across very few mines and generally found the routine dull and extremely monotonous. The Harwich and Dover Flotillas were worked a lot harder and an additional complication was the severity of the first winter of the war, with ice floes reported in Harwich Harbour on one occasion.

Most of the paddlers were manned by RNR and RNVR officers, among them one or two former excursion steamer masters and, in other cases, peacetime skippers who went to war with their vessels. Fairly typical of such ships was the *Devonia,* previously a well-known member of the Bristol Channel fleet of P. & A. Campbell. All the large saloon windows were plated over, the main saloon aft becoming – as in most paddlers – the wardroom and officers quarters, whilst fairly basic messes were provided for the rest of the crew by dividing up forward saloons. As ships designed largely for summer operations, few had any sort of heating and this omission was solved by installing cast iron stoves whose chimneys went straight up through the deck head. Apart from the skipper, only the steamer's telegraphist lived in comparative luxury in the wireless cabin below the bridge.

Devonia's crew immediately before the call to Dunkirk was made up of the following: Captain – a retired paddle steamer skipper with the rank of Lieutenant-Commander, RNR; First-Lieutenant (RNR); Sub-Lieutenant (RNVR); Chief Engineer (Lieutenant RNR); Second Engineer (Sub-Lieutenant RNR); Coxswain (Petty Officer pensioner); Buffer (PO); Leading hands (one RN and one RNR); three able seamen (all RN); PO steward; PO cook; telegraphist (RNVR) and Signalman (RNVR). *Devonia* also carried five Hull and three Stornoway fishermen and a dozen Maltese from Cardiff on T124 engagement for engine room and stokehold duties.

The paddlers which came through Operation Dynamo returned to minesweeping, although from the following year as more purpose-built minesweepers were completed, most of them were adapted to serve as coastal auxiliary anti-aircraft vessels or 'Eagle Ships', a term taken from a trio of paddlers from the General Steam Navigation Company's Thames-based Eagle Steamers fleet. They were designated 'Thames Special Service Ships' before the end of 1939 and given extensive anti-aircraft armament for coastal convoy escort work and in this guise *Royal Eagle*, *Golden Eagle* and *Crested Eagle* all saw service at Dunkirk, the latter becoming one of four paddle steamers to be lost or abandoned.

The minesweepers and special service ships were supplemented by two further paddle steamers called from the Southern Railway's Isle of Wight ferry service. Although hurriedly commissioned into the Royal Navy, both *Whippingham* and *Portsdown* went to Dunkirk without any armament and with time for little more than basic additional protection to their wheelhouses. Ten of the paddle steamers each carried more than a thousand troops during the course of Operation Dynamo and made several crossings – the *Medway Queen* going to Dunkirk Harbour or the beaches on no fewer than seven occasions.

Bunkering the coal-burning steamers was a problem while the evacuation was at its height. Refuelling the oil-burning ships direct from tankers specially brought in for the task was fairly straightforward and at Dover tugs became highly proficient at manoeuvring vessels requiring fuel into position. *Medway Queen* would never have managed all those trips had she been a coal-burner and, at Ramsgate, the arriving steamers unloaded their troops and then already exhausted crews had to turn to and man-handle sacks of coal onboard – and sometimes the fuel had first to be put into bags on the barge or collier.

Although four excursion paddlers were built between the end of the war and the early 1950s, and some of the Dunkirk survivors went back into civilian service, the side-wheeler's day was over. As far as even large screw vessels are concerned, the traditional pleasure cruise trade has virtually disappeared. Nevertheless, two of the best-known Dunkirk paddlers have managed to repeatedly cheat the shipbreakers. The *Medway Queen* is now moored in Damhead Creek off the River Medway and undergoing an extensive programme of restoration while the *Princess Elizabeth*, after many years as a floating restaurant on the Thames in central London, is to be found as an arts and cultural centre on the River Seine in Paris.

BRIGHTON BELLE

A steamer of handy size for secondary services, *Lady Evelyn* joined the Campbell fleet after a major competitor in the shape of Tucker's Yellow Funnel Fleet was seen off in 1922. Renamed *Brighton Belle* she was sent to the Sussex station but the problem caused by giving steamers local names was brought into focus from 1934 when the vessel was recalled to the Bristol Channel.

Built: 1900 by J. Scott & Co, Kinghorn, as *Lady Evelyn* for the Furness Railway Company, lengthened by 30 feet at Barrow 1904. Acquired by William Tucker of Cardiff 1919; P. & A. Campbell 1922 and renamed *Brighton Belle*, 1923.
Gross tonnage: 295.
Length: 170 ft.
Width: 29 ft.
Machinery: Compound diagonal, two cylinders.
Speed: 16 knots.
1939 route: Bristol Channel excursions 1934–39; stationed Sussex Coast 1923–33.

Brighton Belle was fitted out as a minesweeper at Penarth and joined the 10th Flotilla based at Dover and worked in the Channel through the first winter of the war. She sailed with the rest of the flotilla on the evening of 27th May and was returning next day with 800 troops when she ran over a submerged wreck near the North Goodwins while coming in for attention from enemy aircraft. As *Brighton Belle* settled by the stern the paddler *Medway Queen* moved alongside and took off the troops and crew.

BRIGHTON QUEEN

After twice running in opposition to P. & A. Campbell, this fine twin-funnelled steamer final-

Less than a year separates these shots of the **Brighton Belle,** *on Bristol Channel service for P. & A. Campbell in the summer of 1939, and going down by the stern on 28th May 1940 after running over a submerged wreck while returning from Dunkirk with 800 troops who were safely taken off by other vessels.* (Author's collection and Imperial War Museum)

A close-up of **Brighton Queen,** *going astern from Eastbourne Pier in 1933, and turned out in typically immaculate Campbell fashion with gleaming brasses and snowy white canvas dodgers around the bridge. The steamer made regular cross-Channel excursions from South Coast resorts until late in August 1939. She was back off the French coast on the last day of May 1940 and made one trip from Bray Beach to land troops at Margate but was hit and abandoned soon after leaving Dunkirk Harbour with a second load on 1st June.* (Robert Brutnell)

Built: 1905 by John Brown & Co, Clydebank, as *Gwalia* for the Barry Railway Company; acquired by Furness Railway as *Lady Moyra* 1910; William Tucker of Cardiff 1919; P. & A. Campbell 1922, renamed *Brighton Queen* 1933.
Gross Tonnage: 519.
Length: 245 ft.
Width: 29 ft.
Machinery: Compound diagonal, two cylinders.
Speed: 18 knots.
1939 route: Summer excursions from Sussex resorts, including cross-Channel sailings.

ly joined the fleet and then became *Brighton Queen* when sent south in 1933, reviving the name of an earlier Sussex favourite lost in the First World War. The second *Brighton Queen* regularly undertook cross-Channel excursions and carried 259 passengers from Brighton, Eastbourne and Hastings to Boulogne for the last time on 28th August 1939. By the time war had been declared barely a week later, *Brighton Queen* and two other Sussex-based Campbell vessels had already been recalled to the Bristol Channel. Fitted out to serve as a minesweeper for the second time in her career, *Brighton Queen* was part of the 7th Flotilla, based on the Forth, and regularly swept with sister ship *Devonia,* another ex-Barry Railway paddler that found her way into the Campbell fleet. Ordered south, *Brighton Queen* called at Harwich for fuel and supplies, arriving off Bray on Friday 31st May and used her own boats to load over 100 men before taking 300 off a skoot which had run aground. After towing the latter for some miles until its engine was started, *Brighton Queen* landed her troops at Margate and then returned to Dunkirk, berthing in the harbour and taking on 600 French and Algerian troops. Twenty minutes after leaving *Brighton Queen* came in for concentrated attention from a formation of German aircraft and, after a direct hit, Captain W. Watson, skipper of the Campbell steamer *Ravenswood* for two seasons before the war, gave the order to abandon ship. Some survivors were machine-gunned in the water while awaiting rescue from a Royal Navy sloop and smaller vessels.

CRESTED EAGLE

The first Thames paddle steamer built with oil-fired boilers, the *Crested Eagle* was designed with a hinged foremast and telescopic funnel to pass beneath London Bridge and berth in the Thames at the Old Swan Pier. Later, when the vessel's base became Tower Pier, a conventional funnel was fitted and, after running to Ramsgate for seven years, *Crested Eagle* was switched to a

Crested Eagle, *seen in the Pool of London, laid claim to be Europe's first oil-burning excursion steamer. After helping Thames pleasure steamers evacuate children from the capital in the opening weeks of the Second World War,* **Crested Eagle** *was converted to operate in the Thames Estuary as an anti-aircraft vessel. Leaving the East Mole crowded with troops on 29th May, the paddler suffered several hits from German Stukas and was soon blazing from stem to stern.* (Frank Pattrick)

daily London–Southend–Clacton–Felixstowe service when the larger *Royal Eagle* was completed in 1932. After the war started, *Crested Eagle* was first used to evacuate children from London before being one of three paddlers from the famous Eagle Steamers fleet to be designated Thames Special Service ships and fitted at Sheerness with special anti-aircraft equipment.

Built: 1925 by J. Samuel White & Co, Cowes, for the General Steam Navigation Company.
Gross tonnage: 1,110.
Length: 299 ft. 7 in.
Width: 34 ft. 6 in.
Machinery: Triple diagonal, three cylinders.
Speed: 18 knots.
1939 route: GSNC 'Eagle Steamers' excursion service from Tower Pier, London, to Southend, Clacton and Felixstowe.

Crested Eagle was recalled from patrol duties to Sheerness on 25th May 1940 but it was not until Tuesday 28th that she was ordered across by Route Y to La Panne. After arriving next morning, *Crested Eagle* was sent on to Dunkirk Harbour and managed to berth on the seaward side of the East Mole, her complement of troops being swelled by survivors from the Manx packet *Fenella* which was hit whilst moored astern. The paddler got underway at 18:00 and was off Malo-les-Bains when attacked by a flight of Stukas and, although the first bombs were avoided, *Crested Eagle* was struck aft of the bridge. Two more bombs ignited fuel oil tanks and the after half of the vessel was quickly a blazing inferno. Lieutenant-Commander B. R. Booth managed to beach her and the minesweeper *Albury* moved in to pick up survivors but many lives were lost.

DEVONIA

Although not used by Campbells during the 1939 season, *Devonia* was requisitioned soon after the war started and sent to Milford Haven to be converted into a minesweeper, a role she had filled with some distinction between 1914 and 1919. Commissioned at the end of 1939, the steamer went to join the 7th Flotilla at Granton and there worked regularly with sister ship *Brighton Queen* apart from a spell in February 1940 when collision damage was repaired at

Built: 1905 by John Brown & Co, Clydebank, for the Barry Railway Company; acquired by P. & A. Campbell in 1911.
Gross tonnage: 641.
Length: 245 ft.
Width: 29 ft.
Machinery: Compound diagonal, two cylinders.
Speed: 18 knots.
1939 route: Laid up throughout season, previously Bristol Channel excursions for P. & A. Campbell.

Another well-known member of the P. & A. Campbell fleet, 1914–18 war veteran **Devonia** *was serving as a minesweeper for the second time when ordered south to Dunkirk. Damaged by bombing whilst lying off La Panne on 30th May,* **Devonia** *was deliberately beached. The second photograph, believed to come from German sources, shows the abandoned wreck from the beach a few days after the end of the evacuation.* (PSPS archives and Author's collection)

Leith. Sent south towards the end of May, coaling en route at Tynemouth and Harwich, *Devonia* crossed to La Panne on 30th May and launched her boat, which made runs to the beach and assisted in loading the skoot *Hilda* which was closer to the shore. *Devonia* came under air attack and after an explosion caused serious leaks astern, the commanding officer, temporary Lieutenant J. Brotchie was instructed to beach the vessel as far inshore as possible in the hope that she could be used as a jetty and boarding point by the troops. *Devonia's* crew crossed to the *Hilda* and were later transferred to the destroyer *Scimitar* and returned to Dover. There were reports that *Devonia* had been salvaged by the Germans and put to work on the Elbe but these were unfounded and the wreck was broken up on the beach.

DUCHESS OF FIFE

Designed for year-round Clyde service, *Duchess of Fife* proved a successful and economical vessel despite having unusual four-cylinder, two-crank machinery. She served for a remarkable 50 years, including spells as a minesweeper in both World Wars and when called up again in 1939, she formed part of the Harwich-based 12th Minesweeping Flotilla which then consisted entirely of Clyde paddlers. *Duchess of Fife* sailed with the rest of the flotilla on 28th May, arriving off La Panne at midnight, and loaded troops from small boats before taking them to Margate. The steamer completed two further return trips without suffering serious damage and landed a total of 1,500 men. Not all troops were eager to board rescue ships and, despite taking lines and assisting *Duchess of Fife* to berth on one arrival in Dunkirk Harbour, none of a mass of French soldiers on the pier made a move towards the vessel and even after being harangued from the gangway by her captain, Lieutenant John Anderson, RNR, only a handful of men came forward. Fast losing patience, Lieutenant Anderson returned to his bridge and shouted for any British officer to come forward. At length, a man emerged to inquire: 'Don't be so windy. What do you want?' Lieutenant Anderson's response said it all: 'Damn you, sir, I am not windy or I wouldn't be here', he boomed back. The army officer confirmed there were no British troops in the area and suggested that as the French would not budge, *Duchess of Fife* should let go her lines and get clear. Anderson persisted, however, eventually leaving with 550 French who were landed at Margate. *Duchess of Fife* was later used

Her decks crowded with troops, the Clyde steamer **Duchess of Fife** *gets underway on one of three trips back from Dunkirk, the smoke billowing from the funnel giving an obvious indication of the efforts by those in the coal-burner's stokehold.* (Times Newspapers)

After enduring the rigours of war service for the second time, **Duchess of Fife** *was almost rebuilt in 1945–46 before returning to Clyde services. The extent of the work carried out is apparent from this view taken at Lamont's Slip in September 1945. She sailed on until 1953.* (Graham E. Langmuir)

Built: 1903 by Fairfield, Glasgow, for the Caledonian Steam Packet Company.
Gross tonnage: 329.
Length: 210 ft. 3 in.
Width: 25 ft.
Machinery: Triple diagonal, four cylinders.
Speed: 17 knots.
1939 route: Clyde services, particularly Wemyss Bay–Largs–Millport–Kilchattan Bay.

as a training vessel at Port Edgar on the Forth until returning to the Clyde and resuming on Cumbrae run. Displaced by new tonnage during June 1953, *Duchess of Fife* was broken up at Port Glasgow. Her bell was presented to Millport, a community served faithfully winter and summer for so many years.

EMPEROR OF INDIA

After a traumatic early career *Emperor of India*

Built: 1906 as *Princess Royal* by J. I. Thornycroft, Southampton, for the Southampton, Isle of Wight and South of England Royal Mail Steam Packet Company but not accepted after failing to meet contract speed. Lengthened by builders and sold in 1908 as *Emperor of India* to Cosens & Co, Weymouth.
Gross tonnage: 482.
Length: 217 ft. 2 in.
Width: 25 ft. 1 in.
Machinery: Compound diagonal, two cylinders.
Speed: 16 knots.
1939 route: Summer excursions from Bournemouth.

operated with success, although never spectacular speed. Prior to the First World War the vessel handled Cosens' longer excursions from Weymouth, including cross-Channel trips to Cherbourg, and between 1914 and 1918 served as a minesweeper, troop transport and hospital carrier, going as far as the Eastern Mediterranean. Mainly based at Bournemouth in summers between the wars, she was requisitioned in November 1939 and fitted out at Southampton as a minesweeper and attached to the 10th Flotilla

Its ornate paddle box crest and name scroll covered in drab grey, the **Emperor of India** *reaches Dover with what, by Operation Dynamo standards, is a fairly modest loading of troops in the early stages of the evacuation. The well-known Bournemouth vessel went as far as the Eastern Mediterranean during the Great War and finished the 1939–45 conflict as a training ship for stokers.* (Times Newspapers)

Pictured in excursion service between the wars, **Emperor of India** *returned to her old haunts in 1948 but with lines rather spoiled by the addition of new bridge and enclosed wheelhouse and a larger funnel.* (PSPS Archives)

based at Dover. *Emperor of India* certainly appears to have crossed to Dunkirk with the rest of the ships of the 10th on the evening of 27th May and her return to Dover was recorded by a well-known photograph in *The Times.* Whether any further trips followed has remained obscure and the vessel's officially recorded total of troops carried, 642, rather suggests that only the one return crossing was completed. Later came a spell of service on the Thames as an auxiliary anti-aircraft ship and *Emperor of India* finished the war as a training vessel for stokers. When returned to Cosens in 1948, the steamer was extensively reconditioned, converted to burn oil fuel and given a large modern-looking funnel. Although having a high standard of interior accommodation, her mechanical performance remained erratic and at times the *Emperor of India* struggled to make 10 knots. She survived to the end of the 1956 season and was scrapped in Belgium the following year.

ESSEX QUEEN

Built: 1897 by Wm Denny & Bros, Dumbarton, as *Walton Belle* for Coast Development Corporation (Belle Steamers). Operated by E. Kingsman 1920, PSM Syndicate 1921–24 and East Anglia Steamship Company 1925. Sold to New Medway SP Company and renamed *Essex Queen* 1926.
Gross tonnage: 389.
Length: 230 ft.
Width: 26 ft. 2 in.
Machinery: Triple diagonal by builders.
Speed: 17 knots.
1939 route: Laid up from September 1938, previously East coast excursions and PLA London Docks cruises.

Although over 40 years old and not commissioned by her owners in the last peacetime summer of the 1930s, the *Essex Queen* had been brought into use by the Port of London Authority as a Thames hospital carrier, a role she had filled following the Great War – but some 2,000 miles from London's river and beyond the

The last of the famous Belle Steamers in commercial service, **Essex Queen,** *originally* **Walton Belle** *of 1897, was reported at Dunkirk by a number of different sources, although her name never appeared in any official lists of participating ships.* (Author's collection)

Arctic Circle! In her original name of *Walton Belle,* the steamer was a minesweeper from 1915 until 1919 and then, equipped as a hospital ship, made a 20-day voyage to the White Sea to carry wounded from the Russian campaign along the River Dvina to Archangel, spending over four months in the area. The name of *Essex Queen* does not figure in official lists of Dunkirk vessels but the late 'Jack' Graves, *Medway Queen's* First-Lieutenant, recalled seeing *Essex Queen* in the Dover area before Operation Dynamo started and in the log of *Princess Elizabeth,* another of the paddle minesweepers from *Medway Queen's* flotilla, the master recorded that small boats used by his vessel to load troops off La Panne on 31st May were handed over to the *Essex Queen.* No other ship with a remotely similiar name was present at Dunkirk and, obviously, it must have been a substantial one to be able to take on men from several boats. *Essex Queen* was reported to have been based at Sheerness in her hospital ship role and was commanded by Captain Branthwaite, a well-known Thames skipper who was master of *Royal Eagle* up to 1939. The *Essex Queen* was sold by the New Medway Company as she lay at Southampton in 1947 to the South Western Steam Navigation Company and used as *Pride of Devon* on cruises from Torquay. After three seasons the veteran failed its survey and was laid up until scrapped at Grays in 1951.

FRESHWATER

Built: 1927 by J. Samuel White & Co, Cowes, for the Southern Railway.
Gross tonnage: 264.
Length: 152 ft. 5 in.
Width: 23 ft. 1 in.
Machinery: Compound diagonal, two cylinders.
Speed: 14 knots.
1939 route: Lymington–Yarmouth, Isle of Wight ferry service.

Freshwater was the largest and last paddle steamer built for the Southern Railway's long-established link between the mainland and West Wight but ceased to be the route's principal vessel in 1938 when a car ferry came into service. *Freshwater* remained on passenger sailings until after the summer of 1939 and was then pressed into service as a naval examination vessel in the Solent. *Freshwater's* name does not appear in any of the official lists of Operation Dynamo vessels

The little Isle of Wight passenger ferry **Freshwater** *is another vessel with claims of a Dunkirk role—despite lack of any official corroboration.* (Author's collection)

although it is fairly certain she made one return crossing at least. The paddler seems to have been sent to Sheerness as late as 1st June and at the same time as the Southern Railway steamers *Whippingham* and *Portsdown*. She was joined by actor and peacetime yachtsman Moran Caplat, an RNVR Sub-Lieutenant who was on leave in London from his own posting, a Royal Navy trawler. Walter Lord, in his book *The Miracle of Dunkirk* (Allen Lane, 1983), tells how Caplat happened to answer a telephone while staying at the Royal Ocean Racing Club. The call was from the Admiralty urgently seeking men to man vessels in the Kent ports and within an hour Caplat was on his way to Sheerness to join *Freshwater*. When the steamer went back to Lymington in 1947 she became second boat and although seeing only limited peak season service, survived until 1957, at which time she was probably the last paddler in home waters to use a sail – a staysail being hoisted at the bow to assist navigation in Lymington River. Even then *Freshwater* saw a little more service, at Brighton as *Sussex Queen* in 1960 and from Bournemouth and Swanage as *Swanage Queen* the following year. More use was planned for 1962 by new owners including Stuart Townsend, founder of cross-Channel operators Townsend Brothers Ferries, but it was found that too much work was needed and, instead of sailing, the vessel went to Belgian breakers.

GLEN AVON

Built: 1912 by Ailsa Shipbuilding Co, Troon, for P. & A. Campbell.
Gross tonnage: 509.
Length: 220 ft.
Width: 27 ft. 1 in.
Machinery: Compound diagonal, two cylinders.
Speed: 16 knots.
1939 route: P. & A. Campbell Bristol Channel excursion services.

Never intended to be a flier, *Glen Avon* joined the Campbell fleet during 1912 and was designed to provide large capacity with economy in operation and, registered at Newport, became closely associated with the Monmouth port. During the First World War *Glen Avon* was a minesweeper from December 1914 until March 1919 and then had a rather uneventful Bristol

Heading for home! The **Glen Avon** *even has troops on the reserved deck above the aft shelter as she pounds away from Dunkirk with some of almost 900 troops transported back to Britain. In happier days of Bristol Channel sailings,* **Glen Avon's** *passengers paid a few pence extra for the privelege of enjoying the passing scenery from this elevated position.* (A. G. Taylor)

Channel career until called into minesweeping service for a second time in September 1939. *Glen Avon* and other Campbell paddlers were based at North Shields, forming the 8th Flotilla, and they were ordered south to assist in the evacuation as the enormity of the Dunkirk situation became apparent. *Glen Avon* made at least two trips to the beaches near La Panne and transported a total of 888 men. Although most of the paddlers switched to other duties as the war progressed, the *Glen Avon* continued as a minesweeper and was lost in severe weather in the Bay of the Seine, off the Normandy coast, on 2nd September 1944.

GLEN GOWER

Campbell's first new steamer after the Great War did not appear until 1922, *Glen Gower's* construction being delayed by shortages of materials and shipyard strikes. The vessel received second-hand machinery from the paddler *Albion* scrapped in 1920 and, although *Glen Gower* was some 35 feet longer and broader in the beam, the engines served her well and produced a trial speed in excess of 17 knots. *Glen Gower* was stationed at Swansea in most of her early seasons and was transferred to the South Coast in 1934 to take her share of the longer excursions, including cross-Channel trips. Her final pre-war sailing to Boulogne was from Eastbourne and Hastings on 27th August 1939, when a meagre loading of 173 passengers reflected the public's growing unease over the international situation. *Glen Gower* was programmed for three more Boulogne sailings in the following week but these were cancelled and Campbell's closed their entire Sussex operation and recalled the steamers to the Bristol Channel the day before war was declared.

Glen Gower was fitted out as a minesweeper and attached to the 8th Flotilla on the Tyne,

Built: 1922 by Ailsa Shipbuilding Co, Troon, for P. & A. Campbell.
Gross tonnage: 553.
Length: 235 ft. 1 in.
Width: 28 ft. 5 in.
Machinery: Two-cylinder compound diagonal, built 1893 for steamer *Slieve Donard,* later *Albion,* broken up 1920.
Speed: 17 knots.
1939 route: Summer excursions from Sussex resorts.

Glen Gower *made one of the 1st pre-war cross-Channel excursions on 17th August 1939 and then had the distinction of re-opening the route to Boulogne in July 1954 after a break of 15 years. The P. & A. Campbell paddler, requisitioned for minesweeping, made three crossings to Dunkirk and was active right through to 1945, latterly as an anti-aircraft ship on the east coast.* **Glen Gower** *is seen below at the Underfall Yard in Bristol immediately after being returned to her owners in 1945* (A. G. Taylor) *and (bottom) back in peacetime colours approaching Brighton in 1950.* (John H. Meredith).

becoming the Senior Officer's ship. The flotilla was brought back from a sweep in the North Sea and ordered south, *Glen Gower* sailing in the company of fellow Campbell paddlers *Glen Avon* and *Waverley,* which had been renamed *Snaefell,* presumably to avoid confusion with the Clyde steamer *Waverley* which was also serving in the North Sea as a minesweeper. *Glen Gower* became *Glenmore* later in the war but made three trips to Dunkirk under her own name, transporting a total of 1,235 men according to Admiralty records. On one of the crossings *Glen Gower,* carrying around 500 men, ran aground off La Panne but the *Snaefell,* also loaded, succeeded in passing a line and then towed her off as both ships came under aerial attack. The *Glen Gower* was then signalled to make a detour to pick up a further 300 troops further down the coast but arrived at the rendezvous some three hours before the soldiers and, during the wait, occupied the attention of more German aircraft and shore batteries. During the whole operation the paddler received only a single direct hit, a shell passing right through the deck before exploding below and killing twelve sleeping troops. *Glen Gower's* skipper, Acting Commander M. A. Biddulph, was awarded the DSC and Leading Seaman J.Fleming from North Shields received the DSM for his work as coxswain of a small boat which made a dozen trips between ship and shore and ferried well over 400 troops.

Named *Glenmore* from 1941, the vessel was commanded by Lieutenant-Commander Lachlan McLean-Sheddon, who had been her chief officer in 1937. During this period the paddler ploughed through a sea of timber to rescue the crew of a torpedoed Dutch freighter that had been carrying pit props, and she also went to the aid of a Norwegian steamer. On another occasion *Glenmore* towed the damaged paddle minesweeper *Laguna Belle* back to the East Coast, both vessels being repeatedly attacked by German aircraft. *Glenmore* finished the war as an auxiliary anti-aircraft vessel based at Harwich and from November 1944 was sent to the Scheldt Estuary. After her release in 1945, *Glen Gower* was put through a thorough overhaul in time to re-open the South Coast station for Campbell's in May 1947. Apart from 1950, the paddler, still a coal burner, stayed on the Bristol Channel for each season from 1948 to 1953 but was back in Sussex for 1954 when, on 21st July, she ran a first cross-Channel trip to Boulogne for 15 years. 'No passport' trips were possible in the following year and proved a great success, with *Glen Gower* crossing on 37 occasions, often with loads up to the 562 allowed by her certificate. Bad weather ruined the 1956 season, 23 days being lost, including 17 cross-Channel trips, and *Glen Gower* then stayed on the Bristol Channel for what turned out to be a final year in service. She was broken up in Belgium in 1960.

GOLDEN EAGLE

Golden Eagle brought triple expansion engines to the Thames excursion fleet and quickly became one of the most popular vessels. Taken over by the Admiralty in September 1915, *Golden Eagle* spent the rest of the First World War as a transport and when released in November 1915 had carried 518,101 troops from Felixstowe and South Coast ports to places including Dunkirk, Calais, Boulogne, Le Havre and Rouen. On a number of occasions the paddler also conveyed aircraft to the Continent as deck cargo. *Golden Eagle* returned to the London–Margate–Ramsgate run between the wars and was converted to burn oil fuel in 1934. In the autumn of 1939 *Golden Eagle* was selected to join the other Eagle Steamers paddlers *Crested Eagle* and *Royal Eagle* in the Thames Special Service Flotilla, based at Sheerness. *Golden Eagle's* first crossing to Dunkirk was on 29th May, when she was able to pick up survivors from the Clyde paddler *Waverley* and land them, together with her own complement of men, at Ramsgate. *Golden Eagle* crossed again to Bray on 31st May and worked two boats to and from the beaches before moving to Dunkirk Harbour to take on further men to boost the loading to more than 1,000. The paddler was back in Dunkirk

Built: 1909 by John Brown & Co, Clydebank, for the General Steam Navigation Company.
Gross tonnage: 793.
Length: 275 ft. 7 in.
Width: 32 ft. 1 in.
Machinery: Triple diagonal, three cylinders.
Speed: 19 knots.
1939 route: GSNC 'Eagle Steamers' excursions from Tower Pier, London, to Southend and Ramsgate.

There is certainly a difference between these pictures of the **Golden Eagle** *setting off past the Tower of London with a crowd of day trippers for Margate and Ramsgate* (Author's collection) *and a wartime view of the same vessel bristling with anti-aircraft weapons following conversion to operate as a Thames Special Service Ship. In this guise* **Golden Eagle** *brought back 1,751 men loading both from Bray Beach and Dunkirk Harbour.* (Imperial War Museum)

Harbour in the early hours of 2nd June and returned safely, although at reduced speed after getting a rope entangled in the port paddle wheel. *Golden Eagle* carried a total of 1,751 men and returned to Thames pleasure cruises in 1947 but was laid up after the 1949 season as GSNC brought in new motor vessels and she was scrapped at Grays in 1951.

GRACIE FIELDS

The Southampton company's long tradition of royal or geographical names for its ships was broken in 1936 when the entertainer Miss Gracie Fields launched a new multi-purpose paddle steamer named in her honour and gave a rendering of 'Sing as we go' while the vessel was sliding down the Thornycroft slipway at Woolston and into the River Itchen. *Gracie Fields* was designed to run on the Southampton–Cowes

Built: 1936 by J. I. Thornycroft, Southampton, for the Southampton, Isle of Wight & South of England Royal Mail Steam Packet Co. (Red Funnel Steamers).
Gross tonnage: 393.
Length: 195 ft. 9 in.
Width: 24 ft. 9 in.
Machinery: Compound diagonal, two cylinders.
Speed: 14 knots.
1939 route: Southampton–Cowes ferry, Solent excursions and tender duties.

This postcard showing the Red Funnel paddler **Gracie Fields,** *and the star in whose honour she was named, was a popular buy among passengers after the vessel's debut in 1936. Hit and disabled when returning from La Panne with 750 troops on 29th May, she sank despite an effort by the sloop* **Pangborne** *to secure a tow. Some reports suggested that the* **Pangborne** *might have assisted the final demise of* **Gracie Fields** *with a few four-inch shells to stop the wreck from becoming a danger to other ships of the evacuation fleet.* (Author's collection)

ferry, carrying cars on her foredeck, as well as performing summer excursions and, at times, acting as tender to ocean liners in the Solent. During her first season she made a special visit to Brighton to take Miss Fields and children from an orphanage she supported on a sea cruise and, later in the same summer, the paddler was based at Bournemouth during the time the star was appearing in the resort. *Gracie Fields* was very quickly requisitioned when the war started in September 1939 and after conversion for mine-sweeping duties, became part of the 10th Flotilla, based at Dover. The steamer's popular peacetime master Captain N. R. Larkin, stayed with the rank of Temporary Lieutenant, and it was on the evening of 27th May that he took her across to the beaches east of Dunkirk for the first time, *Gracie Fields* loading 281 men and successfully transporting them to Dover. A second visit to the beaches next day produced a load of 750 men at La Panne and the steamer was heading back when bombed near Middel Kirk Buoy and hit in the engine room. Steam escaping from burst pipes swept the engine room and upper deck and with no way of stopping the engine and the rudder jammed, *Gracie Fields* began to circle at six knots. Two skoots managed to get alongside in turn and take off troops before the sloop *Pangbourne* transferred the remainder of the men and then took the damaged vessel in tow. Progress was painfully slow and in the night, as *Gracie Fields* filled with water, the remaining skeleton crew were taken off shortly before the vessel sank. Captain Larkin was among the survivors and, after the war, returned to serve Red Funnel until retirement in 1961, his commands including *Princess Elizabeth*, another of the company's vessels at Dunkirk.

LAGUNA BELLE

Another of the famous Belle Steamers, the old *Southend Belle* served as a minesweeper from April 1916 to November 1919 and changed hands several times between the wars, becoming *Laguna Belle* in 1930 when bought by Mr H. E. Kingsman, owner of Clacton Pier, to run a special cheap service from Tower Pier to the Essex resort and calling en route only at Greenwich and North Woolwich. *Laguna Belle* continued to serve Clacton after joining the General Steam Navigation Company fleet in 1936 and her run was also extended to include Walton-on-the-Naze. She operated right up to the start of the war in September 1939 and despite being over 40 years old was again taken for service as a minesweeper, joining the Dover-based 10th Flotilla. *Laguna Belle* is not officially listed among the Operation Dynamo ships but the late 'Jack' Graves, First-Lieutenant of the *Medway Queen*, was always adamant that all the 10th Flotilla's eight vessels left Dover for the beaches on the night of 27th May, the line-up also including *Thames Queen*, another former Belle steamer just two years *Laguna Belle's* junior. As recorded earlier, there was a later occasion when the Campbell paddler *Glen Gower*, then serving as *Glenmore*, assisted a damaged *Laguna Belle* back to port, the Thames veteran finishing the war as an accommodation ship. She was technically returned to the General Steam Company at Southampton in 1945 but they sold her as she lay to Dutch breakers early in 1946.

Built: 1896 by Wm Denny & Bros, Dumbarton, as *Southend Belle* for the London, Woolwich and Clacton-on-Sea Steamboat Company (later Belle Steamers); acquired by East Anglian Steamship Company, 1925; East Anglian Hotels 1929; H. E. Kingsman 1930, when renamed *Laguna Belle;* General Steam Navigation Company. 1936.
Gross tonnage: 617.
Length: 249 ft.
Width: 30 ft.
Machinery: Compound diagonal, two cylinders.
Speed: 16 knots.
1939 route: London–Clacton–Walton-on-the-Naze excursions and Port of London Authority docks cruises.

The Belle steamers were considered quite trim in their day but conversion for wartime duties made them look hideous. Compare this picture of **Laguna Belle** *as an anti-aircraft vessel after Dunkirk with the earlier view of near-sister* **Essex Queen.** (Imperial War Museum)

MARMION

Designed for the North British Company's Loch Long service, the *Marmion* was an attractive single-funnel steamer with much gold embellishment on the black hull and paddle boxes. But she was never the same following First War service as a minesweeper from February 1915, for which the promenade deck was extended to the bow and plated in. *Marmion* returned to Clyde services in this condition in 1920 but the draught had increased, with a resulting drop in speed, and there were such stability problems that the steamer was withdrawn from service at the end of the season. Her exasperated owners eventually told the Admiralty that *Marmion* had been rendered useless and demanded that either the ship be put back to its original condition at Admiralty expense or be taken off the railway company's hands with suitable compensation paid. Alterations, financed by the Admiralty, were finally put in hand in 1923 – by which time the North British had been absorbed into the London and North Eastern Railway - and *Marmion's* promenade deck was shortened by over 60 feet. Surprisingly, the steamer was not brought into service for another four years, then performing general duties until going back on the Arrochar run in 1938 and 1939. *Marmion* was requisitioned as a minesweeper within a few weeks of the start of the war and, after fitting out on the Clyde, made the long haul round to the East Coast and a place, along with other Scottish paddlers, in the 12th Flotilla at Harwich. She sailed direct from the Essex base to Dunkirk with *Waverley, Duchess of Fife* and *Oriole,* arriving off the beaches in the early hours of 29th May, and transported a total of 713 men back to England. *Marmion* returned to Harwich and was bombed during an air raid on the port on 9th April 1941, sinking in shallow water. The wreck was raised, but *Marmion* was not worth repairing and was scrapped.

Built: 1906 by A. & J. Inglis, Pointhouse, for the North British Railway Company; ownership transferred to London and North Eastern Railway, 1923.
Gross tonnage: 409.
Length: 120 ft.
Width: 24 ft.
Machinery: Compound diagonal, two cylinders.
Speed: 16 knots.
1939 route: Clyde services from Craigendoran and Greenock.

Marmion *sailed with other Clyde steamers of the 12th Minesweeping Flotilla to Dunkirk and came through the evacuation unscathed. But this was how she finished up after being bombed at Harwich in April 1941. Although raised, the vessel was not considered worth putting back into service.* (Rev. Wm. C. Galbraith collection)

MEDWAY QUEEN

Medway Queen's Dunkirk exploits made her the most famous of all the paddle steamers and ferries participating in Operation Dynamo and, half a century on, she is the largest survivor of the vessels which brought back troops. *Medway Queen* completed no fewer than seven return trips to Dunkirk and although officially recorded as landing 3,046 men, the vessel's officers calculated that the true figure, including survivors taken from the sinking *Brighton Belle,* exceeded 6,000 and was probably closer to 7,000. Built for the New Medway Company and at first placed on the Rochester–Southend–Clacton summer service, *Medway Queen* later became closely associated with the Herne Bay run – although there were times when visits to Margate and Felixstowe fully utilised a certificate allowing operation inside a line from the North Foreland to Orford Ness. Able to carry up to 980 passengers, she received a new oil-fired boiler in 1938.

After the start of the war curtailed 1939 sailings, *Medway Queen* was requisitioned during September and conversion for minesweeping began during the following month in Deptford Creek. Although commissioned in November, it was January 1940 before *Medway Queen* joined the 10th Flotilla at Dover and became sub-divisional leader. The steamer first sailed for Dunkirk with the remainder of the flotilla on the evening of 27th May and, after loading from the beaches during the night, began a return crossing soon after 7 a.m., shooting down a German aircraft as air raids developed. *Medway Queen* took troops and crew off the sinking *Brighton Belle* on the way back to Dover. The flotilla left Dover again in the evening and this time went to Dunkirk Harbour, but thereafter vessels operated independently and *Medway Queen* slotted into a routine of sailing in the evening, loading during the night and returning at dawn. From the second day onwards the paddler used Ramsgate, which was less heavily congested than Dover, and her trips were almost equally divided between Dunkirk Harbour and the open beaches. *Medway Queen's* last crossing on the evening of 3rd June saw her reach the Harbour at around midnight and some 400 French troops were taken aboard during heavy shelling. Then, a destroyer moored astern was hit and flung forward, badly damaging the steamer's starboard paddle box and sponson. But at 1 a.m., following some feverish work by the crew to cut away buckled steelwork that was obstructing the wheel, *Medway Queen* was nursed away from the Mole by her skipper, Lieutenant A. T. Cook, and slowly crossed to Dover – the crew hearing a BBC radio broadcast reporting their ship's loss on the way! When the paddler finally limped in to Dover ships large and small sounded their whistles in salute and a 'Well done *Medway Queen*' signal was received from Vice Admiral Ramsay. The Admiralty, having previously listed the vessel among Dunkirk casualties, quickly issued an additional bulletin stating: 'The paddle mine-sweeper *Medway Queen,* believed lost, has now arrived safely in port.'

The paddler resumed minesweeping duties after repairs and crew leave, continuing until 1942, first at Dover and later based on the Tyne. While many of her contemporaries became auxiliary anti-aircraft ships, *Medway Queen's* minesweeping gear was retained when she became a training vessel. She was finally handed back to the New Medway Company at Southampton and was reconditioned there by the Thornycroft yard before going back to the Medway and returning to the excursion service in May 1947. Ill-health prevented *Medway Queen's* pre-war skipper Bob Hayman from resuming and his place was taken by Leonard Horsham, who remained in command until the vessel's last sailing to Southend and Herne Bay in September 1963. The old steamer was laid-up and despite preservation efforts she appeared to be destined for Belgian breakers until she was bought by a group of Isle of Wight businessmen and towed to the River Medina and moored in a former mill pond as centrepiece of a marina development at Binfield. An impressively restored *Medway Queen* was opened in May 1966 by 'Jack' Graves, her First-Lieutenant at Dunkirk, and for a time the operation prospered to such an extent that two more paddle steamers, *Ryde* – sister ship of Dunkirk paddler *Sandown* – and the little former River Dart vessel *Kingswear Castle,* arrived on the scene. As the 1970s progressed the marina business changed hands on several occasions and *Ryde* became the headquarters ship. Then the whole operation went into liquidation and after being removed from the mill pond and placed in the River Medina itself, *Medway Queen* became increasingly neglected.

Built: 1924 by Ailsa Shipbuilding Co, Troon, for the New Medway Steam Packet Company.
Gross tonnage: 316.
Length: 179 ft. 9 in.
Width: 24 ft. 2 in.
Machinery: Compound diagonal, two cylinders.
Speed: 15 knots.
1939 route: Summer excursions from Chatham to Southend, Herne Bay and Clacton.

The 40th Anniversary of her Dunkirk heroics in 1980 found the vessel almost derelict and four years passed before the rusted wreck was eased on to a submersible pontoon and towed 'home' to the River Medway. Alas, those responsible for moving the ship lacked resources to proceed with restoration and *Medway Queen* lay in a Chatham mud berth and filled with water on each successive tide. Fortunately, paddle steamer enthusiasts from the Medway area felt it unthinkable that such a famous vessel should be allowed to rot and in June 1985, after a public meeting, the Medway Queen Preservation Society was

Four distinct phases in the career of **Medway Queen,** *perhaps the most famous of all the paddle steamers which went to Dunkirk:* **Left** *The vessel is seen at Ramsgate as a minesweeper earlier in 1940 and looking very much as she did when making seven crossings during Operation Dynamo* (J. G. Graves); **Top right** *Twenty-two years on, and the indefatigable Leonard Horsham brings his charge towards Herne Bay Pier on a July afternoon in 1963, just one year before the* **Medway Queen** *was taken out of service* (Cedric Greenwood); **Centre** *After some years of successful static operation as centrepiece of a marina in the Isle of Wight,* **Medway Queen** *became neglected and the almost derelict steamer is seen arriving back on the River Medway on a submersible pontoon in 1984 (Bernie Thompson);* **Bottom** *Only in more recent times has restoration work started and, as this April 1989 photograph reveals, the Medway Queen Preservation Society has a long way to go* (Author)

formed. In the next couple of years tons of mud was pumped from the hull and holes patched while problems over legal ownership of the *Medway Queen* herself were sorted out. The vessel was finally refloated on 1st November 1987 and, a week later, she was towed down the Medway to a new and sheltered berth in Damhead Creek, on the Hoo Peninsular, where a major restoration effort then got into its stride. Membership of the Preservation Society swelled to more than 700 and, during 1988, the body received financial backing from local authorities. It is still surprising, however, that Chatham Historic Dockyard has never seen fit to offer facilities.

ORIOLE (EAGLE III)

Eagle III was the last Clyde steamer to be built with a single diagonal engine and also had an equally outmoded haystack boiler. During the First World War she served as a minesweeper from 1916, based first at Grimsby, then Harwich, and it was to Harwich that she was sent in 1939 when fitted out for minesweeping again, this time renamed *Oriole*. After reaching La Panne with other units of her flotilla early on 29th May, *Oriole's* skipper, Lieutenant Edwin Davies, saw the problems being encountered by small boats working off the beach and ran his vessel aground in 10 feet of water. Although she was high and dry for much of the day, when the tide came back an estimated 2,000 men were able to wade out to the steamer and cross her decks to board other vessels and be ferried to larger ships. The *Oriole* had dropped two kedge anchors on the way in and was able to haul herself off and sail to Margate with a full load of 700 troops, among them patients and nurses from one of the final field hospitals to be evacuated. Even amid the chaos of the moment, Lieutenant Davies thought fit to advise the Admiralty of his actions and sent his now famous signal, 'Deliberately grounded HMS *Oriole* Belgian coast dawn on May 29th on own initiative, objective speedy evacuation of troops. Refloated dusk same day, no apparent damage. Will complete S.232 when operations permit—meantime am again proceeding Belgian coast and will run aground again if such course seems desirable,' which produced a reply that was a classic of simplicity: 'Your action fully approved.' Davies was as good as his word and beached the *Oriole* a second time, again using kedge anchors, when she sailed in the evening of 31st May and arrived off La Panne at 4 a.m. next day. After returning to Margate the steamer made two more trips to Dunkirk Harbour before a fifth crossing on 3rd June when her entire crew was relieved by that from the paddle minesweeper *Plinlimmon* which had moved down from Granton with the rest of the 7th Flotilla but had not been sent over because of defective degaussing equipment. *Oriole* came back with around 50 Dutch and French men just before the signal concluding the operation and the two crews again changed back to their original ships. The officially recorded figure of men transported by *Oriole* was put at 2,587, but a rough tally kept by Davies produced a figure closer to 5,000 and did

Built: 1910 by Napier & Miller, Glasgow, for Buchanan Steamers; acquired by the Caledonian Steam Packet Company, 1935 and then transferred to Williamson-Buchanan Steamers (1936) Ltd.
Gross tonnage: 441.
Length: 215 ft.
Width: 25 ft. 1 in.
Machinery: Single diagonal.
Speed: 16 knots.
1939 route: Glasgow to Lochgoilhead, Dunoon, Rothesay and the Kyles of Bute.

not include those who crossed the decks of the paddler to reach other craft when she was beached at La Panne. Later in the war the vessel was used as an accommodation ship until released in 1945 and laid up in Holy Loch. By then her boiler was in need of replacement. Because of the problems of obtaining a new haystack boiler, and the high cost, reconditioning was ruled out and in

Eagle III, *distinctive through having a promenade deck carried right to the bow over an open foredeck (above left), was forced to discard her Clyde finery for austere grey before 1939 was out and on the 29th May 1940 the steamer, by then HM minesweeper* **Oriole,** *could be found high and dry at La Panne after being deliberately beached (left). As the safety valves lift and a plume of steam is released from behind the funnel, troops are congregating at the stern and, during the day, an estimated 2,000 crossed her decks to board other vessels.* (P. A. Vicary and J. Rutherford Crosby) *Time finally caught up with* **Eagle III** *when the war ended. The boiler was in need of replacement and with other expensive work unavoidable it was decided that the breakers' yard was the only alternative. The veteran of two world wars is seen (below) forlornly awaiting her fate at Port Glasgow in 1946* (Rev. Wm. C. Galbraith collection)

1946 she was towed to Port Glasgow to be broken up.

PLINLIMMON (CAMBRIA)

Built: 1895 by H. McIntyre & Co, Alloa, for P. & A. Campbell.
Gross tonnage: 433.
Length: 225 ft.
Width: 26 ft. 1 in.
Machinery: Compound diagonal, two cylinders.
Speed: 18 knots.
1939 route: Bristol Channel excursions.

For the best part of the 50 years since Dunkirk, the paddle minesweeper *Plinlimmon*, better known as the crack P. & A. Campbell steamer *Cambria*, has been at the centre of one of Operation Dynamos' greatest debates. It has never been proved really conclusively whether or not she actually crossed to the French shores, despite appearing in the official list of participating ships and being credited with transporting 900 troops! With claims to being the fastest paddler in British waters, *Cambria* was the vessel chosen by Campbell's to compete around the turn of the century for a share of the South Coast trade with the other well-established operators at Southampton and Bournemouth. After being re-boilered in 1912, *Cambria* served as a minesweeper from 1914 to 1919 and was again prominent on long distance Bristol Channel excursions through the 1920s and '30s, receiving another new boiler during the winter of 1935–36.

When the war started, *Cambria* was requisitioned once more and fitted out in Bristol before going to Granton as part of the 7th Minesweeping Flotilla. She was certainly ordered south with other ships of the Flotilla as the evacuation began, but from there the picture becomes cloudy. Lieutenant Edwin Davies, skipper of the Clyde paddler *Oriole*, was sure *Plinlimmon* did not cross owing to a fault with her degaussing equipment. He explained: '*Oriole*, under my command, and completing her fourth trip, berthed alongside at Margate to disembark 750 officers and men at 8.20 a.m. on 3rd June. After the troops were off-loaded and we had replenished essential supplies, I was instructed to take my ship to an anchorage where *Plinlimmon* came alongside and the entire ship's companies exchanged vessels. The exchange was made without incident and with *Plinlimmon's* crew the *Oriole* sailed on her fifth trip. We, as we stood, walked on board *Plinlimmon* and I took her to anchor where we all dropped in our tracks.' Davies was quite certain that *Plinlimmon* had not previously carried troops and remarked on the contrast between her onboard condition and that of his own ship. However, there are claims that *Plinlimmon* was at Dunkirk on 31st May, a dim photograph coming to light and purporting to show her alongside the Mole. The picture was taken from the bridge of *Queen of Thanet* by one of her officers and while the paddler seen stern on certainly appears to have Campbell lines, it could just as easily have been *Westward Ho* or even *Snaefell*. After completing minesweeping duties, *Plinlimmon* was used as an accommodation ship for the remainder of the war and was then laid up in London docks where she was severely damaged by fire in August 1946. Handed back to the Director of Sea Transport in the following November, the *Cambria* never returned to the Bristol Channel and was sold for breaking up at Grays, a process assisted by a further fire on board in December 1946.

PRINCESS ELIZABETH

One of only two surviving Dunkirk paddle steamers, *Princess Elizabeth* is to be located on the River Seine in Paris and used as a cultural and arts centre. Although appearing in 1927, the steamer was virtually a copy of the *Princess Mary*, completed in 1911 and lost during the First World War and included the by then outdated feature of having side alleyways around the main saloon. In addition to regular work on the

Built: 1927 by Day, Summers & Co, Northam, for Southampton, Isle of Wight & South of England Royal Mail Steam Packet Company.
Gross tonnage: 371.
Length: 195 ft.
Width: 24 ft. 2 in.
Machinery: Compound diagonal, two cylinders.
Speed: 14 knots.
1939 route: Southampton–Isle of Wight ferry services and summer excursions from Bournemouth.

Princess Elizabeth *back in Dover Harbour for the first time since her spell as part of the 10th Minesweeping Flotilla in 1940. The vessel was sheltering from severe gales in December 1987 while being towed from the Thames to Rouen for conversion into an arts centre on the River Seine. During Operation Dynamo* **Princess Elizabeth** *completed four crossings to the beaches.* (Dover Harbour Board)

Southampton–Cowes ferry run, when ten or more cars were carried on the open foredeck, she was useful for excursion work and was at Bournemouth in the summer of 1939. Quickly taken over by the Admiralty during September, the *Princess Elizabeth* was equipped for minesweeping at Southampton and found her way to Dover and a place in the 10th Flotilla. All of the vessel's four evacuation crossings were to the beaches east of Dunkirk, the first two being to La Panne on the evenings of 27th and 28th in company with other ships from the flotilla. When loading on the morning of Wednesday 29th, *Princess Elizabeth* was ordered to the assistance of another Southampton vessel, *Gracie Fields*, which had been bombed. However, she was sent back to the beach when other vessels reached the damaged paddler first. The *Princess Elizabeth* made two further crossings to Bray and, in all, transported 1,673 men. After more minesweeping the paddler became an auxiliary anti-aircraft ship until returned to Southampton in 1944.

She resumed excursion sailings in the summer of 1946 after a refit which included conversion to burn oil fuel and extension of the main saloon to the full width of the hull. Although based at Southampton, *Princess Elizabeth* went as far as Bournemouth each week and became the first excursion vessel to use the pier there since 1939 and also re-opened the pier at Yarmouth, Isle of Wight. *Princess Elizabeth* was Red Funnel's last paddle steamer when withdrawn in 1959 but she ran for a further six years for different owners, putting in two seasons at Torquay, one from Bournemouth and then three based at Weymouth. Sale in 1966 for use as a floating casino began a chequered period for *Princess Elizabeth* during which the engine and boiler were removed and the vessel was at one time in shipbreakers' hands. Eventually she was bought and moved to the River Thames, opening in June 1970 as a floating restaurant and pub exactly 40 years to the hour of the final Dunkirk departure from Bray beach. Originally moored below Tower Bridge, the *Princess Elizabeth* moved in 1975 to a berth at the Old Swan Pier above London Bridge, continuing until 1987 when taken downstream prior to reported conversion as a yacht club headquarters near Gravesend. The plan did not materialise and after being on the market she was sold to the Association de Défense des Arts Typographiques and towed to Rouen to refit before being finally established in Paris. During the tow, in December 1987, the *Princess Elizabeth* was forced by bad weather to shelter at Dover, her first visit to the port since being based there during the Second World War.

PORTSDOWN

Portsdown was one of the older Portsmouth ferries left to keep open the passenger service to Ryde after other vessels were taken away for minesweeping. *Portsdown's* own call came at the end of May: from the 30-minute run through Spithead, the paddler was taken to Sheerness and hurriedly commissioned under the command of RNR Sub-Lieutenant R. H. Church, hoisting the white ensign on 1st June. She was still in peacetime colours and during the first crossing members of the crew tried to camouflage as much of the white superstructure as possible, also packing the wheelhouse with kapok to give some protection against splinters. Then, a dummy gun was made from wood and canvas to defy the might of the Luftwaffe! Shells landed astern and alongside as the steamer tried to enter Dunkirk Harbour before being taken further east. There *Portsdown's* two 15-foot lifeboats were launched and began to bring troops out from the beach, one boat being blown from the water after three trips while the other sank due to an accumulation of damage following four runs. Without boats, Church solved the problem by putting *Portsdown's* bow on to the beach and holding it there until the tide began to ebb, finally pulling away at 4 a.m. as dawn was breaking. On the way back, the paddler assisted a French ship to refloat to the west of Dunkirk and then took 25 men off a motor boat. *Portsdown* next went to the aid of a heavily laden lighter that was in difficulties and embarked its complement of troops and Commander Clouston and some of his pier party who were returning for a break from their work in Dunkirk. By then carrying over 600 men, *Portsdown's* progress was hampered by a defective compass but directional guidance was received from the anti-aircraft cruiser *Calcutta* and the steamer reached Ramsgate safely. A brief moment of glory over, *Portsdown* returned to the Isle of Wight ferry until mined and sunk off Southsea when making an early morning run to Ryde in September 1944.

Built: 1928 by Caledon & Co, Dundee, for the Southern Railway.
Gross tonnage: 342.
Length: 190 ft.
Width: 25 ft. 1 in.
Machinery: Compound diagonal, two cylinders.
Speed: 14 knots.
1939 route: Portsmouth–Ryde ferry service.

The Southern Railway steamer **Portsdown** *was still in peacetime colours when called from the Isle of Wight ferry service to join the evacuation fleet. After surviving an eventful trip visiting Dunkirk Harbour and Bray Beach,* **Portsdown** *returned to Portsmouth and was lost off Southsea after hitting a mine while taking the mail run to Ryde in September 1944.* (Author's collection)

QUEEN OF THANET

Built: 1916 by W. Hamilton & Co, Port Glasgow, as HM paddle minesweeper *Melton.* Sold as scrap in 1927 to Hughes Bolckow Shipbreaking, but re-sold in 1929 to the New Medway Steam Packet Company and rebuilt as passenger steamer *Queen of Thanet.*
Gross tonnage: 792.
Length: 234 ft. 9 in.
Width: 29 ft. 1 in.
Machinery: Compound diagonal, two cylinders.
Speed: 16 knots.
1939 route: Laid up 1939, previously excursions from Thames and Medway.

The only two vessels from a large class of First World War paddle minesweepers to be converted for civilian use, both *Melton* and sister vessel *Atherstone* were acquired by the New Medway Company and rebuilt to enter service as *Queen of Thanet* and *Queen of Kent. Queen of Thanet* was actually bought from shipbreakers and made an excursion debut in 1929 and although not particularly fast offered large capacity and was used on cruises to French ports or Dover from Gravesend, Southend or Clacton, as well as some even longer hauls from Sheerness and Southend to Great Yarmouth and back. Neither of the Queens was in service during 1939, partly due to the availability of a third large motor vessel in the Thames fleet, yet both were quickly requisitioned after the war started and restored to their original role as minesweepers. *Queen of Thanet* became senior officer's ship of the 7th Flotilla, based at Granton, and sailed south in the final week of May when called upon for Dynamo. The steamer made four crossings in all, transporting 2,500 troops to Margate, plus a further 2,000 taken off the personnel vessel *Prague.* This was on 1st June during *Queen of Thanet's* third crossing and represented an excellent piece of seamanship by her commanding officer, Commander S. P. Herival, who put the paddler alongside the damaged ferry while both continued to steam towards the English coast. Naval vessels had taken around 500 men off and after inquiring how many were left, and being told 2,000, Commander Herival said *Queen of Thanet* would take them all.

After further minesweeping work, *Queen of Thanet* was Control Ship, Selsey, during the Normandy Landings and was responsible for the assembly and dispatch of the Phoenix and Whale sections of the Mulberry Harbour. Both *Queen of Thanet* and her sister resumed Thames excursions in 1946 but were replaced by motor vessels and sold in 1948 to the Southampton, Isle of Wight and South of England Royal Mail Steam Packet Company, the *Queen of Thanet* becoming *Solent Queen* in the Red Funnel fleet and entering service at Whitsun 1949. The vessel was on the slip being prepared for 1951 sailings when the after end was badly damaged by fire. She was declared a constructive total loss, and was broken up at Dover later in the year. *Queen of Kent,* which had become *Lorna Doone,* saw service with Red Funnel to the end of the 1951 season before she too was scrapped.

The French tricolour fluttering at the yard arm, opposite the New Medway Steam Packet Company's own house flag, indicates a cross-Channel destination for **Queen of Thanet** *as she pounds away from Southend for a 1930's summer day-trip. Four years after bringing back 2,500 men from Dunkirk in four crossings – and also taking another big load from the damaged personnel carrier* **Prague** *– the* **Queen of Thanet** *was to play a part in the Normandy Landings.* (Imperial War Museum)

ROYAL EAGLE

The GSNC still remained loyal to paddle propulsion for their first large vessel of the 1930s and, although shorter than her immediate predecessor, *Crested Eagle*, the Mersey-built *Royal Eagle* had a much more substantial superstructure and, if anything, looked larger than her 1,539 tons. Like earlier steamers her open bridge was positioned behind the funnel and immediately over the paddle boxes, a feature useful in the evenings when it was usual for the vessel to turn below Greenwich and complete journeys astern. With luxurious facilities and dining saloons seating over 300, *Royal Eagle* became understandably popular on the traditional Thames service from Tower Pier to Southend, Margate and Ramsgate. When war came in September 1939, *Royal Eagle* made some evacuation trips from London and was then sent to Sheerness for conversion to serve as an anti-aircraft vessel in the Thames Special Service Flotilla. The steamer

Built: 1932 by Cammell Laird, Birkenhead, for the General Steam Navigation Company.
Gross tonnage: 1,539.
Length: 292 ft. 1 in.
Width: 36 ft. 7 in.
Machinery: Triple diagonal, three cylinders.
Speed: 18 knots.
1939 route: Excursion service from Tower Pier, London, to Southend, Margate and Ramsgate.

Largest of the Dunkirk paddlers, **Royal Eagle,** *seen above in 1938, was really rendered obsolete by large motor vessels introduced to Thames excursion routes before the war and enjoyed a peacetime career totalling only 13 seasons until taken out of service in 1950. In addition to three trips to Dunkirk, the rest of the war, and a role in the defence of London as an anti-aircraft vessel, was probably her finest hour. Despite the camouflage paint, she retained her distinctive eagle emblem at the front of the superstructure right through from 1939 until 1945.* (Author's collection and Imperial War Museum)

crossed to La Panne on 29th May 1940 and after loading from small craft through the day, left during the evening and landed 900 men at Margate the next morning. On 31st May the paddler reached Sheerness with an estimated 1,900 aboard, including 40 seriously wounded. *Royal Eagle* went direct from Sheerness to the beaches for a third trip on 1st June and, all told, was attacked from the air on 43 occasions during her crossings. Officially recorded as transporting 2,657 men, *Royal Eagle* returned to anti-aircraft duties until released and hurried back into service for the summer of 1946, although her trips went only as far as Margate. She switched to the Southend and Clacton run in 1950 but ran only for a few weeks in the peak season and was then laid up, never to sail commercially again. The largest British post-war paddler languished until sold for scrapping in November 1953.

When completed in 1934, the **Sandown** *represented considerable advances in size and facilities for the Isle of Wight ferry run, and in her early years also did some excursion work. After the war, the ship's appearance was marred when the pole mast was replaced by a tripod structure topped by a radar scanner.* (PSPS Archives)

SANDOWN

Built: 1934 by Wm Denny & Bros, Dumbarton, for the Southern Railway.
Gross tonnage: 684.
Length: 216 ft.
Width: 29 ft. 1 in.
Machinery: Triple diagonal, three cylinders.
Speed: 14 knots.
1939 route: Portsmouth–Ryde ferry year round with occasional summer excursions.

After introducing *Portsdown* and two other 1920s paddlers which were little changed in design and appearance to vessels brought out before the First World War, the Southern Railway received a much more modern and advanced steamer when Dennys delivered the *Sandown* in 1934. Although designed for year-round work on the Portsmouth–Ryde ferry, on which 974 passengers could be carried, the *Sandown's* early summers included some excursions to Isle of Wight piers. Requisitioned on 27th September 1939, *Sandown* went to Thornycroft's Woolston yard at Southampton and was converted for minesweeping before going round to Dover to become senior officer's ship of the 10th Flotilla under Acting Commander K.M. Greig. Apart from often strenuous minesweeping work in the bitter first winter of the war, *Sandown* was involved in covering the evacuation of Dutch ports immediately prior to Dunkirk. Commander Greig led the flotilla away from Dover on 27th May and they crossed as a unit again next evening. After that, vessels usually operated independently and *Sandown* had a particularly hectic day on 1st June. While crossing to France the paddler answered a distress call from the flare-burning drifter *Golden Girl*, aground on the Goodwin Sands, and, in darkness, used her motor boat to ferry 250 troops across in five trips. *Sandown* took the men to Ramsgate before setting off again at 11 a.m. and within three hours was off Bray beach and had

The black top of the funnel marks **Sandown** *as senior officer's ship in the 10th Minesweeping Flotilla in this 1940 picture taken from* **Medway Queen,** *with the* **Gracie Fields** *beyond.* (J. G. Graves)

commenced loading from small boats. By this stage of the operation the German batteries at Nieuport were getting too accurate for comfort and twice *Sandown* up-anchored and altered position to upset the aim of the gunners. Magnetic mines were also dropped nearby before the paddler finished loading and headed for home half an hour before midnight with 910 troops. Most of the time while small boats were working between the shore and the *Sandown* their task was made more difficult by heavy swell and, in his log, Commander Greig noted with obvious pride that ratings from the stokehold had volunteered for extra duties to help man them. *Sandown* transported 1,861 men and returned to minesweeping based at Lowestoft and Granton before being re-armed for anti-aircraft work on the Thames. In 1944, *Sandown* moved to the South Coast to play a part in naval operations supporting the Normandy Landings and after further service in the Scheldt Estuary was released to return to the Ryde ferry route in 1945. Although thoroughly reconditioned the vessel was not converted to oil-firing and remained a coal-burner. For a few years immediately after the war the Isle of Wight enjoyed a holiday boom and huge queues became the weekend norm at Portsmouth and Ryde as ferries ran a shuttle service. Following the arrival of two new motor vessels during 1948, the Sandown was no longer required for winter work but sailed on each summer until 1965 and was sold to Belgian breakers and towed away to Antwerp in February of the following year.

SNAEFELL (WAVERLEY)

This popular steamer had an eventful career in both World Wars and, although surviving Dunkirk, was bombed and sunk off the North East Coast in 1941. Built for a triangular service on the Bristol Channel and linking Barry with Minehead and Weston Super Mare, the *Barry* joined the Campbell fleet towards the end of 1911. Used as a transport in 1914 and 1915 she went to the Mediterranean and was a transport and store carrier at Gallipoli and was the last ship to leave Suvla Bay following the evacuation.

Built: 1907 John Brown & Co, Clydebank, as *Barry* for the Barry Railway Company; operated by Bristol Channel Passenger Boats 1910–11; acquired by P. & A. Campbell 1911, renamed *Waverley* in 1926.
Gross tonnage: 497.
Length: 225 ft. 6 in.
Width: 26 ft. 6 in.
Machinery: Compound diagonal, two cylinders.
Speed: 17 knots.
1939 route: Summer excursions from Sussex resorts.

Later there was service at Salonika and the name was changed to *Barryfield* in 1917. Following reconditioning, she returned to Bristol Channel services until renamed *Waverley*—after the pioneer Campbell steamer—and being sent to the South Coast in 1926. Apart from 1934 and 1935 she undertook secondary services from the Sussex resorts right through to 1939 and was called back to the Bristol Channel on 2nd September 1939, the day before the war started. After conversion for minesweeping she was commissioned as *Snaefell* and attached to the 8th Flotilla at North Shields. Having been ordered

Built alongside the famous Cunarder **Mauretania** *and a veteran of Gallipoli in 1915, the Campbell paddler* **Waverley** *approaches Eastbourne Pier a few short weeks before World War II started. Appearing as a minesweeper before the end of 1939, she was named* **Snaefell** *to avoid confusion with the Clyde paddler* **Waverley** *which had also been requisitioned. In the second photograph* **Snaefell** *is seen heading for the beaches to the east of Dunkirk and towing a string of small boats for use in ferrying troops. In all she carried 981 men to safety.* (Robert Brutnell and A. G. Taylor)

south, she crossed to the beaches with *Glen Gower* and *Glen Avon* from the same flotilla and at one stage succeeded in hauling off a grounded *Glen Gower* when both vessels were loaded with troops and coming under fire. *Snaefell* went on to return almost a thousand men to English shores and continued minesweeping from the Tyne until sunk 13 months later.

Built: 1898 by Wm Denny & Bros as *Yarmouth Belle* for Coast Development, acquired 1921 by PSM Syndicate, sold 1925 to East Anglian Steamship Company, and in 1929 to the New Medway Steam Packet Company and renamed *Queen of Southend.* Name changed again in 1938 to *Thames Queen.*
Gross tonnage: 517.
Length: 210 ft.
Width: 28 ft. 1 in.
Machinery: Compound diagonal, two cylinders.
Speed: 16 knots.
1939 route: New Medway Steam Packet Company summer excursions from Chatham and Southend to Herne Bay, Margate and Ramsgate.

THAMES QUEEN

Although her name never appeared in any official records, men who were there at the time were quite certain that *Thames Queen* played a part in the early stages of Operation Dynamo at least. The vessel's first years as *Yarmouth Belle* in the well-known Belle Steamers fleet were interrupted by the Great War and service as a minesweeper from 1916 to 1919. She changed hands several times during the 1920s, finally appearing in New Medway colours as *Queen of Southend* from 1929. In the winter of 1935–36, when almost 40 years old, the steamer's old narrow forward saloon was removed and the promenade deck extended to the bow and plated in. Two years later she switched to London Docks cruises and was given the more appropriate name, *Thames Queen,* although evidence of the steamer's early years remained with the CDC initials of the Coast Development Company still appearing on the saloon carpets. Although the extensive forward alterations were not entirely successful and tended to put the vessel down by the head and affected her speed, *Thames Queen* was again commissioned as a minesweeper towards the end of 1939 and stationed at Dover as part of the 10th Flotilla, with which she is reported to have sailed for Dunkirk on the night of 27th May 1940 at least. After more minesweeping *Thames Queen* was at Southampton in a static role in 1945 and was retained by the Royal Navy until released early in 1947 when sold for scrap and broken up at Dover.

WAVERLEY

For many years the *Waverley,* the first steamer built for the North British Railway Company specifically for Clyde cruising as opposed to railway connection runs, was acknowledged among the fastest paddlers and, in her prime, was well capable of 20 knots. The *Waverley's* best years probably ended with the start of the First World War, during which she was taken for conversion into a minesweeper in September 1915, the work including extension of the promenade deck to the bow. The extension, which was plated in, was retained when the steamer resumed service and, although her accommodation was increased, the alterations caused a loss of speed. *Waverley* remained an extremely comfortable vessel and was used on the Loch Long excursion run in the 1930s until withdrawn at the end of the 1938 season. Surprisingly, she was not scrapped but remained laid up at Bowling Harbour on the Clyde and was called up with other active members of the Craigendoran fleet almost as soon as the war started. After working-up based at Ardrossan, *Waverley* had a spell in the English Channel before being based at Harwich as leader of the 12th Flotilla and with responsibilities for sweeping the East Coast shipping lanes from Harwich as far north as Great Yarmouth. *Waverley* and her flotilla were on a sweep when instructed to put into Yarmouth to refuel and take provisions before sailing south to rendezvous with a motor torpedo boat in the Thames Estuary to collect secret orders. These directed the Flotilla to the beaches east of Dunkirk.

Captain John Cameron, *Waverley's* Clyde skipper in 1938 and who went to war with the vessel, never forgot the sight that greeted those on the paddler as dawn broke on 29th May, with hundreds of men formed up in orderly lines waiting on the beach for rescue. Loading was

The Clyde favourite **Waverley** *as she appeared until 1936 (left), with striking red, white and black funnel and black paddle boxes embellished in gold leaf. For her last couple of active seasons the hull became light grey. The deck saloons were removed during conversion for minesweeping and* **Waverley** *was photographed from (centre left)* **Marmion** *during one of the 12th Flotilla's patrols in the North Sea in April 1940 with* **Duchess of Fife** *the vessel astern.* (Clyde River Steamer Club and Rev. Wm. C. Galbraith collection)

A bow close-up of **Waverley** *with the 12-pounder gun crew closed-up at action stations.* (Rev. Wm. C. Galbraith collection)

Captain John Cameron, **Waverley's** *Clyde skipper in the 1930s, went to war with the vessel and stepped off the bridge and into the sea as she went down after being bombed while sailing home from Dunkirk. Captain Cameron commissioned the replacement* **Waverley** *in 1947 and is seen on this vessel, now the only sea-going paddle steamer in the world, during the Dunkirk 40th Anniversary cruise in 1980. Captain Cameron died in 1988, at the age of 81.* (Author)

very slow and to speed up the process the *Waverley's* crew ran lines to the shore, and troops in the small boats were able to haul themselves out hand over hand. There were frequent visits from German aircraft on bombing and machine-gun attacks and *Waverley* had to be moved on several occasions to avoid being left high and dry by the ebbing tide. The steamer got underway with an estimated 600 troops in the early afternoon and about half an hour into the voyage was caught in the same aerial assault that claimed the personnel vessels *Lorina* and *Normannia.* A dozen Heinkels attacked *Waverley.* At first, sudden course alterations dodged the bombs, and all the time the steamer kept up sustained fire with her 12-pounder, machine guns and even the rifles of rescued troops, and claimed to have shot down two enemy aircraft. Eventually, however, three bombs struck in succession, the last one jamming the *Waverley's* rudder and putting steering gear out of action. When the steamer was abandoned the lives of many troops and crew were saved by peacetime buoyant seats that floated free as the ship went down, these having been retained at the insistence of Captain Cameron when *Waverley* was at the yard of her

Built: 1899 by A. and J. Inglis, Pointhouse, for the North British Steam Packet Company, transferred to London and North Eastern Railway (Clyde Section) in 1923.
Gross tonnage: 537.
Length: 235 ft.
Width: 26 ft. 1 in.
Machinery: Compound diagonal, two cylinders.
Speed: 19 knots.
1939 route: Laid up in 1939, the vessel was used on LNER Craigendoran–Kyles of Bute sailings in 1938 and for Craigendoran–Arrochar excursion until 1937.

builders, Inglis, and fitting out the previous autumn. Small craft were on the scene in about half an hour and were later joined by a French naval vessel and the Thames paddler *Golden Eagle*.

Captain Cameron spent the remainder of the war on minesweeping trawlers and was awarded the DSC. In 1946 he was back at the Inglis yard to stand by during construction of the *Waverley's* replacement, the present vessel of the same name which he took on its maiden voyage in 1947. Captain Cameron commanded most of the principal vessels of the Clyde fleet until retiring in 1970. Ten years later, flanked by members of the Dunkirk Veterans' Association, he proudly cast a wreath on to the waters of the English Channel off the French coast after *Waverley* had made a special crossing to mark the 40th Anniversary of the evacuation. Captain Cameron died in 1988 at the age of 81. In recent times the wreck of the earlier *Waverley* was discovered by a Dutch diving enthusiast and several relics subsequently brought to the surface were presented to the Paddle Steamer Preservation Society.

WESTWARD HO

Built: 1894 by S. McKnight & Co, Ayr, for P. & A. Campbell.
Gross tonnage: 438.
Length: 255 ft.
Width: 26 ft. 1 in.
Machinery: Compound diagonal, two cylinders.
Speed: 18 knots.
1939 route: Bristol Channel excursions.

With 46 years of service behind her, *Westward Ho* was the oldest paddle steamer taking part in Operation Dynamo. Diverted from a second spell of war service as a minesweeper, the Campbell veteran more than played her part by transporting 1,686 troops to safety. *Westward Ho* was the first of the famous Bristol Channel fleet to have a full-length promenade deck and was commanded in her first season by Captain Alec Campbell himself. She was named *Westward Queen* and later *Westhope* during the First World War and returned to excursions following a major reconditioning on the Clyde in 1920. The steamer was quickly requisitioned again in the autumn of 1939 and became part of the 7th

Before and after the war views of Westward Ho*—in the late 1930s during a Bristol Channel excursion (below), and in March 1946 being towed back to Bristol (above right). Alas, the oldest paddler to take part in Operation Dynamo proved beyond economic repair and was soon hauled down the River Avon on a sad final voyage to Newport shipbreakers.* (A. G. Taylor)

Flotilla based on the Forth at Granton. By the time *Westward Ho* arrived on the scene at Dunkirk, the evacuation was well in progress but she is reported to have completed two or possibly three crossings, the first on 1st June when 900 French troops were loaded at Margate. It is also recorded that *Westward Ho* broke off from loading on 2nd June to go to the assistance of the War Department launch *Haig* which was sinking after being struck by different tugs close to Dunkirk. The *Westward Ho* returned to mine-sweeping until a major boiler failure, after which she was relegated to accommodation ship duties at Dartmouth. Although towed back to Bristol in March 1946, Campbell's decided that the cost of reconditioning would be prohibitive and *Westward Ho* was moved away to Newport on the last day of July 1946 to be broken up.

WHIPPINGHAM

The largest of the Portsmouth railway paddlers, *Whippingham* and a sister ship *Southsea,* were built with an eye to summer excursion work and became well-known along the South Coast during the 1930s. When the war started, *Whippingham* was left on the Ryde ferry service until called away to assist at Dunkirk, stopping en route only long enough for an RNR Lieutenant named Eric Reed to be put in command. She appears to have crossed just once, but what a trip it turned out to be. Designed to take up to a maximum of 1,183 passengers on short summer runs to and from Ryde, more than twice that number were squeezed aboard *Whippingham* on 1st June—an amazing total of 2,700 troops being brought back. There was hardly an inch of space to spare anywhere and, as the steamer laboured home with less than a foot between the sponsons and the sea, Lieutenant Reed nonchalantly described the ship as being 'very much over-loaded'. *Whippingham* went back into service at Portsmouth until requisitioned as a minesweeper the following year and was converted again for use as an anti-aircraft ship in 1942. The paddler was involved in the Normandy Landings of 1944 and returned to the Southern Railway in April 1945 and was quickly refitted and put back on the

Built: 1930 by Fairfield Shipbuilding Co, Govan, for the Southern Railway.
Gross tonnage: 825.
Length: 244 ft.
Width: 30 ft. 1 in.
Machinery: Compound diagonal, two cylinders.
Speed: 16 knots.
1939 route: Portsmouth–Ryde ferry service and summer excursions.

The unarmed **Whippingham** *was called from the Portsmouth–Ryde ferry run to play a part at Dunkirk and brought back an amazing load of 2,700 men. Requisitioned as a minesweeper in 1941 and later used as an anti-aircraft vessel, the paddler returned to Portsmouth for increasingly limited summer use until 1962.* (PSPS Archives)

ferry run. Post-war excursions were confined to the Solent and by the mid-1950s *Whippingham* saw service on only a few peak Saturdays each year and it was no surprise when she was offered for sale at the end of 1962 and went to Belgian breakers the following May.

Surviving passenger-carrying and private craft record their presence at Dunkirk in 1940 by proudly displaying plaques like this one on the Portsmouth excursion vessel **Folkestone Belle**. (Maritime Photographic)

Excursion Ships, Small Ferries and Cargo Vessels

MOST of the larger ferries and paddle steamers which took part in the evacuation were already requisitioned and had been carrying out Admiralty duties of some description. Nearly all the smaller ferries, excursion craft and small cargo vessels were not. They hurried to the Kent ports in response to orders after Operation Dynamo started on the evening of Sunday 26th May 1940 and performed an endless variety of tasks.

Stately steam launches built for work on the Thames above Westminster made their first ever sea crossing to work off the beaches with open excursion boats from Eastbourne or Southend; small ferries plodded up-Channel from as far away as Poole Harbour; five powered lighters left their regular run carrying goods to the Isle of Wight; even a Mersey ferry and some of the Great Yarmouth summer trip boats were represented together with craft from rivers as far west as the Dart and Tamar.

Some vessels, after making their best speed of six or eight knots all the way to Dover or Ramsgate, arrived only to be sent straight back again. Others did not even get that far, one of the large, laborious Woolwich ferries answered the call but was soon forced to turn back because of mechanical trouble.

A Thames stalwart that did go all the way and return for the crew to tell their tale was the London fire float *Massey Shaw*, which was at first sent across in the hope of being able to help bring some of the fires in the port of Dunkirk under control. When it was realised that this was futile, *Massey Shaw's* crew of 13 London fireman went to work off the beaches. After two trips the vessel had sailed again but was recalled.

Not all ships were as lucky and there were losses off the beaches, with further craft simply abandoned after suffering engine or other failures. Although long since retired from fire-fighting, the *Massey Shaw* survives in private ownership in London and is one of a quite large proportion of smaller vessels that are still to be seen. Several are operating commercially on the Thames, or providing trips from resorts on the East and South Coasts, and, in one case as far afield as Gibraltar.

Bat Motor cargo vessel of 51 tons – 86′ × 16′3″ – powered by 100-bhp Kromhout engine, owned by Pickfords: Part of a Pickfords fleet used for the carriage of goods from Portsmouth or Southampton to Cowes, Isle of Wight, going to Dunkirk in company with four other Pickfords vessels – *Bee, Chamois, Hound* and *M.F.H.* – all manned by their civilian crews. Commanded by James Butcher, *Bat* first crossed on 30th May and picked up 15 survivors from the French destroyer *Bourrasque* and landed them at Ramsgate. *Bat* went over again next day returning with about 100 men, by which time the crew had been without sleep and the vessel's engine had been running continuously for 92 hours.

Bee Motor cargo vessel owned by Pickfords, built by Timmer & Zoon at Schiedam, Holland, in 1937 – 78′ × 10′: Lay offshore through the night of 30th/31st May before being taken in by skipper Bill Mansbridge to collect 360 British troops who were transferred to a tug. Returned to Ramsgate under her own power.

Britannia IV Eastbourne beach excursion boat – 24′6″ × 8′ – powered by a Thornycroft petrol/paraffin engine of 28 hp, owned by Sayers

The little powered lighter **Bat** *left its cargo run to the Isle of Wight and twice crossed to Dunkirk, with the four-man crew keeping going for 92 hours without sleep. After being held at Ramsgate in the closing stages of the evacuation the* **Bat** *was sent back to Portsmouth and started work again almost immediately. Skipper James Butcher then reported: 'Back again and glad of it, but we are all ready again for another job of the same kind if we are wanted.'* (Ray Butcher)

Brothers: A 41-passenger open launch built in the 1920s which ran until the 1950s.

Britannic Single screw Thames excursion launch, 40′ long, built 1925 and powered by a petrol/paraffin engine. Completed for Richmond owners but used from 1935 by Thames Motor Boats on downstream runs from Westminster. The 63-passenger vessel was towed across the Channel by the skoot *Hilda* together with lifeboats from the Belgian steamer *Flandres* and other small craft, but was reported lost after carrying troops to larger vessels.

Caversham Thames steam launch built in 1884, 55′9″ long and owned by Alfred Crouch: One of the oldest vessels at Dunkirk, *Caversham* was built by East's of Reading for their own services and was used by another local operator before moving down river to run for Harry Hastings of Kingston from 1925, joining the Crouch fleet 10 years later when licensed to carry 104 passengers above Westminster Bridge. *Caversham* returned from Dunkirk but was too badly damaged to resume Thames services and was subsequently broken up.

Canvey Queen Southend pleasure boat owned by F. D. Clyne: Set out direct for Dunkirk on 29th May but had engine trouble and was towed to Margate. Rescued crew of Thames vessel *Queen of England* after it was cut in two by the skoot *Tilly*. Reached beaches after more engine trouble, starting ferry duties on 30th May.

Chamois Motor cargo vessel owned by Pickfords: Skippered by E. Brown, twice beaten back by air attacks when crossing on 30th May. A third attempt succeeded and 130 men were taken off two different transports under fire.

Court Belle II Thames motor launch built 1922, 40′ long, owned by C. Whatford & Sons of Hampton Court: A 36-passenger vessel towed across to work off the beaches which failed to return.

Dreadnaught II Thames motor launch built 1916, 45′3″ long and owned by H. W. and R. T. Redknapp: This 96-passenger single screw vessel, based at Richmond, was lost off the beaches.

Eastbourne Belle Eastbourne beach excursion boat – 25′6″ × 8′6″ – powered by Atlantic petrol/paraffin engine of 30 hp and owned by Allchorn Brothers: A 45-passenger launch dating from the early 1920s and used to provide short cruises from the beach at Eastbourne to Beachy Head or along the coast. Towed over by trawler

Brock in company with yacht *Commodore,* returning to serve Allchorn Bros until the mid-1950s when sold to Hastings owners as *Channel Tripper.*

Eastbourne Queen Eastbourne beach excursion boat – 14′6″ × 8′ – powered by Thornycroft petrol/paraffin engine and owned by Sayers Brothers: A 41-seat launch which crossed with other Eastbourne craft but failed to return.

Empress Thames steam launch built 1895, 88′3″ long and owned by Alfred Crouch: A single screw vessel acquired by Crouch in 1935 and registered for service above London Bridge. Crossed to France but sunk off Calais.

England Thames steam launch built 1900 at Reading. 100′ long, owned by J. Mears, Richmond: Not in official lists but reported lost at Dunkirk.

Enchantress Eastbourne beach excursion boat – 32′6″ × 10′6″ – powered by an Atlantic petrol/paraffin engine of 35 hp and owned by Allchorn Brothers: A larger launch licensed to carry 60 passengers, *Enchantress* was sunk off Dunkirk on 31st May.

Fawley One of two vessels from the Portsmouth–Gosport ferry service requisitioned for Operation Dynamo, although there is no record of either *Fawley* or the other steam-powered *Ferry King* crossing to France, or even being moved to the Dover area.

Felicity Passenger launch – 35′ × 9 ′ – built 1931 for Poole owner J. Davis who delivered her to Navy at Dover. The vessel came back, and now operates as *Wight Rose* for Hurst Castle Cruises, Lymington. ADLS member.

Ferry King Single screw launch of 57 tons, built 1919 – 64′ × 18′ steam reciprocating engine by Plenty & Co, Newbury: Gosport–Portsmouth ferry. Evacuation role never confirmed. Continued on the Gosport ferry until sold in the 1960s to Blue Funnel Cruises of Southampton as *Solent Queen.* At first retained steam engine, then fitted with Gardner diesel. In use until 1984.

Ferry Nymph Poole Harbour ferry owned by J. Harvey: Sailed to Dover on 29th May, crossed next day with naval crew, returning safely and eventually resuming on Poole–Sandbanks ferry.

Fishbourne Double-ended car ferry of 136 tons, built by Wm Denny & Bros, Dumbarton in 1927 for the Southern Railway – 131′ × 26′ – powered by two Gardner oil engines, double twin screw: Left Portsmouth–Fishbourne vehicle ferry service and sailed to Ramsgate. Set off for Dunkirk under tow on 1st June but tug *Duke* was ordered to assist barges *Haste Away* and *Ada Mary* and *Fishbourne* was sent back to Ramsgate under her own power. In service until 1962.

Floss Hilda Thames launch listed as owned by Bond's Boatyard, Maidenhead: Was most probably *Flosshilde,* one of a fleet of electric launches built in the 1890s by the Immisch Electric Launch and Boat Co of Hampton-on-Thames.

Folkestone Belle Motor launch of 17 tons, built 1928 by Thomas Lechter, Cowes – 50′ × 12′8″: Portsmouth–Hayling Island ferry owned by Cecil and George Spraggs. Handed over to a Naval crew who sailed to Dover and on to Dunkirk for work off the beaches. Returned to ferry until sold to M. Pearce of Eastney, renamed *Southsea Belle,* fitted with a Ford-Parsons diesel engine and used for harbour cruises from Portsmouth Hard. The original name, *Folkestone Belle*, was restored in June 1989 immediately before the vessel took part in a gathering of Dunkirk 'little ships' at Cowes, Isle of Wight. ADLS member.

Gondolier King Twin screw motor excursion vessel of 37 tons, built by Husk & Co, Wivenhoe, 1929 – 56′ × 16′: Used by Poole and

Built in 1928 to serve the ferry between Portsmouth and Hayling Island, **Folkestone Belle's** *original name was restored in 1989 after the vessel had spent more that 20 years on cruises around Portsmouth Harbour as* **Southsea Belle.** (Maritime Photographic)

Swanage Motor & Speedboat Company for summer service Swanage-Boscombe 1934-39. After the war became *My Queen* on the Thames, then joined Dart Pleasure Craft with new Ford diesels fitted. Sold to Plymouth Boat Cruises in 1985. ADLS member.

Gondolier Queen Twin screw motor excursion vessel owned by the Poole & Swanage Motor and Speedboat Company.

Good Hope Single screw Thames steam launch built 1921 by Bond's Boatyard, Maidenhead, for their own services. Crossed to Dunkirk but did not return.

Gwenny Listed as owned by W. G. S. Crouch of Greenwich: Most probably the Crouch launch *Gwennie,* built in 1910 powered by a petrol/paraffin engine.

His Majesty Thames steam launch of 53 tons, built 1906 at Maidenhead – 84′2″ × 14′7″ – owned by J. Mears of Richmond: Licensed to carry 306 on up-river services from Westminster Bridge. Came back safely to run for Thames Launches for 20 years from 1946 and was re-engined with diesels in 1949.

Hound Motor cargo vessel owned by Pickfords: Arrived off Dunkirk late on 31st May. Skipper H. Knight sent two crew ashore in a small boat to return with 12 men. *Hound* went to small pier and took aboard 100 French and Belgians.

Hurlingham Thames steam launch of 79 tons, built by Salter Bros, Oxford, in 1915 – 101′6″ × 16′5″ – owned by J. Mears of Richmond: Single screw with tunnel stern to reduce draught for up-river work and licensed to carry 325 passengers. After the war began, *Hurlingham* was one of a dozen larger launches placed in the Thames Hospital Emergency Transport Service, based at Dagenham. Staffed by medical personnel, they patrolled each night in dockland areas at risk from air attacks. *Hurlingham* survived the evacuation and was re-engined with a Thornycroft 760 diesel in 1947, soon after passing to Thames Launches. Now used by Tidal Cruisers on their Westminster–Tower Pier–Greenwich service and for private charters.

Jeff Thames motor launch built by J. Mears at Eel Pie Island in 1923 – 39′9″ × 10′9″ – powered by Parsons petrol engine: Operated above Tower Bridge for Mears and returned to the fleet after

Although long-since converted from steam to diesel propulsion, the launch **Hurlingham** *continues to defy the Thames tides and runs from Westminster Pier in the same pool of operators as several other Dunkirk veterans.* (Author)

This picture was taken less than a fortnight before the Thames excursion vessel **Marchioness** *was sunk with the loss of 53 lives after colliding with the 1,475 ton dredger* **Bowbelle** *just below Southwark Bridge. The tragedy happened in the early hours on 20th August 1989 during an all-night private charter cruise and the skipper of the* **Marchioness**, *Stephen Faldo, was among those who lost their lives. Tidal Cruisers acquired the vessel in 1979 and spent heavily to improve accommodation, the main saloons adopting Edwardian styling. The wreck was raised and towed away to be broken up.* (Walter Sartori)

Dunkirk. Ran for Tidal Cruisers from 1947, fitted with Ford diesel engine 1950 and sold to Arthur Jacobs of Windsor two years later, at first being named *Windsor Four* and then *Windsor Two.* Now owned by Turk Launches of Kingston and restored to original name. ADLS member.

Kingwood Thames passenger launch of 63 tons, built by Salter Bros of Oxford in 1915 – 101′2″ × 16′5″ – single screw with compound engine by W. Sissons & Co: Tunnel stern steamer for 366 passengers, owned by J. Mears, and one of the Thames vessels used as hospital launches from the winter of 1939. Came back from Dunkirk to join Thames Launches in 1947 and received a Thornycroft diesel in 1950. Still in year-round service from Westminster. ADLS member.

Lady Cable Motor boat owned by C. and M. Mott: Transported 40 troops. Now owned by G. Medway of Torquay and used for fishing trips. Previously ran with Class IV certificate for 48 on local cruises to Brixham, the River Dart, etc.

Lansdowne 42′ Thames motor launch, built 1920 and operated from Richmond by E. Messum and Sons with a certificate for 67 passengers. Crossed to operate from beaches but failed to return.

Malden Annie Double ended steam launch built 1921, 56′5″ long and owned by Mrs A. Lamont: Previously worked Westminster–Greenwich. Towed most of the way over, arriving 30th May but abandoned and left to drift after engines failed.

Marchioness Thames steam launch of 46 tons, built by Salter Bros of Oxford, in 1923 – 85′5″ × 14′5″: Owned by J. Mears of Richmond and used as hospital tender before Dunkirk. Passed to Thames Launches in 1947, by whom the steam engine was replaced by a Thornycroft diesel in 1953. Owned by Tidal Cruisers and used on Westminster–Tower Pier–Greenwich service and charters until sunk following a collision in August 1989.

Margherita Thames motor launch built 1922, 39′10″ long and owned by J. Mears. Sunk en route by wash from destroyer.

Mary Spearing Thames motor launch built 1934, 40′10″ long, and owned by W. G. S. Crouch of Greenwich: Diesel powered single screw vessel registered for 57 passengers above London Bridge. Did not return from Dunkirk and listed among vessels lost.

Mary Spearing II Thames motor launch built

Above *The immaculate* **Kingwood,** *emerging from Westminster Bridge after an up-river trip to Kew in May 1989. Although originally twin decked, the tunnel stern former steamer was rebuilt in this form following a major fire while being overhauled in December 1950. In addition to flying the Association of Dunkirk Little Ships ensign at the bow,* **Kingwood's** *'Dunkirk 1940' battle honour plaque can be seen next to the lifebelt at the front of the wheelhouse. The father of* **Kingwood's** *owner, Charles Wyatt, came back from Dunkirk on a naval vessel.* (Author)

Below *Now used for fishing trips from Torquay, the little* **Lady Cable** *was taken to work off the Dunkirk beaches and transported over 500 men in seven trips to and from larger vessels before coming back under her own power with 40 troops aboard.* (Peter Box)

1934, 40′ long, and owned by W. G. S. Crouch of Greenwich: Survived the evacuation but left the Crouch fleet in 1943.

Massey Shaw Thames fire float built by J. Samuel White, Cowes, Isle of Wight, in 1935 – 78′ × 14′6″ – powered by twin Glennifer diesels: Sailed to Ramsgate with Sub Officer A. J. May and a crew of 12 London firemen to fight fires in Dunkirk Harbour but sent instead (on 31st May) to work from beaches three miles east of the harbour, returning with 60 men. Made second trip on 1st June with Royal Navy commander but still eight firemen in crew, ferrying over 500 men to larger craft in 20 trips, before going back to Ramsgate with 46 men on board. *Massey Shaw* set out a third time but was sent back. Now owned by a preservation society, and based at St. Katharine's Dock. ADLS member.

M.F.H. Motor cargo vessel of 48 tons owned by Pickfords: Crossed under skipper W. H. Smith, arriving during bombing raid on 31st, and ferried troops to larger vessels offshore before returning to Ramsgate with 140 men. *M.F.H.* (an abbreviation of *Master of Fox Hounds*) and the other Pickfords ships returned to Isle of Wight services which were taken over by the British Transport Commission in 1948 and British Road Services nine years later. They ceased in 1975 since when all Island goods have gone by car ferry services.

My Queen Wooden steam launch built in 1902, 70′ long and owned by the Oreston & Turnchapel Steamboat Company: One of a fleet of passenger ferries linking the villages of Oreston and Turnchapel with Plymouth. Used as an Admiralty tender HMS *Foliot* after Dunkirk but was hulked in Weston Mill Creek after sinking following a collision with a trawler near Saltash Bridge.

Mutt Thames motor launch built in 1922 by J. Mears and 40′ in length: The first vessel in the Mears fleet powered by an internal combustion engine, this 75-passenger open launch was used on the Westminster–London Bridge service and

A fully laden **My Queen** *leaves Totnes on a return excursion to Dartmouth in the summer of 1988, some 48 years after going to Dunkirk when named* **Gondolier King.** *Until 1939 the motor vessel was used for trips between Swanage and Boscombe.* (Peter Box)

returned safely from Dunkirk. When the Mears fleet was dispersed in 1947, *Mutt* passed to Thames Launches who fitted a diesel engine in 1950. The vessel was then acquired by J. Watson in 1953.

Nemo IV Excursion motor vessel owned by Nemo Motor Boat Co, Clacton-on-Sea: Sunk off La Panne on 2nd June.

New Britannic Passenger launch – 54′ × 14′5″ – built at Chiswick in 1930. Operated at Ramsgate from where taken to ferry from the beaches before returning with 83 men. Now owned by Bryher Boat Services, Isles of Scilly, and named *Commodore*. ADLS member.

New Prince of Wales Wooden excursion vessel of 90 tons, built by Alex Fowler, Bosham, in 1923 for L. E. Goulding of Shoeburyness, and trading as Southend Motor Navigation Company – 104′3″ × 25″ – powered by twin Thornycroft paraffin engines: Previously used for local sea trips from Southend. Bombed and sunk off Dunkirk, crew taken off by motor vessel *Triton*.

New Windsor Castle Thames steam launch of 85 tons, 94′ long, built by Arthur Jacobs Ltd. in 1923 and operated by them at Windsor: Reached Sheerness but boilers could not cope with salt water and the vessel was not allowed to proceed further. Now diesel powered and in the Kingston fleet of Turk Launches.

Norwich Belle Steel excursion steamer of 90 tons, built by Fellows & Co, Great Yarmouth, 1924, for the Yarmouth & Gorleston Steamboat Co – 93′ × 18′ – steam reciprocating engine built by Crabtree Brothers: Originally designed for Yarmouth–Norwich service but used prior to 1939 on local excursions from Yarmouth including circular trips to Lowestoft, out via the Broads and back along the coast. Role at Dunkirk unclear, but records retained by Steamboat Co's successors Southern Coastcrafts, confirmed presence and service from 1941 to 1946 as a fireboat at Lowestoft. Steam engine replaced by Gardner diesels in 1959. Withdrawn after the 1980 season, she was laid-up in London while schemes for static use were considered before being finally sold to Israeli owners and going to the Gulf of Aqaba under her own power in April 1983.

Oulton Belle Double ended steel excursion steamer of 75 tons built by Fellows and Co, Great Yarmouth, in 1935 for Yarmouth & Gorleston Steamboat Co – 84′ × 17′ – steam engine by Elliot & Garrod of Beccles: Built in the same style as nineteenth-century Norfolk steamers with hinged funnel and no wheelhouse to enable them to clear bridges on the Rivers Yare and Waveney. After Dunkirk, used for tender duties on the Clyde until discharged by the Ministry of War Transport at Port Bannatyne, Isle of Bute, in October 1945. Rebuilt the next

Apart from receiving calls from the London and Medway excursion steamers, Southend also boasted some fine locally-based trip boats, among them the wooden-hulled **New Prince of Wales** *which operated from a landing stage close to the beach. Although bombed off Dunkirk, there was time for her crew to be taken off before the vessel went down.* (Ambrose Greenway collection)

The Mersey ferry **Perch Rock** *returned to the Wallasey–Liverpool vehicle service until 1955 and is pictured two years later, soon after commencing service across the Oresund between Sweden and Denmark as* **Betula.** *The hull survives as a pile-driving barge and the superstructure forms part of a yacht club headquarters near Helsingborg.* (Scandinavian Ferry Lines)

year as single ended vessel with fixed funnel, bridge and upper deck and returned to Broads excursions from Yarmouth. Diesel engines fitted in 1955, two years after sale for service at Scarborough as *Regal Lady,* then returned to Norfolk, operating at Norwich for over a decade from 1971 until going back to the North Yorkshire coast to offer short trips from Scarborough.

Perch Rock Mersey vehicle ferry of 766 tons, built by Caledon Shipbuilding and Engineering Co for the Corporation of Wallasey in 1929 – 144′6″ × 48′1″ – powered by triple expansion engine by builders: Used on Wallasey–Liverpool vehicle ferry service until requisitioned by the Admiralty and fitted with a crane to unload cargo from convoy vessels arriving in the Mersey. Although listed by the Admiralty among the evacuation vessels, her presence in the area at the time has never been explained. Withdrawn in 1953 and sold to the Swedish Sugar Company, she was named *Betula,* fitted with rails on the vehicle deck and used to transport sugar beet in rail wagons. Service on Danish routes as a vehicle ferry followed in 1954 and in 1955 the veteran was rebuilt as a passenger and vehicle ferry and served for Linjebus International between Helsingor and Helsingborg until placed in reserve in 1968. Sold in 1972 and converted into pile-driving barge for a Malmo construction company. Wheelhouse and superstructure remain as a yacht club headquarters near Helsingborg.

Princess Freda Thames motor launch of 36 tons, built in 1926 and 63′ in length: Part of the up-river fleet of C. Whatford & Sons of Hampton Court, registered for 140 passengers. Came back safely from Dunkirk and continued in the same fleet after the war until the Whatford business became a subsidiary of Thames Motor Boat Co in 1970 and was later transferred to TMB ownership. Now owned by Phillips of Westminster and still employed on up-river services to Kew. ADLS member.

Although the Thames steam launches that went over to Dunkirk have since altered almost out of all recognition, the appearance of the motor vessel **Princess Freda** *has changed little in a career spanning more than 60 years. Owned by C. Whatford & Sons at the time of the evacuation,* **Princess Freda** *is now operated from Westminster on up-river services by M. & C. W. Phillips.* (Author)

Princess Lily Thames motor launch built as *Majestic* in 1920, 43′10″ long and powered by a petrol/paraffin engine: Renamed *Princess Lily* when acquired by C. Whatford and Sons of Hampton Court in 1924 and licensed for 101 passengers above Richmond. Worked of beaches with Thames vessel *Tigris One* until lost.

Princess Maud Southend pleasure boat owned by W. H. Wilson: Crossed on 29th May with other Southend pleasure boats but ran aground and was lost after going too close inshore.

Q and J.J. Thames motor launch owned by S. Cooper: Further particulars unknown.

Queen Boadicea Thames motor launch of 33 tons, built in 1929, 65′ long owned by Mrs C. Smith of Long Ditton and powered by a petrol/paraffin engine: Used for up-river services from Westminster carrying 173. Returned to operate for P. J. and R. F. Jackson with original engine replaced by diesel in 1952 and was then in the fleet of Thames Pleasure Craft until sold in 1971. Acquired by Dart Pleasure Craft in 1976 and used on the Kingswear ferry service until scrapped 1984.

Queen Boadicea II Thames passenger vessel of 45 tons, built and engined by J. I. Thornycroft, Southampton, 1937 – 63′6″ × 12′6″: A 173-passenger vessel originally part of same fleet as *Queen Boadicea* but bought by George Wheeler Launches in 1938. Worked off Dunkirk on 31st May. Continued in the Wheeler fleet after the war with diesel engine fitted in 1950. Bought by Dart Pleasure Craft in 1976 and operated for a time with fellow Dunkirk veterans *Queen Boadicea* and *My Queen*, serving until sold in 1985 to Tamar Cruising Co and Cremyell Ferry. ADLS member.

Queen of England Thames steam launch of 25 tons, built 1902, 75′ long and owned by Alfred Crouch: Built and operated at Windsor by C. Maynard and Sons, this 260 passenger, single

Seen smartly turned out at Cremyll in 1987, **Queen Boadicea II** *has carried the same name for over 50 years and was originally a Thames launch. She is recorded as having worked off the beaches on the last day of May 1940.* (Peter Box)

screw steamer had later spells at Laleham, Richmond and Kingston before entering the Crouch fleet in 1937. Lost after being cut in two by the skoot *Tilly* while en route to Dunkirk on 29th May.

Royal Thames Thames steam launch built at Molesey by Harry Tagg in 1896, 71′6″ long and owned by J. Mears of Richmond: Returned from Dunkirk but did not operate after the Mears business became Thames Launches in 1947.

St. Patrick Motor launch built 1910, 42′ long and powered by a petrol/paraffin engine: Brought from Ireland by Thompson Brothers in 1930 and placed on the Westminster–Tower service. Crossed to Dunkirk under tow but lost while working off the beaches.

Seymour Castle Wooden passenger vessel of 37 tons, built by Ferris & Blank, Dartmouth, in 1938 for the River Dart Steamboat Company – 60′1″ × 14′8″ – powered by a Glennifer oil engine: Based at Ramsgate with Dart skipper Cyril Roper in command and used by the Admiralty for marking swept channels. Crossed to Dunkirk but was confined to the harbour area. Returned to the Dart after the war and served until sold in 1973, having spells as *Scomber* and *Southern Comfort of Plymstock* before becoming *Dartmouthian*. Now owned by G. H. Ridalls of Plymouth. ADLS member.

Shamrock Southend pleasure boat owned by A. Barrell: Taken across by her owner and skipper but lost on 30th May after being abandoned with a fouled propeller caused by a human obstruction.

Silver Queen Passenger launch – 40′6″ × 12′6″ – built in 1926 by Horn Brothers, Southampton, powered by Atlantic petrol/paraffin engine and owned by Mrs L. Carter of Sheerness. Among the first small craft to be sent across, the vessel returned safely and operated after the war in the Medway area before being sold in the 1950s to Percy Ferguson of St. Peter Port, Guernsey. Now powered by a Sutton Power diesel and named *Fermain V*, the 65-seat launch provides a summer service from St. Peter Port to Fermaine Bay. ADLS member.

Silver Queen Thames motor launch, built 1924, diesel powered, single screw: A 176 passenger launch added to the Thompson brothers' Westminster fleet in 1936. Survived Dunkirk to be shipped out to Freetown, Sierra Leone, for harbour duties, but was so run down when the war ended that it was not considered worth bringing her back.

Skylark I Brighton beach boat owned by N. Knight and W. Stephenson: Lost on 29th May after sinking while under tow.

Skylark II Southend vessel owned by Charles and Arthur Myall. Survived crossing for damage to be repaired by Tough Brothers at Teddington.

Skylark VI Passenger launch built by R. Newman & Sons, Poole, in 1922 for J. Bolson of Poole – 45′ × 12′ – powered by petrol/paraffin engine: Open launch with Class VI certificate for 62 passengers and part of the large Bolson fleet offering excursions from Bournemouth and Boscombe. Reported lost at Dunkirk but later found adrift in the Channel submerged almost to the gunwhales. Resumed excursions in August 1945 but sank in Poole Bay on 21st April 1946.

Skylark IX Passenger launch built and owned by J. Bolson & Son, Poole, in 1934 – 50′ × 14′ – powered by Parsons petrol/paraffin engine driving single screw: Operated by Bolson from Bournemouth until 1939, registered to carry 115 passengers, and then sold after the war for service from Brighton. Now owned by John Sweeney of Balloch and part of a three-vessel fleet offering summer cruises on Loch Lomond. ADLS member.

Skylark X Passenger launch built and owned by J. Bolson & Son, Poole, in 1936 – 48′ × 13′ – powered by Blackstone diesel engine driving single screw: Original engine replaced almost immediately by Parsons petrol/paraffin unit and vessel sold after only one season to the Thames fleet of Jackson Brothers of Hammersmith. *Skylark X*, registered to carry 99 passengers as far downstream as Gravesend, came back safely from Dunkirk and continued for Jacksons until 1957, receiving a new Gardner diesel engine and then having spells with Thompson's Launches, Alfred Crouch, Tideway Passenger Boats and F & B Boats of Kingston, by whom she was sold in 1980 to A. S. Taylor of Hampton Wick to be converted for private use, still remaining on the Thames. ADLS member.

Southend Britannia Motor excursion vessel of 92

Built to compete for local traffic with **New Prince of Wales** *in 1924, the* **Southend Britannia** *held certificates for 400 passengers and, after surviving Dunkirk, saw further service immediately after the war.* (Ambrose Greenway collection)

tons, built and engined in 1924 by J. I. Thornycroft, Southampton, for Charles & Arthur Myall of Southend – 106′3″ × 26′5″: Survived Dunkirk and saw further service from Southend after the war, also spending some years in the Western Lady fleet before almost 20 years at Teddington as Thames TV's restaurant. Replaced in 1987 and present location unknown. One of her lifeboats, sold after the war, is the yacht *Landscaper* (see page 175).

Southern Queen Poole Harbour ferry launch owned by J. Harvey & Sons: Went to Dover with Poole running-mate *Ferry Nymph*, crossing to Dunkirk on 30th May, but sank after being damaged by bombs while working off the beaches.

Southern Queen Passenger motor launch – 51′ × 12′ – built in 1927 and based at Folkestone in the 1930s. Went to Dunkirk commanded by Sub-Lt. B. de Mattos. Sold to Scilly Isles owners in the late 1950s and still used on services from St. Mary's.

Tamar Belle Steel passenger vessel of 26 tons, built in 1927 by H. Gale and Co, Cowes – 54′1″ × 12′2″ – powered by Atlantic diesel engine: Introduced by the Tamar Trading Co for local excursions and sold after two seasons for Thames service. When the war started *Tamar Belle* had been in the fleet of Thames Motor Boats since 1936 and was used on the Westminster–Greenwich service and licensed for 135 passengers. *Tamar Belle* returned from Dunkirk to see further service for TMB until 1974 when sold to Nottingham owners and is still to be found making summer trips on the River Trent, now owned by Tamar Belle Cruises, and bearing her original name after more than 60 years of service.

Tarpon, *seen on the Hayling Ferry slipway for underwater attention in 1955, shared the service with larger consort* **Folkestone Belle** *for many years and the two boats went to Dunkirk together.* (M. Collins)

Tarpon Ferry launch built 1910, owned and operated by Spraggs Brothers on the Portsmouth–Hayling Island ferry: Taken by owners to Southampton with another Hayling Ferry, *Folkestone Belle*, and from there to Dover by naval crews. Towed across to work off the beaches, returning safely to resume ferry duties until service was taken over by Portsmouth Corporation during the 1960s.

The King Thames steam launch of 41 tons, built of teak in half saloon style by Harry Tagg in 1902 – 81′ × 14′6″ – 196 passengers. A distinctive vessel with clipper bow which passed into the Mears fleet in 1916 and spent 30 years with Thames Launches from 1947. Steam engine replaced with Thornycroft diesel in 1948 when bowsprit and other embellishments were removed. A third change of hands in eight years brought *The King* into the Thames Tripping fleet in 1985 and the interior has been impressively restored for services from Westminster to Kew, Richmond and Hampton Court and also private party cruises. ADLS member.

The Mew Passenger ferry of 117 tons, built in 1908 by Cox & Co, Falmouth, for the Great Western Railway – 90′2″ × 22′4″ – with twin compound steam engine by builders: Left Dartmouth–Kingswear ferry and taken to Dover by regular Dart crew at maximum speed – 6 knots! Arrived on 2nd June, but by then the need for small vessels had been met and *The Mew* was sent back to Devon and remained on the Kingswear service until scrapped in the autumn of 1954.

Tigris One Thames passenger launch, converted in 1922 by Tough Brothers, Teddington, from Royal Navy launch built 1918–74′6″ long: Operated by Toughs until sold in 1937 to Harry Hastings of Kingston. Taken to Sheerness and on to Dunkirk by her owner/skipper, *Tigris One* was estimated to have moved 800 troops from the shore to larger vessels, working with other small craft including the Whatford launch *Princess Lily*. Harry Hastings, whose crew included his brother and partner Warren Hastings, was blown overboard by a near miss as *Tigris One* made a fourth run to the beach but clambered back uninjured. After a fifth run Hastings was ordered to beach and abandon the leaking *Tigris One* and his crew were taken off and returned to Ramsgate. *Tigris One* came back too. Troops from a French engineering regiment managed to patch leaks and repair the boat's pump and started out across the Channel. They ran aground on the Goodwin Sands but were towed off and into Ramsgate. *Tigris One* was refitted by Toughs but her hull had been severely strained and after the 1944 season she was sold for use as a houseboat.

Viscount Thames steam launch of 75 tons, built 1908 by Salter Bros, Oxford, for J. Mears of Richmond – 100′6″ × 16′6″: Returned to Mears fleet until taken over by Thames Launches in 1948, when the steam engine was replaced by Gardner diesel. Now used by Thompson's Launches on Westminster–Tower–Greenwich services, although much altered from original appearance. ADLS member.

Watchful Passenger excursion vessel of 72 tons, built in 1935 as *Brit II* by Fellows & Co, Great Yarmouth, for E. W. and S. H. D. Longfield of Great Yarmouth – 88′ × 19′ – compound steam engine, single screw: Used until 1939 by the Longfield Brothers on sea trips from the Town Hall Quay and Britannia Pier, Great Yarmouth. Requisitioned September 1939 as tender and

Coronia, *seen returning to Gibraltar from a short sea trip, flies the Association of Dunkirk Little Ships flag at the bow, although there are no official records to substantiate claims that 900 men were brought back from Dunkirk. Curiously, some local folk insist that the vessel never left the Yarmouth area during the time of Operation Dynamo.* (Alan Sparrow)

nominal base vessel for HMS *Watchful*, Great Yarmouth, and used mainly to ferry supplies to destroyers and other naval vessels lying in Yarmouth Roads. The Longfields remained on board as skipper and engineer and although the vessel does not appear as *Watchful* or *Brit* in any official lists, it is claimed to have ferried 900 troops from off the beaches. Returned to excursion work as *Brit* in 1949 but ran on the Thames in 1950 before going to Scarborough the next year as *Yorkshire Lady*. A change of ownership in 1968 brought the name *Coronia II*, the suffix being dropped before Millet Investors took over in 1980. Since 1985 *Coronia* has been owned by Tommy Hansom of Scarborough and based in Gibraltar for short local cruises. ADLS member.

Wootton Double ended vehicle ferry of 149 tons, built in 1928 by Wm Denny & Bros, Dumbarton, for the Southern Railway – 136′ × 27′ – powered by twin Gardner oil engines: Left Portsmouth–Fishbourne service and travelled to Ramsgate with sister vessel *Fishbourne*, but with a top speed of only 8 knots and limited manoeuvrability there is no confirmation of her crossing. The *Fishbourne* set out for Dunkirk under tow but was sent back and *Wootton* may never have left Ramsgate. The vessel returned to the Isle of Wight ferry service until withdrawn in 1962 and broken up in Holland.

DUNKIRK VESSELS STILL IN COMMERCIAL SERVICE

Amazone Charter cruises world wide as *Welsh Liberty*. Owners: Dragon Yachts of London.

Cabby Charter trips (under sail) on Medway and Thames. Owners: Crescent Shipping, Strood.

Felicity Cruises from Lymington as *Wight Rose*. Owners: Hurst Castle Cruises.

Folkestone Belle Portsmouth Harbour cruises. Owner: M. G. Pearce, Portsmouth.

Gondolier King Local cruises from Dartmouth as *My Queen*. Owners: G. H. Ridalls and Sons, Dartmouth.

Hurlingham River Thames services from Westminster to Tower Pier and Greenwich. Owner: Tidal Cruises, London.

Jeff River Thames services from Kingston to Richmond and Hampton Court. Owners: Turk Launches, Kingston.

Kingwood River Thames services from Westminster to Kew and Hampton Court. Owner: C. H. Wyatt, London.

Lady Cable Local cruises and fishing trips from Torquay. Owner: J. Bolus, Torquay.

New Britannic Scillies inter-island trips as *Commodore*. Owners: Bryher Boat Services, Isles of Scilly.

New Windsor Castle River Thames services from Kingston to Richmond and Hampton Court. Owner: Turk Launches, Kingston.

Oulton Belle Coastal cruises from Scarborough as *Regal Lady*. Owner: T. Machin, Scarborough.

Princess Freda River Thames services from Westminster to Kew and Hampton Court. Owner: M. & C. W. Phillips, Westminster.

Queen Boadicea II Local cruises from Plymouth. Owner: Tamar Cruising, Plymouth.

Silver Queen Cruises from St. Peter Port, Guernsey, to Fermain Bay as *Fermain V*. Owner: Fermain Marine, Guernsey.

Skylark IX Cruises on Loch Lomond. Owner: J. Sweeney, Balloch.

Southern Queen Scillies inter-island cruises. Owner: A. Hicks, St. Mary's, Isles of Scilly.

Tamar Belle River Trent cruises from Nottingham. Owner: Tamar Belle Cruises, Nottingham.

The King River Thames services from Westminster to Kew and Hampton Court. Owners: Thames Tripping, Westminster.

Viscount Thames excursions from Westminster to Tower Pier and Greenwich. Owner: Thompson's Launches, Westminster.

Watchful/Brit II Short sea trips from Gibraltar as *Coronia*. Owner: T. Hansom of Scarborough.

Dutch Schuits (Skoots)

ANOTHER massive contribution to the overall achievement of Operation Dynamo was made by what might at first appear an unlikely assortment of Dutch motor coasters. Known collectively as schuits, they were a self-propelled seagoing development of the towed barges so familiar on European rivers such as the Rhine, Elbe and Danube.

Despite considerable variation in both size and age, almost all were flat bottomed, designed to take the ground at low water, and had operated along the coasts of the Low Countries, mostly owned and crewed by a single family who made their home in accommodation above the engines right at the stern. A large number of these craft crossed to England following the fall of Holland and were moored either on the Thames or in Poole Harbour.

Their potential, initially for transporting supplies, was not lost on Captain J. Fisher, director of the Ministry of Shipping's Coastwise and Short Sea department. As early as 20th May he arranged for 40 of them to be commissioned by Royal Navy crews, and the British personnel quickly translated the Dutch title of 'schuit' to 'skoot!' Chatham crews took over 22 craft lying in London's river and the remaining 18, at Poole, were manned from Portsmouth, mostly with RNR or retired list officers placed in command.

The 40 skoots were available to Admiral Ramsay as Operation Dynamo began and in the next nine days they undertook all manner of tasks. Some worked off the beaches ferrying men to larger ships throughout the operation, others crossed repeatedly towing small craft and several managed to get in and out of Dunkirk harbour itself. Although contemporary accounts claim that *Horst*, abandoned after running aground in

A skoot, its white ensign fluttering at the stern, lies beached off La Panne as troops queue in the water until it is their turn to be hauled aboard. Further on, another knot of men stand patiently awaiting the return of a boat ferrying out to a vessel lying in deep water and, beyond them, what appears to be an abandoned drifter. (J. Rutherford Crosby)

shallows close to the West Mole on 3rd June, was the only skoot to be lost, the Admiralty also listed three others, *Alice, Lena* and *Sursum-Corda,* among the Dunkirk casualties.

Two of the 40 vessels at Dunkirk survive. The British-built *Amazone* is now the luxury charter yacht *Welsh Liberty,* equipped to cruise worldwide, while the *Brandaris,* built in Amsterdam and barely three years old when sent to Dunkirk, is on the other side of the North Atlantic, owned by an American from Rhode Island.

Abel Tasman (Commissioned by Lieutenant-Commander T. Crick, RN, replaced by Lieutenant C. Beal RN, from *Kaap Falga* on 28th May after being wounded): Previously lying London, transported 220 men.

Aegir (Lieutenant Q. Whitworth, RN): Previously lying London, carried 835 men, making no fewer than six crossings.

Alice (Lieutenant H. Slater, RN): Previously lying Poole – worked at La Panne on 1st June, subsequently reported lost.

Amazone (Lieutenant-Commander L.Phillips, RN): Built by J. I. Thornycroft at Southampton in 1936 – 127′ 5″ × 21′ 1″ – powered by two MAN engines. Previously lying Poole, worked off beaches transporting 549 men. Now owned by Dragon Yachts of London and named *Welsh Liberty,* the vessel emerged from a massive three year interior reconstruction in the Bute Dry Dock, Cardiff, to resume cruising in the summer of 1989. Equipped to berth up to 20 with a crew of between eight and 12, the vessel's original hold has been converted into luxury suites and after spending some weeks in Irish waters and, later, the Solent, *Welsh Liberty* headed for the Caribbean.

Antje (Lieutenant M. Buist, RN): Lying London prior to taking supplies of food and water to La Panne on 1st June. Transported 450 men.

Atlantic (Lieutenant-Commander L. Fordham, RNR): Previously lying Poole, transported 590 men.

Bart (Lieutenant E. G. Ball, RN Retd): Previously lying London, worked off the beaches.

Bonrif (Lieutenant A. N. Blundell RNR): Previously lying London, transported 146 men.

Brandaris (Commander C. Euman, RN Retd): Built (and owned) by G. de Vries Lentsch, jun, at Amsterdam in 1937 – 53′ × 16′ 4″ – powered by four-cylinder Thornycroft petrol engine. Previously lying London, worked off beaches transporting 330 troops. Now owned by A. E. Symonds of Providence, Rhode Island, USA.

Caribia (Lieutenant M. Morais RNR, then Lieutenant G. Williams from 29th May): Previously lying London, transported 701 men.

Delta (Lieutenant-Commander D. Lawrence, RN Retd): Built 1898 and previously lying London. Transported 503 troops. Foundered in

Almost certainly the last of the Dunkirk skoots to see service as a cargo vessel, **Amazone** *was virtually derelict when acquired by Dragon Yachts in 1976. Refitted as an ocean-going motor yacht at Cardiff during 1977, emerging as* **Welsh Liberty,** *the vessel retained its original engine until returning to the Bute Dry Dock of an associated company in the C. H. Bailey Group for a three-year reconstruction completed in the summer of 1989. Now she is again cruising worldwide.*

October 1944 when moored at Harty Point, Sheppey.

Deneb (Commanding Officer unknown): Previously lying London, transported 100 men.

Despatch II (Lieutenant-Commander F. Wilmott-Sitwell RN Retd): Previously lying Poole, transported 428 men.

Doggersbank (Lieutenant D. McBarnet RN): Previously lying London. Crossed on 27th May with skoot *Hilda* and made three more trips, carrying 800 men. CO awarded DSO and ERA E. Horne the DSM.

Fredanja (Lieutenant-Commander K. Stewart, RN Retd): Previously lying Poole, transported 1,002 men.

Frisco (Commanding Officer unknown): Previously lying Poole, transported 1,002 men.

Gorecht (Sub-Lieutenant D. Edwards, RNR): Previously lying Poole, transported 47 men.

Hebe II (Lieutenant-Commander J. Temple, RN): Previously lying Poole. Worked West Quay at Dunkirk, transporting 515 men.

Hilda (Lieutenant A. Gray, RN): Previously lying Poole. Completed three trips, transporting 835 men. Towed four lifeboats from Belgian steamer *Flandres* on 27th May. Rescued 30 men from HMS *Keith* on 1st June and towed motor vessel *Bluebird* on the following day.

Hondsrug (Lieutenant F. Renny, RNR): Previously lying London, transported 1,453 men.

Horst (Lieutenant-Commander G. Fardell, RN): Previously lying Poole, transported 1,150 men before running aground at West Mole on 3rd June and being abandoned.

Jaba (Commanding officer unknown): Previously lying Poole, worked off the beaches, transported 469 men.

Jutland (Lieutenant G. Barwell, RN Retd, relieved by Lieutenant-Commander W. Clements, RNR, on 30th May, but re-assumed command on 31st): Crossed at least twice towing small craft, transported 505 men. Sunk 2nd May 1942.

Kaap Falga (Lieutenant H. Beal RN, until transferred to *Abel Tasman* on 28th May, then Lieutenant H. Wykeham-Martin RN): Previously lying Poole, transported five men.

Lena (Lieutenant-Commander R. Hawkins, RN, Retd): Previously lying London, transported 996

Two skoots alongside Margate Pier with **Oranje,** *the outer vessel, still waiting to disembark her complement of troops.* **Oranje** *is recorded as landing 605 men and, judging by the look of those crowded decks, the majority were probably from this one crossing.* (Imperial War Museum)

men. Listed by Admiralty as lost.

Oranje (Lieutenant H. Crispin, RN): Previously lying London, full name possibly *Oranje Yreeswijh*. Transported 605 men.

Pacific (Lieutenant-Commander C. Skrine, RN): Previously lying Poole, transported 945 men.

Pascholl (Lieutenant T. Johnson until transferred to the paddle-steamer *Portsdown*, then Lieutenant J. Wise RNVR): Previously lying Poole, transported 695 men, 300 of them in one of the final departures on 3rd June in spite of damage suffered after being wedged against the West Mole by a destroyer.

Patria (Lieutenant-Commander N. Pisani, RN, Retd): Previously lying London, transported 1,400 men.

Reiger (Lieutenant A. Tyson, RN): A vessel of 48′ × 15′5″ built in 1906 and powered by a Ford petrol engine. Previously lying London. Completed five crossings, transporting 592 men.

Rian (Lieutenant-Commander J. H. Miller, RN): Previously lying Poole, transported 257 men, completing last trip with engine firing on only two cylinders.

Rika (Lieutenant H. Webber, RN): Previously lying Poole, transported 300 men.

Ruja (Lieutenant H. Webber, RN): Previously lying Poole, transported 300 men.

San Antonio (Lieutenant-Commander G. Legassick, RNR): Previously lying Poole, transported 484 men and probably last vessel to work off the beaches.

Sursum-Corda (Lieutenant C. Philpotts, RN): Previously lying Poole, transported 370 men. Listed by Admiralty as lost.

Tilly (Lieutenant-Commander W. Clements RNR, and Lieutenant-Commander C. M. Rasmus, RNR): Previously lying London, transported 602 men. Ran down Thames pleasure boat *Queen of England* on 29th May. Worked with Leigh cockle boats off the Mole on 31st May.

Tiny (Lieutenant-Commander J. Hunter, RN): Previously lying Poole, transported 261 men.

Twente (Lieutenant-Commander H. Boys-Smith, RNR, to 30th May, then Lieutenant A. McMullen, RNR): Previously lying London, transported 1,139 men.

Vrede (Lieutenant-Commander R. Lampard, RN): Previously lying London, transported 473 men.

Zeus (Lieutenant-Commander C. Hoggan, RN Retd): Previously lying Poole, transported 601 men.

Tugs

ADMIRALTY and civilian tugs worked side by side throughout the evacuation, undertaking all manner of conventional, and more than a few unorthodox towing tasks, on either side of the English Channel. Around 50 vessels were involved and Operation Dynamo drew heavily on ship-handling tugs from London's river and docks system with well-known Thames concerns like the Sun tugs of Alexander's and the fleets of Gaselee, Gamecock and William Watkins equally well represented.

Some of the hardest-worked tugs never left the sight of a British shore and were occupied throughout at Dover, Folkestone or Ramsgate. Others crossed and re-crossed to the French coast with tows in the outward direction consisting of anything from sailing barges to ship's lifeboats, or cabin cruisers to sturdy RNLI boats. The returning tugs picked up any vessels to which they could lend assistance, including damaged warships, larger merchant vessel, or simply more small craft.

In the almost total absence of local tugs which had either been withdrawn from the area some days before the evacuation, or were simply marooned on the wrong side of shattered lock gates, the British tugs, and five Belgian vessels, worked throughout amid the turmoil of Dunkirk Harbour helping the troop-carrying warships and merchant vessels to berth or swing in the wreck-strewn approaches. All but one of the Belgian tugs were lost and three of the British vessels also failed to return.

Some tugs even found time to ferry men to vessels lying offshore and a number actually carried men back to the Kent ports, one Watkins tug, the *Racia*, managing to squeeze in over 400 and transport them safely to Ramsgate. Towards the closing stages of the operation, when just about everything which floated had been hauled across, tugs were simply sent out to look for any small vessels needing help.

All of the tugs taking part in the evacuation were steam powered and many of the survivors went on to serve for a further 20 years, and in some cases more. One of the Dunkirk tugs, the *Challenge*, ran until 1973 and has been preserved and is located on the Thames at St. Katharine's Dock.

Aid Steam tug of 134 tons, owned by Risdon Beazley, Southampton: Sunk by gunfire on 29th November 1940.

Betty Steam tug of 119 tons, built by Henry Robb, Leith, in 1907 – 96′ × 25′1″ – owned by Gaselee & Son, master G. Finch: Worked at Ramsgate throughout the operations.

C 9 Admiralty steam tug of 138 tons, built in 1919 as *West Acre* by Yarwood & Sons, Northwich, with engine of 450 ihp – 89′ × 21′ – master C. Treleaven: Portsmouth Naval stores depot tug. Sold to Handcock, Cardiff, as *West Acre* in 1950, and sold out of fleet as *Lavernock* in 1960.

C 11 Admiralty steam tug of 144 tons, built in 1938 as *Foremost 91* by Cook, Welton & Gemmell of Beverley – 91′ × 25′3″: Also operated by Portsmouth Naval stores depot. Renamed *Regard* in 1959, broken up at Antwerp in 1966.

Cervia Steam tug of 157 tons, built 1925, owned by William Watkins Ltd, master W. H. Simmons: Crossed to La Panne on 1st June towing small craft. Took crew off beached sailing barge *Royalty* and was among tugs which went to the assistance of the destroyer *Keith*. *Cervia* also picked up crew of barge *Duchess* and 30 troops from a motor boat. Requisitioned by the Admiralty in 1941, *Cervia* was returned to her owners in 1945.

Challenge Steam tug of 212 tons, built in 1931 by Alexander Hall & Sons, Aberdeen, with engine of 1150 ihp – 100′ × 26′1″ – owned by Elliott Steam Tug Co: Worked at Dunkirk assisting vessels berthing at the East Mole on 31st May, and on 1st June to take small craft in tow. Continued to operate on the Thames until withdrawn and preserved at St. Katharine's Dock in 1973.

Contest Steam tug of 213 tons, built in 1933 by Alexander Hall & Sons, Aberdeen, with engine of 1150 ihp – 100′ × 26′1″ – owned by Elliott Steam Tug Co, master H. J. Bates: Crossed on 31st May and worked off beaches, picking up survivors from sunken drifter. Served on Thames until scrapped at Grays in 1972.

Crested Cock Steam tug of 177 tons, built in 1935 by Alexander Hall & Sons, Aberdeen, with engine of 950 ihp – 96′ × 25′1″ – owned by Gamecock Steam Towing Co, master T. Hills: Arrived at Dover on 31st May towing barges from the Thames and crossed to the beaches towing a lighter loaded with fresh water and food and carrying an Army working party. The destroyer *Basilisk*, which had damaged a propeller, was assisted to turn in a narrow channel before the tug returned to Dover. *Crested Cock* crossed again on 1st June to look for small craft adrift. She was scrapped at Antwerp in 1970.

Doria Steam tug of 150 tons, built in 1909 by

After Dunkirk, the **Challenge** *returned to the Thames but her work hardly lacked variety and the tug is seen later in the war while helping to move a Maunsell Fort into position.* (Imperial War Museum)

Challenge, *the last steam tug in service on the Thames, towards the end of her active career in the colours of Ship Towage (London) Ltd.* (M. J. Gaston)

Philip & Son, Dartmouth – 96′2″ × 20′6″ – owned by William Watkins Ltd, master A. W. Mastin: Served as inspection vessel and was at sea in the Channel for most of the operation, picking up 90 men.

Dromedary Steam tug built 1911, 220 ihp: Belgian tug, probably ex-*President Arnaud Grison,* taken over by the Admiralty in March 1940, commanded by Sub-Lieutenant T. Lawrie, RNVR. Broken up in the Channel Islands.

Duke Steam tug owned by S. Williams & Sons, master B. Mansfield: Left at 9.30 a.m. on 1st June with Williams sister tugs *Prince* and *Princess* towing vessels including the car ferry *Fishbourne. Duke* parted the tow to pick up barges *Ada Mary* and *Haste Away* which had broken adrift from the tug *Sun III* and arrived off Dunkirk in the afternoon. Later a lifeboat was sighted adrift near the Outer Ruytingen Buoy and *Duke* took on its load, assisted by *Sun III.* While returning to Ramsgate *Duke* found another small boat and landed its 10 occupants together with a further 34 troops.

Elbe Steam tug built in Holland in 1905, 150 grt, owned by S/A Helice, Antwerp: One of a fleet of five Belgian tugs which worked in Dunkirk Harbour from 25th May until the closing stages of the operation when all but one was lost. *Elbe* was salvaged by the Germans and put back to work until sunk on 7th October 1942.

Empire Henchman Steam tug of 239 tons, built 1940 by Cochrane & Sons, Selby – 112′ × 27′ – owned by the Ministry of War Transport, managed by United Towing Co, master E. Fisher: Worked small boats from beaches to destroyers on 30th May, staying until the early hours of 1st June. Went back late in the evening towing barges loaded with petrol but forced to return to Ramsgate after being damaged when bombs exploded alongside. Sold to Swedish owners as *Karl* in 1946 and to Italy as *Capo Faro* in 1963.

Fabia Steam tug of 151 tons, built at Milwall in 1919 – 85′ × 20′9″ – owned by William Watkins Ltd, master F. Smith: Formerly HMS *Early,* this tug was requisitioned by the Admiralty in 1939 and not returned until 1945. It crossed to Dunkirk towing various craft and then worked off the beaches. *Fabia* was sold as *Moor Cock* to the Liverpool Screw Towing Company in 1947, surviving until scrapped at Preston in 1956.

Fairplay 1 Steam tug of 191 tons, built as *Fairplay X* in 1911 at Hamburg – owned by Fairplay Towage & Shipping of London, and managed by William Watkins Ltd, masters S. Wright and G. Finch: Escorted skoots from Ramsgate to beaches before making a second crossing towing small craft. Later damaged by a mine at Ostend in November 1944. Returned to Fairplay Richard Borchard, Hamburg, after the war, being renamed *Fairplay XX* in 1951.

Foremost 22 Steam tug of 362 tons, built in 1924 by J. Meyer at Zalt Bomel – 100′4″ × 27′2″ – owned by the Southern Railway, acting master F. Holden: The Southern Railway's Newhaven tug towed HMS *Sharpshooter* to Dover after the destroyer had been damaged in a collision with the personnel carrier *St. Helier. Foremost 22* returned to work in Dunkirk Harbour but was almost stranded on 2nd June when attempting to move the ferry *Rouen* on a fast ebbing tide. *Sun X*, a tug of less draught, also failed. *Foremost 22* served at Newhaven until replaced in 1960.

Foremost 87 Steam tug of 163 tons, built in 1935 by Scott & Sons, Bowling – 88′4″ × 24′6″ – owned by the British Transport Commission, managed by William Watkins Ltd, master J. Fryer: One of the tugs which assisted the damaged personnel carrier *Prague* back across the Channel and subsequently beached her on 30th/31st May. Went over in convoy from Ramsgate towing barges later on 31st and again on 2nd June towing two RNLI boats. Also assisted a launch towing two ship's lifeboats and landed a total of 100 men. Skipper Fryer awarded DSO.

Fossa Steam tug of 105 tons, built in 1929 by Alexander Hall & Sons, Aberdeen – 81′ × 21′6″ – owned by Gaselee & Son, master G. Finch: Towed vessels across including the ketch *Jeanette* with which *Fossa* then worked loading troops ferried from the East Mole. When *Jeanette* developed a steering fault *Fossa* herself went in, later departing towing *Jeanette* and a naval cutter. Then ran aground and cast off tows whose men were transferred to another boat. *Fossa* was refloated but lost on 2nd June after suffering a direct hit.

Goliath Steam tug of 354 tons, built 1921 for the French Government as *L'Etalon:* Renamed after purchase by Antwerp tug operator S/A Helice in 1925, *Goliath* was the only survivor of five Belgian vessels which worked in Dunkirk Harbour from 25th May until *Elbe, Max, Thames* and *Vulcain* were all lost on 2nd June. *Goliath* then worked as *W 121* for the British Admiralty until 1945, returning to Helice until scrapped in 1958.

Gondia Steam tug of 151 tons, built in 1927 by Cochrane & Sons, Selby, with engine of 850 ihp – 100′ × 25′1″ – owned by William Watkins Ltd, master C. Pratt: Crossed to Boulogne on 22nd May with vessels carrying the 20th Guards Brigade and there assisted destroyer *Keith* to berth. In action almost continuously at Dover, working warships and passenger vessels for refuelling.

Hibernia Steam tug of 219 tons, built in 1884 by Maats de Maas, Delftshaven, Holland – 107′1″ × 22′1″ – owned by William Watkins Ltd, master B. Youseman: Worked out of Ramsgate throughout the evacuation. Scrapped at Grays in 1961.

Java Steam tug of 128 tons, built in 1919 by J. Cochrane & Sons, Selby – 94′ × 19′6″ – owned by William Watkins Ltd, master W. Jones: Requisitioned by the Admiralty in 1940, returned 1945. Towed drifters and motor boats on 29th May and next day used own lifeboat to ferry men from beach to motor boats which, in turn, put them on the tug or drifters. Later transferred troops from East Mole to a destroyer off La Panne, then returned to ferry from the Mole all evening. Recorded as carrying 270 troops. Scrapped in Belgium in 1966 after further service on the Thames.

Kenia Steam tug of 200 tons, built in 1927 by Cochrane & Sons, Selby, with engine of 850 ihp – 100′ × 25′1″ – owned by William Watkins Ltd, master W. Hoiles: Requisitioned by Admiralty in 1939, returned 1945. Worked as an inspection vessel off Dover and Ramsgate from 27th May to 3rd June. Sank in collision at Tilbury Docks in 1966 and afterwards scrapped at Newhaven.

Lady Brassey Twin screw steam tug of 362 tons, built in 1913 by J. P. Renoldson & Sons, South Shields – owned by Dover Harbour Board, master F. Hopgood: One of the operation's busiest tugs, working in Dover Harbour and frequently going to sea to tow in damaged or disabled vessels including the *Kohistan* 24th, *Isle*

After sailing to Boulogne in the week before Dunkirk, **Gondia** *worked throughout Operation Dynamo at Dover. Little changed apart from the modern lifeboat some two decades on, and pictured during repainting in the livery of final operators Ship Towage (London) Ltd, the* **Gondia** *was scrapped in Belgium during 1966. Note the open wheelhouse with its canvas awning.* (M. J. Gaston)

of Thanet and *Mona's Isle* 27th. On 29th *Lady Brassey* and the Watkins tug *Simla* were ordered to near Cap Gris Nez where HMS *Montrose*, fully loaded with troops, had her bows blown away. The tugs brought the destroyer back to Dover stern first and later *Lady Brassey* pulled the grounded *Prague* clear at Dunkirk and on 1st June helped to beach her. *Lady Brassey's* distinctive twin funnel profile remained part of the Dover scene until 1958.

Max Steam tug of 177 tons, built 1911 at Goole as *Marino:* Owned by Remorquage Letzer and served at Dunkirk with other Belgian tugs throughout evacuation until lost on final day.

Marquis Steam tug of 49 tons, built in 1902 at Delftshaven, Holland – 65′ 5″ × 15′6″ – owned by Samuel Williams Lighterage Ltd, London: Name appears in Admiralty lists of participating vessels, but role in the evacuation unclear.

Ocean Cock Steam tug of 182 tons, built in 1932 by Alexander Hall & Sons, Aberdeen, with engine of 950 ihp – 96′ × 25′1″ – owned by Gamecock Steam Towing Co, master A. V. Mastin: Left Dover on 31st May towing six motor boats and returned safely, before setting out again next day with orders to search in the Channel for any small boats in need of assistance. Continued in service until scrapped at Antwerp in 1969.

Persia Steam tug of 165 tons, built in 1932 as *Dongara* by Cochrane & Sons, Selby, with engine of 950 ihp – 95′ × 24′1″ – owned by William Watkins Ltd, master A. Aldrich: Renamed *Persia* in 1937. Set off from Dover on 29th May towing barges loaded with food and ammunition, arriving off the beaches at dawn on the 30th, returning with 27 soldiers aboard. On 1st June *Persia* secured a line to HMS *Ivanhoe* which was lying disabled to the west of Dunkirk Harbour but soon after the tow started a bomb between tug and destroyer severed the line. Skipper Aldrich managed to pass a second line and succeeded in towing *Ivanhoe* to Dover. The tug was damaged by a mine at Shellhaven on 9th April 1941 and was rebuilt, resuming Thames service the following year. Renamed *Muria* in 1946, she was scrapped at Antwerp in 1967.

Prima Steam tug of 40 tons, built in 1930 by Yarwood & Sons, Northwich, with engine of 100 ihp – 55′1″ × 15′1″ – owned by James Dredging, Towage and Transport, London, master J. B. Morran: Requisitioned for use at Portsmouth. Sold in the 1950s to W.E. White & Sons, renamed *Doris White.* Withdrawn from service 1975, hull scrapped 1982.

Prince Steam tug owned by S. Williams and Son, master J. Benson: Crossed on 1st June from Ramsgate towing smaller vessels.

Princess Steam tug owned by S. Williams and Son, master J. Wallis: Sailed on 1st June in same convoy as *Prince.*

Racia Steam tug of 163 tons, built in 1930 as *Dilwara* by Cochrane & Sons, Selby, with engine of 950 ihp – 95′ × 24′1″ – owned by William Watkins Ltd, master A. C. Addison: Renamed *Dendera* in 1935 and *Racia* in 1938. Towed over 12 ship's lifeboats on 31st and set off again on 3rd June with an Army party aboard. *Racia* then went independently to Dunkirk Harbour before loading 423 troops to Ramsgate. *Racia* was scrapped at Antwerp in 1967.

Risban French steam tug of 159 grt, built 1924 and with engine of 625 ihp: Escaped to serve with Royal Navy from 1941 to 1945.

Roman Steam tug of 108 tons, built 1906, with engine of 430 ihp, owned by United Towing Co: Worked throughout at Dover.

St. Abbs Admiralty steam tug of 468 tons, built in 1918 by Ferguson Brothers, Port Glasgow, with triple-expansion engine of 1250 ihp – 135′6″ × 29′ – commanded by Lieutenant T. Brooker, RN Retd: Aided survivors of HMS *Keith* on 1st June but bombed and sunk on 2nd with surviving crew members picked up by the tug *Sun XI.*

St. Clears Admiralty steam tug of 468 tons, built in 1919 by Livingston & Cooper with triple-expansion engine of 1250 ihp – 135′6″ × 29′ – master W. J. Penney: Left Sheerness on 28th May in company of *Sun V* and towing 20 naval cutters, arriving safely after coming under fire near Gravelines. Next day cutters were used with the tug to load cargo vessels *Beal* and *Bullfinch* off the beaches, *St. Clears* returning with 70

Racia *set off for the beaches on 31st May towing a dozen ship's lifeboats and was later moving a tow of 17 small craft when ordered to hand over to one of the Sun tugs and proceed to the harbour at Dunkirk. Over 400 men were taken aboard and landed at Ramsgate.* (M. J. Gaston)

The **Sun** *was only a couple of years short of completing 60 years service when broken up in 1964. She twice crossed to Dunkirk in 1940 and also made an up-river trip to collect a string of ship's lifeboats from Tilbury.* (M. J. Gaston)

troops. She was sold in 1948 to Southampton salvage contractor Risdon Beazley.

St. Fagan Admiralty steam tug of 550 tons, built in 1919 by Lytham Shipbuilding Co, with triple-expansion engine of 1250 ihp – 135′6″ × 29′ – commanded by Lieutenant-Commander G. Warren: Blown up near Dunkirk on 1st June.

St. Olaves Steam tug of 468 tons, built in 1919 by Harland & Wolff, Govan, with triple-expansion engine of 1250 ihp – 135′6″ × 29′ – master H. Forrester: Admiralty tug sold 1922 but recalled to service in December 1939. Used as a rescue tug in Channel, landing 200 troops. Wrecked on 21st September 1942 after running aground.

Simla Steam tug of 144 tons, built in 1918 by Lobnitz, Renfrew – 100′4″ × 20′1″ – owned by William Watkins Ltd, master G. Lowe: Worked throughout evacuation at Dover. Scrapped Sheerness 1964.

Sultan Particulars unknown: Transported 193 troops.

Sun Steam tug of 130 tons, built in 1906 by R. Cock and Sons, Appledore, with engine of 550 ihp – 87′3″ × 22′3″ – owned by W. H. J. Alexander Ltd, master H. Cole: After working off Dunkirk on 30th May was sent to collect 20 ship's lifeboats from Tilbury and deliver them to Ramsgate. Left on 1st June towing a launch and two lifeboats, returning with 173 troops, 28 naval ratings and 7 of her own crew aboard. Scrapped in 1964.

Sun III Steam tug of 197 tons, built in 1909 by Earle & Co, Hull, with engine of 750 ihp – 100′ × 25′6″ – owned by W. H. J. Alexander Ltd, master F. W. Russell: Requisitioned by Admiralty in 1939, returned 1945. Crossed on 1st June towing barges. Sold to Grimsby as *Lady Sarah* in 1956. Broken up at Blyth in 1967.

Sun IV Steam tug of 200 tons, built in 1915 by Earle & Co., Hull, with engine of 750 ihp – 105′ × 25′5″ – owned by W. H. J. Alexander Ltd, master G. C. Alexander: Towed nine small boats over on 31st May and returned on 1st June to work off the beaches loading 112 men, during which time the tug's engineer Wally Jones pulled his own soldier brother from the water. *Sun IV* also towed back the Walton on the Naze lifeboat

While **Sun IV** *was working off the beaches on 1st June 1940, her engineer, Wally Jones, pulled his own brother out of the water. The tug worked until 1966, ending her days in the Mediterranean.* (M. J. Gaston)

E.M.E.D. with 39 men onboard. The tug was sold to Italy as *San Benigno* in 1966.

Sun V Steam tug of 200 tons, built in 1915 by Earl & Co., Hull, with engine of 750 ihp – 105′ × 25′5″ – owned by W. H. J. Alexander Ltd, master W. Mastin: Requisitioned by Admiralty in 1939, returned in 1945. Sailed towing cutters with *St. Clears* on 28th May and was back working off Dunkirk on 1st June. Sold in 1966 to Italy with *Sun IV*, becoming *Punta Alice.*

Sun VII Steam tug of 202 tons, built in 1917 by Cook, Wivenhoe, with engine of 700 ihp – 105′ × 25′5″ – owned by W. H. J. Alexander Ltd, master G. Cawsey: Requisitioned by the Admiralty in 1939. Completed a crossing on 31st May with five tenders from RAF Calshot despite the tow breaking on six occasions. Crossed again on 1st June and searched for six hours without finding anything. *Sun VII* was mined and lost in the Thames Estuary on 6th March 1941.

Sun VIII Steam tug of 196 tons, built in 1919 by Cochrane & Sons, Selby, with engine of 750 ihp – 100′3″ × 25′6″ – owned by W. H. J. Alexander Ltd, master S. Smith: Requisitioned by the Admiralty in 1939, returned 1946. Crossed on 31st May in convoy with *Sun IV* and *Sun IX*, going back to the beaches on 1st June and bringing home 120 men. Returned to Thames service until broken up at Antwerp in 1969.

Sun X Steam tug of 196 tons, built in 1920 by Cochrane & Sons, Selby, with engine of 750 ihp – 100′3″ × 25′6″ – owned by W. H. J. Alexander Ltd, master W. A. Fothergill: Tried unsuccessfully to move the grounded *Rouen* in Dunkirk harbour on 2nd June before taking on over 200 of her troops and transferring them to other ships. Sold for breaking at Antwerp in 1969.

Sun XI Steam tug of 183 tons, built in 1925 by Earle & Co, Hull, with engine of 750 ihp – 100′ × 25′6″ – owned by W. H. J. Alexander Ltd, master J. R. Lukes: Left Dover on 31st May towing barge loaded with drinking water and food with orders to beach it two miles east of Dunkirk Harbour, arriving after a passage of six hours, a motor boat taking the barge through shallows to the beach. *Sun XI* spent an hour in Dunkirk Harbour, leaving with 188 men aboard. Out in the Channel on 1st June, skipper Lukes saw lights, and went to investigate and found a broken down lighter full of troops, many of them wounded. Also aboard were survivors from HMS *Keith* and the tug *St. Abbs*. *Sun XI* was sold to Belgium as *Schelde X* in 1964 and later went to Italy as *Andea*.

Sun XII Steam tug of 183 tons, built in 1925 by Earle & Co., Hull, with engine of 850 ihp – 100′ × 25′6″ – owned by W. H. J. Alexander Ltd, master B. Mastin, towing master A. Mee: Crossed with barges on 31st May, returning again on 1st and 2nd June. The tug was requisitioned by the Admiralty in 1942, returning to the Alexander company in 1945 and continuing in service until sold for breaking at Antwerp in 1969.

Sun XV Steam tug of 183 tons, built in 1925 by Earle & Co., Hull, with engine of 750 ihp – 100′ × 25′6″ – owned by W. H. J. Alexander Ltd, master J. J. Belton: Towed six small boats across on 31st May and on 2nd June went to the assistance of survivors of the bombed and abandoned hospital carrier *Paris*, crossing yet again on 3rd June to look for small boats. Sold for scrap in Belgium at the same time as *Sun* XII in 1969.

Tanga Steam tug of 203 tons, built in 1931 by Philip and Sons, Dartmouth, with engine of 950 ihp – 100′ × 25′3″ – owned by William Watkins Ltd, master H. Gouge: Towed six small boats over on 31st May, returning on 1st June with 160 troops loaded from small boats. Also picked up survivors of the tug *St. Fagans* and then towed in the barge *Pudge*. Sailed again in convoy with four small boats and made a further crossing on 3rd June in convoy including Admiral Taylor. Transported 367 troops in all. *Tanga* continued in Thames service until broken up at Antwerp in 1969.

Thames Steam tug of 144 tons, built 1904 in Holland with engine of 525 ihp: Owned by S/A Helice of Antwerp. Lost in Dunkirk Harbour after working from 25th May but later salvaged by the Germans and used until sunk at La Havre on 15th June 1944.

One of 10 tugs from the Alexander fleet to take part in Operation Dynamo, **Sun XV** *went to the aid of survivors of the hospital ship* **Paris** *during one of her several crossings to Dunkirk.* (M. J. Gaston)

Another of the Watkins tugs that was in the thick of the action off the Belgian and French coasts, **Tanga** *performed a number of towing tasks and also played a part as a rescue craft, landing 367 men in England.* (M. J. Gaston)

Trapu French steam tug of 226 grt, built 1919, with engine of 800 ihp: Got away from Dunkirk after assisting in evacuation and then sunk at Le Havre on 15th August 1944.

Vincia Steam tug of 150 tons, built in 1909 by Philip & Sons, Dartmouth – 112′ × 27′ – owned by William Watkins Ltd, master A. Hoiles: Picked up 180 men from the sinking HMS *Keith* on 1st June.

Vulcain Steam tug of 200 tons, built 1903, with engine of 850 ihp: Previously *W. 71* with British Navy during First World War (from September 1917 to January 1919). Later in the Antwerp fleet of Helice. Worked in Dunkirk Harbour from 25th May, lost in final stages of the evacuation.

Fishing Vessels

WITH only a small force of regular minesweepers maintained between the wars, an urgent need for extra vessels arose from September 1939. This was filled by requisitioning many of the paddle steamers mentioned earlier, the remainder of the shortfall being made up from the fishing fleets, with both deep sea and inshore trawlers fitted out for minesweeping and many drifters also slotted into similiar roles or for other specialist duties.

During the Dunkirk evacuation the various minesweeping trawlers and drifters were required for sweeping and patrol duties in the Channel in addition to work off the French coast and at Dunkirk itself. They were supplemented by other vessels direct from the fishing fleets, and the operation received equally wholehearted support from smaller craft including beach fishing boats from South Coast centres and even Essex cockle boats, shrimpers and oyster dredgers.

The small vessels, often manned by their skipper/owners, suffered losses en route to Dunkirk and operating off the beaches and there were casualties among the trawlers and drifters as well with 17 sunk, the most tragic loss being of the drifter *Comfort* which was mistaken for an E-Boat after stopping to pick up survivors from the torpedoed destroyer *Wakeful*. Both HMS *Grafton* and HMS *Lydd* opened fire on the *Comfort* and *Lydd* then sank the drifter by ramming.

No drifters performed with greater distinction than five East Coast herring boats that had been equipped by HMS *Vernon* at Portsmouth to recover grounded mines by trawling. Skippered by RNR men from the Hull or Grimsby deep sea fleets, and based at Ramsgate, the little flotilla consisting of *Fidget, Fisher Boy, Jacketa, Lord Cavan* and *Silver Dawn* had already come to be known as 'Vernon's Private Navy.' They were sent to Dunkirk to ferry from the harbour to larger ships and also returned to Ramsgate with troops, regularly exceeding their official load of 100 men per trip. *Lord Cavan* was shelled and sunk but the other four drifters all came through the operation and between them landed 4,085 men.

TRAWLERS

Alouette Built 1931, 387 tons and owned by Hellyer Brothers: Later sunk by a U-boat off Portugal on 19th September 1942.

Amethyst Built 1934, 627 tons: Mined and sunk in Thames Estuary on 24th November 1940.

Argyllshire Built 1938, 504 tons: Trawler from 11th A/S Strike Force. Worked off beaches on 29th May, sunk by E-boat on 1st June.

Arley Built 1914, 304 tons: Performed minesweeping duties and assisted smaller craft and transported 135 men. Later damaged by mine on 3rd February 1945 and sank whilst under tow.

Artic Pioneer Believed to have served as minesweeper.

Blackburn Rovers Built 1934, 422 tons: Antisubmarine trawler, torpedoed and sunk on 2nd June.

Botanic Built 1928, 670 tons: Towed small vessels from Dunkirk.

Drifters did valiant work ferrying troops out to larger vessels from the harbour area in Dunkirk and here one of their number, possibly either **Lord Cavan** *or* **Jacketa** *from what had come to be known as 'Vernon's Private Navy', is heading out to sea.* (Imperial War Museum)

Breadwinner 59 tons, owned by J. Bellhouse.

Brock Particulars unknown: Worked off the beaches returning with six men.

Calvi Built 1930, 363 tons: Minesweeping trawler lost 29th May.

Cape Argona Anti-submarine trawler: Worked off La Panne.

Cayton Wyke Built 1932, 530 tons: Carried 605 men, including 300 taken off a barge. Sunk by torpedo near Dover on 8th July 1940.

Clythness Minesweeping trawler: Loaded 150 troops off La Panne.

Desiree Built 1913, 213 tons and owned by Grimsby Trawlers: Survived Dunkirk but mined and sunk in Thames Estuary 16th January 1941.

Dhoon Owned by Wyre Steam Trawling Co: Carried 150 troops.

Edwina Owned by Dalby Steam Fishing Co: Transported 120 men before being lost off Bray Beach on 1st June.

Evelyn Rose Trawler: Ferried troops to larger vessels. Brought back 120 men.

Fire Fly Owned by St. Andrews Steam Fishing Co.

Fortuna Built 1906, 259 tons and owned by Dobson Ship Repairers: Survived Dunkirk but sunk by aircraft off St. Abbs Head, 1st May 1941.

Fyldea Minesweeping trawler: Based at Dover, carried 180 men.

Gava Minesweeping trawler: Brought down three planes with fire from own guns. Went alongside Mole to take on 376 French troops, later stopping to pick-up survivors from a French warship, the *Foudroyant*. Also assisted a disabled trawler, taking on 123 men, to land a total of 502.

Golden Lilly Owned by Inshore Trawlers: Towed from Sheerness to Dunkirk by the skoot *Jutland*.

Grimsby Town Anti-submarine trawler: Patrolled in Channel.

Iverforth Minesweeping trawler.

Jacinta Fleetwood trawler owned by J. Marr and Sons: Became stranded on East Mole at Dunkirk on 1st June.

Jasper Built 1932, 596 tons: Survived the evacuation but was sunk by an E-boat in the English Channel on 1st December 1942.

John Cattling Minesweeper. Landed 77 men.

Kestrel Trawler of 75 tons, owned by S. Rowden: Crossed from Ramsgate on 31st May. Bombed and sunk north of Lundy, 28th March 1941.

King George Trawler, other particulars unknown.

Kingston Alalite Built 1933, 550 tons: Anti-submarine trawler, patrolled off La Panne. Mined and sunk off Plymouth, 10th November 1940.

Kingston Andalusite 550 tons: Anti-submarine trawler, patrolled off La Panne.

Kingston Galena Built 1934, 550 tons: Anti-submarine trawler, sunk off Dover on 27th July 1940.

Kingston Olivine 550 tons: Anti-submarine trawler, patrolled with sisters off La Panne.

Lady Philomena Anti-submarine trawler: Worked off Dunkirk on 1st June.

Lent Lilly Trawler of 44 tons: Released on 3rd June but later re-allocated for special army service.

Lord Grey Minesweeping trawler: Patrolled off La Panne and also entered Dunkirk Harbour, transporting 400 men.

Lord Inchcape Built 1942, 338 tons: Loaded troops from Dunkirk Harbour on 28th May, transporting a total of 240. Later lost after striking a mine off Plymouth on 25th October 1940.

Lord Melchett Minesweeping trawler.

Malabar Trawler, further particulars unknown.

Ocean Reward Trawler: Reported lost following collision with hospital ship *Isle of Thanet* off Dover on 28th May.

Olvina Anti-submarine trawler: Patrolled off La Panne. Transported 347 men.

Our Bairns Minesweeping trawler: Operated as minesweeper and patrol vessel. Landed 200 men.

Polly Johnson Built 1918, 290 tons: Minesweeping trawler, sunk off Dunkirk Mole on 29th May.

Relonzo Built 1914, 245 tons: Minesweeping trawler, worked off the beaches. Lost in Crosby Channel, Liverpool on 10th November 1941.

Restrivo Minesweeping trawler: Worked off beaches at La Panne.

St. Achilleus Built 1934, 484 tons: Anti-submarine trawler, lost on 31st May after striking mine.

Saon Anti-submarine trawler: Worked off La Panne, transporting 359 men.

Saturn Minesweeping trawler: Extensively used for ferry duties, carrying a total of 1,177 men.

Shamrock Trawler owned by Consolidated Fisheries.

Spurs Anti-submarine trawler: Bombed and damaged *en route* for Dunkirk on 2nd June, forced to return to Dover.

Stella Dorado Built 1936, 550 tons: Anti-submarine trawler, carried 55 men before being sunk by E-boat on 1st June.

Stella Rigel Minesweeping trawler: Worked off beaches on 31st May.

Strathelliott Minesweeping trawler: Transported 339 men.

Tankerton Towers Motor trawler of 95 tons: Crossed on 31st May and continued loading from beaches despite a fouled propeller. Taken in tow and returned safely with 50 men. Lost after bombing off St. Govans Light on 9th May 1942.

Thomas Bartlett Built 1918, 290 tons: Lost on 28th May, mined off Calais.

Thuringia Built 1933, 550 tons: Anti-submarine trawler, mined and sunk off La Panne, 28th May.

Thyme Owned by Ramsgate Diesel Trawlers.

Topaze Built 1935, 608 tons: Anti-submarine trawler, patrolled off beaches and transported 118 men. Lost on 20th April 1941 following collison on the Clyde.

Velia Trawler: Ferried troops from Mole.

Vivinia Trawler: Ferried troops from Mole on 29th May.

Volante Steam trawler of 226 tons, owned by R. J. Solly: Later lost on 12th July 1940, bombed off Iceland.

Westella Built 1934, 550 tons: Lost on 2nd June, sunk by mine or torpedo.

Wolves Anti-submarine trawler: Worked inside Dunkirk Harbour and transported 50 men.

DRIFTERS AND OTHER FISHING VESSELS

Alcmaria Drifter: Swept mines and assisted small craft off beaches, returned with 32 men.

Ben and Lucy Drifter: Used off beaches, 30th May, carried 100.

Boy Billy Fishing boat owned by J. Adams: Survived Dunkirk but lost 10th April 1943, mined near Dungeness.

Boy Roy Dover Flare-Burning Drifter of 70 tons, built 1911: Lost 11th February 1942.

Britannic Deal beach boat. Later repaired by Tough Brothers at Teddington and returned to Sheerness.

Comfort Drifter of 60 tons: Although loaded with men, stopped to pick up survivors of HMS *Wakeful*, broken in two by torpedo. Was mistaken for E-boat by HMS *Grafton* and HMS *Lydd* which opened fire. The latter continued to ram and sink *Comfort*.

Defender Cockle Boat owned by W. Harvey and Sons, built at Leigh-on-Sea in 1912 – 42′ × 13′ – powered by Perkins diesel engine: Came under air attack near Gravelines during tow to Dunkirk, then worked independently from beaches. Returned to Ramsgate with 68 men. Now owned by Ken Hill of St. Aubins, Jersey. ADLS member.

Dorienta Drifter: Transported 65 men.

Eileen Emma Dover Flare-Burning Drifter: Transported 115 men.

Dumpling Deal beach boat: Made seven ferry trips from beaches to larger vessels before being sunk on 1st June by the wake of destroyers passing at high speed.

Endeavour Sail cockle boat built by Cole and Wiggens at Leigh-on-Sea in 1926 – 35′ × 11′5″: Owned by H. Robinson. Towed across and used to ferry troops from beaches. Now powered by a Ford engine and owned by Graham Thorrington and based at Chatham Historic Dockyard. Still licensed for fishing. ADLS member.

Fair Breeze Motor drifter of 92 tons, built 1925: Owned by P. Watson. Transported 316 men before being lost on 1st June after striking a wreck near Dunkirk.

Favourite Motor fishing vessel owned by B. Allen.

Feasible Drifter: Minesweeper worked in Channel during the evacuation and also patrolled off the beaches.

Fidget Herring Drifter: Originally named *Formidable*. Crossed on 29th May to ferry men to larger vessels before crossing to Ramsgate with 150 onboard. On 1st June assisted in taking men off the personnel vessel *Scotia*, transporting some 568 troops in total.

Fisher Boy Drifter: Ferried troops from beaches between 29th and 31st May, assisted *Fidget* in picking up *Scotia* survivors.

Forecast Drifter: Took 353 men from beaches to larger craft.

Formidable Drifter owned by W. Catchpole.

Genius Drifter: Used to tow small craft across, also for minesweeping. Transported 100 men.

Gervais Rentoul Dover Flare-Burning Drifter: Carried 57 men.

Gipsy King Deal beach boat owned by G. Riley: Taken to Dunkirk by original Deal crew of A. Betts, F. Hook and H. Brown, staying for 48 hours ferrying men from the beaches. Returned on 31st May as one of several vessels towed by the skoot *Hilda*.

Girl Gladys Dover Flare-Burning Drifter: Transported 249 men.

Girl Pamela Dover Flare-Burning Drifter of 93 tons, built 1912: Carried 59 men but lost on 29th May in collision off Dunkirk.

Golden Gift Dover Flare-Burning Drifter of 89 tons, built 1910: Transported 273 men, most of whom were taken off by the paddle minesweeper *Sandown* after *Golden Gift* grounded on the Goodwin Sands on 31st May. Refloated but lost in Oban Bay on 6th May 1943.

Golden Sunbeam Dover Flare-Burning Drifter of 84 tons, built 1920: Carried almost 400 men. Sunk off Dungeness 19th August 1942.

Gula Drifter: Used as minesweeper and helped smaller craft off French coast. Transported 110 men.

Heather Bell Motor fishing vessel owned by R. Williamson.

Industry Drifter owned by R. Irving and Sons.

Jacketa Herring Drifter: An East Coast vessel which was part of what had come to be known as 'Vernon's Private Navy'. Carried 651 men between 29th May and 1st June.

Jackeve Drifter: Loaded 120 men at La Panne.

Jane Hannah Motor fishing vessel, ex-RNLI lifeboat *Jane Hannah MacDonald* which had been based at Eastbourne and Flamborough: Owned by Bernard Chase.

Jeannie McIntosh Drifter: Requisitioned as a minesweeper.

John and Norah Drifter: Requisitioned as a minesweeper. Carried 61 men.

Kindred Star Drifter: Requisitioned as a minesweeper.

Leach's Romance Fishing vessel of 44 tons, owned by Bob Leach & Sons: Survived Dunkirk but sunk by mine on 29th July 1940.

Letitia Leigh-on-Sea cockle boat, owned and skippered by A. Dench: Sailed on 31st May with five other Leigh vessels and ferried from Mole before being towed back by a trawler. Still used for fishing by owner Simon Frost. ADLS member.

Letitia II Fishing smack owned by F. Browning: Towed over by tug *Sun XV* on 3rd June. Ferried troops from Mole to gunboat *Locust* before taking demolition crew to manhandle depth charges aboard damaged gunboat *Mosquito*. Was caught in subsequent explosion while withdrawing and had to be abandoned.

Little Admiral Fishing vessel owned by C. A. Pegg.

Little O'Lady Fishing vessel owned by Bob Leach & Sons.

Lord Barham Drifter: Crossed to Bray Beach on 31st May with food and fresh water, returning with French troops. Carried a total of 388 men.

Lord Cavan Herring drifter of 96 tons, built 1915: Another of the Vernon flotilla. Ferried troops from Dunkirk Mole on 29th May, staying while sister vessels escaped. Sunk by shore fire on 1st June, crew all rescued.

Lord Collingwood Drifter: Transported 332 men.

Lord Hood Drifter.

Lord Howard Dover Flare-Burning Drifter of 98 tons, built 1918: Transported 379 men.

Lord Howe Dover Flare-Burning Drifter: Transported 277 men.

Lord Keith Drifter: Worked off beaches, ferrying 323 men.

Lord Rodney Drifter: Requisitioned as minesweeper. Worked off the beaches on 1st June.

Lord St. Vincent Drifter of 115 tons, built 1919: Worked off beaches transporting 120 men. Sunk by mine in Thames Estuary on 7th July 1941.

Mare Drifter: Transported 219 men.

Maretta Drifter: Loaded troops from small boats at La Panne 2nd June.

Midas Dover Flare-Burning Drifter of 89 tons, built 1910: Carried over 360 men but lost following collision near Dungeness on 3rd February 1941.

Monarda Drifter of 109 tons, built 1916: Transported 390 men but later foundered in Thames Estuary on 8th November 1941.

Nautilus Drifter of 64 tons, built 1929: Lost on 29th May.

Netsukis Dover Flare-Burning Drifter: Transported 483 men.

Ocean Breeze Drifter: Ferried off Bray Beach, carried 259 men.

The flare-burning drifter **Lord Howard** *(with name suitably abbreviated for naval purposes), returning to her home port of Dover with some of a total of nearly 400 men transported. Note the forest of funnels and masts belonging to vessels of all sizes in the background.* (Times Newspapers)

Ocean Reward Drifter of 95 tons, built 1912: Lost with all hands on 28th May in collision with personnel ship *Isle of Thanet.*

Overfall Drifter: Worked off Malo Beach.

Paxton Dover Flare-Burning Drifter of 92 tons, built 1911: Bombed and sunk off Dunkirk on 28th May.

Pearl Motor fishing vessel owned by G. Pounds.

Pearl Drifter owned by A. Sutton.

Pearl Motor fishing boat owned by J. Sinclair.

Providence Motor fishing vessel owned by W. Hogarth.

Quicksilver Motor fishing vessel of 31 tons, owner A. Fletcher.

Reed Drifter of 99 tons, built 1911: Worked off beaches. Mined in the Thames Estuary 7th November 1940.

Reliance Cockle boat from Leigh-on-Sea, owned by W. Kennedy: Sailed with the rest of the Leigh fleet, skippered by A. Legget.

Rememberance Fishing boat of 7 tons: Sunk by mine on 7th July.

Renascent Drifter: Worked off La Panne transporting 260 men.

Renown Leigh-on-Sea cockle boat owned by Osbourne Bros: Towed back by *Letitia* on 1st June, later mined and lost in Thames.

Resolute Another Osbourne cockle boat from Leigh-on- Sea, built in 1927. Now converted for cruising. Owned by A. C. Miller and based at Rye. ADLS member.

Rewga Drifter: Picked up troops at Bray, carrying 162 in all.

Rig Drifter: Loaded 60 men from smaller boats.

Rob Roy Drifter.

Robert Cliff Drifter.

Rose Fishing vessel owned by A. Large.

Rowan Fishing smack.

Sarah Hyde Drifter: Took 100 men off Bray Beach, 31st May.

Officially drifters were not supposed to carry more than 100 men but there appears to have been something of a miscalculation as this vessel arrives in Dover with a load looking like at least double that, and with an equally well-laden motor yacht in tow. The yacht is most probably the **Nydia** *which still survives under her original name (see page 172).* (Times Newspapers)

Seasalter Oyster dredger built at Whitstable by Anderson, Rudgen and Perkins in 1931 – 39′5″ × 10′ – powered by Thornycroft diesel engine: Owned by Seasalter and Ham Oyster Fishing Co Sailed to Dunkirk overnight on 29/30th May with skipper L. Salmons, Dick Cook engineer and Bill Bridge, accompanied by another oyster boat *Vanguard* and the motor yacht *Ma Joie.* Went first to harbour, then to beaches, using rowing boats to load men who were ferried to skoots and the armed yacht *Grive. Ma Joie* was abandoned but both *Seasalter* and *Vanguard* reached Ramsgate under their own power with troops. Later owned as pleasure boat by S. Anderson of Kent, *Seasalter* was lost off the Channel Islands in 1980.

Shipmates Dover Flare-Burning Drifter of 89 tons, built 1911: Transported 196 men. Lost 14th November 1940 in air attack on Dover.

Silver Dawn Herring drifter: Another one of the 'Vernon's Navy' drifters with *Lord Cavan, Fisher Boy, Jacketa* and *Fidget.* Returned with 150 men on 29th May, made second trip on 1st June but lost a propeller blade in Dunkirk Harbour during third trip. Transported 694 men, the highest total of any drifter.

Starlight Rays Drifter: Also carried over 600 men, mainly working off the beach at La Panne.

Strive Drifter: Towed lifeboats on 1st June. Carried 243 men.

Suffolk's Rose Fishing vessel owned by Jubilee Fishing Co.

Swift Wing Drifter: Performed ferry duties on 30th May.

Taransay Drifter: Ferried from beaches, carrying 162 men.

The Boys Dover Flare-Burning Drifter of 92 tons, built 1914: Lost in heavy weather in the Downs on 14th November 1940.

Thomsons Drifter: Worked off Bray Beach.

Three Kings Drifter: Ferried off Bray Beach, carried 350 men.

Thrifty Drifter: Ferried off the beaches.

Tony Fishing vessel owned by T. Neilson.

Torbay II Dover Flare-Burning Drifter of 83 tons, built 1910: Transported over 300 men. Sunk in air raid at Dover on 1st November 1940.

Tweenways Drifter: Worked in Dunkirk Harbour, lifting 126 men.

Unicity Drifter of 96 tons, built 1919: Patrol duties before loading 225 troops. Capsized and sank off Blyth on 31st January 1942.

Ut Prosim Dover Flare-Burning Drifter of 91 tons, built 1925: Transported 457 men, including survivors from French destroyer *Bourrasque*. Later sunk at Dover on 2nd March 1942.

Vanguard Oyster dredger owned by Smith Bros, Burnham- on-Crouch: Crossed with dredger *Seasalter* and motor yacht *Ma Joie,* but told to keep out of Dunkirk Harbour so went without orders to beaches. Reached Ramsgate with troops on 31st, continuing on to Burnham. Now converted for shrimping, owned by Douglas Whiting and based at Rochford. ADLS member.

Victoria Oyster dredger owned by Smith Bros, Burnham- on-Crouch.

Volvo Fishing vessel owned by G. Denny: Torpedoed 28th December 1941.

Willanne, Willdora, Willmarie Three 55′ Scottish yawls that crossed to work in the La Panne area. *Willdora* survived the war and was later used as a pleasure craft. Found semi-submerged at Sunderland, the wreck was raised by the Ousebourne Water Association who have plans for restoration.

Yorkshire Lass Dover Flare-Burning Drifter: Transported 469 men including full load on final trip when engine failed and vessel was taken in tow by the tug *Sun XV*.

Young Mon Dover Flare-Burning Drifter: Transported 120 men.

A drifter arriving at Dover's Admiralty Pier with troops packed into every available foot of deck space, several even in the vessel's dinghy. (Times Newspapers)

Barges and Lighters

THAMES sailing barges made up one of the more unlikely elements of the Dunkirk fleet and some historians believe it was the first occasion since the Anglo-Dutch campaigns that so many spritsail-rigged vessels had gone to war! One third of more than 30 barges failed to return, some being lost on the way, others deliberately beached and abandoned after the supplies they carried had been removed.

The shallow-draught barges were ideally suited to take much needed food and water to the beaches, especially as their holds were large but still comparatively easy to unload. Although most were towed across, some of the larger barges with auxiliary engines went in one or both directions on their own using a combination of sail and power.

Three of the barges that had been abandoned on the beaches turned up again, the most unusual story surrounding the Ipswich- based *Ena* whose re-appearance, empty and virtually undamaged on Sandwich Flats, has never been entirely explained. Now preserved at Ipswich, the *Ena* has since been back to Dunkirk with other vessels from the ranks of the Association of Dunkirk Little Ships.

The barges *Glenway* and *Beatrice Maud* were both found and boarded by troops who somehow managed to master the complications of their rig and set off for home. *Glenway* was towed in with 160 men on board and the *Beatrice Maud*, also still in existence and based at Maldon, was found under full sail in the middle of the Channel on 5th June 1940, two days after Operation Dynamo was officially over!

Dumb barges and lighters from various Thames companies were towed across and just about every available lighter from the naval dockyards at Chatham and Sheerness – perhaps the most remarkable feature of the whole evacuation being the number of these unpowered craft that actually survived to be towed all the way back again.

Ada Mary Sailing barge owned by Leigh Building Co: One of four barges towed from Ramsgate on 1st June by tug *Sun III*. Now used as Sea Scout Headquarters, Newhaven.

Advance Self-propelled barge owned by W. J. Woodward-Fisher.

Aidie Sailing barge of 144 tons: Deliberately run ashore on 1st June by skipper Harry Potts, loaded with supplies of fresh water, food and ammunition. Subsequently abandoned.

Anee Wherry owned by A. Biddle: Sunk off La Panne on 1st June.

Barbara Jean Sailing barge of 144 tons: Run ashore on 1st June by skipper C. Webb and set on fire after food, water and ammunition had been unloaded.

Basildon Sailing barge owned by Leigh Building Co.

Beatrice Maud Sailing barge built by A. White at Sittingbourne in 1910 – 88′ × 21′5″: Anchored off beaches on 31st May and thought to have been abandoned. However, she was picked up under sail in mid-Channel on 5th June carrying 260 men. Later based at Maldon, Essex, and used as a houseboat.

Burton Sailing barge owned by Leigh Building Co: Another of the barges towed from Ramsgate

Several of the 30 sailing barges listed as being involved in one way or another with Operation Dynamo still survive. Among them is the **Cabby,** *seen (left) in the Thames whilst still trading* (E. H. Cole), *and on the Strood slipway of owners Cresent Shipping in April 1989* (Author). *Crescent, successors to* **Cabby's** *original owners, the London and Rochester Trading Company, have converted the hold to seat passengers, who can enjoy the exhilaration of charter trips under full sail.*

by *Sun III* on 3rd June.

Cabby Auxiliary sailing barge owned by the London and Rochester Trading Company, and built at its Frindsbury yard on the River Medway in 1928 – 91′6″ x 21′: Although used to carry supplies including ammunition at the time of the evacuation, it is not clear whether an actual crossing to Dunkirk took place. *Cabby* continued to trade under sail for Crescent Shipping of Strood, successors to her original owners, until converted by them in 1980 for passenger charter work with the hold adapted to seat 36. *Cabby* sails in the Medway and Thames Estuary and makes annual summer visits to the Solent.

Charlotte Dumb barge owned by John Harker Ltd.

Clara Bell Wherry owned by A. Biddle: Lost on 1st June.

Claude Sailing barge owned by T. Sargent: Crossed with supplies of fresh water and worked in Dunkirk Harbour.

Dawn Sailing barge owned by London & Rochester Trading Co.

Doris Wherry of 83 tons owned by T. H. Read: Beached loaded with supplies of fresh water, food and ammunition and later abandoned, although Admiralty listed cause of loss as a mine.

Duchess Sailing barge of 91 tons: Skippered by H. Wildish, ferried 90 troops to a destroyer on 31st May. Abandoned next day with crew picked up by tug *Cervia.*

D1, D4, D7, D9, D16 Dumb barges owned by Silvertown Services.

Edina Wherry owned by T. H. Read: Sunk off beaches on 1st June.

Ena Spritsail sailing barge built by W. B. McLearon at Harwich in 1906 – 88′ × 20′5″: Taken to Dunkirk with supplies by skipper A.Page on 31st May and although abandoned as instructed, was later found stranded and empty on Sandwich Flats. One theory is that the barge was found and re-floated by soldiers who crossed the Channel under sail, but *Ena* could just have easily have drifted back unaided. Now sail and diesel powered, owned by Brian Pinner and based at Ipswich. ADLS member.

Ethel Everard Sailing barge of 190 tons owned by F. T. Everard and Sons Ltd: Towed across by tug *Sun XII* in company of the barge *Tollesbury* to be beached but the tide took her broadside and troops waded out and climbed aboard. They had to be removed, with skipper T. Willis and crew, before the *Ethel Everard* could be set on fire. After the war a German propaganda magazine came to light showing a picture of the barge's charred wreck with a caption claiming that this was what happened to the British Navy when it tangled with the Nazis!

Ethel Maud Sailing barge built at Maldon in 1889. Believed to have crossed with supplies. Traded into the 1960s, now a houseboat at Rochester for David and Jean Maude. ADLS member.

Foremost 89, 101 and 102 Steam hopper barges owned by Tilbury Dredging Co: Dispatched with the company's *Lady Southborough* from dredging in Portsmouth Harbour, the four vessels went to Ramsgate and from there, having taken motor boats in tow, to Malo-les-Bains, arriving on the morning of 31st May. *Foremost 101* returned to Ramsgate with 400 British, French and Belgian troops and *Foremost 102* brought back 206.

F.W. 23 Dumb barge owned by Frazer and White Ltd: Towed back with 13 men aboard.

Gallion's Reach Steam hopper barge: Transported 123 troops.

Glenway Sailing barge: Towed across by the tug *Crested Cock* on 31st May loaded with supplies and beached by skipper H. Easter as instructed. Later refloated and boarded by 160 troops who were half way home under sail when taken in tow. Now owned by Elizabeth Poore and based at the Dolphin Barge Museum, Sittingbourne. ADLS member.

Grappler Lighter, other particulars unknown.

Greta Sailing barge owned by London and Rochester Trading Co, built in 1892. Now a houseboat at Rochester, but still seen in large races. ADLS member.

H.A.C. Sailing barge: Beached with supplies before skipper R.Scott and crew were taken off by the barge *Thyra.* After food and water had been unloaded *H.A.C.* was refloated and towed back with 100 men. Now used as a dredging hopper at Ramsgate.

Haste Away Sailing barge owned by Peters and Co: Another of the barges towed from Ramsgate by *Sun III* and then picked up by the tug *Duke* after breaking adrift. Returned to owners on 5th June. Believed broken up in 1972 following fire damage.

Hopper Barge 24 and 26 Particulars unknown.

James 67 Lighter: Chatham dockyard lighter, stood by at Ramsgate but was not taken across.

Kitty Dumb barge owned by E. Blows and Co.

Lady Richmond Sailing barge of 109 tons, owned by Sam West Ltd: Crossed with stores 1st June but blown up before being unloaded.

Lady Rosebery Auxiliary barge: Skipper W. Ellis. Sunk by mine activated by tug while under tow to Dunkirk.

Lady Southborough Steam Hopper barge owned by Tilbury Dredging Co: Crossed with other hopper barges towing smaller boats and still wearing the red and white funnel colours of the Tilbury company. After loading from boats off-shore, skipper Anthony Powell drove the vessel bow first on to the beach at Malo-les-Bains to allow 350 troops to wade out. *Lady Southborough* was refloated as the tide rose and steamed slowly back to Ramsgate.

Lark Sailing barge of 67 tons, owned by A. Fayers: Towed with supplies by tug *Crested Cock* on 31st May, abandoned next day.

Mary Barge owned by Nash and Miller.

Medora Wherry owned by T. H. Read: Sunk off the beaches 1st June.

Monarch Sailing barge.

Mousma Auxiliary barge owned by C. Barber, built by Hutson at Maidstone, 1924 – 84′4″ × 19′5″ – sail powered and Ferry engine: Now powered additionally by a Kelvin 4 engine and owned by Mrs C. Bennett of Hammersmith, London.

Plinlimmon Auxiliary spritail barge built by G. Curel, Strood, in 1886 – 80′ × 17′6″ – Bergius petrol engine: Owned by Capt. G. Wilkinson of Rochester.

Pudge Auxiliary barge owned by London and Rochester Trading Co, built 1922 – 82′ × 21′: Crossed under skipper W. Watson. Now owned by the Thames Barge sailing club and based at Maldon. ADLS member.

Queen Sailing barge owned by H. Murrell.

Queen Alexandra Sailing barge owned by Turmaine and Jones.

Royalty Sailing barge of 101 tons: Towed by *Cervia* to Malo Beach and ran aground loaded with supplies by skipper H. Miller.

Sark Dumb barge.

Seine Auxiliary barge owned by London & Rochester Trading Co: Taken across by skipper C. Cogger on 31st May, returning under own power with 352 men. Made two more crossings, landing 793 in all.

Shannon Sailing barge owned by W. McCormack: Towed over by *Sun III* on 1st June, returned in damaged condition.

Sherfield Auxiliary barge: Sailed from Sheerness on 1st June. During return trip German aircraft appeared and crew and over 70 troops lay still to give the appearance of an abandoned vessel until the planes made off.

Shetland Dumb barge: Towed across by tug *Persia* together with barge *Sark*.

Spurgeon Sailing barge: Suffered near miss and splinter damage when bombed whilst under tow to Dunkirk.

Surrey Dumb barge owned by J. Stratford & Sons.

Thyra Auxiliary sailing barge owned by London & Rochester Trading Co: Taken across by skipper E. Filley, towed home loaded with troops on 1st June.

Tollesbury Sailing barge owned by Paul's Maltsters, built by W. Fellow, Sandwich, 1905 – 84′2″ × 20′6″: Towed across loaded with stores and dynamite by *Sun XII* on 31st May. After unloading, an estimated 200 troops were taken on board and the vessel was pulled off the beach by the tug *Cervia* and then towed home. Now powered by a Ruston and Honsby engine and owned by Mrs D. Tonkin of Pin Mill, Suffolk. ADLS member.

Unique Sailing barge of 51 tons, owned by J. Churchill: Survived the evacuation but later sunk by mine on 2nd May 1942.

Viking Auxiliary barge of 63 tons, built 1895. Transported 70 men. Lying in the Medway awaiting restoration.

Warrior Sailing barge.

Westall Spritsail sailing barge owned by London & Rochester Trading Co: Now owned by John Drew, Hoo Marina, Rochester. ADLS member.

W 24, W 26 Hopper barges.

X 95, X 134 Chatham Dockyard lighters.

X 149 Sheerness Dockyard lighter: Reported sunk.

X 209 Royal Clarence Yard, Gosport, lighter.

X 213, X 217 Chatham Dockyard lighters: *X 213* reported sunk.

YC 63, YC 71, YC 72 Chatham Dockyard lighters.

Small Craft

ONE of the most widely accepted myths of Dunkirk is that scores of boat owners from the south-eastern corner of England suddenly leapt into their craft and, burning with patriotic fervour, headed out across the English Channel. It is true that a lot of men bravely took their own boats over but most of the small craft were in the hands of a wide assortment of Naval personnel, and some even went to Dunkirk and back without their true owners knowing what was happening.

That the huge number of small craft which played such an important part in Operation Dynamo, particularly working right in the firing line ferrying men from the beaches to larger ships offshore, came together was due to a piece of almost totally unrelated planning by an Admiralty department known as the Small Vessels Pool. Under the direction of Admiral Sir Lionel Preston, the pool's principal role was to supply small vessels for harbour duties and other auxiliary tasks. Although a building programme had been started, the greater part of its output was geared to providing wooden coastal minesweepers to deal with a growing threat posed by magnetic mines dropped by German aircraft and laid from E-boats.

Preston reasoned that, in the short term at least, the pool's other requirements could be best filled by requisitioning civilian-owned pleasure craft. Accordingly, the BBC's morning news at 9 o'clock on 14th May 1940 included an Admiralty order, confirmed some four days earlier, requesting the owners of all self-propelled pleasure craft from 30 to 100 feet in length, to send particulars within 14 days, if the vessels had not already been offered or requisitioned.

The fact that owners were allowed a full fortnight to submit information tends to refute a quite widely held view that this order was really the beginning of plans for an evacuation. It was also put forward by French historians, and in my view equally lamely, as evidence that the British decision to evacuate had been taken early and without any consultation with their ally. Whatever the background, by the time that fortnight was up, many vessels were already heading for Dunkirk.

The Ministry of Shipping, responsible for the management of the British merchant fleet since the beginning of the war, had its own small craft section whose key men, Mr A. L. Moore and Mr H. C. Riggs, worked closely with the Admiralty Small Vessels Pool. As the situation worsened in France and Operation Dynamo began, Rear-Admiral Alan Taylor was brought from semi-retirement and a desk job in the London-based Admiralty Economic Warfare Section and sent to Sheerness as Maintenance Officer. His job was to receive craft collected from the Thames and other East Coast rivers, service them and send them mainly to Ramsgate to be towed across the Channel by fishing vessels, Dutch skoots or tugs.

But the task of contacting individual owners who had sent in details of their craft in the preceeding couple of weeks proved painfully slow and at Sheerness it soon became apparent that vessels were not coming through quickly enough. Mr Riggs, after spending hours trying to contact owners from the department's London office, decided that as the majority of vessels had been laid up since the start of the war it would be far quicker to deal direct with boatyards where quite large numbers of craft were to be found.

Yards like that of Tough Brothers at Teddington were asked to act as agents and round up craft in their own area. Douglas Tough, whose family had been on the river for three generations, proved an ideal choice. What he did not know about about Thames pleasure boats was hardly worth knowing and, leaving the staff at his yard working on over a dozen boats already to hand, Tough went up and down the river himself in search of further suitable candidates. The majority of owners co-operated willingly, some even joining volunteer crews assembled at the Tough yard to take the vessels to Sheerness. There, officially, Royal Navy personnel took over but more than a few owners managed to keep contact with their vessels and go all the way. If no owner could be traced and the boat looked right for the job, it was taken anyway – a number of owners subsequently reporting imagined thefts to the police after turning up to find their mooring empty.

Other boatbuilders and repair yards fulfilled a similar function to Toughs and while, officially, each of the small craft was chartered by the Ministry of Shipping, quite often such details as the necessary paperwork was not completed until weeks afterwards. It was typical of the manner in which restrictions and red tape were abandoned, the Ministry accepting the full responsibility for getting each individual craft to Sheerness and for any damage or even total loss that subsequently occurred.

Admiral Taylor's small team at Sheerness had to provide the vessels with fuel, provisions and crew – finding the latter at times proving almost as difficult as obtaining the vessels had been. But somehow men were found, Naval reservists and retired personnel being supplemented by the amateur weekend sailors and fishermen from ports as far afield as Lowestoft who readily put their names to T124 papers which made them subject to Royal Navy discipline for a period of one month – and for a payment of £3!

As many of the small craft had been inoperative for months, their engines caused problems and, of course, quite a few were possessed of quirks known only to their owners. To solve the chronic shortage of men with even the most rudimentary knowledge of machinery, an appeal went out from Admiral Taylor to the Shipping Federation which somehow produced over 300 with marine engineering experience.

When every single serviceable craft had been sent off from Sheerness, Taylor went to Ramsgate and then managed to persuade Admiral Ramsay to allow him to cross the Channel on a special mission to try and pick up a pocket of men reportedly holding out on the beach at Malo-les-Bains but unable to get into Dunkirk. Getting together a small flotilla of three skoots and some fast motor launches he set out, crossing in *White Lady,* a vessel under the command of journalist David Devine, who later wrote what has come to be regarded as one of the classic accounts of the maritime aspects of Operation Dynamo.

About half the 1,300 vessels taking part in the operation can be classed as small craft and a surprising number of the survivors are still in existence. They have been traced by the Association of Dunkirk Little Ships, a body formed in 1967 to keep alive the spirit of Dunkirk by perpetuating for posterity the identity of those little ships which went to the aid of the British Expeditionary Force. The Association's interpretation of the term 'little ships' is to include all of what were originally privately owned participating vessels such as motor cruisers and yachts, barges, pleasure steamers and motor vessels together with British, French, Belgian and Dutch fishing boats. Membership is also extended to a few former service craft, now privately owned.

One of the craft which crossed to Dunkirk was a 30-foot motor launch called *Surrey.* It was bought in 1964 by writer and broadcaster Raymond Baxter, whose son suggested they should visit Dunkirk at the end of May 1965 to mark the 25th Anniversary of the evacuation. After a letter had been published in *The Sunday Times,* whose then editor, Dennis Hamilton, had himself been rescued from the beaches, 42 of the original little ships made the crossing. The Association of Little Ships came into being following a further meeting of boat owners and some 120 vessels are now in membership.

The Association remains a unique collection of boats rather than people and it stages a weekend rally at a British centre each year. There have also been subsequent visits to Dunkirk in 1970, 1975, 1980 and 1985, with special plans being made for a 50th Anniversary crossing in 1990.

Aberdonia Motor cruiser – 48′ × 11′ – built 1935. Now owned by Paul G. King and based at

Coming home! Twenty-two of the little ships of Dunkirk passing through London's Upper Pool on their way back to up-river berths on 9th June (Times Newspapers). *The same flotilla is seen later (below) getting a wave from Sunday afternoon strollers at Richmond. Apart from* **Rapid 1** *in the middle of the centre trio, the names of other craft in the first couple of rows are frustratingly indistinct* (Popperfoto).

Kingston on Thames. ADLS member.

Ace Twin screw ketch, built by Ramparts, Southampton in 1938 – 45′ × 10′1″: Owned by Ralph Banks, Wimborne, Dorset.

Adeline Motor boat owned by the late G. H. Kent.

Adventuress Schooner with single oil-engine, built Murdoch & Murray, Glasgow in 1898 – 135′ × 24′1″: Owned by Colonel B. Millard of Shanklin, Isle of Wight. Reported lost.

Ahola Twin screw ketch built by G. de Vries Lentsch, Jun, at Amsterdam in 1936 – 67′ × 13′ – powered by two oil engines: Owned by F.J. Spickernell of Southsea and requisitioned as an Auxiliary Patrol Yacht. Ferried troops from beaches with crew of Able Seamen Hollands and Finch, both mentioned in despatches.

Aide Motor-launch.

Albatross III Harbour launch owned by Dover Harbour Board: Used as Dover patrol craft.

Aljanor Former Royal Navy pinnace powered by two Ailsa Craig oil engines: Owner J. K. Mann of London W14. Reported lost.

Aloc-Oc Small craft owned by Mr Bodley.

Aloha Twin screw vessel built by Vosper, Portsmouth in 1932 – 56′ × 11′8″: Owned by J. E. Pearce of Thames Ditton and powered by two Gardner four-cylinder Patricroft engines.

Alouette II Twin screw schooner – 68′3″ × 14′ – powered by twin Davey Paxman engines: Owned by C. B. Colston of Penn, Bucks and requisitioned as Echo-Sounding Yacht. Worked off beaches with crew including A. F. Wyatt who was awarded DSM.

Alusia Built by Ramparts at Southampton in 1938 – 45′ × 10′ 6″: Owned by J. F. Alexander of London and powered by twin Morris Commodore Mk II engines. Now owned by M. Woods, moored at Cuxton and powered by twin BMC diesels. ADLS member.

Amity Auxiliary Bermudian cutter, built at Farilie by W. Fife & Son in 1926 – 53′7″ × 12′5″: Owned by G. Levey of Paris.

Andora Particulars unknown.

Andora II RAF launch: Used to ferry troops from beaches and then crossed to Ramsgate with 23 Frenchmen aboard.

Angler 14-foot rowing boat owned by F. Wells of Margate.

Angler II Motor boat owned by W. M. Hart.

Anlah Portsmouth A/P yacht.

Ankh Twin screw schooner built by G. de Vries Lentsch, jun, of Amsterdam in 1939 – 70′ × 14′7″ powered by two Gleniffer oil engines: Owned by F. J. Spickernell, Southsea. Used off beaches.

Anne Twin screw motor boat built F. Curtis, Looe, 1925 – 30′4″ × 8′9″ – powered by Ailsa Craig engines. Owned by P. J. Darby of Stourbridge. Now owned by H. W. Bambridge of Bristol. ADLS member.

Anne Motor boat owned by L. Basso.

Anne Twin screw schooner built by Camper & Nicholson at Gosport in 1925 – 98′7″ × 17′4″ – powered by two Gardner oil engines: Owner J. S. Highfield of Cookham Dean, Bucks.

Anne Ketch built by Elco & Co., Bayonne, New Jersey, USA, in 1916 as *ML 104* – 79′9″ × 12′ – Gardner Patricroft engine: Owned by W. Woellworth of Long Ditton, Surrey. Sailed from Teddington, returning there from Ramsgate on 17th July 1940.

Anthony Twin screw motor yacht built by Husk & Sons Ltd at Wivenhoe, 1933 – 32′ × 9′2″ – powered by Morris petrol engines: Owned by F. Winter of Surbiton. Loaded troops off La Panne on 1st June. Now named *Huntsman,* owned by Malcolm Taylor of Marple Bridge, Stockport, and powered by BMC diesels. ADLS member.

Antionette Owned by A. Albert: Retained Gravesend on APS work.

Aquabelle Twin screw motor yacht built by William Osbourne Ltd., Littlehampton in 1939 – 45′3″ × 11′9″ – powered by two three-cylinder Ailsa Craig oil engines: Owned by B. Taylor of Hampton Wick. Now with two six-cylinder Ailsa Craig engines and owned by P. D. Lostuzzo of Port de Plaisance, France.

Ashington Particulars unknown.

Athola Particulars unknown.

Auntie Gus Owner S. Long.

Aura Motor vessel of 35′ × 10′ – owned by Lord Moyne. Reported lost.

Autricia Twin screw cutter built by Elkins, Christchurch, in 1939 – 42′ × 10′8″ – powered by Gray petrol engines.

Balquhain Twin screw motor yacht built by J. Norris, Gosport, 1936 – 33′2″ × 9′6″ – powered by Morris petrol engines: Owned by Dr P. Mitchell of London. Now powered by Perkins oil engines and owned by G. Douglas of Twickenham. ADLS member.

Barbara Owned by A. E. Johnson.

Barbill II Single screw sloop built by Kris Cruisers, Isleworth, in 1933 – 24′ × 7′6″ – powered by Parsons petrol engine: Owned by Colonel H. Roberts of London.

Bendor Single screw motor yacht built by G. Woodstock, Woodbridge, in 1933 – 35′ × 9′ – powered by a six-cylinder Brooke petrol engine: Owned by G. G. Ireland of Nassau, Bahamas.

Berkshire Lass Motor boat powered by a car engine adapted for marine use: Taken to Dunkirk by owner A. Harris of Twickenham, completing many ferry trips to drifter offshore. During an air attack Mr Harris was shot and thrown into the water. He was rescued and put aboard a hospital ship but his vessel sank.

Bessie Small craft owned by W. R. Cox.

Betsy Nora Particulars unknown.

Betty Built by Walton Yacht and Launch Works, Shepperton in 1933 – 40′ × 9′5″ – powered by a three-cylinder Ailsa Craig oil engine: Owned by R. F. Skinner of Wargrave, Berks. Now named *Nyula*, powered by a Mercedes engine and owned by Peter Packard of Woodbridge, Suffolk. ADLS member.

Betty Motor boat owned by W. Kennedy.

Beverley Owned by F. Robinson, sunk off La Panne.

Bhurana Owned by W. Grint.

Black Arrow Single screw sloop built by F. Maynard at Chiswick in 1912 – 33′2″ × 8′ – powered by Kermath petrol engine: Owned by P. Wilkinson, St. Margarets, Middlesex. Lost during evacuation.

Black Java Particulars unknown.

Blackpool Particulars unknown.

Bluebird Twin screw motor yacht built/engined by J. I. Thornycroft at Hampton-on-Thames in 1939 – 52′ × 11′: Owned by Captain A. Fuller of Marlborough, Wilts. Now named *Bluebird of Chelsea*, powered by Perkins oil engines and owned by Summers of London. ADLS member.

Bluebird I Twin screw motor yacht built by Jas. A. Silver Ltd at Rosneath in 1933 – 43′5″ × 10′1″ – powered by Morris engines: Owned by Lieutenant-Colonel R. Chadwick of Rhu, Dumbartonshire.

Blue Bird Owned by C. P. Evinson and H. J. Adam.

Blue Bird II Twin screw schooner built by Goole Shipbuilding Co, in 1938 – 103′7″ × 20′1″ – powered by Ruston Hornsby engines: Owned by Sir Malcolm Campbell of London. Became *Janick*, with twin Badouin engines when owned by French car company supremo Jean Renault. Now owned by Robert Harvey-George and based at Falmouth. ADLS member.

Boat Owned by W. Robertson: 16-foot boat, sunk at La Panne.

Bobeli Single screw motor yacht built by Kris Cruisers at Isleworth in 1938 – 30′5″ × 9′1″ – powered by Grey petrol engine: Owner A. Cox of Coombe, Surrey. Moored alongside a destroyer off Dunkirk but wrecked when the naval vessel moved off at full speed during an air raid without cutting lines.

Bonnibell Auxiliary ketch built by D. Hillard at Littlehampton in 1937 – 35′ × 10′3″ – powered by Morris engine: Owned by C. Patey of Gerrards Cross, sunk off La Panne on 1st June.

Bonny Heather Owned by A. Zoccola: Left Ramsgate on 30th May as leader of convoy of 10 motor boats all towing ship's lifeboats, worked from the beaches to transports and destroyers off shore.

Bounty Twin screw motor yacht built Camper & Nicholson, Gosport, 1936 – 77′2″ × 15′ – powered by two Gardner oil engines: Used as A/P yacht commanded by peacetime owner Lieutenant C. A. Lundy, RNVR. Left Hamble on 29th May with others of inner patrol group

Now **Bluebird of Chelsea** *and originally owned by Sir Malcolm Campbell, this attractive twin screw vessel went to Dunkirk as* **Bluebird.** *Now Owned by art dealer Martin Summers, she often cruises with another Dunkirk veteran,* **Lazy Days,** *also pictured. When not venturing to more distant waters, both vessels lie in the heart of London at Cadogan Pier, Chelsea.* (Author)

and after calling at Dover, reached La Panne at 5.30 a.m. on 31st. Commodore Stevenson boarded from HMS *Keith* to take command of *Bounty* as his flagship. Later *Bounty* transferred Lord Gort from HMS *Hebe* to HMS *Keith.* On 1st June *Bounty* worked from 1 a.m. to 8.30 a.m. taking 1,000 men to destroyers before fouling her propeller. Commodore Stevenson and Lundy moved to yacht *Seriola* which towed *Bounty* to Ramsgate. Now owned by Nigel E. Harvey. ADLS member.

Bou Saada Twin screw motor yacht built by W. King and Sons, Burham-on-Crouch, 1935 – 33′ × 9′6″ – powered by Morris engines: Owned by E. Dreyfus of London. Now powered by twin Perkins oil engines, owned by Miss C. Khaan of Weybridge, Surrey.

Boy Bruce Owned by C. Haynes.

Boy Fred Owned by C. Good.

B.P. One Particulars unknown.

Braymar Auxiliary ketch built by Courtney & Newhook, Lymington, in 1919 – 49′3″ × 10′1″ – powered by Chrysler petrol engine: Owned by A. Bray of Marylebone. Now owned by A. Pay of London and powered by a Perkins oil engine. ADLS member.

Brenart Owned by K. Frisby and A. Harrison.

Britannia Owned by H. & J. Budd: Sunk at Bray Dunes, 31st May.

Brywyn Built by Kris Cruisers, Isleworth, 1934 – 20′9″ × 7′6″: Owned by C. Priestly-Mist, London. Now named *Birwyn*, with Austin engine, owned by Brian Wheeler of Northmoor, Oxfordshire. ADLS member.

Buffin Cabin cruiser owned by Mr Sharp of Bracknell.

Bull Pup Auxiliary yawl built by J.Hinks and Son, Appledore, in 1935 – 35′2″ × 9′8″ – powered by Berguis petrol engine: Owned by A. Smith of Seaford, Sussex. Lost off Dunkirk on 30th May.

Burgonia Owned by G. W. Burgoyne – other particulars unknown.

Bystander Twin screw motor yacht built by Camper & Nicholson, Gosport, 1934 – 80′5″ ×

15′ – powered by twin Gardner diesels: Owned by W. Roome of Hampstead Heath. Used as Echo-Sounding Yacht. Now based at Gibraltar and owned by Bystander Yacht Company.

Cachalot Auxiliary gaff cutter built by R. Sanders at Folkestone in 1900 – 30′ × 9′8″ – powered by Stuart Turner petrol engine: Owner Mr Spurling. Now owned by Ian Kiloh of Maldon. ADLS member.

Cachalot Owned by J. Powers.

Cairngorm Owned by H. W. S. Wright.

Caleta Twin screw schooner built by Philip & Sons, Dartmouth, 1930 – 115′5″ × 18′ – powered by twin Gardner diesels: Owned by Sir W. Burton of Burstall, Suffolk and requisitioned as Harbour Defence Craft. Came under heavy fire from shore batteries on 31st May but continued ferry duties through to 1st June. Now named *Atlantide*, re-engined with new Gardner diesels and owned by BBJ Houses and Shipping, Bishopsgate, London. ADLS member.

Camellia Twin screw motor yacht built by Hayward & Croxon at Southend in 1919 – 36′7″ × 8′7″ – powered by two Thornycroft petrol engines: Owned by R. F. Money of London.

Carama Punt owned by RNLI acting Second Coxswain A. Moody: One of a number of small craft towed back by motor vessel *Rian*.

Caraid Owned by P. Jeffs.

Carmen Owned by H. Garnett.

Carolina Row boat owned by H. E. Parker.

Caronia Auxiliary ketch built by H. T. & S. Peak, Newlyn, 1927 – 39′9″ × 11′4″ – powered by National oil engine: Owner G. Burleigh of Enfield. Now powered by Gardner oil engine and owned by W. A. Ord of Brightlingsea. ADLS member.

Caryander Twin screw motor yacht built by G. de Vries Lentsch, jun, of Amsterdam in 1938 – 70′ × 14′ – powered by twin Glennifer diesels: Owned by E. R. Colman of London and used as an Auxiliary Patrol Yacht. Ferried troops from beaches.

Catherina Yacht built by Elkins, Christchurch, 1939 – 46′ × 10′7″ – powered by Parsons petrol engines: Owner W. Corby, Bournemouth.

Cecilie Owned by M. Markham.

Cervantes Owned by V. H. Cooper.

Chalmondesleigh Launch built at Algonac in 1935 – 25′ × 7′7″ – powered by six-cylinder Chrysler engine: Taken to Dunkirk by her owner, the entertainer Tommy Trinder. Now named *Chumley* and owned by Alan Rhodes of Aylesbury. ADLS member.

Chantecler Converted Dutch eel boat built at Lemmer in 1919 – 50′ × 13′3″ – powered by paraffin engine: Owned by H. Dipple of Thanet. Towed by skoot *Jutland* on 29th May, ferried until engine trouble next day but returned under own power with 30 men.

Chico Twin screw schooner built by Jas. Miller, Monace, in 1932 – 73′ × 16′ – powered by Glenniger oil engine: One of a trio of *Bluebird* yachts owned by Sir Malcolm Campbell. Named *Chico* when taken for Naval service as an Echo Sounding Yacht early in 1940. Crossed on 30th May under Sub-Lt. J. Mason to bring back over 200 men and, next day, returned to ferry over 1,000 from the beaches to larger vessels. Since the war she has been used as a private yacht and for chartering and, now owned by Philip Goddard, is based at Southampton. ADLS member.

Christabell II Twin screw motor yacht built M. Dickie, Tarbert, 1928 – 90′ × 17 5″ – Gardner engines: Harbour defence craft.

Commodore Owned by W. A. Davy.

Commodore Twin screw motor yacht built by Berthin Boat Co, at Lymington, 1939 – 39′5″ × 10′ – powered by two Chrysler petrol engines: Owned by M. Pemberton-Billing of Shepperton, Middlesex.

Conidaw Twin screw ketch built by James A. Silver at Rosneath in 1939 – 80′ × 16′3″ – powered by Morris/Henty/Gardner engines: Owned by E. Waddilove of Ilkley, Yorks. Entered Calais on 25th May, leaving with 165 men, including survivors of Royal Marine Guard. Crossed to Dunkirk on 30th, returning with 80 soldiers. Now named *Thomasine*. Owned by J. L. Green. ADLS member.

Constant Nymph Motor cruiser owned by Dr Basil Smith of London: One of the first Thames vessels to be ready. Taken to Sheerness by her owner and skipper, Dr Smith, on 27th May, leaving Ramsgate for Dunkirk towed by the skoot *Jutland.* Patrolled off beaches assisting small boats and swimmers. Suffered a near miss from shellfire on 31st. Dr Smith awarded DSM.

Cora Ann Auxiliary ketch built by Lune Valley Engineering, Glasson Dock, Birkenhead, 1921 – 54′ × 12′ – powered by Atlantic Wishaw engine: Owned by Commander F. Newhouse, Thorpe St. Andrew, Norfolk. Survived Dunkirk and war but lost in October 1973.

Cordelia Twin screw motor yacht built by Staniland & Co., Thorne in 1934 – 36′ × 9′6″ – powered by Hyland petrol engines: Now powered by BMC oil engines, owned by J. K. Fuller and moored on the River Weaver in Cheshire. ADLS member.

Cornelia Auxiliary boiler, built Sliderecht, Holland – 49 8″ × 13′3″ – with Gray petrol engine: Owner E. Bushill of Coventry.

Corsair Built by Hornby & Son, Wallasey, 1937 – 28′4″ × 9′2″ – powered by Thornycroft petrol engine: Owner Dr R. Tivy, London.

Count Dracula Launch built in Germany 1913 – 50′3″ × 9′3″: Former Admiral's barge from First World War German battleship *Moltke,* salvaged and sold after the High Seas fleet was scuttled at Scapa Flow in 1919. Owner in 1940, K. A. Kreiner. Now powered by Kelvin petrol/paraffin engine and owned by Michael Hamby of Purley and based at Brighton. ADLS member.

Creole Owned by D. M. Clarke of London.

Cruiser Single screw motor yacht built H. McLean, Govan, 1929 – 37′ × 8′6″ – Gray petrol engine: Owner Dr A. Seymour of Belfast.

Curlew Dinghy owned by W. Gibson.

Curlew Twin screw motor yacht built by Vosper & Co., Portsmouth, in 1929 – 37′ × 9′3″ – powered by Morris engines: Owned by Sir R. Holme of London. Crossed with *Cairngorm,* returning with 24 men.

Curlew II Motor vessel built/owned by J. Bolson and Sons, Poole.

Curlew Owned by Cruiser Hire Co. Possibly ex-naval vessel, sold and renamed *Daisy.* Original name restored after requisitioning.

Curlew Owned by I. C. MacFarlane.

Cyb Owned by Chelsea Yacht Boat Co: Lost at Dunkirk.

Cygnet Owned by J. McLure.

Cygnet Owned by P. M. Lea.

Dab II Twin screw motor yacht built and engined by J. Brooke and Co, Oulton Broad, 1931 – 52′2″ × 12′7″: Owner Lieutenant-Colonel C. Hardie of Chelmsford. Now named *Breda,* powered by Perkins oil engines and owned by Peter Farrant of Teddington. ADLS member.

Dandy Former RNLI lifeboat built Thames Iron Works, Blackwell, in 1901 – 43′1″ × 12′4″ – powered by two Ailsa Craig diesels: Owned by J. M. Ponsonby of London.

Daphne Motor yacht built and engined by J. I. Thornycroft in 1932 – 25′ × 7′: W. J. Harkness believed owner. Now owned by John Mills of Kemsing, Kent, and based on the River Medway. ADLS member.

Daphne Owned by F. Kinson and Son.

D.C. 715 Harbour launch.

D.C. Motor Boat Anti-submarine boat: Transported 15 men.

Deenar Converted Admiralty vessel – 30′1″ × 7′2″ – powered by a Thornycroft petrol engine: Owned by W. G. Dunbsbier. Now powered by Scammell marine petrol engine and undergoing restoration at Weybridge.

Desel II Motor sailer built by Vosper-Thornycroft, Devonport, 1934 – 30′ × 9′3″: Owner Dudley Stone. Now named *Delise,* with a Riccardo diesel engine, owned by Rory Maher of Solihull and based at Lampeter. ADLS member.

Desiree Sloop built by A. Wood, Whitstable, 1925 – 37′8″ × 10′8″ – powered by Universal petrol engine: Owned by N. Dore, Ramsgate.

Devil Fish Owned by P. Knapp.

D.G. 694, D.G. 715 and *D.G. 950* Royal Navy harbour launches.

Diamond Auxiliary sloop built by Crossfield, Arnside, 1912 – 23′ × 7′ – Ailsa Craig petrol engine: Owner F. Bury of Lancaster.

Diana II Further particulars unknown.

Together again! Some of the fleet of more than 40 of the little ships at Dover before making a weather-delayed 45th Anniversary return crossing to Dunkirk in May 1985. From left to right they are **Firefly** *and* **Daphne,** *both still bearing their original names, plus* **L'Orage** *and* **Riis 1** *which, in 1940, were named* **Surrey** *and* **White Heather** *respectively.* (Byrne Craigie Photos)

Diana Mary Cruiser dispatched from Tough Brothers, Teddington.

Diante Cruiser owned by R. W. Taylor of Chislehurst: Survived Dunkirk but sustained damage and was repaired by Tough Brothers.

Dianthus Motor cruiser built at Staines in 1938 – 30′ × 11′ – powered by Chrysler petrol engine: Owned by J. Timms and Son. Now owned by Clive Anderson and undergoing restoration at Falmouth. ADLS member.

Dinky 10-foot boat owned by H. Miramo: Sunk on 1st June.

Dolphin Lugger built by Shelley, Gosport, 1932 – 31′ × 8′5″ – Thornycroft engine: Owner Captain J. Gwyn-Jeffries of Sussex.

Dolphin Converted Admiral's pinnace built at Portsmouth Dockyard, 1940 – 41′ × 11′ – powered by Ailsa Craig oil engine: Built for HM submarine base Gosport. Now owned by D. A. Allen, Hampton Court.

Doreen Owned by Captain C. R. Kettlewell.

Dorian Ex-naval vessel, built Portsmouth Dockyard 1918 – 46′ × 12′1″: Owner E. Webberley, Bognor Regis. Now lies on the Thames but without engines.

Dragonfly Motor boat built/engined by Thornycroft, Hampton, 1933 – 30′ × 9′: Owner C. Taverner, Highgate. Now named *l'Adventure* and owned by J. Cameron Graham, Manotick, Ontario, Canada. ADLS member.

Dreadnought III Owned by G. Murrell: Lost 1st June off the beaches.

Duchess of York Owned by W. & P. Robinson of Thorpe Bay, Essex.

Edna Owned by H. V. Little.

Edward and Mary Owned by C. Adams.

Elia II Twin screw motor yacht built G. de Vries Lentsch, jun, Amsterdam, 1931 – 70′ × 14′5″ – Glennifer oil engines: Owner Stafford Bourne, London. Army Personnel Yacht at Portsmouth.

Elaine Twin screw motor yacht built/engined by

J. I. Thornycroft, Hampton-on-Thames, 1927 – 40′ × 8′ 8″: Owner I. R. Brown, London.

Elizabeth Green Twin screw motor yacht built by H. Milland at Twickenham, 1935 – 42′6″ × 11′6″ – with Morris petrol engines: Owner H. T. Green, London. Made two crossings and was one of the last small ships to leave. Now powered by BMC oil engines, owned by Alan Jackson of Ascot, and based at Wraysbury. ADLS member.

Ella Owned by David Dunnett.

Ellaline Twin screw motor yacht built at Medway Yacht Basin, Rochester, 1937 – 40′ × 5′5″ – powered by Austin petrol engines: Owned by G. M. Ainger of London.

Ellen Mary Motor vessel: Abandoned following collision.

Elsa II Twin screw motor yacht built/engined by J.I.Thornycroft, Hampton-on-Thames, 1929 – 32′ × 8′5″: Now owned by Fred Bourne and based on the River Thames. ADLS member.

Elvin Twin screw yacht built/engined by Hyland Ltd, Barton-on-Humber, 1937 – 35′ × 9′: Owner E. Vincent of King's Norton. Sent from Lowestoft but was at first turned away at Ramsgate. Crossed 1st June and entered Dunkirk Harbour, returning with 23 French troops. Now powered by Ford oil engines and owned by E. H. Serra-Brando of Lisbon, Portugal. ADLS member.

Emile Particulars unknown.

Emprise Motor launch.

Encore Single screw yacht built/engined by J. I. Thornycroft at Hampton, 1930 – 48′ × 9′5″: Owner T. Thistlethwayte, Burseldon. Landed 44 men.

Endeavour Owned by J. Watson.

Endeavour Owned by T. H. Turner.

Endeavour II Bermudian cutter built Camper & Nicholson, Gosport, 1936 -135′8″ × 21′5″: Owned by Thomas Sopwith.

Enterprise Owned by G. J. Kent. Reported lost.

Eothen Launch built by Davie, Quebec, Canada, 1916 – 80′1″ × 12″ – powered by Djinn petrol engine: Owner Lieutenant R. Edmead of Chiswick. Now owned by Mr France of London. ADLS member.

Eric Owned by H. S. Redman.

Erica Crewman C. Greenwood mentioned in despatches.

E.R.V. Owned by E. Harvey.

Esperanza Twin screw motor yacht built/engined J. I. Thornycroft, Hampton, 1929 – 47′ × 9′5″: Owned by T. Norman, Walsall.

Ethel Ellen Owned by E. D. Amey.

Eve Motor boat: Used on 30th May to ferry troops from beaches, completing six trips before being rushed by French troops who overloaded and sank her.

Excellent's Motor boat Anti-aircraft motor-boat from HMS *Excellent,* Portsmouth: Used to patrol off the beaches.

Ex-Service dinghy Owned by 6th Ramsgate Sea Scouts.

Faith Auxiliary cutter built by Shuttlewood, Paglesham, 1933 – 23′ × 7′2″ – powered by Fair engine: Owner K. Romyn of London.

Falcon Single screw motor yacht built by Camper & Nicholson at Gosport in 1921 – 48′3″ × 7′9″ – powered by Gray petrol engine: Owned by R. Teacher of Rhu, Dumbartonshire.

Falcon Steam launch owned by Union-Castle Mail Steamship Company.

Falcon II Schooner built by Vosper & Co at Portsmouth in 1898 – 55′ × 13′1″ – powered by McLaren-Benz engine: Owned by S. Hudson of Liss, Hants. Now named *Alabama,* powered by General Motors engines, owned by M. Hamby and based at Teddington. ADLS member.

Fedalma II Bermudian schooner built by Chas. H. Fox & Sons, Ipswich, in 1936 – 47′5″ × 11′ – powered by Gray engines: Owner Claud Scrutton of Thorpe Bay. Now powered by twin BMC engines and owned by John Knight of Toddington, Beds. ADLS member.

Felicity Owned by J. O. M. Turnball.

Fervent Motor yacht built by Thornycroft, Hampton on Thames, in 1939 – 50′ × 11′9″ – powered by twin diesels: Used as communications launch at Dunkirk throughout evacuation, later being taken to Russia for harbour duties at

Archangel until shipped home with bow damage. Renovated and used on the Thames for many years as *White Marlin*. Now owned by Richard Thompson and based at Marlow. ADLS member.

Firefly Motor yacht built by Cole and Wiggins, Leigh on Sea, in 1923 – 26′ × 7′9″ – single screw: Dunkirk role uncertain but came back with shrapnel embedded in hull. Now owned by Brian Green and based at Walton-on-the-Naze. ADLS member.

Firefly Harbour launch owned by Fowey Harbour Commissioners.

Fire Fly Twin screw motor yacht built by W. Roberts at Chester in 1900 – 80′ × 11′6″ – powered by Gardner-Patricroft: Owned by Lieutenant-Colonel R. Wynn, Corwen, North Wales.

Fleetwing Twin screw motor yacht built by Watercraft of East Molesey in 1939 – 38′6″ × 8′6″ – powered by Fireball engines: Now owned by D. Stringer of London. ADLS member.

Fleury II Twin screw motor yacht built by Elkins, Christchurch, 1936 – 38′6″ × 11′6″ – powered by Fireball engines: Owned by A. Adams, Sandbanks, Dorset. Now named *Mada* and owned by John Loch-Lack of Kingston-on-Thames, ADLS member.

Florientina Ship's lifeboat.

Formosa Motor launch owned by T. Errington.

Forsa Particulars unknown.

Forty Two Twin screw motor yacht built by Strood Yacht and Boat Building Co in 1936 – 46′5″ × 11′2″ – powered by six-cylinder petrol engine: Owned by N. West of Strood.

Fram Motor boat.

Frances Auxiliary yawl built by Howard & Sons at Maldon in 1909 – 48′ × 12′4″ – with Gray engines: Owned by J. Stevens. Now named *Lady Frances,* powered by Newage engines, owned by Jeremy Lamb and based at Yarmouth, Isle of Wight. ADLS Member.

Frans Particulars unknown.

Frightened Lady Motor Cruiser: Ran aground and abandoned after fouling propeller while crossing to Dunkirk.

More of the 'Little Ships' gathered at Dover in May 1985. In front from the left are **Mada** *(ex-***Fluery II***),* **Ona II** *and* **Iorana.** *Visible to the left immediately astern are* **Nydia** *and* **Ryegate,** *while across the Wellington Dock is a further group of vessels including* **Alabama** *(ex-***Falcon II***) and the fire float* **Massey Shaw**. (Dover Express)

Gavine Motor cruiser owned by Dr F. Cooper of Buckhamstead.

Gay Fly Craft owned by Noel Gay.

Gay Crusader Single screw motor yacht built by Gibbs, Teddington, 1935 – 35′ × 9′ – powered by Gray engine: Owned by A. Foster of Plaistow. Now owned by Ronald Matthews, Kent. ADLS Member.

Gay Venture Twin screw ketch built by Watercraft, East Molesey, 1938 – 45′2″ × 12″ – powered by Gray petrol engines: Owned by D. Briault of Pinner. Now powered by twin BMC oil engines, owned by Don and Joan Waddleton of Allington, Kent, and based in the Isle of Wight. ADLS member.

Gertrude Owned by D. Kirkdale.

Girl Nancy Converted drifter built by John Chambers, Lowestoft, 1910 – 80′6″ × 17′9 – powered by Elliot & Garrod engines: Owner

Mrs F. Mitchell of Thorpe St. Andrew, Norwich.

Girl Vine Owned by W. Light.

Givenny Particulars unknown.

Glala Twin screw motor yacht built by Luke & Co/Camper & Nicholson, 1915 – 78′ × 12′5″ – AEC engines: Owned by Associated Equipment of Southall. Used as harbour defence and patrol craft. Now owned by Messrs Wynter and Nachman and used as a charter yacht. ADLS member.

Glitter Single screw motor yacht built/engined J. I. Thornycroft, Hampton, 1930 – 35′2″ × 8′: Owner P. Coode of St. Austell. Ferried off beaches, towed to Ramsgate after losing rudder on 29th May.

Golden Eagle Small craft from Littlehampton: Crossed in convoy with skoots *Tilly* and *Hilda* but sank off the beaches on 31st May.

Golden Spray Motor vessel owned by J. W. Pocock.

Golden Spray II Motor boat owned by F. Roberts: Towed over by skoot *Hilda*. Lifted six loads from beaches before being swamped by wash of destroyer taking evasive action during an air raid.

Good Luck Owned by C. A. Simmons.

Gourka Particulars unknown.

Grace Darling Owned by Sayers Brothers: Possibly Eastbourne beach boat.

Grace Darling IV Owned by C. E. Cundy.

Grave Owned by A. Brown.

Green Eagle Twin screw motor yacht built by William Osborne at Littlehampton in 1938 – 40′ × 10′3″ – powered by Morris petrol engines: Owned by D. Hudson, sent for Dunkirk service from yard of builders but lost during the evacuation.

Grey Mist Schooner built by Camper & Nicholson, Gosport, 1920 – 128′ × 19′5″ – two Gardner diesels: Owned by Lady Maud Burton of London. Requisitioned for use as danlaying vessel.

Grive Twin screw steam schooner of 687 tons built by Fairfield, Govan, 1905 – 224′7″ × 27′7″: Owned by Captain Oswald Liddell of Chepstow. Steam yacht used for Fleet Air Arm and tendering duties under the command of 67-year-old Captain the Hon. Lionel Lambert. Lost off Dunkirk with all hands on 1st June.

Grouse War Department launch: Transported 35 men.

Gulzar Twin screw schooner built J. I. Thornycroft, Southampton, 1934 – 115′9″ × 21′1″ – powered by MAN diesels: Owned by Z. Couyoumdjian of Paris. Fitted out for minesweeping duties. Went to the assistance of launch *Marlborough* which was towed to Dover. Sank at Dover during air attack on 29th July 1940.

Haig War Department launch: Transported 60 men.

Halfway Particulars unknown.

Handy Billie Owned by F. Minson & Sons. Lost.

Hanora Twin screw motor yacht built by J. I. Thornycroft, Hampton-on-Thames in 1930 – 30′5″ × 8′5″ – powered by Thornycroft petrol engines: Owned by D. Tough of Teddington. Beached and abandoned near La Panne on 2nd June.

Harmony Particulars unknown.

Hawfinch Particulars unknown.

Hazard Motor vessel dispatched by Tough Brothers: Broke adrift during tow and sank off Dunkirk.

Hendrika Single screw motor yacht built by J. Akerbook, Boskoop, Holland, 1916 – 42′ × 14′1″ – powered by Parson paraffin engine: Owned by G. Merton of London.

Henry Harris Owned by C. W. and C. Haste.

Hilda Owned by Captain C. Barclay.

Hilda Owned by J. G. Taylor: Requisitioned from Littlehampton together with *Green Eagle* and *White Lilly*.

Hilfranor Twin screw schooner built by Walton Yacht and Launch Works, Walton-on-Thames, 1933 – 42′1″ × 9′ – powered by Morris petrol engines: Owned by F. B. Parnham of Gillingham. Now owned by Norman Watling and based at Swanwick. ADLS member.

Hornet 10-foot speedboat.

Idaho Single screw motor yacht built by Camper & Nicholson at Gosport in 1919 – 74′3″ × 13′4″ – powered by Philip & Son petrol engine: Owned by O. Mocetta of London.

Imshi Bermudian sloop built by McGruer & Co at Clynder in 1937 – 29′2″ × 6′3″: Owned by R. H. Law of Glasgow.

Inspiration Twin screw motor yacht built by William Osborne at Littlehampton in 1931 – 30′9″ × 9′ – powered by Morris petrol engines: Owned by E. A. Manns of West Norwood. Now owned by Dennis Wells. ADLS member.

Iolanthe Single screw motor yacht built and engined by J. W. Brooke at Lowestoft in 1918 – 36′6″ × 7′7″: Owned by A. W. Rowan of Belfast.

Iorana Twin screw motor yacht built by D. Hilliard, Littlehampton in 1935 – 40′ × 10′ – powered by Brooke petrol engines: Owned by P. Lewns of London. Now powered by twin Newage petrol engines and owned by Percy and Joan Beaumont of Chigwell, Essex, and based at Staines. ADLS member.

Iot Auxiliary Bermudian cutter built by Camper & Nicholson, Gosport, in 1897 – 41′ × 10′ – powered by Gray petrol engine: Owned by R. Crofton-Atkins of Weybridge.

Iote Owned by A. Bell. Reported lost.

Irenic Owned by G. Coyde.

Iris Motor launch.

Irma Twin screw motor yacht built by J. I. Thornycroft at Hampton-on-Thames in 1931 – 40′ × 9′1″ – powered by Thornycroft petrol engines: Owned by E. Phillips of Madrid, Spain. Now named *Nottac,* powered by twin BMC oil engines and owned by Keith Slaughter and based at Twickenham. ADLS member.

Irma Marie Particulars unknown.

Isa Particulars unknown.

Island Queen Owned by J. Davies: Survived Operation Dynamo but sunk by aircraft off Folkestone on 14th July 1940.

Janis Motor boat: Disintegrated after direct hit by bomb while working off East Mole.

Jeanette Auxiliary ketch built by Everett of Woodbridge in 1911 – 33′ × 7′ – powered by Universal petrol engine: Towed across by tug *Fossa.*

Jetsam Single screw motor yacht built by Sandbanks Yacht Co in 1938 – 33′9″ × 9′8″ – powered by Morris petrol engine: Owned by Major J. Laurence of Round Island, Dorset.

Jockett II Twin screw motor yacht built by Watercraft at East Molesey, 1938 – 30′3″ × 9′3″ – powered by Morris petrol engines: Owned by A. Partington of Westcliff-on-Sea. Now powered by twin BMC oil engines and owned by the Gingell family of Cheam. ADLS member.

Jong Twin screw motor yacht built by J. I. Thornycroft at Hampton on Thames in 1931 – 40′ × 9′1″ – powered by Thornycroft petrol engines: Owned by D. A. Addington of Dorking. Now named *Gentle Ladye,* powered by twin BMC petrol engines, owned by Paul Rainbow of Gillingham and based on the River Medway. ADLS member.

Jordan Further particulars unknown.

Josephine Twin screw motor yacht built/engined by Thornycroft, Hampton, 1926 – 30′ × 8′: Owned by J. Stanley of Blackpool. Lost.

Karen II Twin screw motor yacht built by Ray Motor Co, Maidenhead, in 1933 – 39′7″ × 9′1″ – powered by Morris petrol engines: Owner Captain F. Vaughan of Harrow. Now owned by J. Bennett, Epping, Essex.

Karina Motor vessel owned by Captain E. F. Ragger of Ewell, Surrey.

Kaydee Motor cruiser built by Ramparts, Southampton, in 1937 – 43′ × 10′ – powered by twin Morris Commodore petrol engines: Owned by K. Davies. Destroyed in fuelling accident.

Kayell Twin screw motor yacht built by Thames Launch Co, Walton-on-Thames in 1930 – 38′ × 7′ – powered by Gray petrol engines: Owned by J. Senior of Claygate, Surrey.

Kestrel War Department launch: Transported 55 men.

Kingfisher Owned by E. Saville. Transferred troops to French vessel.

Kintail Twin screw motor yacht built by J. & N.

Forbes, Sandhaven, in 1922 – 59′6″ × 11′1″ – powered by Morris petrol engines: Owned by W. E. Turner of Hove.

Kitkat Ketch, converted from Royal Navy pinnace – 37′ × 9′2″ – powered by Studebaker petrol engine: Owned by J. Swain of London. Worked independently off beaches after losing convoy.

Kitty Single screw cruiser built Ramparts, Southampton 1930 – 30′ × 9′5″: Owned by H. Wilkinson. Now named *Aureol,* Perkins engined and owned by Jean Jones of Wallingford. ADLS member.

K.N. Cabin cruiser of 20 ft. owned by A. Porter of Weymouth.

Kongoni Twin screw schooner built by J. Taylor at Chertsey in 1937 – 65′ × 14′5″ – powered by two Gardner diesels: Owner Commander F. T. Hare of London.

Lady Carson Former ship's lifeboat owned by C. Nash of Brighton.

Lady Delft Twin screw motor yacht built by Timmer & Zoon at Delft, Holland, 1938 – 48′ × 11′5″ – powered by Junkers oil engine: Owned by W. Purser of St. Albans. Now based at Gibraltar.

Lady Gay Motor cruiser built by King of Westcliffe in 1934 – 36′ × 11′ – Morris petrol/paraffin engine: Built for tobacco company chairman Lord Dunhill and performed various duties during the war. Now named *Mehatis*, powered by Perkins diesel engines and owned by M. Dodds and based at West Mersea. ADLS member.

Lady Haig Owned by H. Meakins: Towed over by skoot *Tilly* on 31st. Now owned by J. Burbridge and moored at Port Richborough. ADLS member.

Lady Inez Motor vessel built Ramparts, Southampton, 1937 – 43′ × 10′ – powered by Gray petrol engine: Owned by Brigadier-General Harding Newman of Warminster, Wilts.

Lady Isabelle Motor launch built by H. Gibbs at Teddington in 1932 – 29′ × 6′6″ – powered by Gray engine: Owned by T. Westhead. Now owned by J. Richards, powered by 8-horsepower Stuart engine and moored on the Thames at Shepperton. ADLS member.

Lady King Particulars unknown.

Lady Lou Twin screw yawl built by Ramparts, Southampton, 1936 – 40′ × 10′: Owned by H. C. Rutter. Now owned by G. J. Boorsman and moored on the Thames at Shepperton. ADLS member.

Lady Nancy Owned by Mr Richards, other particulars unknown.

Lahloo Twin screw schooner built by G. de Vries Lentsch, jun, at Amsterdam in 1937 – 70′ × 14′1″ – powered by Glennifer engines: Owned by R. Steele of Arlesford, Hants. Used as Auxiliary Patrol Yacht at Portsmouth. Worked off beaches and brought back 15 men.

Lamouette Converted naval launch – 112′ × 12′1″ – owned by R. S. Wayland of Southsea: Now powered by Newage and Thornycroft engines, owned by Ian Rennie and based at Ramsgate. ADLS member.

Laroc Twin screw motor yacht built by Camper & Nicholson, Southampton in 1939 – 87′7″ × 15′ – Gardner oil engine: Taken by owner G. Butler of Yarmouth, Isle of Wight. Carried 147 men.

Latona Single screw motor yacht built by Boats & Cars, Kingston, 1938 – 30′ × 9′ – Gray petrol engine: Owned by E. Wood of Esher. Now owned by Bill Williams of Plymouth. ADLS member.

Laudania Particulars unknown: Transported 900 men, including those picked up by *Constant Nymph* from grounded coaster.

Laurel Leaf Prepared by Cosens & Co, Weymouth.

Lavinia Owned by A. Hurley.

Lazy Days Motor yacht built 1930 – 34′ × 8′8″ – owned by M. Lazarus. Used for ferry duties at Dunkirk. Now owned by Walter and Deborah Raven and moored on the Thames at Chelsea. ADLS member.

Leading Star Owned by E. J. Breeds.

Leila 4 Owned by L. Burway of Palmers Green: Sustained damage later repaired by Tough Brothers at Teddington.

Libestraum Owned by H. Hunt of Twickenham:

Returned 19th June 1940.

Lijns Motor vessel built by G. de Vries Lentsch, jun, in Amsterdam – 42′ × 10′ and owned by C. O. Powis: Now owned by Morris J. Tolhurst. ADLS member.

Little Ann Auxiliary Bermudian yawl built by William Osborne, Littlehampton, in 1938 – 28′1″ × 7′9″ – powered by Morris petrol; engine: Lost on 1st June after running aground. Commanded by writer David Devine who went to Dunkirk on T124 assignment and was awarded DSM.

Little Mayflower Owned by F. G. Barton.

Llanthony Twin screw schooner built by Camper & Nicholson, Southampton, in 1934 – 73′ × 14′6″ – powered by Glennifer oil engines: Owned by Major L. Beaumont-Thomas of Great Bampton, Herts. Examination service vessel, ferried troops from beaches and eventually returned with 280 men aboard. Now named *Golden Era* and a charter yacht in the Greek Islands. ADLS member.

L.N. 85 Particulars unknown.

Loranda Particulars unknown.

Lorna Doone Owned by N. Wilkinson Cox.

Lorna Doone Owned by H. Pengelly.

Lotus L. W. Parr.

Lotus Cunard Line tender.

Lurline Auxiliary ketch built by T. Howard of Woodbridge in 1914 – 37′ × 9′7″ – powered by Glennifer paraffin engine: Owned by E. Monkhouse of Bromley. Now powered by Perkins diesel engine and owned by M. Simcock and moored on the Thames at Chelsea. ADLS member.

Madame Pompadour Twin screw ketch built by G. Timmer & Zoon at Schiedam, Holland, in 1938 – 34′6″ × 19′ – powered by Ailsa oil engines: Owned by Lieutenant-Colonel H. Day of West Malling, Kent.

Madame Sans Gene Twin screw motor vessel owned by Guy Shelley: Fouled one propellor while being towed across by *Sun XV*, fouled the other when working from beaches and was abandoned.

Madic Twin screw motor vessel built by Ramparts at Southampton in 1938 – 45′ × 10′6″ – powered by Morris engines: Owned by H.Percy of Hungerford. Lost off Norway, circumstances unknown.

Maid of Honour Single screw motor yacht built and engined by J.I.Thornycroft at Hampton-on-Thames in 1928 – 30′ × 8′5″: Owned by H. Beamish of London. Crossed in convoy on 30th May, lost on 2nd June.

Ma Joie Auxiliary ketch built William Osborne, Littlehampton, in 1939 – 40′ × 9′2″ – powered by Thornycroft paraffin engine: Owned by Mrs L. Clarbour of Burnham-on-Crouch. Left on 30th May with skipper G. Harvey and crew of Walter Amos and Bertie Payne, in company with oyster boats *Seasalter* and *Vanguard*. In the absence of orders *Ma Joie* went in and ferried from beaches until fouling propeller and suffering broken rudder. Vessel abandoned and crew brought back by *Vanguard*.

Major Auxiliary yawl built by F. Miller, Oulton Broad in 1905 – 45′ × 9′5″ – powered by Kermath petrol engine: Owned by R. Bunn of St. Albans.

Malden Further particulars unknown.

Malvina Steam lugger built by R. McAlister & Son, Dumbarton, in 1893 – 55′3″ × 10′4″: Owned by R. Wilcock, Garelochead.

Marasole Particulars unknown: Transported over 400 men in seven or eight trips from beaches between 30th May and 1st June when holed and sunk when attempting to go alongside East Mole.

Mare Nostrum Single screw yawl – 55′ × 10′7″ – powered Berguis paraffin engine: Ex-RAF launch owned by B. Carter of Kirby.

Margaret Mary Twin screw motor yacht built by Husk & Co. at Wivenhoe, Essex, in 1927 – 43′ × 9′3″ – powered by Atlantic Wishaw engine: Owned by G. Chantry of London.

Margo II Twin screw motor yacht built by Richardson, Hamworthy, 1931 – 33′6″ × 9′8″ – with Dorman petrol engines: Owned by J. Ward Cox of Canford Cliffs, Dorset. Now owned by Duncan and Geoffrey Prater and based on the Thames at Putney. ADLS member.

Marianne II Twin screw motor yacht built Ramparts, Southampton, in 1938 – 45′ × 10′6″ –

Few small vessels had more adventures during Operation Dynamo than the motor yacht **Marsayru.** *The sturdy Dutch-built vessel survived and, now based in Ramsgate, is owned by Gareth and Yvonne Roe who provided the picture.*

powered by Morris Commercial engines: Owned by G. Desty of Southampton. Destroyed by bomb on beach.

Marina Owned by L. Basso.

Marlborough War Department launch: Left with other WD craft on 31st and crossed at 18 knots, collected troops and returned. Back on 2nd June to ferry from beaches, leaving on 3rd to rendezvous in mid-Channel with Admiral Taylor. Ordered to pick up French naval personnel from Quai Felix Fauré but scraped on concrete from bombed quay when departing and lost rudder and propellers. *MASB 7* tried to tow but rammed *Marlborough* before motor yacht *Gulzar* got a line aboard and towed her back to Dover.

Marsayru Twin screw, ketch rigged, motor yacht, built by Timmer and Zoon at Schiedam, Holland, in 1937 – 40′ × 10′6″: Served as Army Personnel Yacht prior to crossing from Sheerness on 31st May under the command of her civilian skipper G. D. Olivier and together with the Chatham Dockyard lighters *X 213* and *X 217*, and Sheerness lighter *X 149*. Two of the lighters were lost and the other ran aground as the vessels came under air attack off Malo-les-Bains, but the *Marsayru* was able to transfer 200 French troops to larger ships, Mr Olivier later being awarded the DSM. Whilst being taken back to Britain empty, *Marsayru's* tow broke and, in darkness, the yacht drifted away. She was found near La Panne next day and boarded by Sub-Lieutenant T. E. Goodman, RNVR, and after taking on 19 troops waited until nightfall to be towed to Ramsgate by a trawler. *Marsayru* appears to have crossed again on 2nd June and was machine-gunned for almost half an hour until the attacking German aircraft were chased off by RAF Hurricanes. First registered in Gloucester and capable of 11 knots, new machinery was fitted in 1947 and the present BMC oil engines were installed in 1962. She was renamed *Billowin* in 1955 but the present owner, Gareth Roe of Ramsgate, restored the original name in December 1987. ADLS member.

Mary Auxiliary cutter built at Fowey – 30′ × 10′6″ – powered by Berguis petrol engine: Owned by G. Shaw of London.

Mary Owned by Mrs Irwin.

Mary Irene Owned by H. Cartridge.

Mary Jane Converted naval pinnace, twin screw – 42′7″ × 13′ – Berguis petrol engines: Owned by Lieutenant-Colonel H. Richardson of Ballinamallard, Northern Ireland. Now owned by D. Bowderey of London. ADLS member.

Mata Hari Owned by J. W. Lintott.

Matilda Owned by Chelsea Yacht Club.

Matoya Twin screw motor yacht built by Husk & Co., Wivenhoe, in 1930 – 50′5″ × 11′25″ – powered by Hyland petrol engine: Owned by Lieutenant-Commander Grain of London. Now powered by BMC Commodore engines, owned by Bill Finch of Teynham, Kent, and based at Hoo Marina, on the Medway. ADLS member.

Mavis Half-decked cruiser owned by J. Pierce of Margate.

Mayflower Owned by J. Runcie.

Mayspear Particulars unknown.

Meander H. Graham.

Mermaiden Motor launch built by Kieken, Warmound, 1939 – 69′ × 13′7″ – diesel powered: Owner Lieutenant-Commander P. Filleul. Left Ramsgate on 3rd June carrying Admiral Taylor, then made four trips to vessels lying off the harbour. Now named *Amazone*, and powered by Cummins diesel and owned by Jan Rouschop of Maastrich, Holland. ADLS member.

Mersey Steam launch owned by HM Customs, Liverpool.

Millicent D. Leach Owned by Harry Leach.

Mimosa Owned by A. Gordon.

Minikoi Single screw motor yacht built by British Marine, of Old Kirkpatrick, in 1918 – 26′1″ × 7′1″ – powered by Hercules paraffin engine, owned by P. Mackay: Run down and sunk by *MASB 6* when leaving Downs on 29th May.

Minnedoas Owned by E. White and F. Rising.

Minnehaha Twin screw motor yacht built by J. Samuel White, of Cowes, in 1936 – 40′5″ × 10′2″ – powered by two Thornycroft engines: Owned by E. Tanner of London. Now named *Thamesa,* owned by R. Tough of Teddington. ADLS member.

Minoru II Owned by J. W. Cottrell.

Minotaur Ex-Royal Navy pinnace built in 1916 – 45′ × 10′ – owned by T. Towndrow. Converted into Sea Scout training craft and taken to Dunkirk by Mr Towndrow, scoutmaster of 1st Mortlake Sea Scouts. Crossed from Ramsgate ferrying French troops to larger vessels. Now owned by P. Jackson of Chertsey. ADLS member.

Minwood Particulars unknown. Landed 51 men.

Minx Owned by S. W. Willis.

Miranda Small boat owned by W. H. Goldsmith. Lost.

Mirasol Auxiliary Yawl built by Pasco & Sons, of St. Just in 1924 – 28′5″ × 9′5″ – powered by Gaines Universal engine: Owned by R. Kyle, Isleworth.

Mireille Motor vessel repaired by Toughs.

Miss Madge Motor vessel – 36′ × 8′5″ – powered by Gray petrol engine. Owned by Reg Marden, Windsor.

Miss Margate Built by Hoyle Craft of Nottingham in 1937 – 24′ × 7′5″ – powered by petrol engine: Now powered by 20-cc outboard engine and based in Norfolk.

Miss Ming Built by Kris Cruisers.

Miss Modesty Owned by S. C. Nott.

Mizpah Twin screw motor vessel built by Newport News, USA, 1926 – 185′ × 27′2″ – powered by Winton engines: Owner J. Ovett.

Moiena Twin screw motor vessel built by Jas. A. Silver, Rosneath, 1934 – 54′1″ × 12′1″ – powered by Gardner oil engines: Owner P. Trower of Worplesdon. Now named *September Tide,* owned by Eric H. Zandwijk of Brussels, and based in Ibiza. ADLS member.

Monarch Beach trip boat converted to motor yacht by Haywards, Southend, 1936 – 41′6″ × 13′3″: Owners T. & G.Baker. Now owned by Frank Hutchinson, Kegworth, Derby. ADLS member.

Montagu Whaler owned by 6th Ramsgate Scouts.

Moss Rose Owned by A. Abiett: Towed over by skoot *Hilda* to work off the beaches. Later lost.

Motor Boat Owned by R. Noyes: Towed to La Panne on June 1st.

Motor Boat 42 Particulars unknown.

Motor Boat 278 Royal Navy pinnace built by W. White, Gosport, 1914 – 30′ × 7′8″ – powered by Ferry engine: Now named *Susan K,* powered by Perkins diesel engine and owned by K. Duffy of Pocklington, North Humberside. ADLS member.

Murius, or *Murious* Owned by Vectis Shipping.

Naiad Errant Twin screw motor vessel built by W. Osborne Ltd, Littlehampton, 1939 – 32′ × 8′6″ – powered by Morris engines: Owner Major R. K. Taylor-Nightingale. Left Ramsgate in convoy on 1st June but fouled propeller working off beaches. Although abandoned by crew, soldiers freed screw and crew returned. Engine failed in fairway but again the trouble was rectified by troops and the vessel eventually reached Ramsgate on the morning of 2nd June. Now owned by Sandy Evans and based at Maidenhead. ADLS member.

Nancibell Auxiliary twin screw yawl built at Sittingbourne, 1930 – 40′ × 11′4″ – Thornycroft engine: Owner A. L. Wilcox, London. Still in existence as a houseboat in Cornwall.

Nanette II Owned by E. G. Baxter: Left Sheerness on 1st June, later rescued survivors from *Clan MacAlister* and HMS *Keith.*

Narcissa Owned by H. Allbrow.

Nayland Built by Perkins & Son, Whitstable in 1937 – powered by Thornycroft engine: Owned by Walker Motor boats. Now named *Peggotty*, powered by Chrysler diesel and owned by Miss J. Eves of Twickenham.

Nelson Motor boat and picket boat: From battleship HMS *Nelson* at Portsmouth.

Nin Owned by J. Emons, Holborn: Ferried off La Panne.

Nirvana Single screw schooner built by J. Samuel White, Cowes, Isle of Wight, 1892 – 69′ × 11′6″ – with Beardmore oil engine: Owned by F. May, Twickenham. Dispatched from Thames by Tough Brothers but became a total loss.

No Name II Motor Cruiser built and owned by W. Mason, Hadleigh – 36′6″ × 10′6″: Now named *Don Trevice*, powered by Ford diesel and owned by Eric Barnes, Leigh-on-Sea. ADLS member.

Noneta Twin screw schooner built by J. Samuel White, Cowes, Isle of Wight, 1935 – 61′ × 14′5″ – powered by Gardner oil engines: Owner W. Evans, London. Now based in Pawla, Malta. ADLS member.

Nydia Twin screw motor yacht built by Thornycroft 1939 – 30′ × 9′ – powered by Handy Billie engine: Now owned by Peter Cherry and based at Faversham. ADLS member.

Offenua Auxiliary boiler built by J. A. Holtrop, Joune, in 1901 – 60′ × 16′4″ – powered by petrol engine: Owned by J. Shakespeare of Romford.

Olivia Auxiliary Bermudian ketch built by W. Reekie, St. Monace, 1926 – 57′4″ × 14′ – powered by Gardner oil engine: Owner Mrs J. De Winton Kyffin of Upminster. Ferried off La Panne on 2nd June.

Omega Single screw ketch built at HM Dockyard, Devonport, 1917 – 43′ × 11′7″ – powered by Gardner/Patricroft engine: Owned by A. Forman of Twickenham. Now owned by G. Rouse and based on the River Severn. ADLS member.

Ona Twin screw vessel built by Staniland & Co, Thorne, 1931 – 36′ × 9′5″ – powered by Morris Navigator engines: Owner H. Payne. Now owned by Keith Carter and based on the River Humber. ADLS member.

Orellana Single screw motor yacht built Jas. A. Silver, Rosneath, 1933 – 30′1″ × 8′7″ – powered by Morris petrol engine: Owned by Mary Galbraith of Glasgow. Now named *Romassa*, powered by BMC oil engine and owned by J. Kelleher of Cork.

Orellena Built at Portsmouth in 1907 as naval steam pinnace – 41′ × 9′6″ – later fitted with Dorman diesel engine: Owned by R. Joynson. Now powered by Ford diesel and owned by John Fincham and based in Cornwall. ADLS member.

Ortrava Owned by H. J. Gallop.

Oulton Breeze Particulars unknown.

Our Lizzie Auxiliary ketch built by W. Oliver, Porthleven, 1920 – 46′ × 14′2″ powered by Thornycroft paraffin engine: Owned by H. Becan, Ingatestone, Essex. Now named *Freebooter*, powered by Perkins diesel and owned by R. Barrett of Dartmouth. ADLS member.

Palmerston Motor launch owned by Risdon Beazley, Southampton.

Pandora Twin screw motor yacht built by Elco, Bayonne, 1915 – 75′5″ × 12″ – powered by Berguis engine: Owner D. Hilliard of Littlehampton. Destroyed by fire.

Papillion Twin screw vessel built by Leslie Harris, Burnham-on-Crouch, 1930 – 33′5″ × 8′7″ – powered by Morris petrol engines: Owned by C. Makenrot of Westcliff, Essex. Returned on 3rd June, later re-allocated for A/P duties. Now owned by R. A. Huggett. ADLS member.

Patricia Single screw Ketch built by J. Adam of Gourock in 1919 - 41′4″ × 10′ 2″ – powered by Thornycroft petrol engine: Owned by A. Wilson, Whitecraigs, Renfrew.

Patricia Trinity House Tender, built 1937 at Middlesbrough. Operated off beaches, sending her two 27′ launches to ferry troops from the shore. When *Patricia* was retired in 1982 and went to Sweden for use as a floating restaurant in Stockholm, one of the launches was sold for private use and, named *Patricia*, is owned by Ken and Phyllis Brewer and based on the River Trent at Farndon, Notts. ADLS member.

Pauleter Owned by S. C. Aston.

Pearl Owned by A. Briggs.

Pearl Dispatched by Cosens & Co., Weymouth.

Peggy IV Owned by F. Bridge: Sunk off Dunkirk.

Pelagia Auxiliary ketch built at Woodbridge, 1932 – 29′ × 9′ – powered by Kelvin engine: Civilian owner Major Warnford took vessel from Harwich to Dunkirk but was turned back by naval craft. Now owned by John Holman of Faversham. ADLS member.

Pellag II Twin screw motor yacht built by A. Dickie, Tarbert, 1937 – 60′7″ × 13′5″ – powered by twin AEC oil engines; Owned by Major J. Holt of Lincoln. Failed to return, presumed lost.

Petra Owned by R. Lewis.

Pigeon War Department launch: Transported 60 men.

Pioneer Owned by R. F. Ricketts.

Polly Auxiliary cutter built by Cockerel Cruisers, Rochester, in 1931 – 28′ × 8′2″ – powered by Hyland petrol engine: Owner J. Shanahan of Seven Kings, Essex.

Pompadour Owned by Mr Ager of London.

Pride of Folkestone Owned by J. Brazier.

Princess Eleanora Particulars unknown: Collided with personnel ship *St. Helier* on 30th May.

Providence Auxiliary gaff cutter built by Gilbert & Pasco at Porthleven in 1934 – 38′3″ × 11′3″: Owned by H. Warrington-Smyth of London. Now powered by Perkins diesel engine and owned by Jonathan Minns and based at Falmouth. ADLS member.

Providence Owned by J. Walker.

Quest Cabin cruiser built at Teddington, 1936 – 30′ × 9′6″ – owned by H. Bidgood of Burnham, Bucks: Now owned by Alexander Patch and moored in the River Severn at Hawford. ADLS member.

Quicksilver Twin screw motor yacht built Jas. A. Silver, Rosneath, in 1939 – 64′5″ × 11′2″ – powered by Morris petrol engine: Owned by Lieutenant-Colonel G. Deakin of Birmingham.

Quicksilver Owned by F. Jones.

Quisiana Twin screw motor vessel built/engined by Thornycroft, Hampton-on-Thames, 1927 – 30′ × 8′5″: Owned by A. F. Eldridge. Now owned by Nicholas Lidiard and being restored on the Thames. ADLS member.

Rapid 1 Owned by P. G. Broom. One of a batch of small vessels returned to the upper Thames on 9th June 1940.

Rayon Built by Elco, Bayonne, New Jersey, powered by Beardmore engines: Owned by L. Glover of London.

Reda Twin screw ketch built by Whisstocks of Woodbridge, 1938 – 45′ × 12′: Owned by C. A. Reed. Sailed from Sheerness on 28th May, worked for three hours ferrying to larger craft off Dunkirk before returning to Ramsgate with 21 men. Crossed again on 1st for ferrying, bringing back 23 men. Now named *Janthea,* owned by Norman Cannell of Rickmansworth and based at Marlow, Bucks. ADLS member.

Requin Twin screw motor vessel built by C. Englebrecht, Zeuthen, 1914 – 60′ × 10′5″ – powered by Daimler/Morris engine: Owned by L. M. Wacherm, Herne Bay.

Ricas Particulars unknown.

River Toy Owned by G. H. Elkington.

Roberts Owned by J. Waterson.

Robina Tenant Owned by Harry Leach.

Rocinante 26-foot converted lifeboat owned by R. Fryars.

Rosabelle Schooner built and engined by Ramage & Ferguson at Leith in 1901 – 202′ × 26′4″: Owned by Lieutenant-Colonel J. Abraham of Finchley. Survived Dunkirk but lost in Straits of Gibraltar on 11th December 1941, possibly by torpedo.

Rosa Mary Particulars unknown.

Rose Motor boat owned by A. Mitchell and others.

Rose Motor boat owned by George G. Brown.

Rose Motor launch owned by Lord Moyne of London.

Roselyne Owned by Capt C. Dines.

Rose Marie Twin screw schooner built by J. Crossfield, Conway in 1926, powered by Gray petrol engines: Owner L. Freeman of Birmingham. Towed to La Panne by *Tilly*. Now powered by Perkins oil engines, owned by Major J. Westerman, Wareham.

Rose Marie Owned by J. Boyer, Sheerness.

Rosura Vessel of 20 tons, further particulars unknown: Made three crossings from 30th May to 2nd June, finally picking up 33 French and 3 officers from the Mole. Propeller shaft broke during return crossing and vessel drifted for almost three days until seen by RAF launch and taken to Ramsgate.

Rummy II Built at Bangor, Co. Down in 1930 – 30′ × 8′2″ – powered by Hyland petrol engines: Owned by A. G. Smith. Taken to Ramsgate by Lieutenant N. Sidmouth-Willing of Twickenham Sea Cadet Corps. Given naval crew but he stayed with the vessel to take ashore two lifeboats that had been towed across, 140 men being lifted off with them. Now powered by BMC diesels, owned by D. Teare, London. ADLS member.

Ryegate II Twin screw motor yacht built by H. Gibbs, Teddington in 1937 – 36′7″ × 9′7″ – powered by Gray petrol engines: Owned by A. Ryeland of Banstead. Now powered by Perkins diesels and owned by David Pamment and Jeremy Roger of Rochester and based in the Medway. ADLS member.

St. Patrick Sloop built by W. Fife & Son, Fairlie 1919 – 24′5″ x 6′: Owned by W. Thornhill of London. Reported lost.

Sally Forth Owned by Dr Purvis.

Salvor Former RNLI lifeboat built by Watson, Blackwell, in 1910 – 40′ × 11′6″: Now powered by Perkins diesel and owned by Reginald Cornwell of Ramsgate. ASLS member.

Sandown Owned by G. Alexander.

Santosy Owned by L'Odell, lost May 1940: Place and cause unknown.

Sarah and Emily Owned by J. Todd: Lost, place and cause unknown.

Sargasso Twin screw diesel yacht of 223 tons, built in Germany in 1926 as *Atlantis*: Owned by Sir Loel Guinness, member of Parliament for Bath. Requisitioned for minesweeping duties in 1939, commissioned as *Sargasso* under the command of Lieutenant C. C. L. Gaussen and based at Dover. Used mainly as a danlayer but sent to Boulogne to help bring out troops immediately before Dunkirk. Made at least two visits to the beaches, loading off La Panne on 1st June, and then completed a further crossing to Dunkirk Harbour and was officially credited with landing 605 troops at Dover. Following a spell of patrol work from Ramsgate the *Sargasso* moved further west and was sunk off the Isle of Wight after striking a mine on 6th June 1943.

Satyr Built in Sweden in 1923 – 51′2″ × 10′9″ – powered by Buffalo & Thorn engines: Owned by G. H. Masters of Hatton Garden, London.

Savior Particulars unknown.

Scene Shifter Twin screw motor vessel built by Borwick & Sons, Bowness in 1919 – 40′ × 9′1″ – powered by Morris petrol engines: Owned by S. Longman, Esher. Lost May 29th after being swamped by French personnel vessel.

Schedar Twin screw sloop, built by Osborne, Littlehampton, 1938 – 39′ × 8′9″ – powered by Morris petrol engine: Owned by F. Drake of Horsham, lost during evacuation.

Sea Foam Owned by W. Clayton.

Seagull Owned by E. King: Returned to owner 6th June.

Seagull Owned by C. Loose: Returned to owner 7th June.

Sea Hawk Owned by Alex Ogilvie.

Sea Lord II Particulars unknown.

Seamew Twin screw motor vessel built by Williams & Parkinson, Degawny, 1936 – 37′3″ × 9′6″ – powered by Gray petrol engine: Owned by O. Smith of Liverpool.

Sea Roamer Converted naval pinnace – 43′ × 11′8″ – powered by Morris oil engine: Owner Major J. Wheatley of Walton-on-Thames. Crossed with Naval party who searched beaches 2½ miles east of Dunkirk on 2nd June but found no troops. Also searched wrecks offshore and picked up Frenchmen who had swam the previous day. Then went to Dunkirk harbour, colliding with a destroyer, but suffered no serious damage. Eventually towed back.

Sea School Shipping Federation training vessel.

Sea Swallow Owned by Captain R. Drake.

Seriola Twin screw motor yacht built by G. de Vries Lentsch, jun, Amsterdam, 1938 – 72′ × 14′7″ – powered by AEC oil engine: Owned by J. Bravery, Parkstone, Dorset.

Shamrock Motor yacht owned by W. Scott: Recorded as being lost.

Shamrock Motor yacht owned by Morgan Giles Ltd.

Sheldrake Twin screw motor vessel built by Giles, Teignmouth, 1925 – 40′ × 9′6″ – powered by Parsons petrol engines: Owner H. Davis of London.

Sheldrake Owned by H. Thew.

Shunesta Twin screw schooner built by H. McLean & Sons, Govan, in 1936 – 56′ × 12′ – powered by Parsons paraffin engines: Owned by F. Allen of Thorpe Bay.

Silver Foam Owned by W. H. Dick.

Silver Moon Twin screw motor yacht built by W. Osbourne, Littlehampton, in 1930 – 40′ × 9′5″ – powered by two Schripps petrol engines: Owned by W. Ware of Rustington, Sussex. Now powered by Chrysler diesels and owned by C. Goss of London.

Silver Spray Owned by J. McQueen.

Silver Spray Owned by W. Dick.

Silver Spray Owned by W. A. Eagles.

Silvery Breeze Owned by A. Verley.

Sinbad II Owned by E. A. Hare.

Singapore Single screw motor vessel built by Walton Engineering Co in 1934 – 32′3″ × 9′ – powered by Morris petrol engine: Owner D. Bostock of Ipswich. Ran aground off the beaches on 2nd June, refloated with tide and then broke down and was towed home by ketch *Kitkat.* Now powered by Sutton oil engine and owned by Vassos Zacharakis of Athens. ADLS member.

Singapore II Motor cruiser built at Walton, 1937 – 32′ × 8′6″ – based on the Orwell: Now owned by Richard Moss and moored at Woodbridge. ADLS member.

Skylark Twin screw motor yacht built and engined by Thornycroft, Hampton-on-Thames, in 1922 – 60′ × 13′1″ – Owner by Myalls Ltd. Now named *Tahilla,* powered by twin Gardner engines, owned by Peggy and Jerry Lewis and based at Warsash. ADLS member.

Skylark III Owned by W. Coisan.

Skylark III Owned by F. T. Collins.

Skylark IV Owned by S. B. Leverett.

Small Viking Particulars unknown.

Smiling Through Owned by H. Cartridge: Lost 5th June.

Smolt Twin screw motor vessel built by H. Gibbs at Teddington in 1936 – 39′ × 12′ – powered by Gray petrol engines: Owned by A. Williams of Roehampton. Now powered by diesel engines and believed to be in the Mediterranean.

Smuggler Twin screw vessel built by C. Barker, Maldon, in 1930 – 32′4″ × 8′9″ – powered by Thornycroft petrol engines: Owned by G. D. Tayte.

Snow Bunting Twin screw vessel built by R. Prior at Burnham-on-Crouch in 1938 – 40′ × 11′ – powered by Berguis paraffin engine: Owned by F. P. Wray of London. Now owned by Vic North. ADLS member.

Sonia Owned by Loft West Ltd.

Southend Britannia Former ship's lifeboat built by Thornycroft, 1938 – 17′3″ × 6′ – powered by oars and sails: Later named *Landscaper* and owned by J. Sharman-Courtney of Dunfold Common, Surrey. ADLS member.

Southern Queen Motor vessel of 35′ × 9′ owned by executors of the late E. Saunders of Folkestone. Reported lost.

South Ray Owned by T. Shaw.

Southern Star Motor vessel built by Bates of London in 1928 – 33′ × 9′6″ – powered by Gray petrol engine: Owned by Bates and Co. Now powered by BMC diesel engine and owned by D. McGinley of Twickenham. ADLS member.

Speedwell Single screw auxiliary sailing vessel built by A. Burgoine at Kingston-on-Thames in 1911 – 28′2″ × 7′7″: Now named *Moonraker,* powered by Stuart Turner petrol engine and owned by M. Riggs of Weybridge.

Spinaway Owned by S. Figg of London.

Spindrift Open 20-foot boat owned by Mr Shrubshall of Margate.

Sprite Harbour launch built by Ashton & Kilner at Poole in 1911 – 24′ × 8′ – powered by Stuart Turner petrol engine: Owner R. Parke of Blandford, Dorset.

Starfish Owned by T. Brown: Returned to owner on 5th June.

Stonehaven Owned by W. Stonehouse: Listed as lost.

Summer Maid Twin screw ketch built at Delfizijl, Holland, in 1938 – 46′ × 11′: Owner F. Brown.

Sundowner Bermudian schooner built by G. Cooper at Conyer – 58′ × 12′2″ – powered by Gray engine: Designed by owner, Commander C. H. Lightoller, who in 1912 was the senior surviving officer of the loss of the White Star liner *Titanic.* Taken by Lightoller with a crew consisting of his son and a Sea Scout, *Sundowner* sailed from Chiswick to Southend and then Ramsgate as part of a convoy of some 40 Thames craft before crossing with five other small vessels. En route they picked up the *Westerly's* five-man crew who had to abandon their burning vessel. Finding no one left on beaches, *Sundowner* went to Dunkirk Harbour and succeeded in squeezing in 122 troops who were landed at Ramsgate. Now owned by the East Kent Maritime Trust and based at Ramsgate. ADLS member.

The 14-foot dinghy **Tamzine** *pictured at the Imperial War Museum, Lambeth, London, where she occupies a central position in the newly-established large exhibition hall that was opened by the Queen in June 1989.* (Imperial War Museum)

Sunshine Owned by R. Verrion: Despite having engine out of action, was towed across by lifeboat *Lord Southborough* and worked from the beaches, being hauled back and forth by lines. The vessel was lost returning home when the tow broke.

Surrey Twin screw motor yacht built by Boats & Cars, Kingston, 1939 – 29′ × 8′ – powered by Morris petrol engine: Owned by E. Thomas of Kingston. Now named *L'Orage,* powered by BMC petrol engine and owned by Raymond and Sylvia Baxter of Denham, Bucks, and based at Henley. ADLS member.

Swallow War Department launch: Transferred between 600 and 700 men to HMS *Impulsive* and HMS *Winchelsea* before returning to Ramsgate. Made a second trip on 2nd June, bringing back 68 men.

Sylvia Single screw motor yacht built Southampton 1930 – 44′7″ × 9′8″ – powered by Gray petrol engine: Owned by W. Astley of Maidstone. Now named *Wendy Ken,* rebuilt with twin screws and BMC engines and owned by Ian Pearson and based at Cuxton. ADLS member.

Sylvia Owned by R. Tonkin.

Tamzine 15-foot dinghy owned by Ralph Bennett and built by Brockman and Titman at Margate in 1937. One of the smallest boats in Operation Dynamo, it was towed across and used to ferry men from the beaches to larger craft offshore and survived to be hauled back to Britain by a Belgian trawler. In 1981 Mr Bennett gave *Tamzine* to the Imperial War Museum and, superbly restored, it is now on show in the large exhibition hall of the museum's redeveloped Lambeth premises in South London. ADLS member.

Tarifa Twin screw motor yacht built/engined by J. I. Thornycroft, Hampton-on-Thames, 1932 – 48′5″ × 10′6″: Owned by L. Curtis of London. Now powered by twin Perkins diesels and owned by Mrs E. Lewis and moored at Cowes. ADLS member.

Tarrett Particulars unknown: Worked off beaches on 31st May. Ferried 550 troops.

Tenias Particulars unknown.

Thame II Launch built by Gill & Sons, Rochester, 1909 – 52′ × 10′7″ – powered by Bergius paraffin engines: Port of London Authority survey launch. Worked in Ramsgate area but probably did not cross. Used as a houseboat from 1952 and later as a yacht, but broken up after sinking at Sunbury.

Thark Twin screw vessel built by H. Gibbs, Teddington, 1930 – 32′2″ × 8′7″ – powered by Gray & Morris engines: Owned by G. Thompson of Sydenham.

Thele Twin screw motor yacht built by G. de Vries Lentsch, Amsterdam, 1938 – 72′ × 14′7″ – with Glennifer oil engines: Owned by Montagu Abraham, of Parkstone, Dorset, used as an Auxiliary Patrol yacht at Portsmouth.

Thelmar Twin screw cutter built at Sittingbourne 1936 – 39′ × 9′ – powered by two Morris petrol engines: Owned by C. E. Millson of Goudhurst, Kent. Now powered by BMC engines, owned by J. L. Sands and moored at Canvey Island. ADLS member.

Thetis Owned by H. Eaton: Lost while under tow to Dunkirk.

Three Brothers Ketch built by G. Smith at Rye 1896 – 51′5″ × 15′: Owned by R. Arbuthnot, London.

Thurn Owned by F. Schofield.

Thyforsa Particulars unknown.

Thyra Single screw yacht built and engined by Thornycroft at Hampton-on-Thames in 1921 – 45′ × 8′9″: Owned by A. Clements. Lost since the war due to broken back.

Tom Hill Owned by T. Hill, further particulars unknown.

Tom Tit Motor cruiser built by R. Skentlebery, Plymouth in 1938 – 38′9″ × 11′1″ – powered by petrol engines: Now named *Melinda Margot,* and powered by Leyland diesel. Owned by Stephen Lucas, based at Folkestone. ADLS member.

Tortoise Particulars unknown.

Trillene Owned by Dr. Everard Williams: Returned 19th June 1940.

Triton Twin screw motor yacht built by Jas. Taylor, Chertsey in 1935 – 54′8″ × 12′6″ – powered by Gardner oil engines: Owned by A. Ehrman of Beaulieu, Hants. Leader of a convoy of eight small craft which left Sheerness on 29th May and one of only five vessels to reach Dunkirk. Towed small boats to and from larger craft on 30th May but ran aground after being boarded by Vice-Admiral Stephenson. Refloated at 04:00 on 31st, and continued to ferry. Later renamed *Charmaine,* owned by Lieutenant-Commander R. Elsworth but lost on 8th January 1981 in storm off Kalkara.

Two Rivers F. Fothergill.

Two Sisters R. Haynes.

Usanco L. Hailes.

Valerie II Single screw yacht built by Osborne, Littlehampton, 1939 – 26′ × 8′ – powered by Gray petrol engine: Owned by A. Fuller of London.

Val Ross Particulars unknown.

Vanitee Owned by D. V. Johnson: Failed to return.

Vedettes Owned by F. Lycett.

Venture Owner Mr Donaldson, other particulars unknown.

Venture Owned by Isabella Horn.

Vera Owned by P. Hatch.

Vera Owned by A. F. Self.

Vere Cabin cruiser converted from naval pinnace, built 1905. Recorded as transporting 346 men. Now owned by J. G. N. Perfect. ADLS member.

Vernon Pinnace from HMS Vernon, Portsmouth: Ferried from the beaches on 29th May.

Viewfinder Owner L. A. London: Failed to return.

Viking III Dinghy with outboard motor owned by J. S. Houlton: Lost off beaches.

Vulture War Department launch: Performed ferry duties before returning with 86 men.

Wairakei Twin screw ketch built Jas. A. Silver, Rosneath, 1928 – 42′ × 11′ – powered by Morris petrol engine: Now named *Vivanti*, owned by Russell Harris and based at Ramsgate. ADLS member.

Wairakei II Twin screw ketch built by Jas. A. Silver, Rosneath, 1932 – 52′ × 11′ – powered by Glennifer petrol engines. Brought back 150 men. Now owned by M. Lewen and based at Worcester. ADLS member.

Walker I Owned by Walker Motor Boats.

Walker II Owned by Walker Motor Boats.

Wanda Twin screw ketch built by Elkins, Christchurch, in 1935 – 38′ × 9′6″ – powered by Morris petrol; engine: Owned by H. Maxim of London. Now powered by Perkins oil engine, owned by David Rolt of Hallerton, Leicestershire, and based at Weymouth. ADLS member.

Warrior Twin screw ketch built by Risdon Beazley, Southampton, in 1939 – 69′5″ × 13′5″ – powered by Russell Newbury engine: Owned by W. Loudon Douglas of London. Now owned by J. Hornshaw of Torquay. ADLS member.

Warrior Twin screw schooner of 1,124 tons, built by Ailsa Shipbuilding Co, Troon, in 1904 – 298′7″ × 32′7″ – steam engine by A. & J. Inglis: Owned by Rex Hoyes of Winchester. Lost in air attack off Portland on 11th July 1940.

Wave Queen Owned by G. H. Kent: Returned in sinking condition.

Wayfarer Particulars unknown.

Welcome Owned by E. J. Pitman.

Westerly Motor yacht owned by R. A. B. Christie: Caught fire and had to be abandoned after leaving Ramsgate for Dunkirk on 1st June, five-man crew taken-off by *Sundowner*.

Westgrove Particulars unknown.

Westward Owned by F. Porter of Barking.

Westward Twin screw ketch built by J. Noble at Fraserburgh in 1935 – 42′7″ × 13′6″ – powered by Berguis petrol engines: Owned by E. Kennedy of Killearn, Stirlingshire.

West Wind Particulars unknown.

Weymouth Queen Motor vessel, particulars unknown: Prepared at Weymouth by Cosens and Co, released 3rd June.

White Bear Steam yacht, particulars unknown.

White Heather Twin screw motor yacht built by McGruer & Co, Clynder, 1920 – 57′2″ × 10′1″ – powered by Thornycroft petrol engines: Owned by W. Wright of Pollockshiels. Now named *Riis 1*, powered by twin Thornycroft engines, owned by Ted and Pat Fellows of Ware and based at West Mersea. ADLS member.

White Heather Single screw motor vessel built by Morgan Giles, Teignmouth, in 1939 – 44′ × 10′ – powered by a Parsons paraffin engine: One of eight boats to leave Ramsgate on 1st June in convoy including *Sundowner* and *Naiad Errant* but suffered damage and was abandoned.

White Heather Owned by A. Davidson.

White Heather Owned by V. C. Hay.

White Heather Owned by J. Rainie.

White Heather Owned by S. Worth.

White Lady Owned by W. and B. Peters.

White Lily Prepared by Osborne Brothers at Littlehampton.

White Orchid Twin screw motor yacht built by Jas. A. Silver, Rosneath, in 1932 – 36′ × 9′ – powered by twin Morris petrol engines: Owned by C. Chapman of London. Later named *Doutelle* and powered by Newage oil engines, she survived until broken up in 1986.

White Water Twin screw motor vessel built by J. Despujols at Neuilly-sur-Seine, France, in 1930 – 47′3″ × 9′6″ – powered by Gray petrol engines: Owned by W. Richards of Sutton, Surrey.

White Wing Twin screw cutter built by W. Osborne, Littlehampton, in 1939 – 27′ × 8′ – powered by Morris petrol engines: Owned by F. Cook of Purley. After being forced to abandon his earlier command, *Little Ann*, writer David Devine 'stole' this Thames motor cruiser and was on the point of leaving Ramsgate when ordered to take Vice-Admiral Taylor across to patrol off the beaches and supervise small boat operations.

Willie and Alice Owned by W. G. S. Crouch of Ramsgate: Failed to return.

Windsong Auxiliary ketch built by D. Hilliard, Littlehampton, 1931 – 35′3″ × 9′6″ – powered by Ailsa Craig petrol engine: Owned by G. Dalton of Brighton. Crossed to beaches but forced by air attacks to return. Now powered by Petters oil engine, owned by Col. M. Duddridge and based at Roesmond, Holland. ADLS member.

Wings of the Morning Auxiliary ketch built by D. Hilliard at Leith in 1933 – 35′ × 9′6″ – powered by a Thornycroft petrol engine: Owned by Lord Dunboyne of Chelsea.

Winmabet Owned by J. Gummerson.

Winston Owned by A. Fuller.

Wolfe War Department launch: Crossed on 31st May and also 2nd June, on each occasion in company with other War Department launches. *Wolfe* brought back a total of 69 men.

Wolsey Single screw cruiser built at HM Dockyard, Devonport – 30′2″ × 7′1″ – powered by Berguis petrol engine: Owned by A. Malcolm of Hampton Wick. Set out from Ramsgate on the night of 30th May as one of a convoy of 10 small vessels, all towing ship's lifeboats but broke down en route owing to a blocked carburettor and tied up for the night alongside the North Goodwin lightship.

Yola Bermudian sloop built at the Arendal Yard, Gothenburg, Sweden, in 1932 – 29′2″ × 6′3″: Owned by C. Heywood of London.

Zela Twin screw motor yacht built by Ramparts, Southampton, in 1937 – 45′ × 10′3″ – powered by twin Morris Commodore engines: Owned by H. McLoughlin. Renamed *Rania* for war service. Now powered by twin Ford engines, named *Arkian*, owned by Ian Davidson and based at the Exeter Canal. ADLS member.

SHIP'S LIFEBOATS

More than 50 life-boats were collected from vessels lying in London Docks and at Tilbury. They were moved to Ramsgate and from there crossed the Channel towed by a variety of craft including tugs, skoots and drifters, all but 19 subsequently being lost.

Owner	Number of boats	Lost
Blue Star Line	4	4
British India Steam Navigation Co	10	10
Butchers	2 motor lifeboats	—
Canadian Pacific Steam Ship Co	1 from *Beaverdale*	—
Englis & Mills	4 from *Dunbar Castle*	4
Englis & Mills	1 from *Lolworth*	1
Englis & Mills	1 from *Parales*	1
Unknown	4 from *Flandres*	2
Houlder Bros & Co	4 from *Upway Grange*	1
Orient Line	1 ML/B from *Orient IV*	—
P & O Steam Navigation Co	16	10
Ropner Shipping Co	1 from *Hawnsby*	1
Unknown	4 from *Roslin Castle*	2
Royal Mail Line	5	3

RNLI Lifeboats

NINETEEN of the Royal National Lifeboat Institution's familiar blue-hulled boats took part in Operation Dynamo, with every station from Great Yarmouth round the coast as far west as Bournemouth represented. First to cross were the Margate and Ramsgate craft manned by their regular volunteer crews but later boats to reach Ramsgate and Dover were taken over by Royal Navy personnel, although in some cases RNLI mechanics stayed aboard to look after the engines.

Many of the experienced RNLI coxswains arriving at Kent ports with the lifeboats had serious misgivings about their suitability for working off the beaches. Of necessarily heavy construction with a resulting deep draught, the lifeboats had not been designed to take the ground, but so desperate was the need that the Admiralty simply took control and sent them anyway. A number went in both directions under their own power while others were towed across to conserve fuel and enable them to stay longer off the French coast. Several boats belonged to RNLI classes which were still additionally equipped with sails.

Various lifeboats suffered damage yet, despite all the problems, only a single boat, *The Viscountess Wakefield* from the Hythe station, was a total loss. Half a century on, a remarkable number of these sturdy craft remain in private hands at various places right around the British coast and in the Channel Islands, and one, *Thomas Kirk Wright*, Bournemouth's lifeboat in 1940, is owned by the National Maritime Museum and based at the RNLI's national headquarters in Poole.

Abdy Beauclerk Official number 751, stationed at Aldeburgh: Built 1932 – 41′ × 12′3″ – powered by two 35-hp AEC Weyburn petrol engines:

The **Abdy Beauclerk** *was one of the two lifeboats from Aldeburgh, Suffolk, to go to Dunkirk. The boat, one of a number taking part still provided with sails, was off the French coast from 31st May to 4th June under the command of Able Seaman Charles Strudwick, pictured above right at his Portsmouth home in 1988.*

Named by Prince George in May 1932 and paid for from a private legacy, *Abdy Beauclerk* was taken to Dover where Able Seaman Charles Strudwick was put in command as coxswain with support from one ordinary seaman and a stoker to run the engines. They were towed across the Channel by drifters arriving on 31st May at a beach just east of Dunkirk harbour and told to 'remain until ordered to return.' The boat transferred men to larger vessels anchored in deeper water, staying in case stragglers reached the beach until late on 4th June, crossing to Ramsgate and arriving in the early hours of the following day. No record of the number of troops transported was kept but the figure probably totalled several hundred. *Abdy Beauclerk* returned to Aldeburgh until withdrawn from RNLI service in 1959 after saving 141 lives. She was sold for use as a pilot vessel at Cork.

Cecil and Lilian Philpot Official number 730, stationed at Newhaven: Built 1930 by J. Samuel White & Co, Cowes – 45′5″ × 12′5″ – powered by twin petrol engines: Crossed on 30th May, returning towed by tug *Foremost* on 2nd June. Now named *Stenoa,* owned by Dr Oliver Dansie of Welwyn and based at Walton-on-Thames. ADLS member.

Charles Cooper Henderson Official number 761, stationed at Dungeness: Built 1933 by Groves & Gutteridge, Cowes: Worked with other RNLI boats off the beaches on 31st May. Found broken down with four ratings aboard on 1st June and sailed back by crewmen from Margate lifeboat *Lord Southborough.* Now named *Caresana,* owned by Ron Wylie and based in Guernsey. ADLS member.

Charles Dibdin Official number 762, stationed at Walmer: Built 1933 – 41′ × 12′5″: Holed in two places but returned safely. When stripped for survey after the war, a tracer bullet was found amid charred timbers behind one of the fuel tanks. Went to the Mediterranean in the late 1950s.

Cyril and Lilian Bishop Official number 740, stationed at Hastings: Crossed under the command of Acting PO W. Adkin. Became a fishing vessel in the 1950s and now lies out of use at Port Askais, Islay.

Edward Z. Dresden Official number 707, stationed at Clacton-on-Sea: Built 1928 by J. E. Saunders, Cowes – 45′5″ × 12′5″ – powered by twin petrol engines: Now named *St. Peter,* powered by two Parsons Baracuda engines and owned by Mr and Mrs W. G. Arnold of Irvine, Ayrshire. ADLS member.

E.M.E.D. Official number 705, stationed at Walton-on-the-Naze: Arrived off beaches on 31st May with RNVR Lieutenant R. Mead in command. The vessel failed to return and was believed lost until found with a fouled propeller on 1st June and towed to Dover by the tug *Sun IV* where 39 men were landed, together with the body of Lieutenant Mead who was killed in action. After being withdrawn in 1956, the vessel was sold to the Chilean Government.

Greater London Official number 704, stationed at Southend-on-Sea: In command Sub-Lieutenant W. Clayton, RNR. Still thought to be afloat in Montevideo where she was sold in 1957.

Guide of Dunkirk Official number 826, station not allocated: Built 1940 by Rowhedge Iron Works, Essex – 35′6″ × 9′10″ - powered by AEC Weyburn engines: This new and then unnamed self-righting boat was taken from the builders to Sheerness and then Ramsgate before crossing on 30th May with a crew of naval ratings to work from the beaches to vessels standing offshore. In

1941 *ON 826* took its place at Cadgwith in Cornwall and there, on 14th June 1947, was named *Guide of Dunkirk*, the Girl Guides of the British Empire having presented £5,000 of a £50,000 total raised to help the war effort in its 1940 gift week from 19th to 25th May to the RNLI. Taken out of commission in May 1963, the vessel was bought by A. J. Moore of Mevagissey, Cornwall, and is now named *Girl Guide*. ADLS member.

Jane Holland Official number 673, stationed at Eastbourne: Built in 1922 by J. Samuel White and Co, Cowes – 40′ × 10′6″ – powered by a 45-hp Tylor engine: Served from new at Selsey before going to Eastbourne in 1929. Taken across by a naval crew on 30th May but abandoned after being hit by a French destroyer and then a British MTB. Later found in a waterlogged state but still afloat and towed in. Repaired and returned to serve Eastbourne until 1949 and then in RNLI reserve fleet until sold in 1953.

Lord Southborough Official number 688, stationed at Margate: Left on 30th May with RNLI crew and worked throughout the next day ferrying an estimated 500 troops from La Panne beach to the destroyer *Icarus* and a barge. Returning to Margate to refuel, coxswain Edward Parker stopped to pick up two officers and 15 ratings who were all that remained of a party of 150 who had been working on the beach for four days. After only a few hours the *Lord Southborough* returned to Dunkirk and brought away French troops who had been fighting on the perimeter. Now owned by B. High. ADLS member.

Louise Stephens Official number 820, stationed at Great Yarmouth: Built in 1939 by J. Samuel White & Co, Cowes – 46′ × 12′ – powered by twin Ferry engines: Transported 49 troops. Now named *Tyne Star* and based at Starcross, South Devon. ADLS member.

Lucy Lavers Official number 832, stationed at Aldeburgh: Went across with Sub-Lieutenant T. Betts, RNVR, in command. A Jersey pilot boat from 1968 and now used as a diving training ship at St. Helier.

Mary Scott Official number 691, stationed at Southwold: Built in 1925 by J. E. Saunders, Cowes – 47′3″ × 13′3″: Crossed as part of a second batch of RNLI boats sent on 30th May and ferried from the beaches throughout the 31st until breaking down and being abandoned. Subsequently returned after engine was restarted. Now named *Atanua* and based on the Medway at Gillingham.

Michael Stephens Official number 838, stationed at Lowestoft: Built by J. Samuel White & Co, Cowes – 46′ × 12′ – powered by Ferry diesels: landed 52 men in addition to work off Dunkirk. Now owned by C. Cave of Flax Bourton, Bristol. ADLS member.

Prudential Official number 697, stationed at Ramsgate: Built in 1925 by S. Saunders, Cowes, and powered by diesel engine: Sailed on 30th May under coxswain Howard Knight and towing a ship's lifeboat and eight wherries loaded with cans of drinking water and coils of rope. Naval crews manning the wherries had difficulty in handling them in rough water caused by the sea breaking in shoal water approaching the beach and members of *Lord Southborough's* crew gave assistance. Despite the night being pitch black, an estimated 800 troops were brought out, eight at a time, in the wherries and transferred by the lifeboat to larger vessels further out. Now named *Trimilia*, owned by Richard Rothery and based at Woodbridge. ADLS member.

Rosa Woodd and Phyllis Lunn Official number 758, stationed at Shoreham: Built in 1932 by Groves and Gutteridge, Cowes, powered by two Weyburn diesels: Now named *Dowager*, powered by two Paxman diesels and owned by Tom Lawrence of Canvey Island. ADLS member.

The Viscountess Wakefield Official number 783, stationed at Hythe: Sailed 30th May but disappeared without trace the following day.

Thomas Kirk Wright Official number 811, stationed at Bournemouth: Crossed towed by tug *Foremost 87* with Leading Seaman H. Huntington in command. Returned damaged on 31st May with 12 inches of water in the hold. Now owned by the National Maritime Museum and based at the RNLI's national headquarters in Poole.

In addition, the reserve lifeboat *Agnes Cross* was used for a variety of duties at Dover.

Small Foreign Vessels

BY no means all the small craft which took part in the evacuation were British and, in addition to the participation of a handful of French and Dutch vessels, the former mostly as minesweepers or patrol boats, a major contribution was made by boats of the Belgian fishing fleet.

Some vessels were met in the Channel by British or French patrol craft while fleeing from their home ports following the capitulation of Belgium and diverted to the beaches or Dunkirk Harbour. Others that had already passed through the Straits of Dover, having left earlier carrying refugees and families of the owners and crew members, turned back to sail for the beaches.

Although mostly used for ferry duties off the French coast, some vessels completed two or three crossings to Ramsgate or other Kent ports and carried large numbers of men. The majority of the Belgian fishing vessels were small and well under 100 tons and one of them, the *Maréchal Foch,* was actually sunk in Dunkirk Harbour by the sheer weight of the numbers of men who swarmed aboard. Not to be beaten, her skipper and crew waited until the tide went out and salvaged the vessel, which transported 300 men the next day.

A 5 Belgian fishing vessel, built 1917: Made one crossing, landing 234 troops on 31st May after damage by bombing.

A 73 Belgian fishing vessel: Used as patrol craft.

Abdel Dewulf Belgian fishing vessel of 29 tons, built 1937, skipper H. Beyen: Made two trips, rescuing 15 men.

Alex Rachel Belgian fishing vessel, built 1913, skipper H. Ackx: Completed two crossings, picking up 116 men at sea.

Amblève Belgian launch: Towed to Dunkirk by HMS *Skipjack,* collected full load of men but ran aground and was lost.

André Louis French fishing boat. Carried 761 men.

André Lucienne Belgian fishing vessel of 30 tons, built 1937, skipper L. Decreton: Used as patrol craft, made one crossing.

André Marcel French fishing boat. Landed 50 men.

Angèle Aline Dundee sail trawler, built Fécamp in 1921 – 65′ × 8′6″ – with auxiliary Deutz engine: Two-masted ketch of an 1860s design to trawl for herring in Scottish waters in summer and later off the Normandy coast. Built as *Jules Talleux* for French owners but sold to Belgians in 1931, renamed and based at Nieuport. Requisitioned by French Navy to take part in Dunkirk evacuation but was sunk later in 1940. Refloated and returned to fishing in 1941 and then seized by the Germans in 1944 and used to block the entrance of Nieuport harbour. After the war, she continued to fish until 1963 and then, for 20 years, was home for a Dutch family. Now powered by a Perkins diesel engine, the *Angèle Aline* was bought by George and Meriel Thurstan in 1984 and since a two-year refit has been based at Bodrum, Turkey. ADLS member.

Angèle Lizette Belgian fishing vessel of 29 tons, built 1937: Made one crossing.

Angèle Marie French fishing boat. Carried 421 men.

Anna Belgian fishing vessel of 21 tons, built 1934: One trip.

Anna Léopold Belgian fishing vessel of 53 tons, built 1936: Made three crossings, saving a total of 270 men from the beaches and at sea. Aground and refloated, also bombed and shelled.

Anna Marie Thérèse Belgian fishing boat of 18 tons, built 1935: Completed one crossing.

Anne Marguerite Belgian drifter of 37 tons, built 1911: Rescued some of the 80 survivors from the 500 troops aboard on French minesweeper *Emile Deschamps*, mined on 3rd June within sight of the British coast.

Antonius van Padua Belgian fishing vessel of 17 tons, built 1928: Made one crossing.

Arc en Ciel French fishing vessel: Worked ferrying troops from beaches to larger craft.

Ausa Particulars unknown.

Ave Maria Gratia Plena French Fishing vessel: Ferried troops from Malo beach to Dutch skoots.

Barbara Auguste French fishing vessel.

Belgica Belgian fishing vessel of 36 tons, built 1924, skipper L. DaPaep: Made one trip with 118 men taken from beaches.

Bernadette de Liseux French vessel.

Bertha Léon Belgian fishing vessel of 24 tons, built 1927: Made one trip, landing 13 men.

Besta Dutch barge: Used to ferry troops from the beaches.

Blanche Marguerite Belgian fishing vessel of 102 tons, built 1939: Made a single trip.

Blauvoët Belgian fishing vessel of 73 tons, built 1931: Made one crossing.

Bordeaux French vessel.

Caporal Peugeot Landed 105 men.

Chalutier Particulars unknown.

Chasse Rave Particulars unknown.

Chasseur Particulars unknown.

Chasseur 7th Particulars unknown.

Chasseur Maree Made four crossings.

Ciel de France French fishing vessel: Loaded men at Malo beach.

Commander Delage Particulars unknown.

Constant Léopold Belgian fishing vessel of 35 tons, built 1911.

Cor Jésu Belgian trawler of 97 tons, built 1931: Landed 274 troops on 31st May. Lost in air attack on Alnmouth, 8th June 1941.

Dame Franche Particulars unknown.

Débra Huyseune Belgian fishing vessel of 46 tons, built 1922: Made one trip.

De Hoop Belgian fishing vessel of 91 tons, built 1913: One trip.

Denis Papin French fishing vessel: Sank in 30 seconds during air attack near Buoy No. 6.

De Ruyter Fishing vessel, built 1928: Made one crossing, 90 men landed.

Drifter 145 Belgian craft.

Duperée French trawler.

Dutch Daffil Particulars unknown.

Edmond Rene French vessel. Landed 210 men.

Elona Constance Belgian fishing vessel of 30 tons, built 1937, skipper F. Rameldo: Completed one crossing, landing 73 men.

Emile Lastus, Emile Louise Particulars unknown.

Emma Léon Belgian fishing vessel of 34 tons, built 1932, skipper J. Vlietinck: Completed one return trip.

Escaut Belgian launch: Lost on 30th May.

Florient-Juliette Belgian fishing vessel of 23 tons, built 1936: Completed one crossing.

Frieda Belgian fishing vessel of 98 tons, built 1929, skipper L. Verpoorter: Shell-damaged while picking up 11 men from beach.

Gamboul, Gaston River, Gativois Particulars unknown.

Georges Edouard Belgian trawler of 217 tons, built 1938: Landed a total of 1,007 men on two crossings.

Gérard-Léon Belgian trawler of 77 tons, built 1936: Two trips.

Getuigt voor Christus Belgian fishing vessel of 40

The Belgian fishing vessel **Elona Constance** *preparing to move alongside the paddle minesweeper* **Oriole** *while en route for the Kent coast. Some of the troops from what appears a mixed load of British and French personnel already have a makeshift gangway ready.* (J. Rutherford Crosby)

tons, built 1937: Lost 2nd June after collision with patrol boat near Dover.

Gilda Belgian fishing boat of 69 tons, built 1936: Survived severe air attacks, during which her Belgian Naval officer, Commander Ghesselle, was seriously wounded, to land British and French troops.

Ginette Belgian fishing boat of 24 tons, built 1928: One trip.

Gods Grenade 61-ton fishing vessel, built 1928.

Graaf van Vlaanderen Belgian trawler of 324 tons, built 1926.

Guido Gazelle Belgian trawler of 86 tons, built 1936: Carried over 400 men in two crossings.

Gustaaf Belgian fishing vessel of 38 tons, built 1928, skipper G. Serie: Machine-gunned from the air during one of three trips, landing 130 men in all.

H17, H78, H79 Belgian fishing vessels.

Hdaya Particulars unknown.

Henri Belgian fishing vessel of 25 tons, built 1927: One of the last ships to leave Dunkirk Harbour staying to ferry troops to larger craft.

Henri Louis French vessel.

Henri Yvonne Belgian fishing vessel of 18 tons, built 1922: Made one trip from the beaches.

Icompas Belgian fishing vessel of 22 tons, built 1928: Made one trip.

Ingeniur Cachin French vessel, particulars unknown. Sailed to Le Havre on 1st June.

Irma Belgian fishing boat of 29 tons, built 1937, skipper R. Claeys: Lifted 130 men from beaches.

Jacomina Belgian fishing vessel of 44 tons, built 1930, skipper P. Vandierendonck: Completed three crossings, carrying over 200 troops.

Jean Antoine French fishing vessel: Worked offshore with Belgian drifters.

Jean Bart Dutch auxiliary ketch built by G. de Vries Lentsch, jun, at Amsterdam in 1934 – 37′ 2″ × 10′ 3″ – powered by Niagara engines: Owner J. S. van Mesdag of Hilversum.

Jean Ribault French vessel, carried 100 men.

Jeune France French, particulars unknown.

Johanna Converted Dutch eel boat, built Alkmaar 1937 – 51′ 1″ × 12′ 7″ – powered by Deutz oil engine: Owned by J. de Louwer of Amsterdam.

John Belgian fishing boat of 45 tons, built 1900: Picked up 45 men at sea, but later sank at Ramsgate following bomb damage.

Jolie Mascotte French fishing boat, rescued 77 survivors from HMS *Basilisk* on 1st June.

Jonge Jan Belgian trawler of 81 tons, built 1933, skipper M. Nys: Landed 270 men on 31st May.

Joseph Marcel Belgian fishing vessel of 67 tons, built 1926. Carried 150 men.

La Cerf French craft, crossed twice.

Léopold Raymonde Belgian fishing vessel of 20 tons, built 1926: Completed one trip.

Louise Irène Belgian fishing vessel of 60 tons, built 1937: completed one trip, with 79 men.

Louise Marie French fishing vessel of 68 tons, built 1929: completed one trip.

Lucien Gougy French fishing vessel, carried 361 men.

Lutter Belgian fishing vessel.

Lydie Suzanne Belgian fishing vessel of 26 tons, built 1936, skipper J. Ragaert: First carried Belgian refugees to England and then made four trips to Dunkirk, starting on 30th May when ferrying an estimated 1,000 troops from the beaches to larger vessels. Landed 105 men at Ramsgate on 31st May, 98 on 2nd June and a further 10 on the 3rd.

Madeline Kamiel Belgian fishing vessel of 74 tons, built 1937, Skipper R. Beyen: Completed one trip, landing 300 men.

Maréchal Foch Belgian fishing vessel of 87 tons, built 1930: Sank in Dunkirk Harbour on 30th May by the sheer weight of men on board, but crew returned at low tide and refloated the vessel which returned next day with 300 men. *Maréchal Foch* was lost on 1st June after colliding with HMS *Leda* off the Goodwin Sands.

Marie Elena French fishing boat, carried 120 men.

Marie Jeanne Belgian fishing vessel of 20 tons, built 1924: Made one trip.

Marie Rita Belgian fishing vessel of 26 tons, built 1931: Made one trip.

Mariette Bertha Belgian fishing vessel of 57 tons, built 1905: Made one trip.

Meuse Belgian launch: Later sunk from the air off Folkestone on 14th July 1940.

Monique Camille French fishing boat, carried 45 men.

Moussaillon French vessel: Lost on 1st June crossing in convoy.

Moya Particulars unknown.

M 2 French trawler.

Niger French tanker: Attacked near Dunkirk, finally sank off Gravelines.

Normanville French fishing vessel, carried 458 men.

Onze Lieve Vrouw van Vlaanderen Belgian fishing vessel of 40 tons, built 1934: Sunk by shellfire when crossing with cargo of ammunition on 2nd June.

Onder Ons Belgian fishing vessel.

O 87, O 92, O 318 Belgian fishing vessels.

Patrie French trawler. Carried 1,190 men.

Pharailde Belgian trawler of 49 tons, built 1929.

Pierre Marie French drifter, ferried 396 men.

Pinette Particulars unknown.

Président Buars French patrol boat.

Président Briand French patrol boat. Carried 283 men.

Princess Juliana Dutch coaster – 44′6″ × 10′ – built by Scheeps de Viljt, Aalsmer, 1928.

Dunkirk is the setting for the long-term restoration of the local fishing vessel **Ste. Denise Louise**, *a gaff ketch of the Dundee type which took part in the evacuation of 1940. What was little more than an abandoned hulk was taken over in 1986 and work is progressing steadily on shore in a corner of one of the basins of the inner harbour, as can be seen in this shot from April 1989.* (Author)

Prins Bodewijn Belgian fishing vessel of 90 tons, built 1930, skipper J. Viaene: Picked up 180 men from beaches and 30 at sea.

Puisse Marie Particulars unknown.

Reine de Flots French fishing vessel. Ferried 1,312 men.

Rockall Belgian fishing vessel of 114 tons, built 1930. Carried 150 men.

Saint Bernadette de Lourdes French fishing vessel: Used as minesweeper. Carried 80 men.

Sainte Denise Louise Dundee sail trawler built for Dunkirk owner Victor Marteel at Ostend in 1936 – 90.6 metres × 5.25 metres – with auxiliary engine. Participated in Operation Dynamo, crossing to England on 3rd/4th June but in the confusion of the period her name was recorded as *Sideres Louise* and appears as such in official lists. Resumed fishing after the war but found abandoned and almost derelict in 1986. A restoration programme started under the auspices of the Dundee/Dunkirk Association later in the year and the vessel has since been taken out of the water and the timbers are gradually being renewed near the edge of Number Two Basin in Dunkirk Harbour.

Sainte Elizabeth French drifter. Carried 64 men.

Sainte Eugénie Belgian fishing vessel of 13 tons, built 1922.

Sambre Belgian launch.

Sarzik Particulars unknown.

Savorgran de Brazza Designated headquarters vessel for Rear-Admiral Landriau.

Semois Belgian launch: Took part in the evacuation of Calais, four times entering harbour on 25th May to bring out wounded, but lost at Dunkirk on 30th May.

Simoun Auxiliary cutter built by A. Paumette, Le Havre, 1893 – 50′ × 13′ – powered by Baudouin oil engine: Owned by Leon Chrisis of Paris.

Strijdt vor Christus Belgian fishing vessel of 73 tons, built 1938: Completed one trip.

Sunnyisle Belgian fishing vessel: Sank after collision with HMS *Niger*.

Sucouf de Guesclin French vessel.

Thérèse Louise Particulars unknown.

Triomphant French fishing vessel. Crossed under sail after engine failed.

Vénus French patrol boat: Sank 1st June by shore fire after carrying 218 men.

Victor Erna Belgian fishing vessel of 45 tons, built 1931, skipper L. Ackx: Completed two trips.

Voor Vrouw en Kimas Belgian fishing vessel of 24 tons, built 1928: Completed one trip.

VP 19 French barge.

Watonprise Particulars unknown.

Yser Belgian launch: Lost 30th May after running aground.

Yvonne Belgian fishing vessel of 22 tons, built 1927, skipper A. Moers: Completed one trip.

Yvonne Sail lifeboat of Bruges.

Yvonne Maurice Belgian fishing vessel of 53 tons, built 1918.

Zee Meerin Belgian fishing boat of 63 tons, skipper A. Vandierendonck: Completed one trip.

Z 25, Z 26, Z 40 Belgian trawlers.

Zon Dutch houseboat.

Zwaluw Belgian fishing vessel of 23 tons, built 1931, skipper J. Serie: Returned on 31st May with 58 men and made a second trip to pick up 225 troops, before adding three Frenchmen from a canoe, ten from a destroyer and seven from a pontoon.

Naval Vessels

TO deal in full with the Dunkirk contribution of the 'little ships' it has been necessary to apply some fairly arbitrary definitions. As will have been seen, many of the craft in preceeding chapters participated in Operation Dynamo as units of the Royal Navy, and in the context of this book they have been categorised largely according to type or duties performed. The fact that what can be best described as the 'purpose-built' warships are often mentioned only in passing, in no way minimises their role – but the part played by such vessels and, in particular, the British and French destroyers, is already well recorded. The 56 destroyers – 41 from the Royal Navy supported by 14 French and one Polish vessel – were undoubtedly the mainstay of the operation and transported almost a third of the total number of troops landed in Britain. That so many destroyers were scraped together at short notice was an achievement in itself as, even before Dunkirk, the Royal Navy's total 1939 strength of 202 destroyers had suffered 14 losses and, apart from those deployed abroad, many more vessels were in dockyard hands for repairs or modifications. Home fleet flotillas were also heavily involved in Norwegian waters during April and early May, before evacuations from Boulogne put such pressure on the Dover-based destroyer force that all but one of this force was either sunk or out of action through damage sustained.

Six British destroyers were sunk during Dunkirk operations and a further 23 suffered

The only surviving Dunkirk warship, **MTB 102**, *now in more relaxed surroundings as a Sea Scout training ship in Norfolk. The Vosper-built vessel is still sea-going and returned to Dunkirk for the 40th Anniversary of the evacuation in 1980.* (Peter Box)

serious damage. Major naval losses also included one fleet minesweeper, five paddle minesweepers, an auxiliary anti-aircraft paddle vessel, one gunboat, 12 trawlers and five drifters. A single naval vessel from Operation Dynamo remains in existence, *MTB 102* serving as the training ship of the 1st Brundall Sea Scouts in Norfolk. Built in 1937 by Vospers of Portsmouth for demonstration purposes, the wooden hulled *102* was the prototype for numerous Royal Navy MTBs and was powered by three Italian Fraschini engines. Now powered by one of the original engines and two Perkins diesels, *102* has returned to Dunkirk with vessels of the ADLS.

The following Royal Navy vessels appear in the Admiralty's list of participating ships, and the names of many vessels requisitioned for minesweeping or other auxiliary duties will already be familiar. The figures following the names of larger vessels are of troops transported – although their accuracy has been questioned, not least by men serving on some of the personnel vessels and paddle minesweepers, whose own recollections were of substantially greater totals being landed.

BRITISH WARSHIPS

(Number of troops transported in parenthesis – L denotes vessel lost)

ANTI-AIRCRAFT CRUISER

Culcutta (1,856)

DESTROYERS

Anthony (3,107)
Basilisk (1,115 – L)
Codrington (5,677)
Esk (3,904)
Express (2,795)
Gallant (1,880)
Grafton (860 – L)
Grenade (1,000 – L)
Greyhound (1,360)
Harvester (3,191)
Havant (2,432 – L)
Icarus (4,704)
Impulsive (2,919)
Intrepid (661)
Ivanhoe (1,904)
Jackal (–)
Jaguar (700)
Javelin (1,400)
Keith (1,200 – L)
Mackay (581)
Malcolm (5,851)
Montrose (925)
Sabre (5,675)
Saladin (–)
Scimitar (2,711)
Shikari (3,589)

Some of the troops had quite hair-raising trips back to England. They were crowded on to every available foot of deck space on destroyers which then raced across the Channel at maximum speed and often in excess of 30 knots. Here some of the 5,677 men returned by HMS **Codrington** *wait their turn to disembark in Dover, while another equally heavily laden vessel is moored alongside. Note the pile of discarded rifles at the* **Codrington's** *stern.* (Times Newspapers)

Another of the older destroyers at Dunkirk, HMS **Vanquisher**, *carried almost 4,000 troops to safety. She is seen from the paddle minesweeper* **Oriole** *leaving Dunkirk with the decks from the funnels to the stern solid with men.* (J. Rutherford Crosby)

Vanquisher (3,941)
Vega (–)
Venemous (4,140)
Verity (504)
Vimy (2,976)
Vivacious (1,999)
Wakeful (639 – L)
Whitehall (3,453)
Whitshed (1,038)
Wild Swan (12)
Winchelsea (4,957)
Windsor (3,991)
Wolfhound (130)
Wolsey (3,337)
Worcester (4,545)

SLOOP

Bideford (436)

CORVETTES

Guillemot (460)
Kingfisher (640)
Mallard (–)
Shearwater (–)
Sheldrake (–)
Widgeon (–)

GUNBOATS

Locust (2,329)
Mosquito (1,183 – L)

Despite the intense pressure, with almost continuous air attacks and artillery bombardment, the discipline of the British troops was remarkable. In most cases the men waited calmly before moving in orderly fashion on to units of the rescue fleet such as the destroyer HMS **Vanquisher**, *pictured with troops filing towards the stern whilst berthed well into Dunkirk Harbour.* (Imperial War Museum)

Older destroyers from 'V' and 'W' classes were the mainstay of Operation Dynamo, and included HMS **Wakeful** *which had landed over 600 troops in Dover before being lost on 29th May when torpodoed by an E-Boat. After loading from small boats at Bray Beach, the* **Wakeful** *was steaming at 20 knots off Nieuport when hit amidships. She broke in two and sank in a matter of seconds with heavy loss of life.* (Imperial War Museum)

THAMES SPECIAL SERVICE SHIPS

**Crested Eagle (– L)*
**Golden Eagle (1,751)*
**Royal Eagle (2,657)*
**Snaefell (981)*
Speedwell (1,688)
Sutton (1,371)
**Waverley (– L)*
**Westward Ho (1,686)*

MINESWEEPERS

Albury (1,536)
**Brighton Belle (– L)*
**Brighton Queen (160 – L)*
**Devonia (– L)*
**Duchess of Fife (1,801)*
Dundalk (1,129)
**Emperor of India (642)*
Fitzroy (867)
**Glen Avon (888)*
**Glen Gower (1,235)*
Gossamer (3,169)
**Gracie Fields (281 – L)*
Halcyon (2,271)
Hebe (1,140)
Kellett (1,456)
Leda (2,848)
Lydd (1,502)
**Marmion (713)*
**Medway Queen (3,064)*
Niger (1,245)
**Oriole (2,587)*
Pangbourne (1,020)
**Plinlimmon (900)*
**Princess Elizabeth (1,673)*
**Queen of Thanet (2,500)*
Rodd (1,096)
Salamander (1,161)
Saltash (800)
**Sandown (1,861)*
Sharpshooter (373)
Skipjack (865 – L)

(*see 'Paddle Steamers')

MINESWEEPING CRAFT

Alcmaria
Arley
Botanic
Brock
Calvi (L)
Clythness
Chico
Comfort (L)
Conidaw
Dorienta
Feasible
Fidget
Fisher Boy
Fyldea
Genius
Gula
Gulzar
Inverforth
Jacketa
Jackeve
Jeannie Macintosh
John and Nora
John Cattling
Lord Barham
Lord Cavan (L)
Lord Collingwood
Lord Grey
Lord Hood
Lord Inchcape
Lord Keith
Lord Melchett
Lord Rodney
Lord St. Vincent
Mare
Maretta
Nautilus (L)
Olivae
Our Bairns
Overfalls
Polly Johnson (L)
Reed
Relonzo

Renascent
Restrivo
Rewga
Rig
Sarah Hyde
Sargasso
Saturn
Silver Dawn
Starlight Rays
Stella Rigel
Stathelliot
Strive
Swift Wing
Taransay
Thomas Bartlett (L)
Thomsons
Three Kings
Tweenways
Unicity

MOTOR TORPEDO AND ANTI-SUBMARINE BOATS

MTB 16
MTB 22
MTB 67
MTB 68
MTB 102
MTB 107
MASB 5
MASB 6
MASB 7
MASB 9
MASB 10
ML 100

ANTI-SUBMARINE TRAWLERS

Argylshire (L)
Blackburn Rovers (L)
Cape Argona
Catton Wyke
Grimsby Town
Kingston Alalite
Kingston Andalusite
Kingston Olivine
Lady Philomena
Olivina
St. Achilleus
Saon
Spurs
Stella Dorado (L)
Thuringia (L)
Topaze
Westella (L)
Wolves

DOVER FLARE-BURNING DRIFTERS

Boy Roy (L)
Eileen Emma
Forecast
Gervais Rentoul
Girl Gladys
Girl Pamela (L)
Golden Gift
Golden Sunbeam
Lord Howard
Lord Howe
Midas
Netsukis
Paxton (L)
Shipmates
The Boys
Torbay II
UT Prosim
Yorkshire Lass
Young Mun

PORTSMOUTH AUXILIARY PATROL YACHTS

Ahloa
Anlah
Ankh
Bounty
Caryanda
Eila II
Lahloo
Marsayru
Noneta
Seriola
Thele

MISCELLANEOUS HM SHIPS

ALC 3, 4 (L), 5
ALC 8 (L), 10
ALC 15 (L), 16 (L)
ALC 17, 18 (L)
Allouette II (Echo-Sounding Yacht)
Amulree (Harbour Defence Craft – L)
Aronia (Yacht)
Ben And Lucy (Drifter)
Bluebird (Motor Boat)
Bystander (Echo-Sounding Yacht)
Caleta (Harbour Defence Craft)
Chrystobel II (Harbour Defence Craft)
Dolphin's (Motor Boat)
Evelyn Rose (Trawler)
Excellent's (Anti-Aircraft Motor Boat)
Gava (Trawler)
Glala (Harbour Defence Craft)
Grey Mist (Danlaying Vessel)
Grive (FAA Yacht – L)
Kindred Star (Drifter)
**King Orry (Armed Boarding Vessel – L)*
Llanthony (Examination Vessel)
**Lormont (Armed Boarding Vessel)*
Monarda (Drifter)
**Mona's Isle (Armed Boarding Vessel)*
MLC 12 (L), 17 (L), 21, 22 (L)
***St. Olaves (Rescue Tug)*
Turret (Anti-Submarine Yacht)
Thrifty (Drifter)
V.4 (HMS Vernon's Pinace)
Vella (Armed Trawler)
Viviana (Anti-Submarine Trawler)

(* see 'Armed Boarding Vessels'; ** see 'Tugs')

WAR DEPARTMENT MOTOR LAUNCHES

Grouse
Haig
Kestrel
Marlborough
Pigeon
Swallow
Vulture
Wolfe

RAF SEAPLANE TENDERS – LAUNCHES

ST 243 (L)
ST 254 (L)
ST 276
ST 291
AMC 3 (L)
HSL 120

FOREIGN WARSHIPS

DUTCH

Motor Boat M.74

FRENCH

Amiens
Amiral Mouchez
Arras
Belfort
Bouclier
Bourrasque (L)
Branlebas
Cyclone
Diligente
Epervier
Floré
Foudroyant (L)
Impetueuse
Incomprise
Léopard
Marceau
Mistral
MTB 24
Simone
Siroco (L)
T.112
T.113
T.143

POLISH

Blyskawica

The Seafarers' Stories

EVERYONE who went to Dunkirk returned with a story to tell. Here are the recollections of men from all walks of life who sailed across the English Channel in an equally varied selection of vessels including paddle steamers, a passenger ferry, an RNLI lifeboat and even a little cargo boat from the Isle of Wight.

The name of no ship is woven more inextricably into the story of Dunkirk than that of the *Medway Queen*, the Thames Estuary paddler that completed an incredible seven crossings. Three men who went to the beaches or Dunkirk Harbour and back on every one of those trips provide views of Operation Dynamo from the bridge, galley and deck of the steamer.

John D. Graves was rising 21 and an RNR sub-lieutenant when the war started. He commissioned *Medway Queen* in October 1939, having been appointed First-Lieutenant while the steamer was undergoing conversion for minesweeping at Deptford, and served as second in command to Lieutenant A. T. Cook, RNR, throughout the evacuation. After devoting time and energy to the campaign to secure the preservation of *Medway Queen* it was fitting that, some 25 years later, 'Jack' Graves officially opened the vessel in its role as a yacht marina club ship in the Isle of Wight. He died in 1985 after the steamer had been returned to the Medway for the fresh restoration initiative that still continues. It was during the 1970s that he wrote the following:

All ships acquire a personality and sometimes this is so strong as to become evident even to strangers. Such a ship was the *Medway Queen*. I first found her lying in Deptford Creek refitting as a minesweeper and she looked very small, dirty and quite inadequate to her task as, somehow, ships always do in a dockyard. Our company represented almost all the classes being mobilised for the Royal Navy in war. As for the officers, it was curious that our ranks were exactly reversed. The Captain, R. D. C. Cooke, a paddle minesweeping veteran of the First World War and a merchant service master of no mean experience, was a Sub-Lieutenant RNVR. Next there was myself, also with one ring, but RNR, and hence just that bit senior to the Captain. Thirdly we had Lieutenant Leonard Jolly, RNVR, a peacetime yachtsman and now our navigator who, with two rings on his sleeve, was senior to both of us! Lastly, Lieutenant. Keilly, RNR, a tough old deep-water sailor, 66 years young, had persuaded the captain to sign him on as junior officer. This reversion of rank was typical of the disturbed state of minor naval affairs in those early days of the war, but it worked – and it worked well.

For a while *Medway Queen* swept the lower reaches of the Thames Estuary based on Harwich as a single ship attached to no particular flotilla. The winter seas found weaknesses in the hull and machinery of a ship used only to summer sailings

A stern view of **Medway Queen** *at Dover in the spring of 1940 which reveals the way the after saloon was cut back to make room for minesweeping gear. The samson post derrick 'found' by the* **Medway Queen's** *crew at Chatham can be seen clearly.* (J. D. Graves)

in protected waters so, in December 1939, we were ordered to Chatham. When the Dockyard had finished and the crew returned from leave, *Medway Queen* joined the 10th Minesweeping Flotilla in January 1940 and at once our minesweeping gear excited much interest. We had discarded the lifeboat-type davits supplied for launching floats and kites and had 'found' – something we became quite good at – a tall samson post derrick in Chatham Dockyard which we carried aboard one night at the cost of a case of whisky, and welded it to the after deck abaft the minesweeping winch. This structure improved the handling of the heavy equipment so much that we had not been in the flotilla more than a week or two before every record for fast and efficient handling of the sweeping gear was in *Medway Queen's* possession – and remained there.

During the latter half of May 1940 it became the practice, after the day's work of sweeping was over, for us to anchor in various roadsteads to act as spotting craft for mines laid by aircraft. It was at such an anchorage on 27th May that orders came to proceed to some beaches north of Dunkirk to embark troops who would be waiting there. Eight ships weighed anchor that night comprising *Sandown, Gracie Fields, Emperor of India, Thames Queen, Princess Elizabeth, Laguna Belle, Brighton Belle* and *Medway Queen.* In line ahead we steamed through the night to a point half a mile from the shore where, in the first faint light of dawn, could be made out long lines of men standing still like human piers stretching out into the water – knee, waist and even neck high in it; standing so patiently there in full equipment, boots, rifles, packs, tin helmets and all, with sergeants passing or rather swirling their way up and down the lines with a word of encouragement here and a command there.

Medway Queen's *gun crew, right, at action stations during the paddler's first trip to Dunkirk, and below sporting an assortment of uniforms.* (Roger Matthews)

Orders were to leave by daylight but in the face of what we found this was not possible, and as dawn broke the ships put off their lifeboats to be rowed or towed to the head of the human queues.

The anti-aircraft cruiser *Calcutta* stood by, giving support against any German aircraft which ventured over, but apart from a few bombs which went wide, there were no untoward incidents and by 7 a.m. *Medway Queen* and the rest of the flotilla left and headed for Dover. On the way back a heavy air raid developed during which *Medway Queen* shot down a German fighter. In the confusion, *Brighton Belle* drifted over a submerged wreck, tore her bottom out and began to sink. We went alongside and took off her crew and soldiers before the old ship subsided to the bottom. We then continued to Dover and disembarked the soldiers, who were mostly base personnel, line of communications troops and anti-aircraft gunners. One wonders who gave the latter priority – they were to be sorely missed at Dunkirk later.

The flotilla re-assembled at 5 p.m. that second day and once again, in line ahead, steamed out from Dover for Dunkirk, this time with instructions to enter the harbour. Off the entrance the flotilla came under very heavy fire from shore batteries, and some ships hauled out of the line as the sea spouted columns of water around them. The scene was awe-inspiring. Rows of great oil tanks were blazing furiously and the glare was reflected on the clouds. Heavy shells plunged in to the harbour, which was littered with wrecks. It was a scene to daunt the stoutest navigator, but still the ships came and went, feeling their way past uncharted obstructions and avoiding each other. By then Lieutenant Alfred Cook was our captain, Lieutenant Cooke having been forced to stand down through ill-health shortly before Dunkirk. After a consultation between the officers it was decided that we should act independently of the flotilla, make our way into Dunkirk, fill up with troops and leave. The other ships of the 10th evidently reached the same conclusion and we did not sail as a flotilla again.

On the way in, that second night, the sea was unusually phosphorescent. Our paddles left broad twin wakes and on two occasions German aircraft followed them and dropped bombs uncomfortably close. We were nothing if not resourceful aboard *Medway Queen* and devised oil bags which were lowered over the bow on either side to break the force of the waves. This was most successful, our brilliant wakes disappeared and *Medway Queen* went on her way in decent obscurity. Then, at the most critical part of the trip, as we were creeping along the French coast past Gravelines, the funnel began to stream sparks, caused by soot catching fire, and which made us a very obvious target. There followed an hilarious half hour, set against the tragic background of burning Dunkirk, with a bucket chain formed from the main deck and up ladders to the funnel. Our tallest sailor took the buckets of water and tried to tip them down the funnel to at least damp down the fire. This was reasonably effective but not much appreciated by the engine room personnel!

That night Dunkirk Harbour presented an appearance to become all too familiar of the wreck of one of the most modern ports in Europe. Docks and quay walls were reduced to rubble, and torn and broken ships lay everywhere. One single pier remained, the outer Mole on the north side of the harbour. Never designed for handling goods or allowing the passage of men, this concrete strip on its concrete piles was all that was left, and the Navy decided to use it. Along its length walked, stumbled or were carried more than half of the nearly quarter of a million men rescued during the nine days of the evacuation. Ships were sunk alongside, putting parts out of use. Lengths were torn away by shells or bombs but the gaps were repaired by mess tables taken from ships, by ladders, wood planking and any other material that could be found from the debris around the harbour.

As the days came and went the drill became familiar. Once alongside, scaling ladders were erected as the height of the Mole was much above the decks of the *Medway Queen*. Some of the crew would go ashore to control and direct the soldiers, assist the wounded and so on. Work went on to an accompaniement of rough oaths and crude instructions, hurrying and harrying, but, in the exhausted state of most of the soldiers, it proved to be the right approach. It went on against a background of blazing oil tanks, the scream, splash and explosion of shells, the roar of bombs and heavy detonations from the city of Dunkirk where demolition was proceeding. Finally, when the old ship was nearly down to her sponsons in the water, word would reach the captain we were full and, freeing ourselves from the berth, we would make our way down the fairway and out into the roads with Lieutenant Jolly navigating – and no better navigator ever conned a ship.

He was quite the best small boat pilot I ever met and how he kept *Medway Queen* moving backwards and forwards for ten long days and nights no one will ever know. He did all the navigation, although I, as the only other officer with any watch-keeping experience, did relieve him from time to time. Undoubtedly what saved the situation on many occasions was the *Medway Queen's* bow rudder. Jolly and I evolved a drill by which I, in the windlass flat forward, and he on the bridge, connected up the bow rudder at the same time as disengaging the after rudder. It might sound simple, but there were heavy pressures on all concerned when there was way on the vessel and, additionally, I often had to almost fight my way to the bow through crowds of soldiers.

The net effect was that with a bow rudder *Medway Queen* could simply steer off the Mole and go backwards down the fairway instead of canting off on a back-spring, turning and then going ahead on standard rudder. As the rudder of a paddle steamer does not operate in propeller wash but in dead water, the bow rudder gave us an incalculable advantage and was, in my opinion, the sole reason we were able to operate in the awful madhouse of a harbour on equal terms with the very latest destroyers or cross channel steamers. Only when we were at anchor in Dunkirk Roads could Jolly leave the bridge, but even then he did not rest, for he was also engineer of the ship's motor boat and busied himself going back and forth to the beaches. Truly a remarkable man, like myself he had many years of minesweeping to go, long after Dunkirk was a memory.

Once clear of the harbour, the *Medway Queen* would pick a way through the cleared channels known as 'X' and 'Y,' or sometimes if the tide was right, slip over the minefields to save time, relying on our shallow draught to get by. After the first day we used Ramsgate as it was much less congested than Dover, usually arriving back between 10 and 11 in the morning. Then, after disembarking the troops and taking on oil, water and stores, we proceeded out to the roadstead to anchor until dusk and the start of the next trip. Some nights we were directed to the Harbour at Dunkirk, sometimes diverted to the beaches, but as day followed night without respite, weariness blurred the outline of events.

At the beaches a different drill applied. As soon as we dropped anchor the boats were lowered, manned and towed away by the motor dinghy to the beaches where the soldiers waited so patiently in the water. When the boats returned, we hauled the soldiers aboard by the sponson doors behind the paddle boxes and away went the boats for another quota of human cargo, continuing through the night until, with the approach of dawn, we sailed for home. By then the decks were crowded and every alleyway choked with troops. On the weather deck forward the 12-pounder gun was always manned as were the Lewis guns on the sponsons, and these were always attended by volunteer groups of soldiers to fill the magazines and thereby feel that they were at least having a crack at the enemy.

About the third trip, there appeared a sandbagged enclosure on the after deck, set up by three army cadets – stout lads, none over 20 – who asked to come aboard, bringing with them two bren guns which they manned to excellent effect for the remainder of the evacuation. On *Medway Queen* we believed in concentrated fire power and I took a party ashore in Dunkirk on one of our trips and succeeded in 'borrowing' a number of abandoned bren guns which we lashed to stays with a single turn of rope. With a pile of ammunition beside each, they were handy for whoever was nearest to use in an attack. Beyond this, all the troops and sailors who had a rifle were encouraged to blaze away at any approaching aircraft on the sound principle that a storm of rifle fire could be just as effective as machine-guns.

Some curious happenings occurred. There was a party of Spanish sailors, refugees from an earlier war and caught in France by the sudden German advance, whom we picked up from the sea. The same night we were hailed by an officer in a small motor boat and told to proceed 12 miles along the coast to pick up a pocket of troops who had been cut off. We set off, but speaking by chance to the Spaniards, they were horrified and gave us to understand the place had been in German hands for two days! Later we heard it said that a destroyer had been similarly hailed that night and torpedoed when it hove to. The abortive trip delayed arrival at the beaches and with the coming of daylight enemy activity further affected loading and we were hours late getting back to Ramsgate. We had been posted missing, but only learned of this the following day when the papers came aboard and reported that *Medway Queen* had, after all, returned safely.

By Monday 3rd June, the Germans were finally closing on Dunkirk and at midday Admiral Ramsay issued orders that all ships were to leave Dunkirk by 2.30 the following morning. *Medway Queen* set out on her seventh trip and when we berthed at the Mole at about midnight, machine-gun fire could clearly be heard. By this time all the BEF had been evacuated while the French had held the shrinking perimeter and we took aboard just over 400 French troops, despite a surly refusal on their part to do anything to help us or themselves. Shelling in the harbour was heavy and a destroyer astern of *Medway Queen* was hit and flung forward against our starboard paddle box and did extensive damage to the sponson. By 1 a.m. the tangled steel had been cut away sufficiently for us to leave and *Medway Queen* made off very slowly down the harbour under the sure hands of Lieutenant Jolly, with the scene still lit by the blazing oil tanks and Lieutenant Keilly strumming a mandolin on the after deck to cheer up the tired Frenchmen.

Among the first to arrive off the beaches, *Medway Queen* was one of the last to leave. Damaged, worn out and very weary we limped back to Dover to receive a 'Well done *Medway Queen*' signal from Admiral Ramsay; and then, as we made for our buoy, all the ships in the harbour sounded their sirens. This was a very proud moment. I lost my personal log and other papers later on but believe that in total we carried a few score over 7,000 men during the evacuation, a record for all ships other than some of the fast Royal Navy destroyers.

After the war I did not see *Medway Queen* again until having the honour of opening the ship in the Isle of Wight in 1966. But, by 1979, when I was there again, *Medway Queen* had become no more than a rusted ruin and I wept for her gallant little soul. As I walked the decks again, thinking of the days and nights they rang to the feet of the soldiers she rescued, the words came to me of an old sea poem I learned as a boy: 'On them the dead lay still, the wounded suffered and the weary slept, as they shook in the fury of the guns . . .'

Thomas Russell was the *Medway Queen's* cook throughout the evacuation and proudly boasted that not one of the thousands of men transported went hungry. Years later when visiting the *Medway Queen* to celebrate his retirement in 1966, Mr Russell signed a visitor's book and later saw that: 'Ship's cook during Dunkirk' had been carefully added in red letters after his name. His widow, Margaret, a great stalwart of the Paddle Steamer Preservation Society, kindly made available this view from the galley:

I swayed on sore feet, my head ached abominably and my body was racked with fatigue as, up until then, I had had no sleep for 72 hours. It was 4 a.m. The end of a bandage was dripping in the mess-tin which was held out to me, but I was unable to stop a robot-like dip and pour rhythm in time to avoid emptying a ladle of stew over it. Curiosity made me look up. The soldier I saw was wounded in the head, his young face pinched and white under a blood-soaked field dressing. Our eyes met as, reaching out, he removed the bandage and then heartily sucked off the gravy before tucking the end of it back into place. It was a savage gesture and I wondered when he had eaten last. He grinned as if it hurt his lips to stretch them saying: 'Thanks mate, tastes smashing.'

Immediately they were marshalled aboard, the troops were invited by our crew to go to the galley if they were hungry or thirsty. If! Most of the 7,000 men accepted the invitation during the days and nights that followed and I was working with just one young assistant cook named Sec. It all began on the last Sunday in May. It was mid-morning and *Medway Queen* was riding at anchor in the shadow of Dover's white cliffs and Sec and I were leaning on the rail before continuing preparation of lunch for the crew of 48 the vessel carried. We could not understand why none of the flotilla were out on the usual daily sweep and every captain, first officer and wireless operator was now on the flagship engaged in a mysterious conference. A naval barge had just finished unloading a tremendous quantity of food supplies, every space being crammed with crates and boxes spilling out on to the alleyways near the galley. Next day news filtered through that the BEF was retreating under orders to the Dunkirk beaches and the whole flotilla was going to move out together at dusk to bring back to England as many of them as we could.

My orders from Captain Cook came at about 5p.m. on Monday 27th May. I was to use the stores that had been put aboard as I thought best and to prepare hot food sandwiches and drinks 'for several hundred men who will no doubt feel somewhat peckish.' The galley of the *Medway Queen*, principally used in peacetime for preparing light refreshments and the fish and chip teas so beloved by Cockney trippers, was not large and it wasn't an easy job to merely cook three square meals a day for our crew in it. Along with the sink, work benches and cupboards, a temperamental and hungry coal range took up a third of the space. There certainly was little room for moving about and Sec and I became adept at working without bumping into each other. The galley lay athwartships on the middle deck with a divided door at port and starboard, each facing an alleyway.

I butchered a whole carcass of mutton and then proceeded to prepare carrots, onions and potatoes – countless sacks of them – to make Irish stew, using the largest pots I had. Sec had the task of cutting up dozens of loaves to make as many sandwiches as he could, using cheeses and tinned meats. We made several pots full of Navy cocoa, opened a dozen or so tins of condensed milk into each one and put water on to boil in several large iron kettles to make tea and coffee. We worked on at a steady pace, undisturbed except for the steward with his bottomless pot of coffee. It wasn't until every available space on the stove was covered with steaming pans, and we had a mountain of sandwiches, that we noticed the time. It was 2.30 a.m. We had been too busy to pay much attention to anything going on outside the galley, but now were acutely aware of the noises – of the whistling of the shells, the crack of explosions and our own ship's guns blazing away.

While I relaxed for a moment, Sec wandered outside for some air. He was back in a flash, urging me on deck, where all of the crew not immediately occupied were transfixed, standing on a blacked-out ship in silhouette one moment, then reflected in the flashes of bombs and gunfire the next. Presently I realised that the launch heading our way which held about 60 men would soon be alongside. Sec came running with the news that we were taking a thousand men, if possible. This was the ship's full passenger capacity in peacetime. I felt panic starting to engulf me. We'll never cope, I thought, we haven't nearly enough food prepared. We flew back to the galley, opening tins of beans, tins of milk, making pots of tea and although we could hardly move because the galley was so full of food, much more would surely be needed.

Suddenly there was a crush at each galley door, with innumerable khaki-clad arms – many dripping wet – waving billy-cans, mugs and mess tins at us. The hubub of voices was clamorous and insistent. These were not 'peckish' men. These were starving animals, most of them too desperately hungry and thirsty to be polite. Someone opened the starboard half door and they started to flood for service right into the galley, then trying to exit from the other door. Sec and I were serving as fast as we could but were getting shoved back and forth and could scarcely manage. Some of the lads started to help themselves. It was pandemonium. I pushed through the crush and pulled at the sleeve of the first ship's officer I saw, although I could never remember whose arm was in it. He was very calm and efficient and soon had the whole thing organised with orderly queues formed at both doors.

When we reached port and the last of the troops had left, there was no time in which to relax. We not only had to prepare normal meals during the day for our crew, but also to start preparations for the coming night. *Medway Queen* would not be going minesweeping again until the evacuation was completed, but the mammoth cleaning-up operation kept all hands hard at work. Mud and sand was everywhere along with countless abandoned rifles and items of kit, empty cigarette packets, bottles and paper by the cartload. Many of the men had also been seasick and there was hardly an inch of the ship that didn't require to be washed down.

My responsibility weighed heavily upon me, as I was the only person in the ship with the experience to cook in quantity. Sec's help was needed and invaluable, but he was only a lad still in his teens and it was up to me to see there was plenty of tasty, hot food. And so there commenced what was to become a marathon of human endurance, not just for Sec and me, but every member of the crew. During the days there was the formidable cleaning-up operation and preparation for the following night. During the nights, our thousand weary, war-torn, hungry guests to collect and care for during the fight to get them home.

The days merged and became like one. Torpor took over. My actions became automatic. My movements became jerky. My attitude to others became anti-social. There were periods of near delirium when I was haunted by visions of satin cool cushions on which to rest my head and feet – but before I could reach them they turned into piles of sandwiches and mess tins of stew being grabbed away by dozens of grubby, disembodied hands. At dawn on 4th June the last muddy, ragged khaki figure, not nearly so hungry and thirsty as when he'd arrived, left *Medway Queen* and a three-day leave was given to the crew. I could not concentrate to pack and simply stretched out. I slept the clock round and then went home – and then slept some more.

Albert Nason was one of ten lads from Teignmouth, Devon, who joined the Royal Navy in November 1939 and he and five others, Roger Matthews, Jim Day, Bill Keyte, Bruce Sutton and Arthur Maraga, were drafted to the *Medway Queen* as able seamen. An enthusiastic supporter of the Medway Queen Preservation Society, Mr Nason's main memory of the evacuation is 'volunteering' to row in one of the paddler lifeboats.

When we came close to Dunkirk on the first trip across there was nothing but smoke, thick black smoke from the port's oil tanks that had been bombed. *Medway Queen* did not pick up any troops from the harbour itself but was sent on to the beach at La Panne, just inside the Belgian border. We had towed some small motor boats over to pick up the troops and the first morning we got down there the boats went off and they started loading us up. When it was finished and we started coming back, there was a girl on the beach dressed as a soldier but they spotted long hair hanging down her back and wouldn't let her come onboard. The last we saw was when she started walking towards Dunkirk.

After another trip to La Panne, from then on it was to Dunkirk, sometimes to the harbour and sometimes off the beaches. Once when it was pitch black, I was sitting on the after deck with Roger Matthews when our Buffer (the Petty Officer in charge of the deck hands) came along. He asked for a couple of volunteers to row the lifeboat – and said we'd do! They were using our motor boat to tow one lifeboat but as it couldn't manage to tow two, we had to row the other one in. As we were rowing towards the shore we heard a whistling sound and ducked down in the bottom of the boat – and this happened on a couple of other occasions before we loaded up with troops. On the way back it happened again and we ducked again, but one of the soldiers said: 'Jack, just keep on rowing. When you hear that whistle the shell has gone by - and if you don't hear it, it either lands short or you don't know anything about it.'

Another return trip to *Medway Queen* with a boat load of soldiers was probably the saddest part of the whole Dunkirk operation for me. We saw a chap trying to swim, still with most of his gear on, and well off the shore line. He was shouting for help and we asked the coxswain if we could go back and pick him up. He told us to carry on rowing and although we called him some names at the time, long after Dunkirk he explained that had we turned back and tried to save him it would have put the lives of everyone in the boat at risk.

Brighton Belle , one of the other ships of our unit, the 10th Minesweeping Flotilla, had left the beach ahead of us and was steaming back with the white cliffs of England in sight when they flashed a signal to us that they had hit a submerged wreck and had torn a hole in the bottom. We took off all their soldiers, crew and even the captain's dog, and completed the voyage home. While we were at Ramsgate and getting ready to go over for what turned out to be the seventh trip, everyone was saying it was getting a bit fierce over there. So the Old Man (Lieutenant Cook) called the crew together and told everyone to write a post card for their families. I was given the job of collecting them up for posting. Then all hands were told to go ashore to the pub on the end of the jetty where the captain bought all of us a drink!

On that last trip, while alongside the Mole in Dunkirk harbour, we were accidentally rammed when a destroyer astern of us was hit. This badly damaged the starboard paddle box. Although we eventually got underway, it took us a lot longer to get back and while on the way we heard on the BBC news via the ship's wireless that the *Medway Queen* had been lost. At first we laughed about it, but then realised that our loved ones at home would have heard this report too. Eventually we reached Dover and having heard the same report, there were some people who were surprised to see us. It had been a close call!

When the Dunkirk operation finished and we were back at Dover, we received a signal saying *Medway Queen* was to proceed to Portsmouth Dockyard to have the damaged paddle box and sponson repaired. After getting there we were delighted to be given, not the 48 hours leave of other Dunkirk personnel and soldiers, but six days special leave, and I will always remember that leave in the glorious sunshine of June 1940.

Southend-born Frank Pattrick was highly delighted when drafted as an ordinary seaman to one of the Thames Estuary's best known excursion steamers, *Crested Eagle,* called up with sister vessels from the Eagle Steamers fleet for a special wartime role. Now living in retirement in Norfolk, he left the ship as a blazing wreck off Dunkirk.

A countermeasure to the menace of magnetic mines dropped by German aircraft consisted of current-carrying cables being fitted right round the sides of ships. This operation was top secret but the effect was to neutralise the magnetic field of the hull thus rendering it unable to affect the magnetic needle of the mine's detonator. The system was known as 'degaussing' and it was responsible for the saving of many ships. To combat the laying of mines by aircraft along the shallow waters of the East Coast, the Admiralty decided to create a special fleet of anti-aircraft ships. They would be armed with ack-ack guns and carry the hitherto unheard of Radar, but needed to be of shallow draft to operate among the shoals and sandbanks of the North Foreland and Thames Estuary. The plan was to anchor these ships in the narrow channels at night to track aircraft with radar and, hopefully destroy them. At least the mines dropped could be plotted and during daylight hours the ships would also undertake contraband patrols and examine foreign ships that might be carrying prohibited raw materials.

The 'Thames Special Service Flotilla' was duly formed with the pre-war passenger paddle steamers *Crested Eagle, Royal Eagle* and *Golden Eagle* which were sent to the Chatham Dockyard to be converted for their new roles. Being Southend-born I had special affection for these ships as had most residents of the seaside towns around the Thames Estuary and, of course, the East End of London. I was delighted to be drafted as an ordinary seamen to *Crested Eagle,* a special favourite as she was one of the fastest paddlers to operate on the Thames. Going aboard for the first time among the tangle of cables and airlines, the ship was hardly recognisable. The luxurious dining saloon, one of the major attractions of these ships, and originally stretching right across the hull, with its imposing entrance directly opposite the wide main forward staircase was completely gutted, with a new central bulkhead built and the whole area forward converted into mess decks. The two main staircases were left intact but the large after saloon was completely rebuilt to accommodate the wardroom, a large diesel generator, extra fuel tanks and store rooms. Other peacetime cabins

With mast and telescopic funnel lowered, **Crested Eagle** *emerges from London Bridge and heads through the Upper Pool towards Tower Bridge at the start of a pre-war excursion. From this angle it is not difficult to see why one of the Luftwaffe pilots attacking at Dunkirk mistook the vessel for a cruiser. The picture is from the collection of Frank Pattrick, who is also seen while serving as an ordinary seaman aboard* **Crested Eagle** *a month before the evacuation.*

were utilised as ammunition stores, ship's store, paint shop and so on. The deck-heads were reinforced to accommodate the ack-ack guns and the arrival of the radar shack gave great cause for speculation. A large wooden structure, still in camouflage colours mounted on a heavy-duty wheeled chassis, it was topped by a large aerial and, as no-one had yet heard of radar the rumours was that it was a form of secret ray-projector capable of stopping enemy aircraft engines in flight – a comforting thought!

Gradually out of the chaos and confusion we saw the emergence of HMS *Crested Eagle.* Gone was the familiar yellow funnel, white upper-works and black hull, instead everything had been repainted with the dull dark Navy grey. Two single pom-pom guns and the radar shack adorned the after deck whilst more pom-poms were mounted forward. Carley floats replaced the peacetime deck seating, deckchair lockers were now steel ready-use ammunition lockers and the old licenced bar now held stocks of paint, rope, deck scrubbers and other less glamorous stores. Our peacetime paddler was almost ready for the task ahead. During the time the conversion work was being carried out, we were billeted in the Chatham Barracks and had grown accustomed to the noise, bustle and confusion of a naval dockyard and looked forward to working about the ship during the day.

This was soon to change. Gradually the shipwrights, welders, rivetters, armourers, electricians and carpenters completed their various assignments, gathered up their paraphenalia and literally vanished overnight. We then officially commissioned the ship and everything was soon made habitable and, after last-minute checks of equipment, final deliveries of stores and spares we finally cast off and made our way down the River Medway for a shake-down routine. Eventually *Royal Eagle* followed us and *Golden Eagle* came some time later as she required much more structural reinforcement due to her age and size. On all three ships a surprise was the selection of Army personnel to man the radar and considerable friction resulted.

Lieutenant Commander Booth, RNR, was given command of *Crested Eagle* and he was supported by other RNR officers. We had no regular Navy personnel but our Petty Officer and ratings were pensioners who had been recalled from retirement. Their experience was invaluable and they did an excellent job. Our first main task was to swing the compass, which entailed our sailing to a fixed spot in the Thames Estuary and spending several hours lining-up with special bearings on land, under the supervision of experts. This done, all that was left was to try out the guns. Our armament was mainly two-pounder pom-poms built in 1916 and the first time they were fired we expected the ship to go straight to the bottom – the terrific noise and huge vibration was quite frightening! But we soon became used to them and took no notice. We did hear that when *Golden Eagle* did her trials with less guns than we had, she had to return to Sheerness for the decks to be recaulked!

We settled down to the dull routine of patrolling the North Foreland during the daylight hours, stopping foreign ships and sending boarding parties to check cargo manifests. At dusk we would anchor in the narrow channels between the shoals and the Army would keep watch with the radar, but being a completely new innovation it was continually breaking down. At that time, when a plane was picked up on the scanner, there was no way we could tell if it was friendly or not. Thus every time an aircraft took off from nearby Manston 'action stations' would be sounded. It was fun initially, but after the alarm started to sound every five minutes or so the popularity of our Army comrades grew less and less. So it went on until, on 10th May 1940, the Germans launched their major offensive against the Low Countries. During the next few days it became evident that things were very serious on the other side of the Channel.

On Saturday 25th May we were on patrol when ordered back to Sheerness with *Royal Eagle*. The ship's company was mustered and informed that orders had been given for all the Army personnel and those crew members who were not esssential for the actual running of the ship, including gunnery ratings, to be put ashore without delay.

In hindsight, this was a serious mistake for the latter were sadly missed later on. Those of us who were retained spent the next two days wildly speculating just what lay ahead until, on the morning of Tuesday 28th May, we slipped our mooring and went alongside Sheerness dockyard wall. Lorries were already unloading hundreds of life jackets and a working party then proceeded to throw these on to our decks. Several hundred had been loaded and stowed when we were ordered to cast off. No sooner had we started to pull away from the wall when an officer shouted from the dockside for us to return immediately. This we did and more life jackets were loaded before, yet again, we were told to leave. This farce continued twice more before Lieutenant-Commander Booth decided enough was enough and, to the accompaniment of shouting from our officer friend ashore, we headed out into the Thames.

To coincide with our departure the heavens opened and we left in a violent thunderstorm which took a heavy toll of the barrage balloons, many of which were set ablaze by the lightning. We set course for Dover which was reached by nightfall. The following morning we were briefed on the role we were to play in a major operation to be known as 'Dynamo'. *Royal Eagle* and ourselves would sail in the afternoon to arrive off the beach at La Panne by nightfall. We would beach and wait for the tide to go down, when as many troops as possible would be loaded before refloating on the rising tide and returning to Dover. The operation would continue as necessary. Our course was code-named 'Y' and took us due east and soon we were passing many other vessels including tugs towing clusters of naval whalers and cutters. To the south we could see a huge pillar of smoke reaching skywards as Dunkirk reeled under continuous attacks from German artillery and Stuka dive-bombers. We reached a point north of La Panne at about 11 a.m. and altered course for the beaches. Then we were told to part company with *Royal Eagle* and proceed instead to Dunkirk Harbour to pick up wounded from the East Mole. *Royal Eagle* continued towards the beach and we saw no more of her. She was to make several successful trips during that week and went on to achieve a distinguished war record for the duration.

About a mile from the Mole we had our first real taste of fire in the form of a salvo from the the German shore battery which had wreaked so much havoc on the harbour the previous night. We survived but the transport *Clan MacAlister* was set on fire and beached about a quarter of a mile from the harbour entrance. We went alongside the seaward side of the Mole. It had not been designed for berthing and as there were no bollards on which to tie up, we utilised a concrete fence which ran the entire distance along the jetty and managed to berth with our bow tied up and an after line from the paddle box. This left the stern projecting out and away from the Mole, a position that was to save us from two direct hits shortly afterwards.

The harbour had suffered heavily during the night and storage tanks were blazing furiously. The French destroyer *Mistral* was sunk inside the harbour together with the British destroyer *Sabre* and many other vessels. It was at this time that we took our first casualty, the coxswain being badly wounded by shrapnel. The destroyer *Grenade* was just about to leave for Dover so we rushed him across on a stretcher, just in time to hand him over *Grenade's* bow guard-rail as she inched astern to line up with the harbour entrance. She never made it. Just as we turned to return aboard, the Stukas attacked again, we dived for cover and heard the bombs explode. As we got up, we saw to our dismay that *Grenade* had been hit amidships and was on fire and sinking. Our coxswain could not have stood much chance.

More Stuka attacks followed and the Isle of Man ferry *Fenella*, berthed directly astern of us, was hit and destroyed. During the attacks two bombs were seen to fall between the Mole and our stern. Had we been able to berth *Crested Eagle* normally we would have joined the rest of the casualties. Being the only seaworthy vessel left we were inundated with survivors from the ships in the harbour, in addition to the walking wounded and stretcher cases staggering along the Mole from the shore. During all the bombing our radio operator worked non-stop in a vain attempt to drum up air support from Dover. Some twelve ships had been sunk in and around the harbour already and we had seen no sign of the RAF.

Suddenly the attacks eased off, the Germans must have thought they had sunk all the harbour shipping and we took full advantage to speed up the loading unmolested. All available space was gradually filled, stretcher cases were carefully packed along the catwalk alongside the engine room, a favourite observation spot in peacetime. More stretchers filled the mess-decks, and the wardroom and every other inch of space was packed with walking wounded and other survivors.

Finally, at 6 p.m. the order was given to cast off, this being done to the accompaniment of loud cheers from the troops and murmurs of relief from the crew. The throb of the engines and the thump of the paddles gave us renewed hope and a fresh breeze was most welcome as we swung clear and left for the trip back to Dover. Around the time we left, the Stuka squadrons were about to launch a new raid. A report released after the war records that their leader had decided to switch his attack from the harbour to shipping which had been reported on the way to the beaches further east. Due to the falling tide we were compelled to head due east running parallel to the beach which was packed with troops who had been arriving all day.

The Stukas flew in at high altitude. At first we thought they were Spitfires arriving at last, but our joy was short-lived and we watched as they peeled off. The same report states that the leader had reported sighting a cruiser. Paddle-steamers make a wake twice as wide as a normal ships and we must have presented him with a perfect target. As we came abreast of Malo-les-Bains the bombs fell and we managed to avoid the stick with an alteration of the helm but, with our guns continually jamming we were at their mercy. Unhindered, they dropped from the sky pulling out of their dives just above mast height, where we could clearly see their crew through the transparent cockpit cover. And for good measure the rear gunner raked us with their machine-gun as they sped away. Suddenly we felt the ship shudder, as if some giant hand had picked us up, when a bomb struck home just aft of the bridge. It was followed by two more further aft which ripped into the oil fuel and the diesel tanks and immediately everything from the bridge to the stern was an inferno.

As we rushed aft we saw men running with skin blasted from their faces and arms, some scalded and badly wounded and our First-Lieutenant only recognisable by the emblem on his steel helmet. The decks had been packed when the bombs struck home and many had little chance. To make matters worse, the areas where stretcher cases were stowed below had received direct hits and, as we made for the main stairway, we found everything a sea of flame and nothing could be done for them. Meantime, those who had survived on deck were getting over the side on ropes to reach the many small boats which were converging on us. Others leapt straight over, still wearing their full packs, some even clutching rifles.

It was only when they reached the sea that they realised that the oil was laying some inches thick on the surface, it had not had time to disperse and they were unable to get their heads high enough to breathe. Others clutched desperately at the rescue boats and several of these capsized, adding their occupants to those already in the water. Lieutenant-Commander Booth somehow managed to run the ship aground and the last survivors crammed the forward deck as the fire gradually crept along, the ammunition lockers and the tanks containing flares and rockets exploding and sending their contents high into the air to add still more to the chaos and confusion. Somehow we eventually got the remainder of the men, the same men who had boarded us earlier that day, back into the sea; as we gazed down we saw them mingle with bodies still being kept afloat by lifebelts, hampering them as they struggled for survival towards the rescue boats. True losses will never be known but the *Crested Eagle's* destruction must have been the biggest single loss of life of any ship throughout the evacuation.

Eventually only three of us remained on board, the Sub-Lieutenant in charge, another seaman and myself. The fire had crept to within 15 feet when we left. Being a non-swimmer I went down a rope directly over the bow and will never forget the scene all around. Looking down from the height of the deck was bad enough, but seeing everything from the level of the water and experiencing the choking oil was horrifying. I clung desperately to the greasy rope until eventually a carley float drifted close enough to get a hand hold.

It was most difficult to maintain a grip on the overcrowded float because of the oil. It was to be a grim two hours later when a small dinghy headed towards us, rowed by a stoker with a colleage standing in the bow who, wielding an oar, announced in no uncertain terms that should anyone as much as raise a hand to grab the dinghy, he would not hesitate to knock it free. The float was taken in tow and our rescuers hauled us slowly out to where the minesweeper HMS *Albury* was waiting. We could see the *Crested Eagle* still burning, here steel hull glowing red in the darkness. As we came alongside the *Albury* those fit enough were able to clamber up the rope netting that had been put over the side. The exertions of the day had proved too much in my case and I was lifted up with a bowline under my armpits to be greeted, as I reached the guard-rail, with a mug containing neat rum. I gulped it down and remembered no more until I was shaken and told that we were about to land at Margate.

John Rutherford Crosby, son of a Glasgow bookseller, joined the RNVR in April 1939 and, granted his commission as a Sub-Lieutenant in December that year, was posted to HMS *Oriole*, a vessel better known from the Clyde of his youth as the veteran paddle steamer *Eagle III.* Not only did he write the following graphic personal account of Dunkirk evacuation, Rutherford Crosby also took some of the most poignant and widely published photographs of the period. The accompanying and previously unpublished pictures have been made available by Mr John Crosby, a son who never knew a remarkable father, Rutherford losing his life when the minesweeper *Horatio* went down off Bizerta on the African coast in January 1943.

We were lying in Haisborough Roads when a signal came through to proceed to Great Yarmouth immediately. It was 1 a.m. on Tuesday 28th May. We sailed there and coaled, provisioned and watered in an air of secrecy. We had no idea what was in the wind until we heard on the wireless that Belgium had capitulated.

That meant the BEF had to be evacuated. An MTB came out when we were a few miles offshore and gave us charts of Dunkirk and neighbouring coasts. We sailed at about midday from a point off Yarmouth, the *Waverley, Duchess of Fife* and *Marmion,* like ourselves Clyde paddle steamers called up for war. Foreign service at last! I wish I could pen the emotions I felt. A sort of tenseness mingled with curiosity. Around midnight we saw flames on the horizon which, at first, we thought was a ship blazing, but which turned out to be my first view of glorious France. It was the port of Dunkirk. The funeral pyre of thousands of women, children, old men and family pets. It was this horrible sight, which we were to see again and again during the next week, that sickened me more than anything else. More than the bombs screaming down, the shells, the machine-gunning, the swarms of German fighters, like wasps streaming out of the sun, the drowned men floating on the water, the wounded aboard, the smell of rancid food, blood and filthy bodies that pervaded the 'tween decks all week, as we had no time to clean up after unloading.

We sailed in through tortuous channels between sandbanks. It was a hair-raising business that first night. When we came to one part where the two channels converged the night seemed pregnant with ships of all kinds – troopers, trawlers, sloops and destroyers. There were, of course, no navigation lights on any of the ships and the first inkling you had of a ship bearing down on you was a suspicion of grey in the black cloak that seemed to engulf us. The grey would formulate into the dirty white of a bone some ship would be carrying in her teeth. With a long-drawn-out howl from her siren, she would shoot across our bows, maybe 20 yards off. We came very close to a destroyer which flashed us the warning: 'I am aground.' I tried to picture what her men were thinking there in the darkness, waiting on dawn to lift the curtain on another day of horror, tragedy, and not a little humour.

They would be wondering whether the tide would lift them or whether they were stuck there, a sitting target for any bombers that might come along. From far out to sea astern of us, flashes would brighten the sky every now and again, to be followed a few seconds later with an ear-splitting roar. It was comforting to know our big ships were somewhere out there and chucking their stuff well inland.

We crept ashore, taking soundings, and finally dropped anchor to wait for dawn. As it approached, a haziness on our horizon began to form itself into low sand dunes. A confused murmur formulated into human voices mingled with shouts took shape and became patches of Tommies. There were 30 or 40 ships either anchored or slowly under way all round us. Destroyers, sloops, paddlers, Dutch skoots and small drifters. A whaler drifted past in the grey light with two bodies wedged between the thwarts. There was a bad surf breaking for about half a cable offshore and none of the ships were sending boats ashore as they would capsize. A skoot under the White Ensign, lying next us, sent a fourteen-footer and after a lot of trouble managed to bring off about six men. *Waverley,* which was senior ship, fooled about and would give us no orders. Our old man was storming.

Eventually he sent me into the first boat with five men and a grass line. We made a sandbank about 15 yards offshore and jumped out. The pongos waded out to us and started to clamber into the boat. Many of them were almost hysterical as they had been bombed ceaselessly for days and nights on end. The grass line was made fast to the mast of a 20-foot sailing sloop that was lying on the beach. We intended to use this to pull ourselves out hand-over-hand with heavy loads on board. The old man semaphored to bring off one officer only, to see the way she would behave coming over the sandbank. I told the pongos to get out. Many, in addition to having their nerves shot to hell, were half-tight; they had been living on whisky and bully for several days. They sat staring at us with blank faces, however, and it was only when we threatened to pitch them over if they didn't hop it, that they moved.

Eventually we got away with one sergeant, but as soon as we were over the sandbank they waded after us. All tried to climb inboard at the one side, and into the drink we went, head over heels. We dragged the boat ashore and baled her with tin hats, sea anchors anything at all, filled her again in an orderly fashion and made it to the *Oriole.* We were, incidentally, anchored off La Panne, seven miles up the coast from Dunkirk. The *'Fife* and *Marmion* were further down the coast. North of us was Nieuport, about five miles away. By this time, all the planes we had seen was a squadron of Spitfires that flew over us at about 5 a.m. We were in comparative peace although there was a never-ceasing rumble and roar occasionally interrupted by the most god-awful crashes from a mile or two inland. I had no idea where Jerry was and, when one particularly frightened looking pongo was trying to get in the boat, I flippantly asked him what the hurry was, Jerry wasn't as near as that. He turned and croaked: 'Christ alive! He's only two miles down the road,' pointing vaguely with his arm, adding 'and he'll be on the beach by midday.' My jaw must have dropped with dismay at that. Fortunately, the man was a pessimist.

By this time the Old Man had run the ship aground and she was in 10 feet of water or so. Many pongos tried to swim out, but hadn't the sense to ditch their gear. It is a wonder many of them did not drown, but I never saw one. I saw one in the process of going down for the last time but fished him out alright. It was now about 6 a.m. but felt more like four in the afternoon. Shortly the troops could wade out up to their necks holding on to the grass line. They came aboard and we acted as a pierhead for several ships anchored offshore. They sent in whalers and pinnaces and loaded from our sponsons. About 2,000 were sent out this way before the tide receded so much that they couldn't reach us with their boats. What a scene of desolation on the beach as the tide receded, leaving rifles, haversacks, coats, pouches lying on the wet sand! Most of the haversacks were burst open and scattered about were photos of wives, mothers and kiddies, toothbrushes, socks, cigarettes, pipes, even a baby cine camera. It was all rather tragic.

I went ashore with young Sam Grace and up the beach to La Panne. There were a lot of Belgians in civilian clothes, many of them women and children, standing around the plage. The sight of a man in a dark lounge suit and soft felt hat standing with his hands in his pockets, idly watching this historic scene as if it was a cricket match, seemed grotesque. Many of the women were hurrying about with stew pans of steaming meat clutched in their hands. Where they cooked the food I don't know. There were a number of families, dressed in their best clothes and carrying pitiful little bundles, hurrying about with tense faces. Where the hell they thought they were going I don't know, as they were absolutely surrounded by Jerry. There were dusty exhausted French and British soldiers sitting in huddles everywhere, some of them stretched out in bathing boxes on the beach. There were overturned cars daubed with khaki paint.

I kept my camera busy the whole time. I had no money so borrowed half-a-crown from Grace and we went to l'Hotel Splendide and had a

Sub-Lieutenant J. Rutherford Crosby, pictured on the beach at La Panne with the **Oriole** *high and dry behind.*

La Panne beach in a photograph taken from outside the Hotel Splendide by Rutherford Crosby. Both the **Oriole,** *to the left of centre, and a Dutch skoot, seen above the back of the abandoned car, are beached; vessels standing offshore include the paddle minesweeper* **Waverley** *(on the right), another skoot and several Royal Navy destroyers.*

conversation with a charming young Belgian woman who was the manageress. She said the money was all right, and we bought a bottle of dry white wine to share with two Tommies who were drinking lemonade in the lounge. There was no beer in the town. A Belgian soldier was drinking vermouth with three women at the next table. I asked him: 'What now?' He shrugged: 'I should like to go to England and fight against the Germans, but . . .' and shrugged again. We spotted a canoe on the beach, carried it to the ship and hauled it aboard. Later in the day I went up to the town again with Sam. We badly wanted French helmets as souvenirs and eventually spotted a crowd of kids playing at soldiers, two of them wearing French helmets. Sam had changed some shillings for francs, and we gave them four francs for each of them, about 4d. each. Then we went into the cafe again, bought some cigars and proceeded to down cognac and Rossi (a kind of vermouth) with some rapidity. The pongos we talked to had had one hell of a time but all said they had mown down Jerry whenever they had had a chance. Outside Arras they had built barricades of German bodies, and I heard they built a pontoon of German bodies to cross a river and ran tanks across them.

We met a major in the RAMC who had some drinks with us and gave us his wife's address and asked us to drop her a line when we got back to Blighty and explain he was taken prisoner and wouldn't see her till after the war, but she wasn't to worry. Just like that, completely stoical about the whole thing. He said he must stay with the wounded and hadn't a dog's chance of getting off. I was surprised at the number of pongos drinking grenadine, a sort of pink, syrupy lemonade, when there were plenty of spirits in the café, I'd have thought they would have needed something to steady them. I went into another café and ordered a cup of coffee. It reminded me painfully of the Hotel de Bruges at Heist in happier times. It was like a cave, open at the front with tables and chairs out on the plage. The blinding sunlight out there was accentuated by the gloom of the cafe itself. But there were no carefree, sunburnt faces laughing over a beer, a gin, or café glace with an orchestra softly playing continental music in the background. Only dusty, tired, serious-faced soldiers, tin hats shoved to the back of their heads, majors and privates alike. There were also many worried-looking Belgian civvies. There was some dicussion about the sixpence I tendered but eventually it was accepted and I got in exchange a cup of perfectly foul coffee.

Suddenly there was a crash, and everybody leapt to their feet and made a rush for the back of the café. I was in the van. My first bomb. The plage outside cleared as if by magic, and everyone sought protection in the cafes and hotels. There were no more, however, and I went outside. People were coming rather sheepishly out of doorways and peering into the sky for the plane, but it had gone. I went for a look at the town and, on going down a side street, arrived at the main street where the trams ran – but not today. There was a roar and a large covered van, daubed with Khaki paint and with tree branches fastened on the roof as camouflage, rushed past. The trees and shrubs that bordered the sandy street were a glorious shade of light green. I could not grasp

Two views of the beach at La Panne, taken by Rutherford Crosby from the decks of **Oriole**. *In the first, only scraps of discarded clothing and equipment give a hint that anything untoward is happening, but then as an air attack developed the young officer fumbled for his camera and the remarkable second picture was the result as two bombs exploded simultaneously on the beach.*

that in a few days field grey would have replaced khaki in the town, and German troops would be drinking cognac in the cafe I had just left.

The ship was still high and dry on the beach and as there was nothing we could do until the tide refloated us, I had no inclination to return. I felt gloriously contented as I strolled along the plage, drawing on a cigar. Whether or not the cognac I had put away earlier in the day had anything to do with feeling of well-being, I cannot say. It was a scorching day and the sun poured on the back of my neck and seemed to run down my back. I was looking for a tobacconists where I could buy some good cigars, but I couldn't find one anywhere. Eventually I returned to the ship. By this time the water was round her again although it was still possible to wade out without water lapping over my sea boots. I went down to the sweep deck to have a look at my canoe. I was bending over it when someone shouted: 'Here the bastards come.' I raised my head and saw a formation of about 50 planes coming from the direction of Nieuport. Fire opened all along the coast, and we heard the staccato bark of Bofors, and balls of black cotton wool starred the sky all round the planes, but none were hit.

The formation broke and the planes came at us every way, like a school of mosquitoes on a still summer evening. They seemed to single out a ship for themselves and went for it. We saw one plane dive vertically on us, and four bombs fell from it. They seemed to float down; they fell so slowly or so it seemed to us. Somebody muttered: 'For what we are about to receive . . .' But no, they were going to miss us. I fumbled for my camera even as the air all round was hideous with the screaming of the bombs. There was a roar and our four burst on the beach alongside. I got my photo as they burst.

This was the last opportunity I had of using my camera, as we had our hands full after this. Several ships were hit. One paddler close to us, I think it was the *Crested Eagle,* caught fire and was beached. When we left later she was blazing from stem to stern, and her plates were red hot. A small drifter caught fire, the crew baled out, and she drifted down to lee, where she grounded and finally burnt herself out. The planes never left us from now on, except for about ten minutes at a time we were still aground.

The *Waverley* pushed off about this time, but was bombed later in the evening and foundered when about 15 miles off the coast. At about 6.30 p.m. we floated and backed off. The Roads were by this time a graveyard of ships of all kinds, many of them burning furiously. I saw four bombs burst on a destroyer about 400 yards from us, and she went up with a roar. I don't see how anyone could have been saved. When under way we had another narrow escape, four bombs landing in the sea about 40 yards on our port side, to be followed by another enormous one which landed on our starboard side. When we got to our rendezvous with the flotilla it was about midnight and there were no ships in sight, only suspicious-looking dark pyramid-shaped objects which looked like the bows of a ship that had foundered by the stern. We didn't loiter as Jerry had E-Boats knocking about, ready to put tin fish into any laggards. We got into Harwich about 9 a.m. and discharged the troops and 14 nurses we'd brought back.

These kids – they seemed just kids – had plenty of what it takes. They sat in the wardroom, some of them curled up on the deck asleep, with bombs dropping all over the place and never turned a hair. We had our photos taken by a newsreel man as the troops were disembarking. We went to the hotel and had a wash and a meal, and then turned in aboard. A shore party more or less cleaned up the ship, which was a shambles of sodden clothes, pieces of bully beef and hunks of bread. It also smelled abominably. We had picked up several thousand rounds of ammunition and most of it seemed to have got scattered all over the deck. When we left La Panne it was still a town with the houses intact although we saw bunch of incendiaries land on a house on the front and it caught fire. About 50 incendiaries were dropped on the beach beside us, just before we left, and they burnt brightly, in spite of the strong sun, like candles decorating a birthday cake. As we left I looked back and the house that was burning suddenly vomited its roof on to the plage in a cloud of dust.

The Glorious First of June. Flaming June. Flaming Hell! That's what we were going back to! We got under way about 2 p.m. and around midnight picked up the angry-looking flames of Dunkirk. There was an offshore breeze and we could smell the burning ten miles off the coast. We had on board one Mr Martin, a newsreel man from Pathé, and I must hand it to him. To come on a trip like this of one's own free will takes a lot of doing. Certainly it was a case of ignorance being bliss, because he had no idea what he was in for.

This time we made for a point of the beach between La Panne and Dunkirk and arrived there at about 4 a.m. We still had about two hours flood, so when we got off a busy-looking part of the beach, *Oriole's* head was brought round until we were facing dead-on to the beach, everybody went aft to raise the bows as much as possible, and we went lickity-spit for the shore and kept her full ahead until we jarred and came to a full stop. As we went in we dropped two 7-cwt anchors from the stern to kedge off. The men waded and swam out, and many of them had to be hauled on ropes straight up the side of the ship and over the rails. The snag was that when a rope was thrown to a man, about six grabbed it and just hung on, looking up blankly with the water breaking over their shoulders, and it was a hell of a job getting them to let go so that the rest could get pulled aboard. It was a case the whole time of 'To Hell with you, Jack! I'm alright.' I understand many were drowned although I never actually saw them.

From Dunkirk dense columns of black, oily smoke rose slowly into the air and then spread out over all the sky, and there were terrific explosions as delayed-action bombs went off. La Panne on our other hand was also well alight, and we could see the jagged skyline formed by roofless houses and ruptured walls. I wondered what had become of the Belgian girl in the Hotel and the white-haired old man who had given us drinks in the basement, and who had proudly shown us some photos of himself taken by English visitors the summer before. Many of them had signed on the back 'Best Wishes'. He would certainly be needing them now.

We were troubled by German ME 110's which machine gunned us regularly, but there were no bombers. There were a number of holes in the decks and boats to show for it. We loaded about 600 troops on board and pushed off at about 7 a.m. The Pathé man got a number of good shots, but when we were bringing the troops aboard he put his camera aside, rolled-up his sleeves and got to work. He was glad to leave the ship. Although he had spent seven months in France he said he had never spent a night like the one we entertained him to. We landed the troops at Margate at about 11 a.m. and turned in without attempting to clean the ship. We were beginning to feel the strain by now, but got a signal: 'Proceed 18:00'. We got what sleep we could, about four hours. The ship was like a pigsty, both in appearance and aroma. Once again we picked up the terrifying crimson glow in the sky, which showed clearly ascending into the sky from a hundred different parts of the town. The sea was a flat calm and appeared black, like tar, except between the ships and Dunkirk, where it reflected orange and crimson. We wound our way in through the channels, which were now made more difficult because of the number of wrecks that had gone down within the last 48 hours. Destroyers shot silently past with great bones in their teeth. The troops on board could be plainly seen silhouetted against the crimson backdrop. In the middle of this hopeless confusion of ships, explosions and darkness, the Old Man turned and remarked: 'I bet you wish you were at Kimbell's just now.' Kimbell's being a dance place we used to go to in Portsmouth.

We arrived at the harbour mouth. An MTB was patrolling there and had a loud hailer on board. With this she told us where to berth. We avoided a trawler that was sunk alongside the wall, with only its superstructure showing starkly, and finally got ropes ashore. We put gangways ashore, and Tommies and poilus began to file on board. It was a most dramatic scene and made me think of Zeebrugge in that other war. The colour scheme was composed of black, crimson and khaki. The stark, black outline of the ferro-concrete railings on the Mole, with the slow, patient line of soldiers shuffling up to the gangway, heads bowed, backs weary and tired under the weight of their packs, rifles slung on shoulders and pointing raggedly into the sky like the fingers of a jury pointing, condemning the work of a mass murderer.

From the town, which we were almost in, came terrific flashes, followed a few seconds later by shattering explosions as our batteries hurled shells at the advancing Jerry. Flames leapt and curled from a hundred rooftops, casting tall chimneys and cranes into silhouette. We waited calmly, silently, as the men came aboard, curled up somewhere on the deck, and promptly fell asleep. An enemy spotting plane came over, very high, and at once the dark curtain seawards was slashed to ribbons with streams of coloured tracers, crimson, orange and white. It was beautiful if we had been in any mood to appreciate it. As we were casting off there was a flash and a roar from the channel seawards. When we passed the spot about 15 minutes later we came on masses of wreckage floating and somewhere in the darkness somebody shouting. To find him, however, was hopeless.

We got into Margate at about 6 a.m. We were told we were going back again, much to everyone's dismay, as we thought we were finished by this time and everybody's nerves were in a bad way. However, we were going and that was all there was to it. Left Margate at 7.30 p.m. No trouble until we berthed alongside the Mole at about 1.15 a.m. Two paddlers abreast of one another were alongside. They turned out to be *Marmion* and *Duchess of Fife*. As we drew slowly past, the Old Man and the CO of the *Marmion* exchanged pleasantries with one another and enquired after each other's health. It struck me as being rather absurd to enquire after anyone's health when under shellfire as we were.

The fires were still raging ashore as they had been for many days now. Nothing had changed from last night except there were no troops. The Mole was deserted. Understandable, as Jerry had the range to a 'T' and was lobbing over heavy stuff every few seconds, which straddled all around us. We got gangways and ladders ashore and lashed them to the railings on the Mole. It was low water and they were very steep. In many places the Mole had been hit with shells and breaches made, but it had all been fixed up in every case with boards and planks. Well, here we were, all ready to embark, and no bloody troops to be seen. The CO and I were standing on the Mole when he turned and said: 'Now, Sub, I want 700, go and get them.' So off I went.

Every time I heard a roar coming over, I ducked and waited. There would be a terrific crash somewhere near. Sometimes I would feel the blast of it, then all was peaceful again. At last, far down the Mole I came on masses of poilus, standing quietly four deep. I tried to find an embarkation officer, but without any luck, so let them have a flood of half-forgotten school French and managed to get a number of them back to the ship. I had to lead them as there was a sloop berthed between ourselves and the *Oriole* and when they saw men coming up the Mole they tried to entice them aboard like barkers at a fairground. First filled-up, first out of this Hell. But I saw that none of them strayed. If they wanted troops they could bloody well go and find them, the same as I was doing.

When going back for more men I tripped in the darkness and broke a very excellent pipe I had in my pocket, which was a minor tragedy. A pongo stopped me on the way. He was wheeling an enormous motor cycle. 'Can I get this on board your ship, mate?' he asked. 'It's only done 280 miles', he added, as if he was a salesman trying to sell me the ruddy thing. I pointed out, rather tersely perhaps, that we had come to save lives, not bikes, told him to ditch it and left him lovingly caressing the gleaming controls.

We were loaded by this time and pushed off. When we reached the roads it was beginning to get light. For the last time we looked astern at the flames disappearing below the horizon and felt thankful, and not a little amazed, that we had come through almost unscathed. We arrived back at Margate at about 6.30 a.m., very glad it was over for us as many of the ship's company were in a really bad way.

Describing himself as a 'very inadequate RNVR signalman,' Leslie Rashleigh joined the paddle minesweeper *Devonia* on New Year's Day in 1940. Five months later he abandoned her on the beach at La Panne when Operation Dynamo was at its height. Now living in retirement at Upminster, Mr Rashleigh recalls his weeks with the former Bristol Channel steamer:

The *Devonia* was on passage to the Firth of Forth from Milford Haven, where she had been fitted out as a minesweeper, when I joined her, my first ship, on 1st January 1940 in West Hartlepool. With the minesweeping gear fitted aft, *Devonia* had a single 12-pounder gun on the forecastle and Lewis gun mountings on each paddle sponson. When it came to accommodation, the ward-room was aft and all other personnel in two messes in what had been the forward saloon, seamen on the starboard side and the Maltese engine room and stokehold hands to port. On the lower deck were the Petty Officers and leading hands, plus additional sleeping accommodation for the seamen's mess. We were on canteen messing but the Maltese maintained a separate scheme with their own unofficial chef – who always seemed more competent than the ship's real cook!

Life on board was quite monotonous. We were in harbour most nights, which was fortunate as on the few occasions we anchored outside we usually found the odd mine floating nearby, having broken adrift from our own field. We swept daily following a regular routine and were usually paired with *Devonia's* sister ship *Brighton*

Devonia *at Milford Haven shortly after being commissioned as a minesweeper in December 1940 – and two views while the vessel was operating in the North Sea from Granton on the Forth. On the left it is 'Sweeps out' with the* **Devonia's** *two floats being streamed. On the right, the First Lieutenant, Chas Cox, surveys the scene from the starboard paddle box.* (Leslie Rashleigh)

Queen. After leaving harbour at Granton and passing through the boom defence from Inchkeith Island to the north shore of the Forth, we proceeded to just off Methil, a rendezvous point for the East Coast convoys. There we streamed sweeps and followed the shipping channel. Sometimes *Brighton Queen*, also to be lost at Dunkirk, broke off and went north of May Island but we always took the southern channel past Bass Rock towards St. Abbs Head before it was 'in sweeps' and home.

In view of the tricky entrance to the harbour at Granton, our skipper was always anxious to get back while it was still light. This called for full speed which, in *Devonia's* case was quite considerable, and she must have made an impressive sight with the two funnels giving forth vast clouds of black smoke and occasional tongues of flame. The heat inside the funnels was intense and, with the paint on the outsides bubbling like lava, passing them meant hugging the ship's rails to avoid being scorched. The only time I tried the stokehole, I got no further than easing open the airlock door before being driven back by the heat from below.

In my time with *Devonia* we never swept a single mine, not even in our own field, the vessel's cutters seeming somehow to be inadequate. Once or twice we stayed out for the night, anchoring inside the Farne Islands, and on one such occasion at the end of May I was roused from my hammock by the lookout who had seen a light flashing from the shore. I answered and received a curt: 'Please man your RT' instruction in return. Having awoken the telegraphist we received a signal for the captain's eyes only and, very early next morning, set off to Tynemouth for coaling. When the First-Lieutenant and a couple of ABs began testing the Holman Projector by lobbing potatoes, we all wondered what was in store. We continued southwards along the coast in marvellous weather, with the sea to ourselves, and nothing eventful occurred until we had a couple of shots across the bows from the shore near Lowestoft. We were interrogated by light signal and allowed to proceed after identification, but we were somewhat amused by the gunfire, all for an old paddle steamer on an otherwise empty ocean. We eventually tied up in Harwich, which was quite congested with vessels of all types, and a fresh arrival from Dunkirk came alongside and painted a lurid description of what was in store for us; and although we had never heard of the place, it was obviously going to be no picnic.

We coaled ready for another early start and sailed along the Essex and Kent coasts until reaching the swept channel across to France. By this time there was considerable two-way traffic, and in addition to tugs towing long strings of motor cruisers and launches, I recall a large French destroyer crossing to England stern first with heavy damage forward. After Dunkirk we continued along the coast towards La Panne

Tin helmeted troops huddle together while a pitiful few strike out from the beach at La Panne in a dinghy. The abandoned **Devonia** *is in the background with the Thames paddler* **Royal Eagle** *seen in the distance.* (Imperial War Museum)

where a hat-less, weatherbeaten commodore, who seemed to be running the show, came aboard. He briefed the captain below and went off in his boat again while we moved slowly in towards the beaches, which seemed alive with soldiers trying to get off in small boats. This was made very difficult by the surf, which tended to beach the boats and strand them. At some stage lorries had been driven into the sea to form a makeshift jetty, but this was not very successful, apparently.

There was a lot of air activity, mainly bombing, and the Germans were also in Nieuport, in sight of the beaches, which they shelled spasmodically. We manned the 12-pounder and popped off a few shells and also the Lewis guns, which helped morale if nothing else. After passing a Clan Line freighter which had been hit and abandoned while at anchor, we launched our boat to make a couple of runs to inshore, off-loading on to the *Hilda*, a small, one hold, high poop Dutch coaster manned by a Royal Navy lieutenant with three ratings. Before long the bombing and shelling came too close for comfort and then we reeled from a stick of bombs immediately astern. This opened up *Devonia's* stern and before long the commodore re-appeared to see the captain.

Because of the severity of the damage we were instructed to beach as far in as possible in the hope that the ship would act as a jetty for the troops – although at that time we were still too far out for the soldiers to wade. When orders came to abandon ship the Buffer passed among us with the rum jar and everyone was told to take a stiff tot in case we ended up in the sea. After we beached I took the ship's confidential books and papers to the stokehold to be burnt and only the second engineer remained to assist, and then open the seacocks. I think he had already seen the Buffer several times, but he was not a happy man. We left *Devonia* – and her unfinished day trip to France – in style and rowed across to the *Hilda*, which was nearly full, and were then transferred with the troops to the *Scimitar*, an old S Class destroyer which sailed late in the evening for Dover, when Dunkirk was like Dante's inferno as we headed for home.

Tom Corteen went to war with his ship, the Isle of Man Steam Packet Company's *Manxman*, and found himself doing the duties of both mate and second mate during Operation Dynamo. Back with the company after the war, he became master of Dunkirk survivor *Lady of Mann* until she was withdrawn in 1971. He retired later the same year but still lives in the Isle of Man where he recounted his experiences:

Acting as both mate and second mate as *Manxman's* original mate had suffered a nervous breakdown, I had everything to see to, and organise, which was more than a full-time job. The ship did four runs to Dunkirk, including one she might not have been credited with, as on arrival the operation was cancelled owing to the very heavy shelling. The five other cross-Channel vessels with us were turned back by a destroyer – the *Lady of Mann* was one of them – but as we had been in the lead we were never contacted owing to the thick, oily haze and heavy smoke drifting down from the burning town and oil tanks, and we entered harbour not knowing that we were on our own.

It was very eerie steaming in with not a soldier to be seen either on the beaches or on the Mole as they had all been pulled back into the town. There was no naval officer to berth us or personnel to take our ropes but we were then surprised to find men packed underneath the Mole, perched and straddled on piles and some up to their chins in water. They had moved underneath to keep out of sight and miss as much of the shrapnel and straffing as possible. Some soldiers had been washed off as the tide made, there being no room for them to climb onto the piles above them. We had quite a job berthing, getting the soldiers to take two or three turns of a light six-inch rope around a pile and then to hang on until we hove alongside so a sailor could jump across and make our ropes secure. We didn't stand on ceremony when leaving, however, simply cutting the ropes with a fire axe. We embarked every soldier who was there, which proved a very long job as they had to worm their

The **Manxman,** *a steamer from the Isle of Man Steam Packet Company fleet, in which Tom Corteen crossed to Dunkirk on four occasions. He recalls how they had no alternative but to sail through bodies of dead soldiers which, kept afloat by their lifejackets, floated in and out with the tide like huge shoals of jelly fish.* (Ambrose Greenway collection)

way along the piles and even came from the inner end of the Mole.

When we arrived back off Dover a destroyer came racing out to meet us as *Manxman* had been given up for lost having been missing all day. As the evacuation had been cancelled that day there was no one to meet us and no trains waiting to take away the soldiers, many of whom just lay down on the quay side and slept while awaiting transport. How anyone arrived at numbers carried by the various ships amazes me as soldiers came on board any way they could and not all by gangways. In any case, we had no time for counting, and on arrival at Dover or Folkestone they swarmed off and often destroyers or other vessels landed their troops across our decks, contributing to one continuous flood of men pouring ashore. It was the actual time spent in Dunkirk that mattered, not the number of times in and out, as the tension on board eased every time one was leaving the place.

Another day, when we were on the point of leaving with a full load of troops, some of the crew who had been standing by to let go came running up in a very disturbed state. A destroyer had tied up alongside and our troops had started swarming aboard her. She took nearly half of them and had to cast off to avoid being overwhelmed. I told the destroyer commander what I thought about the way he had upset my crew when we had been on the point of leaving. This forced us to remain alongside for several more hours awaiting fresh troops who had to be rounded up in the town and sent to the Mole. When the destroyer left we were alone in the harbour with no protection, no guns and not a single tin hat amongst us. While we were waiting, lamp trimmer Hugh Crennell, who had been a gunner in the 1914–1918 war, managed to procure a Lewis gun and some ammunition from the troops. I helped him to set it up on the forward side of the bridge deck and also loaded many pans with tracer bullets. Hugh used that gun to good effect and certainly turned some of the screaming Stukas off course. Without that gun I am sure that we would never have got out of Dunkirk that day. I mentioned this to Admiral Ramsay back in Dover but, unfortunately, 'lamps' had cracked up on the passage back and had to go ashore.

During the early part of the week quite a few soldiers died during the journey home, some of them killed or wounded by their own mates who, after getting on board, were clearing their rifles by placing the muzzles down on the deck and pulling the trigger. The effect on the men below decks was frightening and I was hoarse from going around the upper decks shouting for them to clear their rifles over the side or into the air.

I saw the Steam Packet vessel *Mona's Queen* mined and break in two abaft her main mast. We were very close and had, in fact, passed the same stop shortly before and were just stemming the tide awaiting a berth at the Mole. We could see the survivors standing on the forward section who were able to climb over and stand on the *Mona's Queen's* starboard shoulder as she rolled gently over to port. Although the stern broke away and sank, the bow section stayed afloat for a long time and survivors were taken off by naval cutters sent in to help.

We had problems with the Navy on another of our trips to Dunkirk, again just as *Manxman* was ready to leave. This time the bosun reported that while swinging on a wire hawser in the ebbing tide, a destroyer berthed astern of us had been set so far from the Mole that personnel standing on it had been unable to lift the eye of the mooring wire over the top of a five-foot-high pile around which it had been dropped. The destroyer skipper solved the problem by simply having his end of the wire thrown over the side, but this had the effect of shutting the *Manxman* in as the wire lay in a parabola from the top of the Mole, over 30 feet above the tide level, to well across the channel. I had to call for volunteers to go ashore with me to pull back enough slack to enable us to finally lift the eye over the top of the pile and throw it into the harbour. It was a hard pull over the muddy harbour bottom but without clearing the wire we would almost certainly have picked it up on the propellers when making our own departure stern first.

The most disturbing part of the evacuation was the number of bodies of dead soldiers in the water. Kept afloat by their cork lifejackets, they came in and out with the tide and bobbed up and down with the swell like huge shoals of jelly fish. Towards the end they could not be avoided and we just had to steam through them. The living troops were generally very easily directed when we got them aboard and mostly just glad to be on the last lap home to England – if all went well. Lack of drinking water had been a real problem for them ashore and many men owed their survival to the large freshwater tanks of *Manxman* and the other ferries. But there was no cooked food and, in fact, I don't remember getting a hot meal at any time while we were working in and out of Dunkirk. As we left Dunkirk for the last time *Manxman* steamed straight out to sea. It was a risk, but we saw the state of the tide would probably take us over the sandbanks and by going this way rather than by the wreck, strewn east or west channels, the vessel's stern presented a much smaller target to the shore batteries.

Half way through 14 days survivors' leave after his ship was dive-bombed and sunk off Norway, Ronald Hector was recalled to barracks and within 24 hours found himself heading for Dunkirk in command of the Dungeness lifeboat. After 22 years service as an able seaman he was due for his pension just two weeks later, but discharge was, as he put it, delayed by Hitler for a further five years. The boat itself is also now enjoying an honourable retirement based in Guernsey as *Caresana*:

We lost half the ship's company when HMS *Bittern*, in which I was serving as quartermaster, was bombed off Namsos, Norway, on 30th April 1940. I was rescued by the Tribal class destroyer *Janus* and put aboard the anti-aircraft cruiser *Carlisle* which, with other British and French naval vessels, completed the evacuation of Namsos on 3rd May. Towards the end of the month, and only eight days into my survivors' leave, I was recalled by telegram to Portsmouth and was part of four coach loads of men who left for an unknown destination. We were soon told by the chief in charge that we were going to Dover and as we passsed through the Kent hop fields in fine weather, we sang typical naval songs. We reached Dover Castle at midnight and were bedded down but told we could be required at a moment's notice.

Two hours later we were called out and formed

into boats' crews of three and I was given an ordinary seaman and a young stoker with orders to draw three days' rations and man any boat tied alongside the inner breakwater in the harbour. We drew six loaves of bread, two 4-lb tins of corned beef, 1 lb of dry tea, 2 lb of cheese, 4 lb of sugar and 2 lb of margarine before trooping off to the harbour where I chose a twin-engined boat which turned out to be *Charles Cooper Henderson,* the Dungeness lifeboat. The upper deck was loaded with two-gallon cans of petrol and the cabin was fully equipped with first aid gear, soft drinks and even two bottles of rum, which proved very useful later in the voyage. A stoker Petty Officer started the engines and then announced he was coming with us, so I reported that my boat was ready to the officer in charge, who was occupying a hut on the breakwater, and gave him a list of the names of the crew.

It was then about 4 a.m. and still pitch dark. We were towed out to sea by a tug whose skipper used a megaphone to give us a course to steer. Although we were all complete strangers I told the other three that, as coxswain, I would do my best to get them back safely. The PO stoker, a chap about 10 years younger than me, came from the Royal Yacht *Victoria and Albert,* and said he would run only one engine and keep the other in reserve. There were about 50 two-gallon cans of fuel on the deck we had to pour petrol down a spout in the forepeak every hour or so. By daybreak we were well out into the Channel and as ships passed every so often loaded with soldiers, we could hear the distant gunfire. We sighted land about noon and altered course to starboard but when about a mile from the shore some V and W Class destroyers came up in line at full speed and began a bombardment, their shells screeching over our heads. The assault was over in a jiffy and I carried on in the direction from which the destroyers had come, and within an hour we sighted the breakwater and entered Dunkirk Harbour.

All hell seemed let loose there but I steered for a half blown away pier which was loaded with soldiers waiting to get away. We began our rescue work, getting men aboard and taking them to the nearest available ship. It then became an endless routine which we carried on for three days and two nights. The air attacks seemed to become more frequent but in the first night it was much easier as they temporarily ceased to function and we were able to ferry soldiers out to the ships in quick time. During the second night planes dropped star shells and attacks continued.

We ate very little and gave most of our rations to the troops, although the minerals were useful and the rum proved good for morale. Eventually, both engines refused to function, luckily when we had no troops aboard. Our bowman passed a painter to a passing boat which towed us out of the harbour and set the propellers in motion. The PO was able to keep the port engine running but as we had only six cans of petrol left he recommended that we should return to England. I had been struck in the face by a bomb splinter and the bowman took over the wheel and I told him to steer a course opposite to that given by the skipper of the Dover tug. It was about 3.30 a.m. when we came up against a dark outline we took to be the coast and eventually tied up against a jetty and decided to sleep until daylight and then find out where we were. Within 10 minutes someone was shining a torch down and telling us we would have to move as this was the end of Margate Pier! We cast off and followed his torch beam the length of the pier and, after securing alongside I was told to report to the liaison officer.

When they saw my bandages we were all taken by ambulance to the Winter Gardens, which was laid out as a casualty station, and there an army doctor put several stitches into my chin. I must have slept for over 24 hours before being awakened and told to report with my crew to the naval officer in charge. He arranged for the *Charles Cooper Henderson* to be returned to her station by members of the Margate Lifeboat crew and gave us rail warrants to travel back to Dover where we spent two days in the transit camp before transferring to Chatham Barracks to have lost clothes replaced. After finally getting back to Portsmouth I had to write a report of all the happenings since first setting out, which was a long job. Eventually, I was able to go home to Porchester, but as I entered the living room where my wife was ironing the children's clothes, she promptly fainted!

The *Bee,* 75 feet in length and capable of seven knots, was little more than a powered barge carrying all manner of cargo between the Isle of Wight and the mainland. But, with four similar vessels, *Bee* was taken to Dunkirk by her normal crew of four, including engineer Fred Reynard who made this personal record:

We were unloading iron plates at Portsmouth Dockyard when a naval officer came aboard and informed us that the *Bee* was being taken over by the Navy. He said the task for which she was required was dangerous and the crew could leave for home if they wished and a naval crew would be put aboard. Alternatively, the Navy would be grateful if we volunteered because of our expertise in handling the craft. The crew consisted of Bill Mansbridge, skipper; Ern Downer, mate; myself as engineer; and Marc Hocking, aged 16, as fourth hand. We all agreed to stay with the ship. A Royal Navy Sub-Lieutenant was seconded to *Bee* and four days rations put aboard before we left harbour at 7.30 in the evening. We steamed through the night and all the next day, arriving off Ramsgate at 5 p.m. The officer went ashore for instructions and was back within the hour. He told us the British Expeditionary Force was being driven into the sea and that our task was to lift as many off the beaches near Dunkirk as possible. We were again offered the opportunity of quitting; again we declined and at 7.30 p.m. the *Bee* set off.

Two routes had been offered to the officer and he was free to discuss these with the crew. We could make for Calais, but would come within range of shore batteries, or we could travel by a more northerly route, a distance of 85 miles, but there German E-Boats were making a nuisance of themselves. We opted for the short route via Calais, travelled on our own and timed our arrival for the cover of darkness. We dropped anchor as per instructions to await the dawn. Overhead was the drone of aircraft, the sky was stabbed by dozens of searchlight beams, while all around one could see the dark shadows of ships large and small, all at anchor. We remained unmolested. In the distance one could hear the rumble of guns and the explosion of bombs, while fires raging in the town lit the sky. Dawn was zero hour, 3.30 a.m. Sleep was out of the question and we busied ourselves hanging a scrambling net over the bows. Dawn finally broke, we raised anchor and made for the shore.

What a sight met our gaze. The sea was covered in oil and there was wreckage everywhere. The docks were burning, as were huge oil container and over the town of Dunkirk was a pall of black smoke. The shores were a sea of human beings and there was a constant stream of men coming over the dunes and down to the water's edge. A light from a Very pistol warned us of impending danger. An aircraft appeared, machine-gun fire struck the water close by, but no bombs were dropped. Other planes were busy dropping bombs and machine-gunning along the beach. We proceeded towards the shore, and the nearer we got, the more destruction we saw. Upturned craft and human beings floated everywhere. Men were tending the wounded. Back came the bombers and a near miss shook *Bee* badly. Warships opened up on the planes. After a direct hit on a destroyer and she listed heavily to port. Another destroyer, laden with troops, was hit and sinking. Men swam towards the shore; some were picked up by smaller craft, but a large number, torn and mangled, went down with the ship. Less than an hour since dawn, we were still afloat, yet seemingly had spent a lifetime in hell.

We were now nearing the beach; another near miss; no one could be lucky enough to survive this holocaust. Now a welcome sight. Nine of our fighters arrived and straight into the Huns they went; easy targets those dive bombers. Some scattered and fled, some went down. Our planes could not remain long and back came Jerry with his unceasing bombing, but still that procession of men came down to the water's edge. There was nowhere else to go. Cars, lorries and motor cycles were being driven into the sea or destroyed on the beaches. A lone chestnut horse ran up and down the beach. More RAF planes arrived, one crashed on the beach, but with more of our planes what a different story it would have been. *Bee* drove at full speed on to the shore and grounded; they came towards us, some wading almost to their necks in the water, those men of the BEF, and we realised that our efforts to assist them aboard with ropes and scrambling nets were futile. Waterlogged and utterly exhausted, many wounded, it was impossible for them to make such an effort. We quickly sawed the ship's ladder in two, placing one half on each side of the bow. The success was reward enough to see these men file aboard, some equipped with nothing but a covering of clothing, but all with a determination to live. A pause in loading for another raid. We escaped, but just along the beach there was a terrible toll in life and little ships. Another start and with a few interruptions we filled to capacity. Every spot where a man could stand was packed, both down in the hold and on deck. Their weight was such that we were stuck firm on the beach and for over an hour we struggled to free ourselves until our plight was spotted by a French tug and we were pulled free.

When finally underway our elation was short lived. We were ordered to transfer the troops to a larger vessel lying offshore and not once but twice more returned to the beach for further troops. Fearing that any further grounding might be permanent we used our pinnace to pick up the soldiers, but this proved a painfully slow process amid ever increasing bombing and shelling. Where there had been ten or a dozen enemy planes dive-bombing ships earlier on, numbers now seemed more like 50, and not only was there more shelling, it was also increasingly accurate. When we finally pulled away for the last time and were ordered to continue with our human cargo to Ramsgate, it marked the end of the most unforgettable 24 hours of my life.

We reached Ramsgate and tied up to discharge our troops amidst expressions of gratitude, not solicited and better left unsaid, for simple thanks could move us to tears in the wake of such an experience. The stronger helped the weaker up the gangway and they were met by ladies with cups of tea, cakes and cigarettes while the Red Cross were there to take charge of wounded. So that other vessels could make use of the landing facilities we moved *Bee* into the middle of the harbour and the telegraph finally rang 'finished with engines'. I went up on deck, lay down on a folded canvas and as sleep overcame me I remembered a lad who had knelt by the engine room hatch and recited the Lord's Prayer.

Of the vessels sent to Dunkirk with supplies, few took a more volatile cargo than the old steam collier *Clewbay,* dispatched with over 500 tons of high-explosives. This is how Captain D. B. Ivor reported a highly eventful round trip:

On 22nd May 1940 we loaded a cargo of 572 tons of explosives at Newhaven and were told to proceed to Dover for further orders. Just clear of the piers at Newhaven a dense fog set in and we dropped anchor awaiting a clearance until 4.30 p.m. We arrived off Dover at 1 p.m. and were sent to the Downs to await orders and anchored off Deal at 2.10 p.m. We finally received orders from an Admiralty launch at 9 a.m. on Friday 24th May to proceed to Dover and from there were sent to Dunkirk, sailing at 3.15 p.m. Off Calais, an enemy plane passed close over us and dropped one bomb so we opened fire and he went off and attacked some ships north of our position. I had received orders at Dover not to get to Dunkirk before night and to keep a careful lookout as the Dunkirk Channel was strewn with mines. We were steaming slowly awaiting the time I was told to get there and, arriving off the Dyck Lightship at 9 p.m., I decided to proceed up Channel so that I could get near my destination before darkness set in. We carried on and kept to seaward of the buoys in the channel, passing many mines, but had light enough to steer clear of them all.

At 10 p.m. we arrived off Dunkirk and could plainly see the town was in flames. We could also hear bombs exploding everywhere ashore. At midnight, high water, I steamed *Clewbay* between the piers but no sooner had I done this and was attempting to make fast when two bombs exploded in the channel astern. One was very close as the rebound of the sea came right over our quarter deck. I remained there for about 15 minutes thinking still to make a landing and try and make contact with the British naval authorities, but just as I got alongside the East Pier, two more bombs were dropped ahead of us, one in the channel and one on the pier which shattered it for some distance. We then opened fire on the plane and succeeded in beating it off, at least for the time being.

I could see no chance of getting ashore, nor was there anyone about the place to get

The steam collier **Clewbay** *which, loaded with explosives, made the harrowing trip to Dunkirk described by her skipper, Captain B. Ivor. Dating from 1904,* **Clewbay** *went back to the Irish Sea coal trade and was scrapped in 1959 after spending the last few years of a long career as* **Ballygilbert**. (Roy Fenton)

information from. Bombs were dropping everywhere and my first thought was for the safety of the ship and cargo, so I decided to make a run for it and get back to Dover if possible, and report. I backed *Clewbay* full speed astern between the piers, but no sooner had I got my ship's head pointing down channel and on our course than we were attacked by another plane. We opened fire and gave him a good salvo. He sheered off in a northerly direction and the engines ceased to roar. We saw no more of him so I believe he must have fallen into the sea. When half way between Dunkirk and Gravelines, they opened up on us from some of the shore batteries and many of the shells passed close overhead. But now we had no alternative but to carry on and hope for the best.

After passing the Dyck Lightship and when near No. 1 Buoy, I reported the mines seen earlier to Patrol Boat *WL 158* who went after them and before long we heard three blown up. At 5.30 a.m. another plane came from the direction of Cap Gris Nez and sent a shell across our bows. We opened fire, as did a patrol craft nearby, and the plane cleared off. *Clewbay* anchored off Dover at 10.40 a.m. on 26th May and was sent to the Downs during Sunday morning. On Tuesday 28th May we were ordered to Newhaven, and then on to Littlehampton to discharge, arriving at 5.30 p.m. next day. Unloading commenced at 8 a.m. on the 30th and was completed at 6.20 p.m. on the 31st.

Tugs more than played their part in the evacuation and none was busier than *Lady Brassey*, the Harbour Board tug that was part of the Dover scenery for over 40 years. Captain F. J. Hopgood took over *Lady Brassey* from Captain G. W. Blackmore on 30th May and this is how he recorded the happenings of the next few days:

Left Dover on 30th May to assist the destroyer *Bideford* off Nieuport, Belgium. Weather fine, but while on passage we received a message to proceed to Dunkirk and stand by Naval personnel in charge of the evacuation. During the passage, a German plane came overhead, so we kept our two machine-guns firing at it until it sheared off towards France. On approaching

Dover Harbour Board's **Lady Brassey** *was busy throughout Operation Dynamo, working in the English Channel and at Dunkirk itself. She is seen here near the end of a 45-year career that ended in 1958.* (Skyfotos)

Dunkirk Roads through the marked channel across the sand banks, we sighted a small coaster that had been bombarded and with shell holes through the hull but clear of the waterline. We could also see dense black smoke over Dunkirk, and vessels of all descriptions lying off the sand dunes which were crowded with troops being ferried off by small boats to larger craft in the vicinity. The troops were being bombed, and craters made by the bombs were soon full of troops taking shelter there.

We felt our way past several craft that had been sunk close to the East Pier, and went alongside the west side of the pier. troops were coming down this pier and embarking on various craft – destroyers, mailboats and passenger boats. All of these were shallow-draught vessels, drawing about 13 feet and able to cope with the channel from Dunkirk to England. During the time we were alongside the pier, shrapnel and fragmentation from the explosive charges fired by demolition squads came over the pier and the tug. A piece of shrapnel slid down inside my raincoat without doing any harm. There was a hospital ship moored close to us that found things too warm whilst she waited for wounded, so she cleared out of Dunkirk.

The evacuation continued while we assisted several of the ships leaving the pier. The tide was falling and these vessels were getting too close to the ground. There were also several vessels sunk near the entrance to the pier. When it became dark, we assisted vessels off the jetty, and in addition assisted vessels into and alongside the pier, clear of the wrecks. We continued until 12.30 a.m. on 31st May when I received instructions to return to Dover, but not to take any troops aboard in case I was wanted for rescue duty. Whilst returning, we received a message to go to the assistance of a drifter ashore on the Goodwin Sands. As we approached the north-east end of the sands we could see the drifter on the north-east bank but the tide was flowing and she got off and we proceeded on to Dover.

On 1st June, vessels were lined up loaded with troops off the port of Dover, waiting to disembark in turn at the Admiralty Pier railway berths. The people there were hard at it clearing the troops. Again we received orders to proceed to the Downs and assist the troopship *Prague* which had been mined and was severely damaged. We reached her and took her in tow, despite her damage, and kept her from sinking by grounding her on the Sandwich Flats. Temporary repairs were made while she was grounded and then she proceeded to port for permanent repairs.

On 2nd June I received instructions to go to the assistance of the hospital ship *Paris,* sinking off Dunkirk. She had been bombed en route to Dunkirk and we proceeded at full speed through the Downs and set course for Dunkirk. It was a dark night, but fine, when at about 11 p.m. a dark shadow approached. It was a destroyer steaming at full speed and loaded with troops. Her speed of 31 knots piled a bow wave white and mountainous over her fore deck and it drenched troops who stood there motionless and helpless. It surged around the turret tops and almost reached the navigation bridge and left in broad, pale gushes over the side. She came so close she sent her swell over the tug. It was a near thing, and if she had hit us, it would have been goodbye *Brassey*! We continued on and searched for *Paris* and finally located her by the star shells sent up overhead. We could see that the vessel was sinking and that there was no hope of saving her. But we cruised around, hailing to find out if, by any chance, anyone had been left aboard by the craft that had taken off the crew before our arrival. We kept in touch with the ship until it sank at about 4 a.m. and then reported her position, and the fact that her masts were sticking up out of the water. We then returned to Dover.

London doctor Basil Smith registered his motor cruiser *Constant Nymph* following the Admiralty appeal on 14th May and after warning his partners that he would be 'away for a bit,' was one of the owners who took their boats right through to Dunkirk. Awarded the DSM for his work off the beaches with the *Constant Nymph*, Dr Smith reported his efforts in a matter-of-fact manner and clearly seemed at some pains to play down his personal contribution:

It was shortly after midnight on 26th May when a duty officer at the Admiralty telephoned to ask whether *Constant Nymph* was ready for sea. They called again at 8.45 a.m. and asked me to go to the boat. Having already put a few things in a bag, I went to Isleworth on the Thames as soon as possible and arrived there between 10 and 11. It was obvious that some form of permit would be required as my own permit only carried to Middle Blythe Buoy, and my instructions were to take the boat to Sheerness. I found at the boathouse that a naval officer was expected who would issue the permits and was requisitioning boats in the same yard. He wanted the boats to go down river together, but separate permits were issued by afternoon so I was then ready to start at any time, and the others did not look like being ready for several hours.

At about 5.30 p.m. I tried to ring up my Mate as I felt sure he would want to be in on the game and might at least be able to help me work the boat down to Sheerness. Luckily he was home early and put such a jerk into things that he arrived from Tulse Hill to Isleworth before 7.30 p.m. and we started at 8.30 without waiting for the other boats. After getting to Sheerness it was suggested that I might like to stay with *Constant Nymph* and sign on temporarily with the Royal Navy. The opportunity of playing boats for a month seemed too good to miss in any case, and I had been able to warn my partners that I should be away for a bit. I toured Sheerness Dockyard interviewing numerous people until late in the afternoon, and by about 5 p.m. had formed a pretty accurate idea what the job was and was quite determined not to be put off. So I appealed to Commodore Taylor himself, who was supervising the fuelling and victualling of the motor boats in the basin. Within half an hour I was signed on and back at the basin with a crew of two young naval ratings, a full tank plus a deck cargo of petrol, a waterbeaker and enough provisions to last my little gang for about a week – including a large lump of raw beef and two small sacks of potatoes, also raw. The boat seemed very overcrowded but by 6 p.m. we were making our way out of the basin to go round to Ramsgate.

We were held there until 30th May but then at 3.30 in the afternoon we finally got going and were towed to Dunkirk with other small boats in about six hours by one of the Dutch skoots, the *Jutland*. It was a very uncomfortable trip. Destroyers kept crossing and passing at high speeds making a very heavy wash and we had to try to keep my boat sheered off to port while the cutter and whaler we towed were sheered off to starboard. Sometimes we all came together in spite of all the effort, but no damage was done.

Constant Nymph and the pulling boats were secured to a curious vessel called *Johanna*, and she was on tow to *Jutland* by a wire rope. This parted at about 4 p.m. but *Jutland* was stopped in time to ease the strain before the last single strand went, thus saving some injuries and possibly lives. *Johanna's* crew fell on her deck and I crouched behind my cabin trunk as that wire spun and strand after strand parted. The *Johanna* was like a heavy old cow and the rate we were going the wire was like a banjo string and the whip back if the last strand had gone would have been terrific. At 4.50 p.m. a new manila rope had been passed and we got going again.

We arrived at Dunkirk at about dusk and turned along the beach eastwards for a few miles before *Jutland* dropped anchor. We cast off the tow at once and I took the cutter and whaler in tow myself and set out for the beach. It was slightly misty as well as dark, but it was not really a dark night and visibility was not too bad. As this point had not been worked before we did not know whether Jerry was there or our men. Being quite unarmed we had to be canny about hailing until we knew who was there. At first we could find no life on the beach but after a short time we were hailed by Frenchmen and for a little while found Frenchmen only, and made one or two full journeys back to the ship with them.

The procedure was to tow the whaler and cutter to the beach and swing them round and cast off the tow in about 3 feet 6 inches of water – my draught being 2 feet 6 inches. The cutter then dropped her grapnel and went in as close as she dared without grounding the whaler, and troops waded out to board them. As soon as the two boats were full they called for the motor boat and pulled up on the cutter's grapnel. I would come past and take the cutter's bow rope and swing out towards the *Jutland* which had to lie about three-quarters of a mile to a mile out. While the whaler and cutter were loading I patrolled parallel with the beach, keeping as close as I dared without grounding, it being essential that the motor boat should not take the ground as it was the only motor boat in the area and the cutter and whaler had only three men apiece aboard so that they were not in a position to row out to the ship, except at a great loss of time.

While patrolling my job was to pick up any swimmers or waders and any odd craft which had put out from the shore. There were several of these. After the first few loads had been taken to the ship, all Frenchmen, a British officer waded out and was picked up and reported that a whole British division were waiting to be taken off a little nearer Dunkirk town than we had been working. I took him aboard, went back and picked up the full cutter and whaler and took them all back to the ship, reporting to the captain of the *Jutland* that the British were further up the beach and that I was going there.

A big fire just inshore was my leading mark as the British were just to the east of this. From then on we worked to this point and the French came down the beach and mingled with the British. After we had been going to this point for about three or four trips a German bomber most inconsiderately dropped a large bomb on our fire and blew it out like a candle. This did not matter very much as I had leading marks and the mass of troops had increased so that they were quite visible on the beach. By about 3 a.m. on 31st May the *Jutland* was full with roughly half and half British and French troops and she sailed at once to avoid the dawn bombing. Jerry was trying to bomb the ships as they left loaded. But his efforts through the ten to eleven hours that I worked on the beach were very poorly rewarded.

At about 7.30 a.m. the captain of the *Laudania* told me to come aboard with all my crew to get some sort of meal. The whole of us who had been on the beach work then had our first stand-easy since 9.30 p.m. the day before, and my crew and I had not had anything to eat since 5.30 p.m. the day before and nothing to drink since 3.30 p.m. and had been continuously employed, as had the two naval ratings who remained on each of the rowing boats during the tow across.

Fred Rogers was married on Monday 20th May 1940. Four days later his honeymoon was rudely interrupted with a recall to Dover to rejoin the motor yacht *Sargasso* in which he was serving as an Ordinary Seaman on a T124 engagement for six months. Now retired in

Brighton, his main recollection of the period is of the suberb weather with sunshine every day!

After joining up in the Spring of 1940 I was first posted to Dover and the cable ship *Alert,* which was owned by the Post Office but under Admiralty control. Once there, I came across the *Sargasso* and was quickly persuaded by some old friends on board to seek a transfer. She was a fine twin screw diesel vessel of over 200 tons that had been built, I think in Germany, during the 1920s and was owned by Sir Loel Guinness, who was then the member of parliament for Bath. Originally named *Atlantis,* she had become *Sargasso* after being requisitioned by the navy at the start of the war and was equipped with paravanes for minesweeping duties. From Dover, during my time, *Sargasso* went out early each morning to assist in clearing channels for the day's shipping and was commanded by Lieutenant C. Gaussen, one of three RNVR officers. Apart from a Royal Navy signalman and a gunner, the remaining nine of us in the crew were all from a merchant service background and including the bosun, Charlie de Rouffiniac, who had been skipper of the vessel as a private yacht before the war. An instinctive seaman from Cornish fishing stock, as might have been expected, he always handled the *Sargasso* superbly.

I left the ship to get married on Monday 20th May, only to be called back on the Friday, and when reaching Dover next day found that *Sargasso* had already been sent overnight to Boulogne to help bring out troops who had been cut off by the German advance. There was great activity on that Saturday morning and throughout the weekend as we loaded stores, mainly bread, corned beef and cocoa. By Monday morning Operation Dynamo was under way and we left at about 9.00 a.m. in sunshine. After the passage of nearly 50 years it is difficult to remember all the daily events but I know that all through the operation the weather was perfect. Our first crossing was uneventful apart from a few aerial dog fights well away from our course. After picking up the French coast, we saw a heavy pall of smoke hanging over the town of Dunkirk and then heard a continuous rumble of gunfire. As we made our way past the harbour we saw hundreds of troops scattered over the beaches and in the water trying to get to small craft along the shore. We lowered our dinghy and motor launch and they each made several trips, taking on a full load each time. After about an hour we were overloaded and made our departure.

The conduct of the troops was very orderly and it was pitiful to have to leave so many behind. Several times we saw German planes straffing the beaches and wondered where our own aircraft were, not knowing they were fighting off the Junkers further inland. The *Sargasso* had twin Lewis guns which were used once or twice but were not very effective as when German aircraft did approach they dived out of the sun and were usually gone before we caught sight of him. Not only that, prior to Dunkirk we had done little with the guns except to clean them! Luckily, as the ship was loaded so far down that the portholes in the hull were only just above the water, the first trip back to Dover was uneventful and we were kept busy all the time making hundreds of sandwiches to feed the troops. When they disembarked I had literally thousands of cigarettes, two rifles, loads of 303 ammunition, several Army blankets and packs of emergency rations. The fo'csle was covered with rifles and ammunition but the Army came that evening and commandered the lot. We kept everything else and I didn't have to buy a cigarette for months.

At Dover we tied up alongside a collier called *Ngaroma* that had been towed in after being damaged off the French coast. Several of her crew had been killed and their bodies were lying on the deck covered by tarpaulins. But we had work to do and as soon as the troops were clear we took on stores, refilled the fresh water tanks and got some sleep before going over next day. Once again it was like a pleasure trip until we arrived at Dunkirk in mid-morning. There were not so many troops on the beaches this time and we first picked up survivors, some in a sorry state, after a ship was hit nearby, the *Sargasso's* ward room and the officers' quarters being given over to the wounded.

We also picked up a lot of French and Belgian troops but it took longer to get a full load and this time it was early afternoon before we departed, with the occasional shell to speed us on our way. The crew were kept busy throughout the trip and the troops were more depressed and all very tired. In Dover we tied up against a destroyer which had suffered a shell hit among the depth charges and had been left with no stern. What a mess! We began loading stores right away as Lieutenant Gaussen had orders to take *Sargasso* on another trip starting at sundown and, as soon as we were clear of the coast, I tried to get some sleep, lying fully clothed in the mess room wearing my tin hat and with a gas mask for a pillow! I was awakened by the sound of an explosion and went on deck to find we were entering Dunkirk Harbour. There was a terrific racket going on and the bosun told me we were going to tie up at the quay. Although the water was low we could make out figures on the quay as we approached and threw them lines before making fast fore and aft. We put up a ladder we had onboard and about a dozen men came down, all French. There seemed to be no one else about and the skipper detailed some of us to scout around and lead whoever we could find back to the ship. He gave us 10 minutes and altogether we located about 50 soldiers, again mainly French.

We took the ladder inboard and cut the mooring ropes to make our getaway. As we slowly left the engines stopped – one of the propellers had picked up a wire cable, presumably from the many wrecks in the area. This gave us an uneasy five or ten minutes with shells dropping quite close, but our luck held. With a bit of manoeuvring we managed to get free and were able to make full speed for Dover as soon as we were clear of the harbour. One of the propellers was damaged and later we had to go into dock at Dover for some repairs. *Sargasso* was still fit for duty and after putting our troops ashore we were sitting around awaiting the next day's work when, just as it was getting light, there was a signal that Operation Dynamo was finished. Our next orders took us to Ramsgate and for three months, almost to the end of my assignment, we were on patrol duties in the English Channel.

Despite being painted white and carrying the internationally recognised Red Cross markings, British hospital ships were repeatedly attacked by aircraft and shore batteries during Operation Dynamo. The intense anger and frustration this caused among those aboard such vessels was reflected in a Dunkirk diary kept by Captain John White, a doctor from the Isle of Wight who joined the Royal Army Medical Corps at the outbreak of war and was aboard the *Isle of Guernsey*, a Southern Railway steamer built for the Channel Islands run from Southampton, throughout the evacuation. Later he served with gallantry in France, North Africa and Italy, reaching the rank of Lieutenant-Colonel. After the war, Dr White became a general practitioner in the Isle of Wight, where his widow, Mrs Sheila White, still lives and made available this fascinating day-by-day account of the evacuation:

Saturday May 25th 1940: Left Southampton at 2.30 p.m. On clearing Calshot the CO informed me we were heading for Dover. I wonder what is on? A glorious sunny day as we sped up the Channel past Selsey, Brighton, the Seven Sisters and Eastbourne, all looking peaceful a few miles off our port beam. At Dover we were ordered to Dungeness for the night. We are all alone in the bay, with its wide sweep giving marvellous shelter from the south-west and west, and spent the night at anchor.

Sunday May 26th: We moved to the Downs early, there is a big collection of shipping here: cross-Channel steamers painted grey and being used as troopships, many destroyers, small coastal craft and four other hospital ships, the *Paris, St. Julien, St. David* and *Worthing*. At 3 p.m. we proceeded to Dunkirk via the short sea route to Calais, then turning north-east up the French coast. We followed the *Worthing* as there were not sufficient charts for all the ships. We were enjoying afternoon tea and listening to the gramophone on deck when, suddenly, some shells went whizzing over us to land 100 yards seaward, throwing up a big splash of water. We imagined this was the French practising and carried on with our tea and music but afterwards learned these were German guns firing as they

The hospital ship **Isle of Guernsey's** *Red Cross markings did not prevent repeated air attacks and shore bombardment during the Dunkirk evacuation and, eventually, she had to be taken out of service and sent for repairs.* (Sheila White)

had already captured Gravelines only two and a half miles away. A little later we noticed what appeared to be a derelict boat drifting in a glassy sea and immediately went over to investigate. It was a French fishing vessel and we found eight soldiers, more or less naked, who told us they had got on board two days previously and tried to escape to England after getting caught behind German lines.

Arriving off Dunkirk we entered the harbour between the breakwaters and proceeded right up to the docks behind the *Worthing* and after being turned round by tugs we berthed at a stone quay and started loading stretcher cases from waiting ambulances. The oil storage tanks a quarter of a mile away had been bombed and were emitting a pall of smoke high over Dunkirk and the docks were bombed as we loaded. We completed this by 10 p.m. and left in company with the *Worthing* and with 350 patients on board, travelling back to England completely blacked-out; and as all the light buoys had been extinguished, it must have been a tricky navigation. Spent the night treating the seriously wounded – most of the cases are not too bad and can wait until the *Isle of Guernsey* docks.

Monday May 27th: Arrived Newhaven at 5 a.m. and unloaded at the railway jetty in four and a half hours. We turned for Dunkirk forthwith. This time we went by the North Sea route as the French coast past Calais is in enemy hands. Procedure on arrival as before but everything more unpleasant. We loaded 450 cases and returned to Newhaven at high speed. The destroyers are certainly in force at Dunkirk and their decks crowded with troops. They are going hell-for-leather through the water at 30 knots – a wonderful sight with their high bow waves. I saw one destroyer go up in bits after a dive-bombing attack. Thank goodness the weather is on our side so far. The sea is flat calm, the sun shines continually and the water is warm. Not too bad if one does have to go overboard from one of the small boats helping to take men off the beaches. Had there been heavy surf, scores of these small boats would have been swamped and quite useless – or wrecked on the way across. There must be a guiding hand on our side.

I saw the *Gracie Fields*, one of the Isle of Wight paddle steamers, painted grey and firing her guns at planes bombing the shipping off the beaches. Everything seems to be here except the RAF who are conspicuous by their absence. A screen of fighters is needed over this armada, otherwise most of it is going to be sunk. There are seven of us here, the whole of the hospital fleet left after the loss of *Brighton* and *Maid of Kent* at Dieppe. Then we heard on our return to Newhaven that the pretty little *Paris* had been bombed and sunk today on her way to Dunkirk. There were no

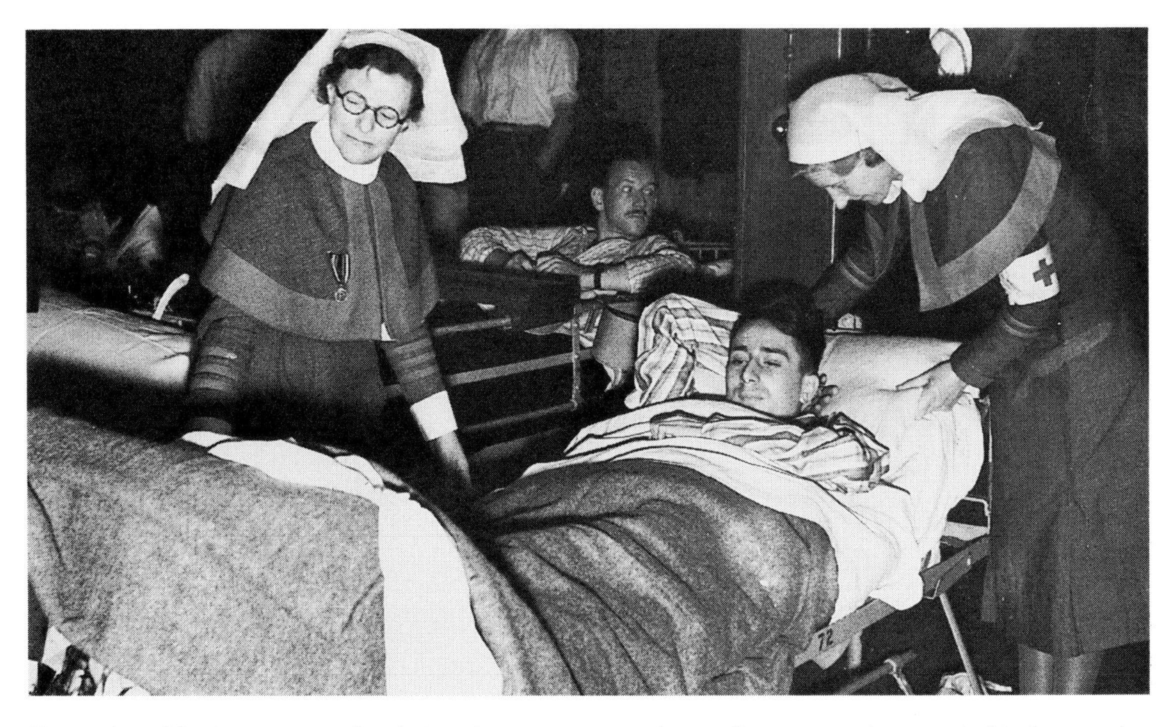

Conversion of ferries to serve as hospital carriers was no more than rudimentary and consisted of little more than replacement of normal saloon furniture with camp beds, as in this view (above) taken aboard the **Dinard.** *As can be seen in the other pre-Dunkirk shot of casualties being landed in England, security was strict, with two armed sentries at the gangway.* (Imperial War Museum)

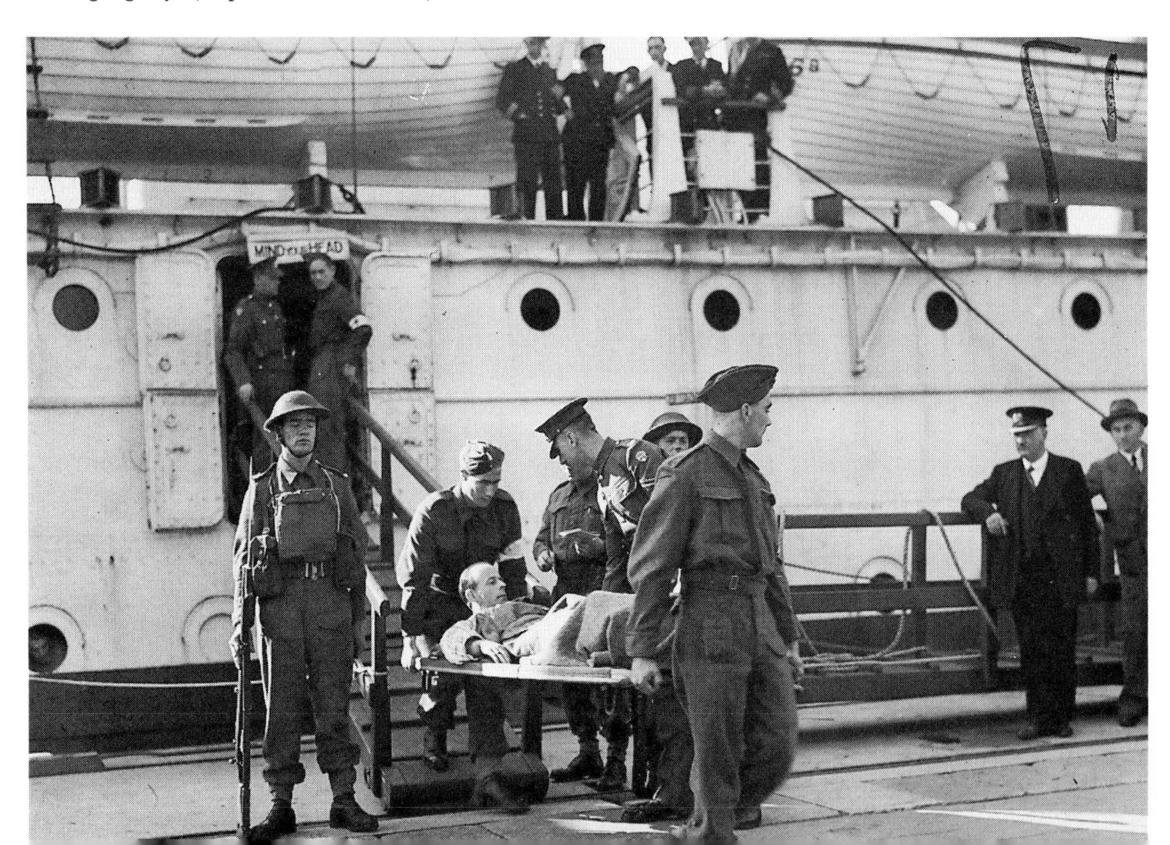

patients on board, fortunately, and three-quarters of the crew were saved, but four sisters are among the missing. All the other hospital ships had tales to tell about being bombed and damaged but none seriously enough to be out of action. Why do we go on with this Red Cross business? We are just sitting ducks. Why not paint us grey and put some guns on board? No guns, I suppose! I am sure all of us on these ships would feel a lot happier. At least we would not feel both helpless and frightened when under attack.

We off-loaded our 450 patients at Newhaven and immediately left for Dover again. The wounded this time were in a much worse condition and many had had little or no attention for days and were in bad shape. On the way we dealt with all the serious cases we could, morphia and new dressings, serum and fluids. The exhausted ones were fed and rested. They were grateful for attention and, strangely enough, felt quite safe with us. Most of them felt and looked better for the trip by the time we had put them off ashore. A few we had to dispatch to nearby hospitals for emergency amputations. We got them back alive, at least. Most to fight again, perhaps? With a dozen it is going to be touch and go I fear. The sisters and orderlies worked like trojans and are splendid when it comes to the real thing. They seem to have the job taped and don't have to be told what to do. This makes the MO's work far easier and I feel we can cope.

Tuesday May 28th: My birthday and this is a new way to celebrate it! We are anchored in the Downs off the Goodwins and there is still a big fleet here including the other hospital ships. This is obviously a very big show and it looks as though we are going to evacuate the whole of the BEF from Dunkirk. Thank God for our sea power and the weather which is still in our favour. The sea is flat calm and the destroyers are going by at high speed, their decks crammed full with troops. German planes attempted to bomb the shipping anchored here this morning but were driven off by ships' guns and AA batteries on shore. But I still haven't seen a British fighter. Have we any left? Belgium's king capitulated today – another gap for our hard-pressed troops to fill.

Wednesday May 29th: Underway 3 a.m. Off to Dunkirk again by the middle North Sea channel. When we were about 20 miles off Dunkirk we saw a pilot bale out after a dog-fight and he came down in the calm blue sea ahead of us. He was one of ours and we heaved-to and threw him a line. Two sailors went out over the side to assist and soon pulled him out. In a flash three German planes were on us and raked the ship with their machine-guns. The two sailors were hit and fell mortally wounded into the water but, by a miracle, the pilot escaped the rain of bullets and was soon on board. He was Flying Officer Ken Newton, a young New Zealander who told us he had been shot down in his Hurricane by a bunch of Messerschmitts.

We then got under way again at top speed and ten minutes later were suddenly dive-bombed by three Stukas. It was a terrifying attack. We felt certain that this really was the end and crouched under any cover available. All hell was let loose as the bombs exploded and the whole ship shuddered and shook like a leaf and lurched hard over as she was given full rudder. The stern seemed to leap out of the water and hit the sea with a thud as each concussion struck us. There were bits of metal and cascading water everywhere. Miraculously we had no direct hit and were still on an even keel but had slowed down percetibly, this we learned later was due to the port engine being lifted off its bed by explosions in the water. There was much damage but nothing vital and the bridge appeared to be completely untouched.

After continuing towards the coast we could see the harbour entrance and a destroyer signalled: 'Harbour cannot be entered, return to Dover.' We turned round, but after an hour's steaming were signalled by another destroyer: 'Turn and make for Dunkirk immediately.' The harbour could apparently be entered after dark and we arrived at 10 p.m. We could see at once the change since our last visit. Fires were raging everywhere in the docks and town which illuminated the place for us and the enemy. There was death and destruction everywhere. The quays were deserted and the harbour empty. We were all alone. We had no bow rudder and with no tugs, had to turn the *Isle of Guernsey* around by hand. This manoeuvre seemed to take an eternity as we were under shellfire but was actually accomplished in three quarters of an hour and we were full of admiration for the way in which the crew carried out this tricky operation with bombing going on all the time. On berthing our gang-planks were hastily put down and loading started at a rush. All hands turned to carrying stretchers – stokers, greasers, stewards, orderlies, even our rescued fighter pilot. We were determined to load and get out. Bombs exploded on the quays and incendiaries showered down on the already gutted warehouses. I noticed men, obviously not wounded, clambering on to the ship but let them get away with it, poor devils. A record loading this time of 45 minutes for 490 stretcher cases and hordes of walking wounded.

Thursday May 30th: At 2 a.m. the mooring lines were cast off and we nosed our way out. What a relief to still be afloat and on our way again. We cleared the harbour entrance in ten minutes but could still see thousands of men on the beaches. Down below, every cot is full and the floors and passageways crowded with stretchers. The dining saloon and smoke room are full of wounded and we gave up our cabins to the walking cases, eight or ten to a cabin. That familiar smell of sweat, dirt and disinfectant fills the atmosphere. The wounded look exhausted, dirty and terribly ill and some of the badly wounded have had nothing done for them for days. A lot of these men will not make it, I fear.

There were some cases of shell-shock this time; terrified, crazed men whose brains had snapped after days and nights of strain, privation and terror. They were put below in one cabin under guard and given sedative injections. Eventually, when all seemed quiet, I went up to visit the wounded on the boat deck. To my horror and distress, eight had died, making a total of 12 on board. We are carrying nearly 1,000 wounded – and the ship was planned to take 250. There are wounded everywhere, even in the lifeboats. We do all we can sorting out the very ill and sending the ones that are not too bad down below to feed them. The ones too ill to move have been made comfortable with pillows and blankets on the deck. This is rough-and-ready doctoring with a vengeance, but at least they are on their way home.

Twenty minutes after leaving Dunkirk there was suddenly an almighty crash. I was below tending the wounded and fell flat on my face. Everyone else did likewise. I picked myself up and rushed on deck. We had hit a sandbank and were stuck fast with 30 feet of our bows almost high and dry. The next 45 minutes was a nightmare of suspense. We were a sitting target for anything that came our way. At last, after what seemed like an eternity, there was more water. The turbines started up, both engines were put full astern and the ship shook and shuddered as we slowly slipped off what could so easily have been our common grave.

Still our nightmare journey was not over. After thick fog came down, we were proceeding slowly when suddenly hailed with a warning: 'You are going right through a minefield. Follow me and I hope to take you safely out of it.' The voice belonged to someone on one of our minesweepers which was another piece of providential luck. Half an hour later we were through the minefield and in bright sunlight. The white cliffs of Dover were ahead and never was a sight more welcome. By midday we had slipped through the harbour entrance and as we started unloading I couldn't help wondering, what next? But the answer was provided for us. *Isle of Guernsey* was too damaged to make another crossing and on Monday 3rd June I left her at Southampton and returned to the Isle of Wight. Arriving home for four days' leave, Dunkirk behind me, I fell into the arms of my family.

Acknowledgements

Despite the many volumes written with Operation Dynamo as a central theme, I find it curious that no detailed record of the part played by individual ships has previously been attempted. This factor, and the way in which some writers almost appear to play down the maritime achievement represented by the evacuation, provided much of the motivation for this book. The rest came from a quite remarkable response to articles I prepared for *Ships Monthly* to mark Dunkirk's 40th anniversary in 1980, and subsequent contact with readers who had been involved in the evacuation, either among the rescuers or the rescued, producing several of the most graphic descriptions in the foregoing pages.

I am particularly appreciative of the interest shown by those individuals, or their close relatives, and, especially, to John Crosby of Glasgow for not only the many truly outstanding original photographs but also letters and the diary kept by his late father, J. Rutherford Crosby, while serving on the paddle minesweeper *Oriole* in 1940. Equal thanks go to Frank Pattrick, Albert Nason, Leslie Rashleigh and Frank Rogers for re-living those harrowing times, and to Margaret Russell and Sheila White for providing detailed accounts of the Dunkirk experiences of their late husbands.

Sadly, several other people who made major contributions to the contents of this book, John Cameron, J. G. 'Jack' Graves and Leonard Baker, have not lived to see their words in print. The trouble taken by Mr Baker of the Portsmouth Branch of the Dunkirk Veterans' Association was typical. After casually mentioning that he was terminally ill with cancer, Leonard gave unstintingly from painstakingly gathered personal records, including the stories of his close friend Charles Strudwick, the able seaman who took the Aldeburgh lifeboat to Dunkirk and back; and that of Ronald Hector who was recalled from his honeymoon to cross to France, also at the helm of a RNLI vessel. In a letter shortly before his death in 1989, Leonard signed off: 'We will always remember the ships and men of Dunkirk – and those who did not return.'

Among others who have given freely of their own specialist knowledge and/or photographic collections concerning specific types of ships represented at Dunkirk are John de S. Winser, M. J. Gaston, Roy Fenton and Richard Osborne. Ambrose Greenway, Peter Box, Clifton Smith-Cox, Ernest Dumbleton, A. G. Taylor, Philip Cone, Harry Burns, Barry Bridges, Ian Muir, Mark Willis, Ray Butcher and Terry Tuck all made valuable contributions together with Richard Danielson who provided photographs of Isle of Man Steam Packet Co. ships and interviewed Capt. Tom Corteen. My thanks are also due to Graham Langmuir for willingly delving into his own extensive collection of negatives and also for making available those from the Rev. William C. Galbraith collection.

Many members of the Paddle Steamer Preservation Society provided information and I was able to draw from the Society's archives for a number of illustrations. My thanks go also to Marshall Vine, Noreen Chambers and Peter Hogwood of the Medway Queen Preservation Society; the staff of Skyfotos Ltd, at their Littleston Road base in New Romney, Kent; Tony Smith for making available prints from some of the 6,000 negatives in the World Ship Photo Library of the World Ship Society; the staff of the Imperial War Museum library and photographic department; the Public Records Office; Jacqueline Treca of Dunkirk Chamber of Commerce; J. L. Pohrel, Dunkirk's Municipal Archivist; and, of course, to the owners of surviving Dunkirk vessels of all shapes and sizes.

Finally, our comprehensive listing of the real 'little ships' was achieved with the considerable co-operation of John Knight, archivist of the Association of Dunkirk Little Ships, who allowed access to a remarkable record compiled by members of his family over a period of years.

Bibliography

A Century of Cross Channel Passenger Ferries, Ambrose Greenway (Ian Allan 1981)

A Century of North Sea Passenger Steamers, Ambrose Greenway (Ian Allan 1986)

British Vessels Lost at Sea 1939–45, HM Stationery Office (Patrick Stephens Ltd 1988)

Clyde River and Other Coastal Steamers, Duckworth and Langmuir (Brown, Son and Ferguson 1939)

Cross Solent Cargo Boats, E. Lee (Newport, IW, 1976)

Dunkerque, Jacques Mordal (Editions France Empire 1948)

Dunkirk, David Devine (Faber and Faber 1945)

Dunkirk – The Great Escape, A. J. Barker (J. M. Dent and Sons 1977)

His Majesty's Minesweepers, Ministry of Information (HMSO 1943)

Island Lifeline, Connery Chappell (T. Stephenson and Sons 1980)

Le Defense de Dunkerque, Blanche (Lille 1950)

Marine Dunkirk, Maurice Guiere (Flammarion 1942)

Railway and Other Steamers, Duckworth and Langmuir (T. Stephenson and Sons 1968)

Red Funnel and Before, R. B. Adams (Kingfisher Railway Publications 1987)

Royal River Highway, Frank L. Dix (David and Charles 1985)

Steamers of the Thames and Medway, Frank Burtt (Richard Tilling 1949)

South Coast Pleasure Steamers, E. C. B. Thornton (T. Stephenson and Sons 1962)

The Miracle of Dunkirk, Walter Lord (Allen Lane 1983)

The Nine Days of Dunkirk, David Devine (Faber and Faber 1959)

The Sands of Dunkirk, Richard Collier (Fontana 1961)

The Second World War (Volume 2), W. S. Churchill (London 1949)

The Thames on Fire, L. M. Bates (Terence Dalton 1985)

The War at Sea 1939–45, S. W. Roskill (London 1954)

The War in France and Flanders, L. F. Ellis (London 1953)

100 Years of Parkeston Quay and its Ships, P. J. Cone (Harwich 1985)

Main Entry Index

The vessels included in this book appear under headings determined by type and/or role during Operation Dynamo. The names of craft known, or believed, to remain in existence appear in **bold type**. The participating Royal Navy vessels and foreign warships are listed according to type in Chapter 18 on pages 190-194.

Armed Boarding Vessels

Barges and Lighters

Cargo Ships

Dutch Schuits (Skoots)

Excursion Ships, Small Ferries and Cargo Vessels

Fishing Vessels (other than Trawlers)

Hospital Carriers

Paddle Steamers

(Pre-Dunkirk role:
PMS – paddle minesweeper;
SSV – Special Service Vessel;
EV – Examination vessel;
HC – Hospital carrier;
CV – Civilian vessel).

Personnel Vessels

RNLI Lifeboats

(with Station in parenthesis)

Small Craft

Small Foreign Vessels

Trawlers

Tugs